Revising Memory

Revising Memory

Women's Fiction and Memoirs in Seventeenth-Century France

Faith E. Beasley

Rutgers University Press
New Brunswick and London

Beasley, Faith Evelyn.
    Revising memory : women's fiction and memoirs in seventeenth-century
France / Faith E. Beasley.
      p. cm.
    Includes bibliographical references.
    ISBN 0-8135-1585-8
    1. Autobiographical fiction, French—Women authors—History and criti-
cism.   2. Women authors, French—17th century—Biography—History
and criticism.   3. Historical fiction, French—Women authors—History and
criticism.   4. French fiction—17th century—History and criticism.
5. Women and literature—France—History—17th century.
6. Autobiography—Women authors.   I. Title.
PQ637.A96B43   1990   90-31075
843'.4099287—dc20   CIP

British Cataloging-in-Publication information available

For My Parents, William and Joann,
and My Grandparents,
Marshall and Evelyn and
William and Henryetta

Contents

Acknowledgments

The present work owes a great deal to the many colleagues and friends who have generously supported me throughout this project. First and foremost, I wish to express my profound gratitude to Joan DeJean, whose inspirational graduate seminars and work first drew me to the world of seventeenth-century France and under whose direction this work originally took shape. Her challenging comments and criticism and her endless patience with my all too numerous questions and doubts have been invaluable from beginning to end. Without her unfailing support and encouragement, this book would not exist.

A number of people have read, discussed, criticized, and encouraged my work, and this book benefited greatly from their generosity. I wish to thank Elizabeth MacArthur for devoting so much energy to reading and questioning this manuscript at every stage. I truly appreciate her intellectual and emotional support. Natalie Zemon Davis carefully read the dissertation, and her insightful comments led to important revisions. Marie-Paule Laden has supported me from the beginning, always suggesting new directions. I am very grateful to Nancy K. Miller for convincing me of the value of the project. The chapter on Lafayette's provocative novel was significantly improved by her suggestions and by the enjoyable discussions we had. That chapter was also developed and strengthened by the challenging questions and remarks of Ann Rosalind Jones and her colleagues in the Comparative Literature Department at Smith College, who graciously allowed me to present my work there twice. Christian Jouhaud provided support in Paris and helped shed light on Montpensier's obscure references. I am indebted to English Showalter for reading the entire manuscript not once but twice, and for making enlightening remarks each time. His insightful suggestions at many different stages helped reshape the original work and led to significant revisions. I would like to thank Charles Bernheimer for his support over the years. Kate Jensen has enriched my work with her sharp insights and was especially valuable in the last stages of the manuscript, as she kept pressing me for the finished product. Sandy Petrey mercifully came to the rescue with a new title when my own imagination failed. Janice Candela has consistently offered encouragement at the most crucial moments. I am grateful to a great many of my colleagues at Dartmouth, who are always willing to discuss subjects often far removed from their own interests, most especially David Rollo, Carla

Freccero, Virginia Swain, and Kathy Wine. Special thanks go to Marianne Hirsch for her reading of Chapter 3, and for her friendship.

I would like to thank my students for their enthusiastic support of my work. Brenda Lunardini's help in preparing the manuscript was invaluable. Nancy Davies's computer expertise was invaluable. Jane Lewin was a scrupulous copy editor whose work greatly improved the book. I sincerely thank Leslie Mitchner for her careful readings, for believing in this project, and for helping me to improve it.

Finally, I wish to thank my family for their patient understanding and constant encouragement.

Portions of articles that previously appeared in *Papers on French Seventeenth-Century Literature* are now incorporated in revised form in Chapters 1 and 4. The Dartmouth Faculty Research Committee provided financial support necessary for preparation of the manuscript.

A Note on Translations

English translations are accompanied by the original French, except that the works of nineteenth- and twentieth-century scholars are given only in translation because the originals are, in general, easily accessible.

I frequently used early editions of French works. When citing such editions, I have reproduced the original punctuation, syntax, and capitalization but have modernized the spelling and accents.

All translations are my own unless otherwise indicated.

Revising Memory

Introduction

In 1929, Virginia Woolf searched in vain among the hundreds of scholarly volumes in the British Museum for a single book that could provide her with a woman's history, the elusive past of the "average Elizabethan woman." She guessed that this life, representative of all past female lives, "must be scattered about somewhere, could one collect it and make a book of it."[1] Woolf not only recognized the gendered void in history, but she also went on to stress the male bias in the genre of history as a whole:

> It would be ambitious beyond my daring, I thought, looking about the shelves for books that were not there, to suggest to the students of those famous colleges that they should re-write history, though I own that it often seems a little queer as it is, unreal, lop-sided; but why should they not add a supplement to history? calling it, of course, by some inconspicuous name so that women might figure there without impropriety.[2]

But maybe Woolf was too quick in concluding that either women's history or history by women was lacking. Perhaps Woolf's female precursors did make an effort to correct the "lopsidedness" of history and disguised their revision with an "inconspicuous name" that would not jump off the shelves as history, even before the eyes of a receptive Woolf.

In this study I will explore the possibility that long before Woolf's illuminating walk through those dusty halls, that territory of no-woman's land, women questioned the revered record of culture and challenged it by creating their own representations of the past. At first glance, the period and place of this investigation would seem the ones least likely to have produced women who dared interrogate the venerable genre of history. Although enough volumes about seventeenth-century France and the patriarchal, absolutist reign of the Sun King, Louis XIV, have been produced to fill many shelves in Woolf's British Museum, those volumes rarely valorize women's roles or even mention women writers. Yet Louis's own Bibliothèque Royale contained not only the names of many of his female contemporaries but also, and more remarkably, their literary works. In fact, the opening years of Louis XIV's reign saw a dramatic increase in the number of women writers. Moreover, if one examines this literary corpus, a striking feature becomes apparent. The overwhelming majority of these works are related to history—whether memoirs that strive to contribute directly to the historical record or novels and pseudomemoirs that posit history as the basis of their fiction. Could memoirs and novels perhaps be the "inconspicuous names" under which seventeenth-century French women chose to challenge history?

Literary historians have long recognized the important increase in the production of these two narrative genres in seventeenth-century France but, not surprisingly, few women's names can be found on the illustrious list of memorialists and novelists. For years the accepted masters of personal memoirs in this period have been Jean-François Paul de Gondi, the cardinal de Retz, and Louis de Rouvroy, the duc de Saint-Simon. Similarly, César Vichard de Saint-Réal is frequently cited for his significant contribution to the genre of the *nouvelle historique,* or historical novel, even though he in fact produced only two such works, one of which for years was mistakenly attributed to a female contemporary.[3] Only one woman from the period, Marie-Madeleine Pioche de la Vergne, comtesse de Lafayette, has succeeded in entering the canon. Her principal work, *La Princesse de Clèves,* is now viewed as the prototype of the modern novel.[4] But her other novels and her memoirs, like the works of all her female contemporaries, have fallen into critical oblivion. The names of her female counterparts—Marie-Catherine-Hortense Desjardins, Mme de Villedieu; Marie-Catherine d'Aulnoy; Madeleine de Scudéry; Françoise Bertault de Motteville; and Anne-Marie-Louise-Henriette d'Orléans, the duchesse de Montpensier, to cite only the most prolific—more frequently evoke salon figures and worldly women than literary works. Their fate clearly illustrates the systematic suppression of women writers from literary history.

Very recently, feminist literary critics have attempted to reverse the burial process that has been occurring over the past two hundred years. The present study owes a great deal to the ground-breaking work of Joan DeJean and Nancy K. Miller, who have led the way in developing a poetics of women writers, especially those in seventeenth- and eighteenth-century France.[5] In contrast to works (such as Micheline Cuénin's enormous study of Villedieu) that, although extremely useful, are efforts to fill in the blanks of literary history, DeJean's and Miller's work presents these early modern texts as self-conscious examples of female authorship that constitute a distinct and cohesive literary tradition.[6] These two critics, joined by others, are not only uncovering previously forgotten women's texts but are also attempting to restore women and their works to the essential place they originally occupied. For many of these women were celebrated in their own time and throughout the eighteenth century as important literary figures who constituted an essential facet of French literary culture.[7] Even as late as 1811, Stéphanie-Félicité de Genlis, novelist and feminist, looked back at the seventeenth century as the golden pinnacle of a female literary tradition. A disproportionate number of the women she cites in *De l'influence des femmes sur la littérature comme protectrices et comme auteurs* are seventeenth-century women who created what she considers an ideal female literary world where women developed the narrative genres in which they were still excelling at the time she was writing.[8] According to Genlis, not only were women recognized as innovators in these genres, but this "multitude of women authors" also received the praise of their contemporaries, who "were happy to show them off" ("se plurent à les faire valoir").[9]

Seventeenth-century French women writers were especially valued for their contributions to narrative genres. Women were drawn to narrative in an age that valued theatre and poetry not because they did not dare enter these male-dominated bastions but because memoirs and novels responded to some of their own specific concerns. As genres in the process of formation, personal memoirs and the novel offered a freedom to experiment and innovate that theatre and poetry did not.[10] In addition, I believe that the specific attraction of memoirs and novels was directly tied to the fact that these genres could be affiliated with a certain vision of history.

Thus far, neither historians nor literary critics have given critical attention to the historical nature of memoirs and novels because it has been generally agreed that, in writing them, women were not really writing history and had no intention of doing so. Women's memoirs, for example, are often considered merely personal reminiscences without historical pretensions.[11] And although an amazing amount of research went into the construction of fictional works (as authors such as Villedieu pointed out at length), the composition of this historical background is neglected.[12] Much of the reluctance to examine history in women's memoirs and novels stems from a deep-seated, stereotypical notion that, because there is no tradition of women's historiography in the conventional sense of the term, women were not interested in history. Too often, the possibility that seventeenth-century women could actually have been seriously drawn to history is seen as preposterous. In his influential study of Saint-Réal, for example, Gustave Dulong denies Lafayette the concern with history that he attributes to her male counterparts—denies it to her precisely because of her sex. "Women, especially worldly women, in general, have a mediocre interest in history. The past, with its crude and old-fashioned elements, appears more ridiculous than appealing to them. They try less to see it as it was than to disguise it following their fancy. . . . Thus in *La Princesse de Clèves* we find the ideal portrait of an aristocratic and worldly society rather than a historically exact painting of the French court in the sixteenth century."[13] Dulong's generalities completely disregard the seventeenth-century context of Lafayette's and other women's works. As a result, he and other critics (albeit less explicitly) interpret the historical content through a grid of preconceptions that inhibits the appreciation of these texts.

Many critics have attempted to account for the general emergence of H/histoire at this time, that is, historical novels that crossbreed the noble genre of Histoire, or history, with fictional histoire, or story. Most critics, however, tend to dismiss the historical nature of these novels either as heavy-handed efforts to adhere to the criterion of vraisemblance, or plausibility, and to fool the reader, or as weak attempts to be realistic.[14] To illuminate the appearance during the classical period of genres related to history, recent critical inquiry has focused on the relationship between memoirs and fictional works.[15] Yet, although much effort has been made to account for the complex relationship between history and fiction in seventeenth-century France and for the development of memoirs and novels, the relationship between women writers and these works at the intersection of history and fiction has remained obscure. Recognized by their contemporaries as the initiators of the historical novel and as innovators with respect to memoirs, these women writers, until very recently, have never been analyzed as a group. Although Marie-Thérèse Hipp, for example, includes proportionately more women than men in her study of memoirs and novels, she does not speculate on the sudden influx of women writers, nor does she view any of the characteristics of their works as gender-specific or even gender-related. Yet, paradoxically, like many other critics both contemporary and modern, she does group female literary works together and often attributes distinguishing characteristics to them. A number of crucial questions thus remain: Why were *women* drawn to history when founding a literary tradition? Why does the period 1660–1680 reveal such a surge of women writing historical narratives, both nonfictional and fictional? Did seventeenth-century women writers have a common conception of history?

I believe one can shed much light on these questions by examining women's memoirs and novels of the period 1660–1680 together, as productions of a specific group of women who dominated the literary scene. I wish to reestablish a conversation between women's memoirs and women's novels, a conversation that has been silenced by strict generic distinctions. Writers such as Villedieu, Lafayette, and Montpensier foster this literary dialogue because they practiced both genres. Moreover, one may view these works as developing from actual, literal conversations among these women, for they all knew one another, came from the same court milieu, and frequently gathered together in the influential literary salons of the period. Thus, even though the memoirs of these women were not actually published until the eighteenth century, it is entirely plausible that they were aware of one another's literary efforts and even circulated their manuscripts.

In fact, I will argue, when these memoirs and novels are read as a literary corpus, they evidence such similar preoccupations with society, literary form, and history that they represent a collective perspective and ideology.

These women's common concerns are especially coherent and well-formulated with respect to history and the relationship between their own literary efforts and the collective record of the past. When one puts aside the common critical coin that history in these novels is just a creative tool and that memoirs are too subjective to be serious history, one can consider these works as nontraditional histories in a dialogue with the traditional and dominant form of history. Such an approach is encouraged and prompted by the influential studies of the feminist historians Natalie Zemon Davis, Joan Kelly, and Joan Scott, who offer an alternative evaluation of women's historical undertakings.[16] They valorize works such as women's memoirs as a form of historical writing and, in so doing, call into question the conventional definition of history itself. This vein of inquiry offers exciting possibilities for the study of women's memoirs as well as women's historical fiction.

A number of other recent trends in historical and literary scholarship encourage the reassessment of seventeenth-century women's memoirs and novels. As historians have attempted to unearth a history of women, a history buried by the officially sanctioned historical record, they have necessarily been drawn to sources that have not traditionally been considered "true history" because they are "unscientific" and "subjective"—sources such as memoirs, autobiographies, and letters. This has led to an examination of the form and content of history itself. Hayden White has greatly advanced this field of inquiry by placing the accent on history's narrativity, its creative and constructed quality, thus undermining the conception of history as the presentation of an inviolable body of fact.

Like the historians who are reevaluating the nature of their discipline and, in particular, are introducing gender as an essential and valid category of inquiry, so, too, feminist critics have been uncovering past female literary productions that call into question the validity of the traditional repressive and patriarchal literary canon. In addition to uncovering women's participation in literature, they have discovered literary creations that have fallen through the crevices left by stringent definitions of genres and "literariness." Women's memoirs and autobiographies have especially profited from this reexamination of genres. Collections such as *The Female Autograph, Interpreting Women's Lives,* and *Life/lines* are all vital efforts to undermine the prevalent critical conviction that women can write only of the self and possess neither the desire nor the ability to transcend the personal in order to enter the "higher" realm of culture.[17] These feminist critics recuperate women's memoirs and autobiographies, long denied status as history because of their first-person subjects and still excluded from the literary canon because they supposedly do not conform to the rules of the genres in which a self is textualized.[18] The feminist critics reevaluate generic categories and examine the criteria used to analyze literary and historical texts. Such an approach is especially useful in my own project, for if there are no women historians in the conventional sense of the term in early modern France, that is perhaps because of our strict generic definitions. But if these women's texts are viewed as powerful and deliberate conflations of conventional generic categories, new possibilities as to the motivation for and purpose of these works become possible. The literary dialogue I am proposing here is feasible only if one follows recent feminist historians and literary critics in disregarding conventional oppositions such as history versus literature and autobiography versus history—dichotomies that, I believe, women such as Montpensier and Lafayette in fact sought to challenge.

In addition to the memoirs and novels themselves, a third component of the conversation among women's literary works is essential to an understanding of how and why these texts function as forms of history. That component is the cultural and historical context in which the works were produced. In many ways, the current discussion of genres and the examination of history reflect the seventeenth-century context, which was far removed from the order and stability conventionally seen as characteristic of the classical age. To interpret these women's writings, it is necessary to examine them in light of the social, intellectual, political, and historiographical movements of seventeenth-century France, for they are products of and responses to the particular period in which they were created. In other words, one must establish the "horizon of expectations," to use Hans Jauss's term.[19]

Georges May and Marc Fumaroli both identify the development of personal memoirs and historical novels as a specifically French phenomenon.[20] I believe that the key to understanding this production is the conception of history that was prevalent in mid–seventeenth-century France—the way history was viewed and the role it played under the Sun King. Too often, critics today consider historical narrative to have been an unproblematic and fixed genre underlying both memoirs and novels.[21] A closer analysis, however, reveals that history, like memoirs and novels, was in a state of transition. Inspired by the critique of historiography epitomized by White's work, many recent critics have delved into the nature of history in seventeenth-century France. Orest Ranum's in-depth examination of historians during the seventeenth century, viewed against the backdrop of their counterparts in the Renaissance, confirms Paul Hazard's previous view of the classical period as "a crisis [in the conception] of history."[22] Intense discussions throughout the seventeenth century focused on the nature and purpose of history. Women's memoirs and novels developed within this "crisis" and reflect and augment the complex changes taking place.

A second important aspect of the sociohistorical climate that fostered women's literary production is the women's own roles as agents in history. In the classical period women emerged as a social force, assuming active roles in the civil war known as the Fronde (1648–1652) that took place during Anne d'Autriche's regency, and establishing influential literary salons (prevalent primarily in the middle of the century). Drawing on the work of a few recent historians, namely, Carolyn Lougee, Dorothy Backer, and Ian Maclean, I propose to read women's history-affiliated works in light of their authors' political and social activity.[23] I believe it is hardly coincidental that the same women who participated in the Fronde and conducted the literary salons were those who turned to writing memoirs and historical novels after the Sun King took power.

It is in light of that crucial historical and literary background, which is elaborated in my first chapter, that I propose to examine the use and conception of history in four representative examples of women's memoirs and novels of the period 1660–1680. The choice of these particular years is not arbitrary. The majority of the women who participated in the Fronde were composing their memoirs during this period, even though the works were generally not published until just after Louis XIV's death in 1715. In addition, 1660 is the accepted date of the decline of the heroic novel, with its reliance on ancient history, and of the birth of the historical novel, with its use of contemporary history.[24] The subsequent twenty years were the apogee of the historical novel, many examples of which were composed by the same women who experienced the Fronde and were dominant salon figures.[25] These twenty years witnessed the emergence of a female literary tradition associated with the two genres of memoirs and the historical novel. Although this tradition continued to flourish well into the eighteenth century, the relationship between the works produced and history changed significantly. Later writers, such as Catherine Bernard, made less of an attempt to deliberately confound fiction with history and tended more to label their fictions "secret history"—a term never used by the preceding generation and one that much more clearly separates literature from history than the earlier titles of choice, namely, *nouvelle historique* or simply *Histoire*.[26] I am especially interested in determining what sparked this particular history-affiliated literary tradition and what inspired women to develop these particular literary genres.

The four works I have chosen can all be viewed as adding to the "crisis of history," for their authors both overtly and covertly probe the general definition of history as "the narration of actions and things worthy of memory [*digne de mémoire*]" (dictionary of the French Academy). Each text proposes a set of revisions to this definition. Each work is also important for its ability to raise issues of current theoretical concern. For example, Montpensier's *Mémoires* has long been dismissed as a self-indulgent, egocentric narrative that epitomizes the genre of personal memoirs. Critics have allowed women to figure "without impropriety" in the first-person works the *Mémoires* represents because they exclude these works from the domains of "real" literature and history. An examination of Montpensier's text within its historical context, however, shows that she uses her voice as a consciously female historian to create a narrative that transgresses the boundaries of "propriety."

Montpensier's *Mémoires* is one of the two texts I analyze at length. The other is the one female-authored work of this period that has been deemed worthy of inclusion in the literary canon, Lafayette's *La Princesse de Clèves*. I focus on the historical narrative, which has traditionally been considered merely a background for the fiction and has been judged the one flaw in a work otherwise viewed as the pinnacle of the genre of the historical novel. In my approach, the historical narrative can be seen as a subtext designed to establish the meaning of the fictional story of the princess. An examination of Lafayette's historical narrative also helps to explain one of the most virulent literary polemics in seventeenth-century France: despite its popularity, the novel was condemned in the seventeenth century as *invraisemblable*, or implausible, and aroused a heated controversy.[27]

My two shorter readings—of Villedieu's *Les Désordres de l'amour* and Lafayette's *Histoire de Madame Henriette d'Angleterre*—are designed to enrich the analyses of Montpensier's *Mémoires* and Lafayette's influential novel. Villedieu has been almost completely ignored, in part because her works, with their historical specificity, are considered unreadable. Yet Villedieu, one of the most prolific authors in the seventeenth century, is even more engaged in her period's debate over history than her now more illustrious counterpart, Lafayette. Her work is thus an essential facet of the overall relationship between literary women and history. Another little-known text, Lafayette's biography of Henriette d'Angleterre, provides a metacommentary on history and is a fascinating counterpoint to women's memoirs and novels.

These four texts were all produced by an elite group of women in response to a specific set of historical, cultural, and intellectual circumstances. When Montpensier's, Lafayette's, and Villedieu's works are viewed in terms of the history they put forward, they illuminate women's literary production, in general, and the development of history-related literary genres, in particular, during this highly creative period. These four memoirs and novels reveal that a group of women were in a dialogue with one another, and with their society, about the form and role of history. Their literary works illustrate the various strategies women of this period used to forge a place in both literature and history for their creativity and, in the process, to challenge the prevailing conceptions of both disciplines.

Perspectives on History in Seventeenth-Century France

*C'est une chose étrange que l'on prenne tant de plaisir de se mettre en
danger, et que le péril soit agréable aux personnes de lettres, comme aux
soldats.*

MARGUERITE BUFFET, *LES ILLUSTRES SAVANTES*[1]

In the early years of the reign of Louis XIV, Charles Le Brun, first
painter to the king, executed a series of drawings to commemorate
the glorious events of the years 1654–1678. After becoming director of
the Manufacture Royale des Gobelins, which produced royal tapestries, Le Brun directed the transformation of these drawings into
tapestries, creating the famous series entitled "L'Histoire du roy."[2]
The fourteen tapestries of the series depict Louis XIV in the military
and civil accomplishments thought to be most worthy of historical
commemoration.[3] This pictorial history begins with the coronation in
1654, portrays Louis's marriage in 1660, immortalizes a succession of
military victories, and ends with the monarch's visit to the Gobelins
ateliers. In each tapestry, the king is glorified as the magnificent, omnipotent ruler of the court, the military sphere, and the realms of both
history and the imagination. The Sun King is placed at the center of
each scene, with almost exclusively male courtiers and military officers radiating from this focal point. With the tapestries, Le Brun
engraved these powerful images upon the collective memory and determined who and what should be transmitted to posterity. Louis XIV
surrounded himself with these images of control, using the tapestries
to embellish Versailles, itself decorated by Le Brun and others, and to
reinforce his royal image. The tapestries reflected the king's image back
at him, functioning much like the mirrors at Versailles. Reproduced a
total of seven times, the tapestries legitimized those moments as the
ones "worthy of memory" ("digne de mémoire"), conforming to the
century's definition of history.[4]

Le Brun's majestic creations communicated not only the king's
accomplishments but also—implicitly—his control over the historical
representation of his reign for future generations. With these scenes,
Louis XIV staged a coup against future representation of his reign by
imposing the only kinds of images that could legitimately be called
history. The omnipotent, patriarchal presence he assumed in the
artistic representations blocked out any other depiction of society.

Louis used such artistic methods to form the historical record in his own image, according to his own desires.

In a society obsessed with *être* and *paraître*—reality and appearance—Louis proves to be the ultimate manipulator of *paraître*, particularly regarding historical representation and discourse.[5] But beneath the Sun King's mastery lies another, rival history, an *être* that awaits unveiling. As Mme de Chartres warns her daughter in Lafayette's *La Princesse de Clèves*, "If you judge by appearances in this place, . . . you will often be mistaken: for appearances are almost never the truth " ("Si vous jugez sur les apparences en ce lieu-ci, . . . vous serez souvent trompée: ce qui paraît n'est presque jamais la vérité").[6] Mirrors can be deceptive. Perhaps Louis's control of historical representation was not as absolute as the tapestries would have us believe.

HISTORY UNDER LOUIS XIV

When Le Brun entitled his series of tapestries "L'Histoire du roy," how was he interpreting the term *Histoire?* What are the importance and function of these artistic representations in relation to the larger domain of history and in relation specifically to narrative history? In the seventeenth century, the boundaries and purpose of history were no longer clear. Critics, theorists, and historians seem to agree with the global definition offered by Richelet in 1680:

> History: A continuous narration of true, great, and public things, written with spirit, eloquence, and judgment for the education of private citizens and princes, and for the good of civil society.

> Histoire: Une narration continuée de choses vraies, grandes, et publiques, écrite avec esprit, avec éloquence et avec jugement pour l'instruction des particuliers et des Princes, et pour le bien de la société civile.

Richelet's contemporary, Furetière, gives a similar description (1690):

> History: A true narrative, coherent and linked together, of many memorable events that have occurred in one or in many nations.

> Histore: Se dit de cette narration véritable suivie et enchainée de plusieurs événements mémorables qui sont arrivés en une ou plusieurs nations.

The adjectives "public" and "memorable" appear consistently here as well as in other contemporary definitions of *Histoire*, and are frequently joined by "general." Furetière's definition of *général*, the qualifier most frequently associated with a global definition of *Histoire*, presents the various qualities associated with the concept:

> General: That which encompasses everything, which extends to everything. . . . People also say that a man, that a work, are generally approved, to say that they are universally esteemed.

> Général: Qui comprend tout, qui s'étend à tout. . . . On dit aussi, qu'un homme, qu'un ouvrage ont une approbation générale, pour dire, qu'ils sont universellement estimés.

In keeping with these definitions of "history" and "general," what can be termed "general history" in seventeenth-century France is a broad view of events that is devoted uniquely to occurrences in the public sector. There is a dominant ideology shaping this narration that is designed to be "universally esteemed." The historian must judge events and choose those that are "great" and "memorable" for the account to fulfill its pedagogical function—"the education of private citizens and princes"—and to offer a model "for the good of civil society."

These universalist, idealistic definitions leave much room for interpretation, a fact implicit in the academy's definition, which enumerates various types of history: general history, universal history, particular history, ancient history, modern history. The academy's list of the several categories points to the variety of ways in which "things worthy of memory" can be inscribed. Although the categories appear distinct and logical, in reality there was much overlap and much indecision about the forms that historical narrative should take. This confusion is reflected in the inflated number of historical avatars during the seventeenth century in France. Although an in-depth analysis of seventeenth-century historiography is beyond the scope of the present study, it is important to isolate certain trends and transformations that influenced the development of narrative genres such as memoirs and the historical novel.

Throughout the seventeenth century, erudite historiography remained alive, and scholars laboriously strove both to continue the work of humanists and to expand upon it. But although this meticulous archival work existed, its influence was negligeable. When courtiers and kings turned to written history, they chose the accounts that were devoted to their own country and written in the tradition of *Les Grandes Chroniques de France*. As Philippe Ariès states, "The history of France is not a scholarly or a literary genre, but it is a traditional genre, for which the rules are well established, the public fairly large, and which varied little from the fifteenth to the nineteenth century."[7] In this tradition, history was not rewritten as people in each century became more illuminated about the events of their past. Rather, the next generation left the account relatively untouched, merely adding its own "events worthy of memory" to the record.[8] This traditional narrative is static, its content determined by preceding centuries. The emphasis is placed on recounting treaties, wars, and other acts of sovereignty.

The most famous seventeenth-century historian in the tradition of *Les Grandes Chroniques* is François Eudes de Mézeray.[9] His *Histoire de France depuis Faramond jusqu'à maintenant* appeared in 1643 and was reprinted six times by 1712. Mézeray's popularity continued into the nineteenth century, which saw two more editions of his work. He was by far the most popular historian during the reign of the Sun King and the one to whom authors of the historical novel turned as their principal source. Mézeray's case is thus important in seventeenth-century historiography, and his work merits our consideration for the innovations he brought to the genre as well as for its ultimate fate under the Sun King.

Mézeray designed his history to appeal above all to a reading public both at court and in the provinces. He attracted readers by promising to include previously undisclosed state secrets, thus going beyond his predecessors' factual accounts.[10] As Ranum remarks, Mézeray "had a keen sense of what might make books sell and seemed willing to do almost anything, including the addition of miracles and prodigies, to appeal to the public."[11] He refrained from listing his sources, out of the same desire to avoid boring his public. He added full-page engravings of each king and queen as well as of the medals and coins of each reign, and commented upon each portrait by placing poetic quatrains underneath it. Mézeray's *Histoire* is thus more lavish than those of his predecessors and is designed to please as well as to inform.

As an astute reader of the book market, Mézeray recognized that women were increasingly drawn to history. In his opening description, he seeks to attract this public by stressing the fact that he grants women their proper place in history: "After the medals come the queens with a summary of their lives, which no author has yet touched, as if ladies were not capable of heroic actions" ("Après des Médailles viennent les Reines avec un sommaire de leurs vies, auxquelles aucun Auteur n'avait encore touché, comme si les Dames n'étaient pas capables de faire des actions Héroïques").[12] Mézeray in fact dedicates his work jointly to Louis XIV and Anne d'Autriche, who was regent at the time of its publication. After inserting a portrait and epigraph glorifying Anne, Mézeray takes the occasion to stress his inclusion of women and to praise their contributions to history:

> This work, which I am bold enough to offer to Your Majesty, has on its cover the name and the portrait of Louis the Just, and was

not undertaken less for your glory than for that of this noble monarch. If Your Majesty deigns to favor it with one of her looks which now watch over the behavior of so many people, she will not only see the kings in their triumphal chariots, she will also see the queens at their sides sharing with them the splendor of the crown and praise for the most royal actions. Certainly I have often been surprised that through negligence our historians have left these illustrious princesses in obscurity for so long: and I was always waiting for one of them to make a point of taking them out [of obscurity] to show that there is now in the world a queen who, herself, possesses more rare qualities than all of them together had.

Cet Ouvrage, que je prends la hardiesse d'offrir à Votre Majesté, porte sur le front le Nom et le Portrait de Louis le juste, et n'a pas moins été entrepris pour votre Gloire que pour celle de cet Auguste Monarque, Si V.M. daigne le favoriser d'un de ses regards qui veillent maintenant à la conduite de tant de peuples, elle n'y verra pas seulement les Rois dans leurs Chars de Triomphe, elle y verra aussi les Reines à leurs côtés partager avec eux l'éctat de la Couronne et les louanges des plus Royales actions. Certes je me suis étonné beaucoup de fois de quoi la négligence de nos Historiens laissait si longtemps ces illustres Princesses dans l'Obscurité: et j'attendais toujours que quelqu'un d'entr'eux prît le soin de les tirer pour leur faire voir qu'il y a maintenant au Monde une Reine, qui possède elle seule plus de rares qualités qu'elles n'en avaient toutes ensemble.

Mézeray seeks to fill a void left in previous histories, as he courts a female public. His innovation is not, however, as revolutionary as his preface would have us believe. He replaces one narrow lens with a wide-angle lens to add "the queens at their sides," but he does not add a second lens focused on women as the first is on men. In fact, the queens and princesses remain to the side, as the placement of their portraits pointedly illustrates. Whereas each king's portrait precedes the history of his reign, the portraits of the women are inserted almost as afterthoughts following the medals at the end of the narrative of each period. Accompanying each woman's portrait is a brief biography. Thus women are mentioned, but they are not fully incorporated into Mézeray's narrative of "memorable events."

Mézeray's history proved to be so popular that in 1667 he produced a shorter, more manageable version, entitled *Abrégé ou extrait de l'histoire chronologique de France*, which was even more widely read. But the popular *Abrégé* proved to be his downfall, for it revealed that he was not the most benign and conventional of historians. In the *Abrégé*, he criticized royal policies of taxation. Colbert quickly warned the historian that he did not receive a royal pension (one that in fact was the highest given to any man of letters at the time) to write such criticism. Mézeray revised his *Abrégé,* but even his corrections were unacceptable; his pension was cut in half and finally withdrawn altogether. The royal historiographer was disgraced. Even his fellow academicians did not support him. In fact, they felt freer to attack his *Histoire* and his *Abrégé* on stylistic grounds: they considered both works too colloquial and not in compliance with the academy's strict standards.

Mézeray's fate provides important insights into the status of historiography under the most absolute monarch. A historian's style was an essential aspect of the work, as history took on literary qualities and pretensions. And both the style and the content of history were more and more subject to surveillance, as Louis XIV began to establish his control over historiography. The timing of Mézeray's downfall is very significant, for it came in the opening years of the Sun King's reign, that is, at precisely the moment when Louis, with the help of Colbert, appropriated the domain of history for his own political ends. In fact, Erica Harth goes so far as to maintain that "when Louis XIV assumed personal rule, . . . official history [in the sense of a general history of France] faded from the literary scene." [13] Histories of France à la Mézeray ceased to be produced and were replaced by accounts consecrated entirely to describing and glorifying Louis XIV.

If the shift from the History of France to the History of Louis XIV as the officially sanctioned and supported narrative appears abrupt, that is because it was. The civil war known as the Fronde prompted this change, for, in the war's aftermath, many nobles were disgraced and thus incapable of supplying support to men of letters. [14] After the arrest of Louis's finance minister, Fouquet, in 1661, patronage no longer came from that central court figure, who preferred poetry and the arts, but from Colbert, who was more interested in history. [15] Colbert recognized the power that lay in properly guided historical narrative. In the 1660s and 1670s, Louis XIV and Colbert engaged a group of writers called *la petite académie* with the express intention of creating a narrative devoted to the glorious moments of Louis's reign. The primary task of the group—which consisted, at various times, of Montausier, Renault, Périgny, Pellisson-Fontanier, Chapelain, Charpentier, Siri, Racine, and Boileau—was to help Louis write his memoirs. [16] Each *historiographe du roi* wrote his own history, which was to contribute to the common objective of producing a complete history of the monarch. The participants in what can be termed this propaganda machine were closely surveyed, and Louis and Colbert carefully monitored the subjects covered and the information included. When, for example, Charpentier asked for secret documents to help him in his historiographical undertaking, Colbert rejected the request—and the historian quit. The topics deemed necessary for inclusion were royal acts of leadership and military deeds that were publicly known. The interior realm of personality traits and state secrets had no place in this conception of history.

Paul Pellisson-Fontanier's history exemplifies Louis's officially sanctioned narrative. The historiographer was chosen to record, in particular, Louis's military campaigns, and he therefore accompanied the king into the field. In the introduction to his history, Pellisson explains the organization of his narrative according to periods of peace and war:

> I am writing the history of France under the reign of Louis, the fourteenth of that name, from the Pyrenees treaty and the death of Cardinal Mazarin, when it can be said that this reign truly began, to the peace of Nimwegen that has just been concluded. This period of eighteen years contains so many remarkable events that it seems that nothing is lacking, either to instruct or to please. . . . In my subject I find, in three almost equal periods, three different revolutions . . . six years of peace, . . . then six years of war suddenly kindled between France and Spain . . . and finally the six last years, when all Europe is in arms.

> J'écris l'Histoire de France sous le Règne de Louis quatorzième du nom, depuis la paix des Pyrénées, et la mort du Cardinal Mazarin, où l'on peut dire que ce Règne a véritablement commencé, jusqu'à la paix de Nimègue, qu'on vient de conclure. Cet espace de dix-huit ans est mêlé de tant d'événements remarquables, qu'il semble n'y rien manquer, ni pour instruire, ni pour plaire . . . je trouve dans mon propre sujet en trois intervales presque égaux, trois révolutions différentes . . . on y verra six années de paix; . . . six années ensuite [de] guerre soudainement allumée entre la France et l'Espagne . . . six dernières années enfin, où toute l'Europe est en armes.[17]

Pellisson's account, intended, like all history, both to "instruct" and to "please," follows the king through all the "negotiations, the military lines, the treaties, the ventures, the sieges, the combats, the battles at sea and on land, as memorable as can be found anywhere" ("négotiations, les lignes, les traités, les entreprises, les sièges, les combats, les batailles sur mer et sur terre, aussi mémorables qu'on en puisse trouver ailleurs") in order to illustrate Louis's great abilities "in governing" ("en la manière de gouverner") and "in making war" ("en celle de faire la guerre") (3). In his introduction, Pellisson uses a tactic common to historians to guarantee the authority of their narratives, stressing that, as eyewitness and the king's confidant, he can recount these memorable events accurately. Not surprisingly, Louis remains at the center of the narrative, as he himself determined which events merited inscription.

Racine's history follows the same path as his colleague Pellisson's,

as he reinforces the patriarchal and political order. Racine had to re-
nounce the theatre to become a royal historiographer, but his history
has much the same laudatory tone as the prefaces to his plays. He begins his *Précis historique des campagnes de Louis XIV* by evoking the king
himself:

> Before the king declared war on the states of the United Prov-
> inces, his reputation had already made all the princes of Europe
> jealous. The tranquility of his people secured, order reestablished
> in his finances, his ambassadors avenged, Dunkerque recaptured
> from the English, and the Empire so gloriously aided, were all il-
> lustrious proof of his wisdom and leadership; and by the speed of
> his conquests in Flanders and in Franche-Comté, he had shown
> that he was as excellent a captain as a political leader.
>
> Thus, revered by his subjects, feared by his enemies, admired
> by the whole earth, he seemed to have only to enjoy in peace a
> glory so solidly established, when Holland offered him new occa-
> sions to distinguish himself by actions whose memory could
> never perish among men.

> Avant que le roi déclarât la guerre aux Etats des Provinces-Unies,
> sa réputation avait déjà donné de la jalousie à tous les princes de
> l'Europe. Le repos de ses peuples affermi, l'ordre rétabli dans ses
> finances, ses ambassadeurs vengés, Dunkerque retirée des mains
> des Anglais, et l'Empire si glorieusement secouru, étaient des
> preuves illustres de sa sagesse et de sa conduite; et par la paridité
> de ses conquêtes en Flandre et en Franche-Comté, il avait fair voir
> qu'il n'était pas moins excellent capitaine que grand politique.
>
> Ainsi, révéré de ses sujets, craint de ses ennemis, admiré de
> toute la terre, il semblait n'avoir plus qu'à jouir en paix d'une
> gloire si solidement établie, quand la Hollande lui offrit encore
> de nouvelles occasions de se signaler par des actions dont la
> mémoire ne saurait jamais périr parmi les hommes.[18]

This history, which borders on panegyric, is representative of the accepted form for general history under the Sun King. It is hardly "general," in that one person occupies center stage and all events are
described with respect to this patriarch. Racine considers the historical scene only from an exterior point of view and places his emphasis
on military exploits. Even the king's character is evoked by these actions, as the "conquests" constitute "illustrious proof of his wisdom
and his leadership." It is these actions, "whose memory [can] never
perish among men," that are "worthy of memory," conforming to the
academy's definition of history.

Louis XIV's own *Mémoires*, composed with the aid of his personal historians, reinforces the exteriorized, military-oriented perspective evident in Pellisson's and Racine's histories. Only five years
are included—1661, 1662, 1666, 1667, and 1668—the years when

Louis was consolidating his power and imposing his views of history. The *Mémoires* was not published until 1806, for it was addressed uniquely to the dauphin with the purpose of instructing him in the art of kingship. The importance Louis attaches to this pedagogical exposition is evident from the opening lines: "My son, many reasons, all very important, made me decide to leave to you, with much work on my part, among all my other important occupations, these memoirs of my reign and of my principal actions" ("Mon fils, beaucoup de raisons, et toutes fort importantes, m'ont fait résoudre à vous laisser, avec assez de travail pour moi, parmi mes occupations les plus grandes, ces Mémoires de mon règne et de mes principales actions").[19]

Judging from the text, Louis considers his "principal actions" to be his consolidation of power around his own person, his military maneuvers, and the royal acts that illustrate his philosophy of government. He does not go into detail in describing these actions, excluding, for example, any discussion of the inevitable decision-making processes behind each royal act. As a result, the *Mémoires* often takes on the appearance of a succinct list of royal decrees:

> I gave to Cardinal Antoine and to d'Auberville, who were in charge of my affairs in Rome, the power to create an opposition group against Turkey, and I offered to contribute my money and my troops, many more than any other Christian prince. I gave one hundred thousand *écus* to the Venetians for their war against Candia. . . . I reestablished, by a new order, the rigor of the former edicts against swearing and blasphemy. . . . I added new precautions to those I had already taken against duels. . . . I applied myself to destroying Jansenism and to dispersing the communities where this spirit of innovation was fermenting. . . . I gave the order that substantial alms be given to the poor of Dunkerque.

> Je donnai pouvoir au cardinal Antoine et à d'Auberville, chargés de mes affaires à Rome, de faire une ligue contre le Turc, où j'offrais de contribuer de mes deniers et de mes troupes, beaucoup plus que pas un des autres princes chrétiens. Je donnai cent mille écus aux Vénetiens pour leur guerre de Candie. . . . Je rétablis, par une nouvelle ordonnance, la rigueur des anciens édits contre les jurements et les blasphèmes. . . . J'ajoutai de nouvelles précautions à celles que j'avais déjà prises contre les duels. . . . Je m'appliquai à détruire le jansénisme, et à dissiper les communautés où se fomentait cet esprit de nouveauté. . . . Je donnai ordre qu'on distribuât des aumônes considérables aux pauvres de Dunkerque. (74–75)

Interspersed among such precise actions are general maxims specifying the absolute monarch's view of the role and character of kings. For example, after recounting the downfall of Fouquet, Louis adds a knowledgeable reflection for his son and for any monarch who desires to learn from his exemplary experiences: "I mean that after having listened to advice, it is up to us to make our resolutions, as no one either dares to or can suggest resolutions to us that are as good or as royal as we can find in ourselves" ("Je veux dire qu'après avoir pris conseil, c'est à nous à former nos résolutions, personne n'osant ni ne pouvant quelquefois nous les inspirer aussi bonnes et aussi royales que nous les trouvons en nous-mêmes" [98]). Louis offers himself as the ultimate exemplum, and his personal actions become the basis for a global notion of the political.[20]

The *Mémoires* is the conclusive expression of the theory of history that, both implicitly and explicitly, underlies Louis's verbal and visual histories. According to this theory, Louis is the only historical subject capable of providing not only "the great events" but also general truths. Louis harnessed the visual power of artistic representations to express this absolutist theory in which one person becomes the raison d'être of a historical narrative. In the early 1670s, the popularity of Racine's historical tragedies, with their glorification of some of Louis's royal predecessors, such as Augustus and Alexander, reached its apogee. Racine's laudatory prefaces frequently compare the Sun King to these monarchs—always, of course, to the ruling king's advantage. The persuasive power of theatrical representations was reinforced by lavish *carrousels* and spectacles in which Louis often played the role of Apollo.[21] These same years witnessed the evolution of Versailles from a small hunting retreat to the king's principal residence, where Louis appropriated historical and mythical images such as Apollo to emphasize his party with such figures and, more often, his superiority.[22] In fact, Louis negated any sense of historical continuity. As Jean-Marie Apostolidès remarks: "From the perspective of the state intellectuals, the strategy consists of closing the historical field in order to prohibit any opposing word. They show that history goes back to a point, a unique, founding event, associated with the first years of the reign. After this coming [*avènement*], history can, at best, only repeat itself. . . . History opens and closes with the present reign."[23]

Succinctly stated, Louis's mythical comment, "l'Etat, c'est moi," can be transformed into "l'Histoire, c'est moi." Louis Marin has pointed out that Louis's model of historical discourse is founded upon a belief in the complicity between the power of royal acts and the equally essential power of the narrative accounts of those acts. According to Marin, "The narrative is that of political power. . . . This complicity is an exchange between . . . the absolute actor of history and the no less absolute writer of the history. Certainly, the historian "needs" the king, because he can tell [history] only if [the king] authorizes him to do so. . . . But the king also "needs" the historian because power cannot attain its absolute culmination unless the historian recounts the power." [24] This reciprocity between Louis and his various historians may have caused other forms of history to be eclipsed, but it did not stifle a debate over the nature of history and the forms it should take.

THE INTERROGATION OF HISTORY

While Louis XIV was creating a strict model for historical narrative, history as a whole was becoming more problematic, as its frontiers were under siege by theorists, commentators, historians, and even novelists wanting to determine its nature and, perhaps implicity, to challenge Louis's exclusive definition. Although questions about the general nature of historiography were raised throughout the century, this interrogation was especially strong in the century's later years, provoked, I would suggest, by Louis XIV's maniuplative claims on the genre. As Louis sought to replace history with his own story, a segment of the intellectual and court community subtly reacted by offering a proliferation of narratives and commentaries that called this exclusivity into question. Significantly, at precisely this time contemporary history became the favorite basis of fiction, as Maurice Lever's bibliography attests. [25] Titles qualified by such phrases as *histoire galante, nouvelle historique, Histoire nouvelle, Histoire véritable,* and *histoire secrète* abound, as writers played with the ambiguity inherent in the French term *histoire,* which can be translated as History and as story. [26] Various critics felt impelled to establish hierarchial rules for the composition, classification, and evaluation of works that, although often not overly claiming to be history, nonetheless had historical pretentions. The development of such narratives and of critiques of history prompted Nicolas Lenglet Dufresnoy to remark in 1713 that "there are fewer excellent Historians than there are writers who have wanted to create a good historian" ("il y a moins d'excellents Historiens qu'il n'y a d'écrivains qui en ont voulu former un bon"). [27]

Among such commentators and critics, François Menestrier stands out as exemplary. His *Les Divers Caractères des ouvrages historiques* (1694) is an effort to classify the various histories of this period by content and by form. [28] The inherent confusion of Menestrier's work is representative of thought about history in the final third of the seventeenth century.

Menestrier begins by announcing his intention to delineate the corpus of historical narrative "according to its content, or according to its form" ("par rapport à sa matière, ou par rapport à sa forme" [7]). Using content as the distinguishing factor, he differentiates six types of history: "natural history, ecclesiastical history, civil history, didascalistic history, curious history, and personal history" ("l'histoire naturelle, l'histoire ecclesiastique, l'histoire civile, l'histoire didascalique, l'histoire singulière," and "l'histoire personnelle" [7]). "L'histoire civile," defined as the histories "of peoples, nations, republics, communities, and towns" ("celles des Peuples, des Etats, des Républiques, des Communautés, et des Villes" [17]), corresponds to *histoire générale*. Formal distinctions prove to be more elusive than those based on content because many histories easily fall into two or three formal categories. The imprecision is evident from the start when Menestrier identifies "twelve or thirteen kinds" ("douze ou treize espèces") of historical forms, showing himself to be incapable even of specifying an exact number. Among these forms, he lists "universal history, particular history, simple history, figurative history, reasoned history, authorized history, and poetic history" ("L'histoire universelle, L'histoire particuliére, L'histoire simple, L'histoire figurée, L'histoire raisonée, L'histoire autorisée, and L'histoire poétique" [33]). When Menestrier turns to actual definitions and examples, the borders become less well defined.

Two general approaches to historiography surface in Menestrier's definitions and are most clearly embodied by his conceptions of *l'histoire simple* and *l'histoire figurée*. *L'histoire simple*, which roughly corresponds to the erudite histories that continued to be produced throughout the period, is defined as

> a *plain* and *faithful* narrative of things past, of the way they happened, *without any artifice* or ornamentation, such as most of the chronicles of the Roman Empire after Constantine, especially those which were written by monks and good religious men, who spoke about things *simply*, . . . with even more of an appearance of truth because there was *less artifice*.

> un récit *nu* et *fidèle* des choses passées, de la manière dont elles se sont passées, *sans aucun artifice* ni ornement de discours comme la plupart des chroniques du bas Empire, particulièrement celles qui ont été écrites par des Moines, et de bons Religieux, qui parlaient *simplement* les choses . . . avec d'autant plus d'apparence de vérité, que l'on y voit *moins d'artifice*. (34–35, my emphasis)

Menestrier places the accent on stylistic simplicity and equates this with veracity. *L'histoire simple* is a chronicle of events that succinctly records what happened, without divulging how occurrences came to pass. In contrast, there is *l'histoire figurée* or *l'histoire raisonnée* (Menestrier's definition conflates these two styles):[29]

> Figurative or reasoned history is that which has received various *ornaments* from the minds and skill of historians, such as for example the political and moral histories of the Greeks and

Romans, and those of the majority of modern historians, who, not content to write down and represent events, look for *the most secret motivations* and, going back to their causes, examine the motives, seek out the circumstances, and draw out certain *reflections*, which are like maxims and salutory teachings for the governance of states and the guidance of morals from the examples of the past. It is a *reasoned history*, which without stopping at the surface and appearance of things goes into the *thoughts of the people* who acted, uncovers their *intentions*, and reveals about the things they undertook the wisdom of their behavior, or their mistakes in judgment. This is why these histories are full of reflections, speeches, dialogue, and consultations.

L'Histoire figurée [or raisonnée] est celle qui a reçu divers *ornements* de l'esprit et de l'adresse des Historiens, comme sont les Histoires Politiques et Morales des Grecs, des Romains, et la plupart des Modernes, qui ne se contentant pas d'écrire les événements, et de les représenter, en cherchent les *ressorts les plus secrets*, et remontant jusqu'à leurs causes en examinent les motifs, en épulchent les circonstances, et tirent de ces principes certaines *réflexions*, qui sont comme autant de maximes et d'enseignements salutaires pour la conduite des Etats, et la direction des Moeurs sur les exemples du passé. C'est une *Histoire raisonnée*, qui sans s'arrêter à l'écorce, et à l'apparence des choses, va jusque dans *la pensée des personnes* qui ont agi, découvre leurs *intentions*, et fait voir sur l'événement des choses qu'ils ont entreprises la sagesse de leur conduite, ou leur défaut de jugement. C'est pour cela que ces Histoires sont pleines de Réflexions, de Harangues, de Dialogues, et de Consultations. (38–39, my emphasis)

Stylistically, *histoire figurée* is more embellished than *histoire simple*. In addition, the narrator of *histoire figurée* adopts a different perspective, delving into the undercurrents of events rather than remaining on the surface. This ornamental history has the merit of being more complete. As it is "l'histoire raisonnée," it gives the "reasons" (in the sense of explanations) for various events and implies, as well, a kind of personalization of the narrative by its author. The narrator of this style of history "reason" (in the sense of *raisonner*, to reflect) about the various events and provides interpretations as well as facts, going beyond a superficial regard to "the most secret motivations," "the thoughts of the people" and their intentions. Mézeray's history can be associated to an extent with this approach, although his perspective is far from all-encompassing, and only certain people's motivations are described. The official histories dedicated to Louis XIV's exploits, however, cannot be entirely subsumed under either the category of *histoire simple* or that of *histoire raisonnée*. As we have seen, Louis's historiographers combine these two categories, as they embellish their narratives with praises and pedagogical maxims yet remain primarily on the surface of events. They certainly would not have imagined going beyond what Menestrier terms "the appearance of things" to unveil "the wisdom of [the king's] behavior, or [his] mistakes in judgment." Mézeray's treating royal taxation in this light is precisely what caused his downfall.

As Louis's historiography superseded histories such as Mézeray's in terms of royal favor, *histoire raisonnée* began to take other forms that, at first glance, seem excluded from canonical definitions of history. Menestrier points to this development when he underscores the danger inherent in *histoire raisonnée* (reasonable history?). This brand of history has a dangerous side because it treads on literary territory, employing "stylistic devices [*figures*]." Too many literary genres can be subsumed under the category of *histoire raisonnée:*

> Whatever advantages history written in this way has, one must not be persuaded that those who lack such charms are not historians, because to merit this title it is sufficient to describe exactly past events in the way they happened, because there are epic and dramatic poems, and even some novels, which are representations and narratives of many things that have happened, but in another way than the way the things came about, because they are accompanied by ingenious fictions, ornaments, and artifice, which are the invention of those who write these things.

> Quelque avantage qu'ait l'Histoire écrite de cette sorte, il ne faut pas se persuader, que ceux à qui manquent ces grâces ne soient pas Historiens, puisque pour mériter ce titre il suffit de décrire exactement les choses avenues et passées, de la manière dont elles sont avenues, parce qu'il y a des Poèmes Epiques, et Dramatiques, et même quelques Romans, qui sont des représentations, et des récits de plusieurs choses avenues et passées, mais d'une autre manière qu'elles ne sont avenues puis qu'elles sont accompagnées de fictions ingénieuses, d'ornements, et d'artifices, qui sont des inventions de ceux qui écrivent ces choses. (44)

Menestrier alludes to the popularity of this more subjective history, which ought to be classified under his rubric *histoire poétique* but which often infiltrates *histoire raisonnée*. Menestrier defines this poetic history as

> that which is accompanied by fiction or which represents the life of a man and his actions under veils and symbols; all epic poems are histories of this kind, as are most novels, where the background can be true even though the circumstances have been changed.

> celle qui est accompagnée de fictions ou qui représente la vie d'un homme, et ses actions sous des voiles et des symboles; tous les

Poèmes Epiques sont des histoires de cette sorte, aussi bien que la plupart des Romans dont le fond peut être vrai quoique les circonstances soient changées. (56–57)

Included in this category of history are memoirs and novels, both of which may have historical pretensions.

It should be noted that Louis XIV himself contributed to the confusion between history and literature by appointing Boileau and Racine, two poets, to the position of royal historiographer.[30] Menestrier, however, attributes the popularity of poetic history to the novel, thus avoiding any critique of Louis's machinations. Works such as *La Princesse de Montpensier* (1662) and *La Princesse de Clèves* (1678), both of which Menestrier mentions explicitly, "created the public taste for these kinds of reading because of the refinement with which the events are brought about" ("ont donné du goût pour ces sortes de lectures pour la délicatesse avec laquelle les événements y sont amenés" [110]). A certain kind of memoirs also responded to this taste for new forms of history. Menestrier singles out those memoirs that unveil court intrigues, as opposed to "state memoirs" ("mémoires d'état") that recount political negotiations (99).[31] According to him, these newer memoirs "are books for which Queen Marguerite gave us the model, which are fashionable because one learns secrets one would never have discovered without the help of these books" ("sont des Livres à la mode, parce qu'on apprend des secrets que l'on n'aurait pas découverts sans le secours de ces Livres, dont la Reine Marguerite nous a fourni le modèle" [100]). Here, as in his examples of novels, Menestrier points to a strong female presence and influence, to which other commentators also refer. The more interiorized perspective resurfaces in this definition, echoing the one we saw in his explanation of *histoire raisonnée.*[32] Poetic history could thus, at times, be conflated with *histoire raisonnée,* as practiced by recognized historians such as Mézeray.

Menestrier ends his exposition of the various forms of history with a warning to critics: "I say that it takes great discernment to judge historical works properly. . . . Before making a pronouncement on a historical work, it is necessary to examine carefully what the content is, what type of history it belongs to, what the author's objective is, and how he aims to reach it" ("Je dis qu'il faut un grand discernement pour juger comme il faut des Ouvrages Historiques. . . . Il faut avant que de prononcer sur un Ouvrage Historique, examiner soigneusement quelle en est la matière, et à quelle espèce d'Histoire il appartient. Quelle est la fin de l'Auteur, et par quelle voie il y tend" [115–116]). The critic's overlapping categories and indeterminate number of supposedly specific forms of history underscore just how great the reader's "discernment" had to be during this time of historiographical questioning, upheaval, and innovation. Menestrier's effort to segregate the various forms of historical narrative was an idealistic venture doomed to failure because of the prevailing uncertainty, discontent, and controversy about the purpose and use of history, especially in the last third of the century.

At the heart of the polemic was the ideological value of two competing perspectives, one more official and exteriorized, the other devoted to divulging motivations and probing secret recesses. A number of critics lamented the incomplete picture transmitted by history as it was conventionally written. For example, Saint-Réal in *De l'usage de l'histoire* (1671) criticizes the general history that Menestrier designates *histoire simple* for its lack of "certain curiosities." [33] He is against histories that focus only on events and actions, and calls for an account that would "make men known. . . . To study history is to study the motives, the opinions, and the passions of men" ("faire connaître les Hommes. . . . Étudier l'Histoire, c'est étudier les motifs, les opinions, et les passions des hommes" [326]). A more detailed account, corresponding in spirit to Menestrier's *histoire raisonnée*, is needed to constitute Saint-Réal's ideal history. Such an account would be more complete and more suited pedagogically to a larger public, in that it would describe

> great people using their most personal qualities and what is most separate from their condition, [describing] the illusions of their mind and the weaknesses of their heart, the detail within, their secret and domestic life; which are all things they have in common with other men, and not at all their good or bad politics, which concern only great people like themselves.

> les Grands par ce qu'ils ont de plus personnel et de plus séparé de leur qualité, par les illusions de leur esprit et les faiblesses de leur coeur, par le détail de leur intérieur, leur vie secrète et domestique; qui sont toutes choses, qui leur sont communes avec les autres hommes, et non point par leur bonne ou mauvaise politique, qui ne regarde que les Grands comme eux. (399–400)

Saint-Réal goes beyond Menestrier in targeting "great people" as the subject of this ideal narrative. His perspective is the opposite of the one held by Racine, who recounts the exploits of one particular "Great"—Louis. Whereas Racine evokes personal traits only as proof of military prowess, Saint-Réal recommends eliminating such exterior elements to concentrate on the "secret life," the "heart," the "detail within" persons and events. It is important to note that Saint-Réal, speaking here as a theoretician and critic, was also a historian and the author of two historical novels. The type of history he is calling for is one that could nourish his fictions and justify their foundation in history. This is not an empirical, objectively verifiable history but, rather, one imagined by an author as s/he fills in the blanks of history.

Thirteen years later, Saint-Evremond echoes Saint-Réal in *Discours sur les historiens français* (1684) and laments the fact that most historians have followed a conventional model and "believed that a precise narrative of events was sufficient to instruct us, without considering that public affairs are conducted by men more often carried away by passion than guided by politics" ("ont cru qu'un récit exact des événements suffisait pour nous instruire, sans considérer que les affaires se font par des hommes que la passion emporte plus souvent que la politique ne les conduit").[34] Like Saint-Réal, Saint-Evremond expresses his public's desire for a history viewed from within, a history that includes "the passion" at the heart of many events.[35] Using a similar line of reasoning, Antoine Varillas describes the two opposing historical perspectives in the preface to his novel *Anecdotes de Florence ou l'histoire secrète de la Maison de Médici* (1685):

> The historian almost always considers men in public, whereas the writer of anecdotes examines them only in particular.[36] One believes he has fulfilled his duty when he depicts them as they were in the army or in the tumult of towns, whereas the other tries in any way to open the door of their study; one sees them in ceremonies and the other in conversation; one primarily follows their actions, and the other wants to witness their inner life.

> L'Histoire considère presque toujours les hommes en public, au lieu que l'écrivain d'anecdotes ne les examine qu'en particulier. L'un croit s'acquitter de son devoir lorsqu'il des dépeint tels qu'ils étaient à l'armée ou dans la tumulte des villes, et l'autre essaie en toute manière de se faire ouvrir la porte de leur cabinet; l'un les voit en cérémonie et l'autre en conversation; l'un s'attache principalement à leurs actions, et l'autre veut être témoin de leur vie intérieure.[37]

Varillas (who, it should be noted, was both a historian in Louis's service and later a historical novelist) posits the "writer of anecdotes" as a historian who adopts a more interiorized perspective. He juxtaposes this perspective against that of the historian as generally conceived, whom he defines as somone who considers only "men in public."

Varillas's terminology is useful for distinguishing between the two principal forms of historical narratives in the seventeenth century and their respective perspectives. In one case, the historian focuses on "men in public," and in the other s/he "examines them only in particular [*en particulier*]." As shall become apparent, "particular" is not synonymous with "private," a term that in these contexts is rarely contrasted with "public." The terms "public" and "particular" are frequently employed to distinguish the historian's focus. In fact, theorists, historians, and commentators in the mid-seventeenth century term the official narration of historical events *Histoire* with a capital H, or *histoire générale* or *publique*. Erudite and court histories, including Mézeray's and those of Louis XIV's band, represent two variations of *Histoire*. Another type of historical narrative with a more interiorized perspective was being formed at this time but had not yet found an official, approved form of expression. It is less politically oriented and more personalized and can be called particular history (*histoire particulière*)—"particular" being the adjective most frequently found to characterize its content. In *De la connaissance des bons livres*, Charles Sorel gives as clear a definition as one can find of each of these two approaches to history: "When one says history, one means the true kind, and that which has the true form of history, which recites the good and bad actions of men, and the success the actions may have had" ("Quand on nomme l'Histoire absolument, l'on entend la Véritable, et celle qui a la vraie forme d'Histoire, laquelle récite les actions des hommes bonnes ou mauvaises, et le succès qu'elles ont pu avoir").[38] Sorel subsumes under particular history all historical narratives that do not limit themselves to public actions and that therefore differ from general history: "Under the title of history, besides general histories, it is necessary to place particular histories, such as the lives of great and less important personages, collections of memorable incidents, and all the other narratives" ("Sous le titre d'Histoire, outre les Histoires générales, il faut comprendre les Histoires particulières, comme sont les Vies des grands personnages et des moindres, les recueils d'accidents mémorables, et toutes les autres narrations").[39]

Particular history is a large subcategory of history. It is difficult to define precisely because it incorporates many different kinds of historical narratives, such as memoirs and accounts that elaborate upon a single event or certain "memorable incidents." Menestrier identifies particular history uniquely with regions, memoirs, and biographies: "Particular histories are . . . the histories of provinces, of cities, of communities, of individual people. These histories are not particular only because of their subject matter, they are particular because of their form, because they refer to particular facts" ("Les Histoires particulières sont . . . les Histoires des Provinces, des Villes, des Communautés, et des personnes singulières. Ces histoires ne sont pas particulières seulement à raison de leur matière, elles le sont à raison de leur forme, parce qu'elles se réfèrent à ces faits particuliers" [33]). In 1685 Adrien Baillet, too, uses the term to refer to histories of provinces and towns.[40] By the eighteenth century, particular history possesses a distinct status within the larger domain of history. Abbé Batteux defines it simply as that which is different from "the general history of the world."[41] In the mid-eighteenth century, Saint-Simon juxtaposes general history and particular history in the *avant-propos* of his *Mémoires:*

> I call general history that which is such because it extends over many nations or over many centuries of the church or of the same nation. . . . I call particular history that of the time or of the country in which one lives. This latter, being less extensive and occurring under the gaze of the author, must be much more detailed and circumstantial.

> J'appelle histoire générale celle qui l'est en effet par son étendue de plusieurs nations ou de plusieurs siècles de l'Eglise, ou d'une même nation. . . . J'appelle histoire particulière celle du temps ou du pays où on vit. Celle-là, étant moins vaste et se passant sous les yeux de l'auteur, doit être beaucoup plus étendue en détails et en circonstances.[42]

In his delineation, the primary distinction between the two kinds of history is in the historian's relation to the events s/he recounts. General history demands a distanced surveyor of past events, whereas the writer of particular history is the eyewitness capable of supplying details.

The adjective "particulier" is defined as that which is diametrically opposed to "général." The many connotations of "particulier" suggest that, when the word is used to qualify "history," it may have more implications than Menestrier, Baillet, Batteux, and Saint-Simon acknowledge. Furetière defines it as follows:

> Particular: a relative term that concerns a type or an individual and that is contrasted to the general, the universal. . . . Also signifies private, that which is opposed to authority and magistracy. The Roman consuls, after their triumphs, returned to a particular life, to the plow. . . . Also signifies that which is uncommon, which is apart and separate. . . . Also signifies specific and is used for a quality, a property that is characteristic of a thing or a person and is not found in others. . . . Also signifies extraordinary. . . . Also refers to the details of things, of circumstances, minute details. . . . Also means intimate, secret.

> Particulier: terme relatif qui regarde l'espèce ou l'individu, et qui est opposé au général, à l'universel . . . signifie aussi Privé, qui est opposé aux Puissances, aux Magistratures. Les Consuls Romains après leur triomphe retournaient à une vie particulière, à la Charruë . . . signifie aussi ce qui n'est pas commun, qui est à part et séparé . . . signifie aussi spécifiquement, et se dit de quelque

qualité, de quelque vertu qui est propre à une chose, à une personne, et qui ne se trouve point en d'autres . . . signifie aussi Extraordinaire . . . se dit aussi au détail des choses, des circonstances, des minutries . . . signifie aussi familier, secret.

Particular history is thus an alternative history, as the synonyms "un-
common," "apart," and "separate" underscore. Many writers of the
period specify that they are recounting "the particularities" of events,
the "minute circumstances of a matter that one examines or recounts
in detail" ("menue[s] circonstance[s] d'une affaire qu'on examine ou
qu'on récite en détail" [Furetière]). This approach to the past amplifies larger, better-known events with specific details, as the author
delves beneath the surface.

In this line of thought, *Histoire,* or general history, can be defined as the account of recognizable, verifiable political events in the
public sector. What I will continue to call particular history, in contrast, is centered on the personal and the less universally known and
can be considered as telling "the secret motivations for the memorable
events we have learned about from general history" ("ressorts secrets
des événements mémorables, que nous avons appris dans l'Histoire"), as Abbé de Charnes defines it in his defense of *La Princesse de
Clèves.*[43] Particular history seeks to reveal the details and reasoning
that underlie the public matters of general history, the motives and
passions that determine officially recorded events, and it includes, in
addition, actions that are excluded from the general record. "Particular history," however, is not synonymous with what modern historians call "private history" because, as will become clear when we
turn to the texts of particular history, the content of this account is not
severed completely from that of general history or from the public
sphere—a severance connoted by the term "private."

During the seventeenth-century polemic, critics not only offered
two perspectives on history, but they also formulated the distinction
on gender grounds. Particular history includes women as motivating
forces, whereas women rarely figure prominently in general history.
The call for particular history in the mid-seventeenth century reflects
the shift of historical events from battlefield to court, from a domain
that traditionally excludes women to one in which they are at the center. As Saint-Evremond remarks:

Let us now turn to the courts, and reflect upon the effects that
passions produce there. In what court have women not had favor;
and in which intrigues were they not involved? And what did the
princesse d'Eboly not do under Philippe the second, as prudent
and as political as he was?

> Venons maintenant à ce qui regarde les cours, et faisons réflexion
> sur les effets que les passions y produisent. En quelle cour les
> femmes n'ont-elles pas eu du crédit; et en quelles intrigues ne
> sont-elles pas entrées? Que n'a point fait la Princesse d'Eboly
> sous Philippe second, tout prudent et tout politique qu'il était?[44]

In effect, Saint-Evremond is not only suggesting that women be included, but he also proposes a narrative where the accent is placed on
the court as opposed to the battlefield and where "intrigues" and "passions" are equivalent to military maneuvers. At the time he was writing, such an account was not yet in existence, despite Mézeray's claim
forty years earlier to have revised his narrative to include women. For
Mézeray does not go far enough below the surface to include most
passions and intrigues because he, like all historians before him, has
a specific conception of what constitutes "valid" history. In focusing
on the king and the king's royal pursuits, he rarely includes women
and is blind to their actual role in public affairs. For this he drew criticism forty years later from Lenglet Dufresnoy:

> But when one reads Mézeray, one finds him to be unfeeling and
> insensitive in this matter [women's roles in history]. He treats
> them less politically and more as a severe casuist.

> Mais qu'on lise Mézeray on le trouvera sec et dur sur cet article. Il
> traite moins en Politique qu'en sévère casuiste ce qui regarde l'in-
> térêt que les femmes prennent dans les affaires publiques.[45]

Lenglet Dufresnoy claims the focus should change to include women
and, in fact, he devotes the major part of *De l'usage des romans* to this
question: "It cannot be denied that the fair sex makes up more than
half of the reasonable world, and that it is the most essential part of
every court. But I dare affirm in addition that it often has more of a
role in important affairs than even ministers do" ("On ne saurait dis-
convenir que le Sexe ne fasse plus que la moitié du monde raisonnable, et qu'il ne soit la portion la plus essentielle de toutes les Cours.
Mais j'ose encore assurer qu'il a souvent dans les grandes affaires
plus de part que les Ministres mêmes").[46] Such a statement calls into
question the traditional conception of historical narrative. This formulation is fallible not only because it limits history to "the important
affairs" but also because it has a narrow view of what these affairs are.

Particular history is proposed as a corrective. As no officially
sanctioned particular history exists, the interiorized perspective can
be found only in certain types of memoirs and in novels that contained history. In fact, the definition of particular history is frequently
founded upon its manifestation in women's works, especially *La Prin-*

cesse de Clèves. Lenglet Dufresnoy identifies women's texts as the best examples of the genres that embody particular history:

> History's imperfection makes novels more valuable. Women, even though they are essential forces in important matters, hardly appear in history. . . . And when you read *Le Portrait des faiblesses humaines* and *Les Désordres de l'amour* of Mme de Villedieu, you are led with such wisdom into the secret recesses. . . . Let us again say it to our shame, it is usually women who raise novels to the highest degree of perfection.

> L'imperfection de l'Histoire doit faire estimer les Romans. Les femmes, quoique mobiles essentiels des grandes affaires, paraissent à peine dans l'Histoire. . . . Et quand vous lisez le *Portrait des faiblesses humaines* et *Les Désordres de l'amour* de Mme de Villedieu, avec quelle sagesse n'êtes-vous pas conduit dans les secrets détours. . . . Disons-le encore à notre honte, ce sont ordinairement les femmes qui les portent à un plus haut degré de perfection.[47]

Women are thus associated with particular history on two levels: as agents behind the scenes, in "the secret recesses" of "the great events," and as writers who choose to focus their narratives on this particular sphere of history. Historical novels merit consideration as history because the novelist builds her/his historical foundation the same way the historian does.

Efforts to revise the conception of history to include the less verifiable aspects of events called into question the truthfulness of the whole genre and gave rise to a vehement debate. Hazard remarks, "How could the true things that Saint-Evremond wanted to be admired be distinguished from the false?"[48] Women writers played an essential role in initiating and carrying on the debate. Memoirs and historical novels, so often considered self-centered or fictional, in fact represented a threatening alternative to official history. The flourishing genre of memoirs and the new genre of the historical novel provided a covert outlet for other viewpoints on history.

MEMOIRS AND NOVELS: A DESIRE FOR DIFFERENCE

The confusion within historiography opened the domain to writers eager to capitalize on the chaos. In fact, the early years of Louis's rule, when the monarchy's hold over historical production tightened, saw a flourishing of two literary genres with historical pretensions. During the last third of the century, the forms of both memoirs and novels changed dramatically, as did the names and gender of their primary authors. Women were in the forefront of the literary scene and helped provoke many of the profound changes in both genres. In fact, the development of the narrative genre that most rivaled history, the historical novel, is attributed to women, and specifically to Lafayette and her now lesser-known contemporary, Villedieu.[49] What changes did these women, among others, initiate that placed memoirs and the historical novel in a position to besiege traditional history's supposedly authoritative account even further?

Literary historians generally view 1660 as the year that marks the death of the heroic novel, as public taste shifted to narratives that purported to be more truthful.[50] In 1683, Du Plaisir attests to the change when he pronounces, "Short stories have completely destroyed long novels" ("Les petites histoires ont entièrement détruit les grands romans").[51] The stories to which he is referring are works that are generally only one or two volumes, such as Lafayette's *La Princesse de Montpensier*, in contrast to the interminable adventures in a heroic novel, which could easily attain twelve volumes. Although length is the most obvious difference, it is perhaps the least important one. With the shortening of fiction came a desire for greater believability. In *Les Nouvelles françaises*, a collection of stories attributed to Montpensier's secretary Jean-Regnault de Segrais, the characters contrast the new novel with the traditional heroic novel. The princesse Aurélie, who represents Montpensier herself, explains the difference between the two types of novels:

> We have undertaken to recount things as they are, and not as they ought to be: And this seems to me to be the difference between the *roman* [heroic novel] and the *nouvelle* [novel]; that the heroic novel writes about things as propriety dictates, and in the style of a poet; but the new novel must be more historical, and try to give images of things as we see them occur ordinarily, instead of as our imagination constructs them.

> Nous avons entrepris de raconter les choses comme elles sont, et non pas comme elles doivent être: Qu'au rest il me semble que c'est la différence qu'il y a entre le Roman et la Nouvelle; que le Roman écrit ces choses comme la bienséance le veut, et à la manière du Poète; mais que la Nouvelle doit un peu davantage tenir de l'Histoire, et s'attacher plutôt à donner les images des choses comme d'ordinaire nous les voyons arriver, que comme notre imagination se les figure.[52]

Montpensier's and Segrais's contemporaries clearly agreed with this formulation and tried to write so that their contributions not only were "more historical" but also appeared to be history itself.[53] Charnes, among others, speaks of this resemblance to history in his definition of the genre. He founds his definition, the clearest during his time, upon the example of a new novel, *La Princesse de Clèves:*

> The gallant (hi)stories that are written today . . . are not among those pure fictions in which the imagination is given free rein, without consideration for truth. Nor are they among those stories where an author takes a subject from history, in order to embellish it and make it more pleasing by her/his inventions. They are of a third type, in which either a subject is invented or one is taken that is not universally known; and it is decorated with several historical characteristics, which create plausibility. . . . These types of works are an invention of our time. . . . They are simple and faithful copies of true history, often so like it that they can be taken for history itself. They are particular actions of private people or of people considered in a private state. . . . The actions [these stories] contain can often be considered the secret motivations for the memorable events we learned about from history.

> Les Histoires galantes qu'on fait aujourd'hui . . . ne sont pas de ces pures fictions, où l'imagination se donne une libre étendue, sans égard à la vérité. Ce ne sont pas aussi de celles où l'Auteur prend un sujet de l'histoire, pour l'embellir et le rendre plus agréable par ses inventions. C'en est une troisième espèce, dans laquelle, ou l'on invente un sujet, ou l'on en prend un qui ne soit pas universellement connu; et on l'orne de plusieurs traits d'histoire, qui en appuient la vraisemblance. . . . Ces sortes d'ouvrages sont une invention de nos jours. . . . Ce sont des copies simples et fidèles de la véritable histoire, souvent si ressemblantes, qu'on les prend pour l'histoire même. Ce sont des actions particulières de personnes privées ou considérées dans un état privé. . . . On peut souvent considérer les actions qu'elles contiennent, comme les ressorts secrets des événements mémorables que nous avons appris dans l'Histoire. (129–130, 135–136)[54]

The novelist takes the stance of a historian, which is why the term *historien* is often used both to designate the authors of historically grounded fictions, such as *La Princesse de Clèves*, and to correspond to the more limited English word "historian."[55]

According to Charnes's definition, therefore, a novelist should appear to be writing an interiorized version of history. Novelists like Lafayette in fact posit court intrigues and love affairs as history that has been eliminated by the official historians. As Charnes explains, "The loves and the intrigues of Henri II's court [1547–1559] are not more clearly known to us than those of King Jean's court [1350–1364]. History does not take account of these kinds of things" ("Les amours et les intrigues de la Cour de Henri II ne nous sont guères plus certainement connues que celles de la Cour du Roi Jean. L'Histoire ne tient point registre de ces sortes de choses" [143]). Whether court intrigues occurred one century ago or three, they are not included in historical accounts. Novelists, in contrast, not only incorporate "these kinds of things," but they also advance these intrigues as the fundamental motivations behind well-known historical events. Their imaginations are constrained, however, as seventeenth-century commentators emphasize the need for the novel to appear *vraisemblable,* or plausible, and the importance of history in creating this plausibility.[56] Charnes refers to this accepted doctrine when he accounts for Lafayette's use of history in *La Princesse de Clèves.* He explains that an author uses history to "make her/his invention more plausible, by relating it to events which are known from history" ("rendre son invention plus vraisemblable, en lui donnant quelque liaison avec les événements qui sont connus dans l'histoire" [63]). This combination of historical fact and an author's fiction, and the resulting aura of plausibility, are seen as the prime distinguishing characteristic of the French novel during this period. Some seventeenth-century critics even attribute the conception of plausibility to the novel and its relationship to history. In *La Bibliothèque française* (1664), written when the novel was just coming into its own, Sorel distinguishes between the new genre and the earlier heroic novel and emphasizes the air of plausibility the novel has because of its kinship to history:

> Many people are looking for believable novels composed as images of history. When people became tired of the heroic novels, authors tried to write others that were more enjoyable, and that were related to truth. . . . People began to recognize what was plausible through short narratives that came into fashion, which were called novels [*nouvelles*]; novels could be compared to true histories of some particular incidents.

> Plusieurs cherchent des Romans vraisemblables qui soient faits pour des images de l'Histoire. Lors qu'on a ésté las des premiers Romans, on a essayé d'en faire d'autres plus agréables, et qui tinssent quelque chose de la vérité. . . . On commençait aussi de connaître ce que c'était des choses vraisemblables, par de petites narrations dont la mode vint, qui s'appellaient des Nouvelles; On les pouvait comparer aux Histoires Véritables de quelques accidents particuliers des Hommes.[57]

Not only can these fictions be "compared" to verifiable history, they can also be mistaken for it, as novelists offer an insider's perspective on the past that is very difficult, if not impossible, to verify.

Although the switch to shorter narratives was relatively sudden, the incorporation of history to create plausibility was also a strategy for authors of the heroic novel, such as Georges and Madeleine de

Scudéry, although a strategy that existed more in theory than in practice. In the preface to *Ibrahim* (1641), Georges de Scudéry offers a miniature critical treatise on the genre in which he stresses the use of history. He isolates *vraisemblance* as the essential rule of literary creation, calling it "the cornerstone" of a literary work, and he advocates the use of history to ensure this solid foundation: "To make things more plausible, I wanted the foundation of my work to be historical, and the principal characters to have been depicted in true history as illustrious people, and the wars to have been factual" ("Pour donner plus de vraisemblance aux choses, j'ai voulu que les fondements de mon Ouvrage fussent historiques, mes principaux personnages marqués dans l'Histoire véritable comme personnes illustres, et les guerres effectives").[58] But history in the heroic novel remains superficial, as Scudéry's comments intimate. History is the framework of best sellers such as Madeleine de Scudéry's *Le Grand Cyrus* and *Clélie*, but it is limited to supplying recognizable names of people and battles. No attempt is made to incorporate the history into the fiction or to pass the work off as history itself.[59]

With the advent of the new novel, however, history became a much more integral element of the creative work. Occasionally the adjective *historique* was even added to qualify "novel" in the title. The new novelists often researched their chosen period thoroughly in order to go beyond recognizable names and battles and include well-known events, such as marriages. They then filled the crevices of general history with their own imaginative history, advancing this as "the secret motivations for history" ("les ressorts secrets de l'Histoire"), as Charnes termed the invention. Saint-Réal and Villedieu were especially ingenious in passing their works off as history that had simply not attracted the historian's attention. Saint-Réal's *Don Carlos* (1672) and Villedieu's *Les Désordres de l'amour* (1675), especially, give the impression of being true history. Saint-Réal scrupulously footnotes his sources, and even the vast majority of the amorous liaisons Villedieu includes in *Les Désordres de l'amour* can be documented in works of general history.

Authors of the historical novel were even more daring than their predecessors in their choice of periods. Antiquity, which had been privileged in the heroic novel, was replaced by recent or contemporary France, most often the sixteenth-century Valois court. Lafayette's *La Princesse de Montpensier*, considered one of the first examples of this new fiction, is set in the court of Henri IV. The move to France made it easier for readers to verify the use of history and, reciprocally, made novelists more cautious in their narrative strategies.

The new genre was extremely popular during the first decades of Louis's reign—proof of the public's thirst for history, and especially for a side of history that did not officially exist under their monarch.

Readers devoured these historical works written from a "particular" perspective, even if the works were fictional. Historians were drawn to the genre as authors, relishing the freedom it afforded them to explore history and include the motivations, personalities, and intrigues that were deemed unnecessary and unworthy in general, official history of all periods, and especially of Louis XIV's. Saint-Réal, Donneau de Visé, and Varillas were historiographers who turned to writing historical novels and had much success. Other practitioners of the genre were historians of a different vein, who composed memoirs concurrently with their historical fictions. Montpensier, for example, composed *La Princesse de Paphlagonie* while she was putting her life on paper. Lafayette's fictional works were interspersed among two memorialistic enterprises, *Histoire de Madame Henriette d'Angleterre* and *Mémoires de la cour de France*. And Villedieu, in the middle of her writing career, took on the role of memorialist for her fictional *Mémoires de la vie de Henriette-Sylvie de Molière*. All these fictional works, which are grounded in history, underscore the public's fascination and the authors' experimentation with the various forms of historical expression.

Like the novel, memoirs were also going through a period of transition and innovation.[60] Until then a genre associated primarily with court officials who gave the historian details, memoirs took on an added dimension, as court figures who held less official positions turned to the genre. Among these figures, the participants in the Fronde top the list. Frondeurs such as the cardinal de Retz, the duchesse de Nemours, the duc de la Rochefoucauld, and Mademoiselle de Montpensier, many of whom were exiled after their treasonous activities, produced lengthy volumes depicting their past. Although most of these works were not published until the early eighteenth century, they were composed precisely during the time when the novel was undergoing its generic transformation and history was being attacked by skeptics and critics. These additions to the tradition of memoirs are thus intimately related to the ideological debate over the forms of history. Some of the many memorialists whose works were produced during this period but published between 1715 and 1730 are Retz, Brienne, Ponchartrain, Lafayette, Motteville, Gourville, Montglat, Lenet, and Montpensier.[61] Given this more-worldly corps of memorialists, the genre became less an addition to official history and more a subjective narrative dedicated, like novels, to revealing the interior story historians had neglected. Memoirs teetered on the border between verifiable history and the more nebulous realms of subjective observation and a created past.

The status of memoirs at this time of creativity in literary and historical narratives was particularly volatile. The genre was then, and to some extent has continued to exist, in a critical void, belonging both to history and to literature but to neither one exclusively. This ambiguity surfaces in Furetière's definition of the genre:

> Memoirs (plural) is the name given to historians' books written by those who were involved in public affairs or were eyewitnesses, or books that contain their lives or their principal actions: the name corresponds to what the Latins called commentaries.

> Mémoires au pl. se dit des Livres d'Historiens, écrits par ceux qui ont eu part aux affaires ou qui ont été témoins oculaires, ou qui contiennent leur vie ou leurs principales actions: Ce qui répond à ce que les Latins appelaient commentaires.

This definition underscores the double status of the genre, as history and as autobiography or biography. One the one hand, memoirs are objective "historians' books," and on the other they are subjective, personal accounts—"lives." Furetière's use of "or" ("*or* books that . . .") indicates a possible incompatibility between these two stances. An account that is too centered on the individual risks losing its historical authority. Only those "lives" that conform to the criteria of general history and recount "public affairs" and the "principal actions" of important events constitute "historians' books."

In the seventeenth century, various commentators such as Menestrier attempt to distinguish between the memoirs of those who "were involved in public affairs" and the more self-centered texts that "contain their lives." Contemporaries commonly refer to two types, state memoirs (*mémoires d'état*) and particular memoirs (*mémoires particuliers*), both of which are viewed as contributions to history.[62] By the beginning of the eighteenth century, when examples of both types abound, Lenglet Dufresnoy can speak of the need for particular memoirs to serve historians. In his opinion, Gabriel Daniel's *Histoire de France* (1696)—the first history of France since Mézeray's—is defective because Daniel chose not to use the various memoirs he was given: "He had all the help and all the time necessary, he was handed memoirs capable of enlightening us. [But] . . . you see only sieges, battles, the movements of armies, attacks, and camps entrenched or attacked" ("Il a eu tous les secours et tout le temps nécessaire, on lui a mis à la main des Mémoires propres à nous éclairer. [Mais] . . . vous n'y voyez que Sièges, que Batailles, que Marches d'Armées, Attaques de Places, Camps retranchés ou forcés").[63] Daniel's history follows the model prescribed by Louis but does not conform to the desires of much of the general public.

Women's memoirs, except Lafayette's *Mémoires de la cour de France*, all find their place under the term "particular memoirs" and are even viewed as models of the genre. In discussing the various types of history, Menestrier, for example, identifies three sorts of memoirs and links women with the third:

> Memoirs are not very different from commentaries, except that we can say there are three kinds. Some are scholarly investigations and historical illustrations. . . . Others are political discussions that are called state memoirs. . . . Finally memoirs of the third type are only court intrigues, which are popular because one can learn secrets one would not have discovered without the help of these books, for which Queen Marguerite gave us the model.

> Les Mémoires ne sont guère différents des Commentaires, sinon que nous pouvons dire qu'il y en a de trois sortes. Les uns qui sont des recherches, et des illustrations Historiques. . . . Les autres sont des négotiations Politiques qu'on nomme Mémoires d'Etat. . . . Enfin les troisièmes ne sont que les intrigues de Cour, qui sont des Livres à la mode, parce qu'on apprend des secrets que l'on n'aurait pas découverts sans le secours de ces Livres; dont la Reine Marguerite nous a fourni le modèle. (99–100)[64]

The pejorative phrase "only court intrigues" reveals Menestrier's cynical attitude toward the category in which most women's memoirs of this period find their place. It is interesting to note that the examples he cites of the first two categories (the ones composed in keeping with the general conception of "important affairs") include only men's memoirs, which, as early as 1694, are viewed as more political than women's. Memoirs modeled on Marguerite de Valois's focus on "secrets" and are thus considered a lower form within the hierarchy of historical accounts in seventeenth-century France; the historical accuracy of these "particular" memoirs is too difficult to judge. Thus the form can be assimilated more easily to fiction than to history. One of the few male authors Menestrier places in his third category is Pierre du Bourdeille, seigneur de Brantôme, whose *Mémoires* illustrate perfectly the intricate ties between particular memoirs and the novel. Significantly, both Lafayette and Villedieu relied heavily on Brantôme for their fictions, excluding many other memorialists.

Writing seventy years after Menestrier, when the memoirs composed during Louis XIV's reign had finally come to light, Joseph de La Porte confirms Menestrier's opinion that more-personal memoirs are not devoted to "historical illustrations . . . [and] political discussions": Marguerite de Valois "left us memoirs which are nothing more than the narrative of her life" ("Elle nous a laissé des mémoires qui ne sont autre chose que le récit de sa vie").[65] La Porte considers particular memoirs an inferior avatar of historiography. As a result, only one work by a female memorialist draws his praise—Lafayette's *Mémoires de la cour de France*. He recommends these memoirs to his public in the following words: "Do not fear that you will find that babble which displeased you so much in Mme de Motteville's memoirs. The reflections are rare, short, and judicious. . . . Besides, do not think that there are only minor court intrigues. There are curious and important things" ("Ne craignez point de trouver ce babil qui vous a tant déplu dans les Mémoires de Mme de Motteville. Les réflexions sont rares, courtes, et judicieuses. . . . Au reste ne croyez pas qu'il s'agisse précisément de petites intrigues de Cour. Il y a des choses curieuses et importantes" [1:495–496]). La Porte considers Lafayette's text more valuable because it does not fall entirely within Menestrier's third category—that is, the category of texts, like Motteville's, that recount "only court intrigues." Critics in the eighteenth century generally value women's memoirs for their interesting anecdotes but do not see them as deliberate additions to the historical record. Claude-François Lambert, in his *Histoire littéraire du règne de Louis XIV*, for example, praises Motteville's account for its inclusion of anecdotes: "The precious memoirs that this illustrious lady left are filled with a great number of anecdotes, as curious as they are instructive" ("Les Mémoires précieux que cette illustre Dame nous a laissés, se trouvent remplis d'un grand nombre d'anecdotes, autant curieuses qu'instructives").[66] La Porte compliments her for the "curious facts" and "interesting details [*particularités*]" that, in his opinion, constitute the primary merit of her account (1:287). Published in the eighteenth century when history was more firmly established on scientific and objective grounds, the memoirs of Motteville and other women could not possibly be viewed as alternatives to history but, as we shall see when we turn to these texts, during the "crisis of history" many of the female authors of memoirs put forth their narratives as serious and necessary contributions to the general knowledge of the past and as alternatives to general history.

Modern critics tend to accentuate the seventeenth-century distinction between state memoirs and particular memoirs and frequently make explicit Furetière's implicit attempt to separate particular memoirs from history, allowing only state memoirs to be considered intentional additions to history. The twentieth-century Robert dictionary, for example, clearly separates the two types of memoirs that Furetière groups together and distinguishes only by "or":

> Memoirs (plural) . . . An account or narrative that a person gives in writing of things and events in which s/he participated or which s/he witnessed during her/his lifetime. Historical memoirs relating historical facts suitable to use for history; see annals,

chronicles, commentaries, and also memorialist. Memoirs more
or less autobiographical; see autobiography, journal, recollection.

It is interesting to note that in the twentieth-century definition, memoirs are defined first as a personal narrative and second as a historical
one. This reverses the order in Furetière's definition, where memoirs
are described as "historians' books" that might contain "lives." The
Robert definition indicates that memoirs are no longer viewed first
and foremost as belonging to the genre of history.

The majority of modern literary critics would agree with the
Robert redefinition of the genre. It is often remarked that the term
"memoirs" was used for works we would now place under the rubric
of autobiography or biography.[67] But until the late eighteenth century,
writers of more personal accounts had recourse only to *mémoires* for
their titles. *Biographie* did not officially enter the French vocabulary
until 1762, and *autobiographie* was accepted even later, in about 1842.[68]
As a result, what we see as "true" memoirs from the seventeenth century are those accounts meeting Furetière's first criterion, that is, they
are works in which the "I" is subordinated to the primary interest—
exterior, historical events of general history. For works meeting his
second criterion, the title *mémoires*—for which, in the seventeenth
century, there was no alternative—is often today considered a mis-
nomer because many such works are centered on the person or personality of the author rather than on exterior events.[69]

With hindsight, some twentieth-century critics have been
tempted to categorize seventeenth-century memoirs under one or the
other of Furetière's two categories. Thus May speaks in terms of authorial perspectives and differentiates three types of accounts subsumed under the common title of memoirs: an account of what one
saw or heard, an account of what one did or said, and finally a narrative of the self, of who one was. He concludes, "To the first two,
contemporary usage tends to give the name memoirs, whereas it
tends to reserve the term autobiography for the third."[70] Similarly,
Hipp classifies seventeenth-century memoirs according to their degree of personalization. In her scheme, there are three categories,
each corresponding to an authorial stance: "historical journals," in
which the author writes as an omniscient narrator about exterior
events s/he could have witnessed or heard about or in which s/he
could have participated directly; "mixed journals," which combine a
historical and a personal stance, and "intimate journals," in which
the emphasis is on the author.[71] For Hipp, Du Fossé and La Rochefoucauld provide examples of the first type, Motteville and Montpensier
of the second, and Madame de Murat of the third. Fumaroli distinguishes between memoirs at the beginning of the century, which he
views as truly historical, and memoirs developing in the middle of

the century, the "worldly memoirs" ("*mémoires mondains*"), of which Motteville and Montpensier present the prime examples. He denies much of the historical character of the worldly memoirs by characterizing them as

> a completely different type of memoirs, written by worldly people who do not consider themselves authors but who find in this hybrid genre that is not very compromising [*peu compromettant*] an occasion to take up the pen and recount their experiences once and for all.[72]

Authors in this category opt for a personal as opposed to a distanced historical stance—and it is significant that the authors of all of Fumaroli's examples are women.[73] Modern critics such as Fumaroli see the vast majority of women's memoirs in mid–seventeenth-century France as autobiographical because of the personal lens through which events are viewed. In contrast, memoirs by men span the entire realm of possibilities, although they include more impersonal than personal memoirs.

Both seventeenth-century and twentieth-century categories take on significance as critical tools when they are used to examine the corpus of seventeenth-century women's memoirs. Although both classifications recognize women's predilection for recounting events from a personal stance, the two do not evaluate the inclusion of the self in the same way. Modern appellations such as autobiography and self-portrait tend to deny historical affiliation to these works, refusing to view a personalized account of events as a different type of historical writing. But when one views particular memoirs in light of the seventeenth-century sense of "particular," one restores the possibility that these works have historical significance. As we have seen, "particular" is associated with an interiorized historical perspective, connoting the private and privileged as well as the personal and detailed. Although a memorialist's inclusion of his or her "life or principal actions" in a historical account was not without controversy in the seventeenth century, particular memoirs were nonetheless considered a type of history, an evaluation that modern critics prefer to avoid. Both the memoirs and the novels that developed primarily after 1660 thus promote the same perspective on history, and the gender of their principal practitioners is the same.

□   □   □

The general climate of historical questioning seems to have responded to a specific desire of many seventeenth-century French literary women. In fact, I will argue, women writers profited from the epistemological crisis in history to redefine it to include women. Because official history, especially under Louis XIV, eliminates most female participation, particular history can be used to tell the other side of the story and thus complete existing accounts. When viewed within the pervading atmosphere of historical questioning, women writers can be seen not as composing plausible fictions and "not very compromising" ("peu compromettant") life histories but, more importantly, as promoting a narrative of the past constructed according to a "particular" theory of history.

FRONDEUSES AND PRÉCIEUSES

The increase in the ranks of women memorialists and novelists in mid–seventeenth-century France attests to the attraction of historical genres but does not explain why such a proliferation of memoirs and novels appeared at precisely this time. The crisis in history was only one of the forces behind this surge in women's literary production. Another was the position women held throughout the century. Especially during the first two-thirds of the century, aristocratic and some bourgeois women wielded considerable intellectual and political power. Various cultural historians have recently begun to bring to light the female sphere of influence in seventeenth-century France. Backer's *Precious Women*, Maclean's *Woman Triumphant*, and Lougee's *Le Paradis des femmes* are the most notable among such studies. My purpose here is not to reiterate their findings but, rather, to discuss the political and social activity that I view as directly fostering the development of women's memoirs and historical novels during the latter part of the century.

To get a sense of the exceptional role played by women in seventeenth-century France, it is necessary to look at the period preceding the time of literary creativity. In that earlier period, a multitude of women participated in creating actual history. Many women writers—such as Montpensier, Lafayette, and Villedieu—experienced certain historical events directly and later used these events as the material for their histories. Two phenomena in particular are intimately related to the historical genres that developed essentially after 1660: women's direct political activity during the Fronde (rebellious actions that occurred when France was governed by a woman) and the salon and *précieuse* culture. In relation to each of these phenomena, it can be argued that women directly influenced the public realm, "the true, great and public things" of general history. Yet today the women's names and contributions to political and cultural history have been obscured or even erased from the collective memory.

The records of the Fronde attest to the fact that even when

women become political agents on the public stage, general historians do not consider their actions worthy of official and authorizing pens. The Fronde provides an excellent example of the systematic exclusion of women from general history. The extent of this deliberate erasure will become clear in the next chapter, when we turn to the memoirs of one of the principal *frondeuses*, Montpensier. To suggest how the women's activities affected the development of narrative genres, I will now briefly examine the role the women actually played.

The Fronde was a civil war that pitted the nobility against itself and divided the populace among various factions. This period of social disorder reached its apogee in approximately 1648 and was brought under control by the crown by 1653. There were urban as well as provincial uprisings, and every sector of French society was affected. The principal charactristic of this civil war is its disunity and confusion. There was no one overriding purpose, except perhaps a general hatred for the regent's (Anne d'Autriche's) foreign-born prime minister, Mazarin. The leaders of the *frondeurs* parties were all from the upper ranks of society—parliamentarians, members of the robe, and members of both the provincial and royal aristocracy. These leaders incited urban citizens as well as rural peasants. But the various factions that composed the *frondeurs*, although united by their chant of "No Mazarin," remained at odds concerning the best way to rid France of this usurper of royal prestige and power. In addition, each group had its own agenda, which frequently conflicted with that of its supposed allies. As a result, many alliances were made only to be broken, and participants often changed factions and sometimes sides altogether.

In general, the Fronde is divided into two relatively equal periods named for their respective leaders. Briefly, the parliament instigated the troubles in 1648 with a series of decrees designed to call royal authority, especially the role of the prime minister, into question.[74] The parliamentary Fronde was, above all, urban and had the support of much of the Paris bourgeoisie. A second wave of protest and rebellion, termed "la Fronde des princes," or the princely Fronde, added to the revolt and enlarged the sphere of participants. This group primarily incited the peasants in the group's various principalities to civil disobedience. The princes' primary objective was to profit from a relatively weak regency to increase their own power. They opposed Mazarin and sought to replace both the regent and the prime minister with a leader from among their ranks who could rule both the country and the young Louis XIV more to their satisfaction.[75] Control shifted continually between the parliamentary and princely parties as well as between the *frondeurs* and Mazarin, whom the *frondeurs* opposed. In an attempt to impose some order, historians have generally divided the two rebellious groups into three clans, named for the male figures who, at first glance, controlled events: Gondi (better known as the cardinal de Retz), the prince de Condé (Louis XIV's cousin), and the duc d'Orléans (Louis XIII's brother).[76] Retz was the coadjutor (the bishop's assistant) of Paris and the primary instigator and organizer of the parliamentary unrest. From 1648 to 1652 he was at various times allied with or against the other clans and with or against Mazarin, depending on what best suited his personal agenda. In the beginning, he set his sights upon Mazarin's position. When this goal became unreachable, he opted to press for a cardinal's hat in order to attain the same rank as the prime minister. In general, Retz's parliamentary coalition did not advocate armed rebellion to dethrone Mazarin, but political maneuvering. They left the war front to Condé and his artistocratic followers.[77]

The prince de Condé's role was equally self-interested. As one historian describes him, the prince was a brave and decisive leader whose lack of a clear objective undermined his strengths.[78] This is evident in his siding first with the regency and then changing strategies and reaching an unstable accord with the parliamentary *frondeurs*.[79] Condé coveted Mazarin's position and, unlike the coadjutor, was more than willing to resort to military tactics. Ultimately he hoped to take the regency away from Anne d'Autriche and impose a group of advisors on the young king. In addition, he wanted Louis's majority to be set at eighteen instead of thirteen in order to extend his own influence.[80] Most of Condé's strength lay in the provinces, in particular in his domain of Burgundy. His brother, the prince de Conti, joined the anti-Mazarin cause and brought with him the support of his province, Champagne. The princely party was further strengthened by the addition of Normandy, governed by the duc de Longueville, the husband of Condé's and Conti's sister, Anne-Geneviève de Bourbon.

The third principal player, the duc d'Orléans, was Montpensier's father. Outwardly the duke chose to play the role of intermediary and peacemaker between Mazarin's, Condé's, and Retz's parties. In reality, he was unable to commit himself to any faction and thus floated from one to the other. A. Lloyd Moote refers to him condescendingly as "the most vacillating of all Frenchmen."[81] In the first years of the Fronde, Orléans served Anne d'Autriche fairly faithfully but, as the strife progressed, he became more and more convinced that Mazarin's policies endangered the monarchy. In 1651 he joined the Condéan coalition to oust Mazarin. When this coalition disintegrated, he vacillated between Condé's and Retz's parties. His indecision kept him from acting, much to the frustration and disgust of his daughter, who was more of a *frondeuse*.

The complex entanglement of personalities and factions created an equally entangled web of events. Anne d'Autriche and Mazarin, with some success, pitted the *frondeurs* parties against one another in an attempt to weaken their power. Mazarin's most costly mistake is now generally considered to have been his imprisonment of Condé, Conti, and Longueville in 1650, a move that fueled the provincial rebellions and drew the duc d'Orléans to the defense of his relatives. Eventually the parliament of Paris petitioned the queen to release the princes and banish Mazarin. In the opening months of 1651, Mazarin was forced to flee Paris. The parliament then sought to force Anne d'Autriche to outlaw clerics from high state offices. The *frondeurs* among the parliamentarians, particularly Retz, did not support this particular solution to rid the realm of Mazarin. The Condéans, in contrast, viewed this ban as their chance to gain power over the regency. Anne d'Autriche, in support of her chief minister, sided with the parliamentary *frondeurs*, thus alienating Condé. Mazarin was restored to power. In response, the Condéans besieged Paris in 1652, forcing Mazarin, Anne d'Autriche, and the young Louis XIV to flee. Eventually the non-*frondeur* parliament was able to end the civil strife and restore the regency to power. Retz was imprisoned and Condé fled to the provinces. Only the duc d'Orléans succeeded in avoiding disgrace. He was exiled to Blois but remained in favor, no doubt because of his nonalliance with any party.

This skeletal structure of events gives little idea of the Fronde's actual power and disruptiveness. Between the lines of this general history reside a number of now-obscure women who played an often determining role in the rebellion and created its particular character. The powerful "Amazons," as they are frequently called, surface when one examines the major events more closely.[82] The duchesse de Longueville was a *frondeuse* even before her brother Condé was. She united with Retz to incite Condé to oppose the crown. She then came to her brothers' and husband's defense when all three were imprisoned.[83] She organized the uprising in Normandy and remained a fervent and politically influential *frondeuse* to the end. Mazarin recognized the duchess's influence and took seriously her maneuvers to have him killed. From her post in Stenay, Anne-Geneviève made a pact with Spanish troops stationed in the Low Countries. Condé's wife, too, took command and, like her sister-in-law, directed the opposition in her own domain of Bordeaux. Not content to remain on the sidelines, the princess even helped fill sandbags to serve as a line of defense. Montpensier, as well, was a vitally active participant, often replacing her weak and indecisive father. She conquered Orléans for the *frondeur* cause and helped Condé's troops enter Paris.

The princesse de Condé, the duchesse de Longueville, and Mademoiselle de Montpensier were not exceptions to their sex. In fact, they were joined by numerous other women—including the duchesse de Chevreuse, who played both sides; the princesse Palatine; the duchesse de Montbazon; the marquise de Sablé; Isabelle de Châtillon, Condé's lover; and Montpensier's friends Mmes de Fiesque, de Frontenac, de Sully, and d'Olonne—who waged battles on the levels of both warfare and political and personal intrigue. Mlle de Scudéry even contributed to the rebellion on a literary level. The first volume of her novel *Le Grand Cyrus* appeared in 1649. Dedicated to the duchesse de Longueville, *Le Grand Cyrus* is a roman à clé whose principal characters are the illustrious and quasi-mythical aristocratic *frondeurs*.

The Fronde was in fact waged primarily on the level of personal alliances and intrigue. Weapons other than those traditionally associated with warfare became the preferred instruments of attack. Marriages, for example, were used to solidify some coalitions and weaken others. The duchesse de Longueville ingeniously arranged a marriage between Anne de Vigean and the marquis de Richelieu, governor of Le Havre, to ensure the marquis's support of the *frondeurs*. She successfully thwarted another marriage between her brother, the prince de Conti, and the duchesse de Chevreuse's daughter—a union designed to solidify aristocratic alliances. Longueville's opposition to that marriage derived from her hatred of the duchesse de Chevreuse, who had preceded Longueville as La Rochefoucauld's lover. In general, the various personages were motivated to act for reasons historians today find hard to comprehend or even take seriously. La Rochefoucauld, for example, joined the *frondeurs* when Anne d'Autriche refused his wife a coveted *tabouret* (a type of chair). The right to a tabouret was a sign of royal favor. Only high-ranking women—duchesses and princesses—were allowed to sit on one in the queen's presence. After Anne's refusal, La Rochefoucauld became an ardent defender of the princely faction. His enthusiasm was increased by his passion for the duchesse de Longueville, who controlled his every move and even bore him a son in the midst of the rebellion.

The intrigues of the Fronde seemingly came to an abrupt end in 1652 when, with parliamentary support, Anne d'Autriche succeeded in regaining control of the government. The political upheaval in which all the aristocratic names of the realm were involved was silenced, as the Longuevilles, Montpensiers, and Châtillons were banished. The Fronde's abrupt failure has led many historians to conclude that this at times novelistic rebellion "adds nothing to history" and "has no creative value," to cite Ernst Kossmann.[84] But such a negative assessment of the Fronde ignores an entire sphere in which it had influence. The *frondeurs* subtly continued their opposition by writing their memoirs. Many of their efforts not only have great "creative value" but also call into question contemporary norms of historiography.

When today's historians turn to women's activity and influence during this period of civil rebellion, they normally refuse to see any significance in the women's actions and portray these Amazons as noblewomen who were only out to play at war at the people's expense. Even Backer, while bringing to light the names of the women involved, undermines any possibility of taking them seriously by contemptuously stating that "none of the ladies fighting this war had any inkling of its larger meanings."[85] In her opinion, they were only trying to live out the adventures they had read about in novels, whereas the male participants were very conscious of the war's causes and implications.[86] Many of their male contemporaries, however, including Mazarin, took the women's actions seriously and realized they were a force to be reckoned with during the war. And one has only to see how many women's memoirs were inspired by the Fronde to perceive that the movement was significant for those who participated as well as for those who looked to history for inspiration for their works.[87] For a select group of seventeenth-century women, the Fronde was proof that they could influence the public events of general history. More important, their activities during the war underscored to an exceptional degree that the "particular" realm of intrigues, passions, personalities, and secret negotiations was an essential and, in fact, decisive force in the public, political sphere. This is the lesson that, as we shall see, frequently resurfaces in women's texts written after the Fronde, while remaining repressed in the official accounts of the past. In addition, female participation in the Fronde brought previous periods of strong political activity by women to the forefront. Women's historical works after the Fronde give special attention to centuries such as the sixteenth, marked by the dominant presences of Marie de Médici and Diane de Poitiers, because the roles of women during these periods foreshadowed some of women's contemporary roles.

Like the Fronde, the salon movement illustrates the influence of the "particular" sector on the public sphere. These gatherings were proof that the "particular" could influence and, in fact, create a public. The salons had a profound effect on literature and on social concerns throughout the seventeenth century, an influence that originated with the marquise de Rambouillet's *chambre bleue* at the beginning of the century and reached its apogee in the 1650s under the guidance of Mlle de Scudéry.[88] Arthénice, as Rambouillet was named by her contemporaries, invited friends and literary figures to her discussions and influenced the tastes and visions of a whole generation of court figures, both male and female. When the *chambre bleue* declined as the marquise grew older, other salons continued the tradition she had begun. Marguerite Thiollier has recently devoted much effort to identifying the various salons in the Marais section of Paris, where the majority of the salon women resided.[89] These gatherings included not only the *ruelles*—as salons were called at the time—of Henriette de Coligny, the comtesse de la Suze, and of the marquise de Sablé, who

collaborated with La Rochefoucauld on his maxims, but also the famous Saturdays/*samedis* of Scudéry. The Faubourg St. Germain also
had its salons, principally that of Montpensier when she was not in
exile. The names of many of the participants in the salons—among
them Lafayette, Sévigné, La Rochefoucauld, Villedieu, and the historian Pellisson, who frequented Scudéry's *ruelle*—have survived, often
thanks to their literary activities. Also active in the salon culture were
academicians, such as Ménage and Huet, and figures known for their
political activities, such as the duchesse de Longueville and Christian
de Suède.

The gatherings in the Marais and in the Faubourg St. Germain
were considered very worthwhile and important and do not conform
to the pejorative image now universally held as a result of Molière's
satirical representations. The salons of seventeenth-century France
were more than polite gatherings of select people around the bed of a
female arbiter of taste. Rambouillet's *chambre bleue* and Scudéry's *samedis* were places of literary innovation and criticism, exclusive meetings
whose influence extended not only beyond the walls of the room but
also beyond the circle of the initiated, to affect the tastes of the reading public as well as the tastes of the authors who wrote to please that
public. In describing the *précieuse* phenomenon in his *La Prétieuse ou
le mystère des ruelles*, Abbé de Pure frequently depicts these women
judging literary works. One character, for example, describes the feeling of exhilaration she experiences as a literary critic: "I take extreme
pleasure in elevating myself to a position of authority on the work of
an intelligent man who presents himself at my court, and who is on
the carpet to await my judgment. My soul is truly thrilled to exercise
this glorious and spiritual influence, and to see myself the arbiter on
such lofty subjects" ("J'ai un plaisir extrême à m'élever en autorité sur
l'ouvrage d'un homme d'esprit qui se présente à mon tribunal, et qui
est comme sur la sellette pour attendre mon jugement. Mon âme véri-
tablement est ravie d'exercer cet empire de gloire et d'esprit, et de me
voir l'Arbitre de ces hauts sujets").[90] To judge by this remark, there is
a reversal of roles in the salons, where women "exercise this glorious
and spiritual influence" over their male subjects. Authors took these
judgments seriously. As Maclean justly notes, "From the authors'
point of view the reception of their work in the salons was crucial to
its failure or success."[91]

In addition to forming the taste of their contemporaries, the *précieuses* of the salons invented and practiced various games that affected
literary style for decades. In particular, the vogue of literary portraits
and the lengthy debates or conversations influenced all types of literature, whether historical or fictional. These games became separate literary genres, best illustrated by Montpensier's *Divers Portraits* (1659)
and her later *Le Recueil des portraits* (1659) and by the numerous vol-

umes of Scudéry's conversations. Even after portraits and conversations declined in popularity as private games, they continued to have a strong place as literary techniques, especially in works written by women.[92]

Portraits and conversations can also be associated with particular history.[93] Montpensier's *Le Recueil des portraits*, for example, is explicitly described as particular history and is especially valued for this perspective. The unknown author of the preface to the *Recueil* gives prime consideration to the merits of particular history, here in the sense of individual or personal:

> Refined and sensible people find more satisfaction in reading about particular actions than about general ones: for the former are so many portraits that paint a man as he is naturally, and give us complete knowledge of him. This is why some assert that a history does not really entertain when it gives us a captain who always has a sword in his hand and has no other occupation than calling his troops to battle. . . . These types of histories . . . do not completely instruct us about the people they discuss.

> Les gens délicats, et bien sensés, ont plus de satisfaction de lire des actions particulières, que celles qui sont générales: parce que ce sont autant de Portraits qui peignent un homme au naturel, et qui nous en donnent une entière connaissance. C'est pourquoi quelques-uns assurent qu'une Histoire ne divertit pas extrèmement, lors qu'elle nous représente un capitaine toujours l'Epée à la main, et qui n'a point d'autre occupation qu'à ranger des Armées en bataille. . . . Ces sortes d'Histoires . . . ne nous instruisent pas pleinement de ceux dont elles nous parlent.[94]

This preface in fact contains the crux of the polemic that we have seen about the different kinds of history and the relative merits of the various approaches. Here, particular history is associated with a court public—"refined and sensible people." The author goes on to extol the virtues of the literary portrait, from which "we can profit considerably" ("nous en tirons un profit considérable"). S/he concludes by asserting the affiliation between portraits and history, thus effectively elevating what began as a game of the *mondains*: "They can be called short histories, summaries of our life, and a type of general confession. . . . Thus one cannot speak highly enough of them" ("On les peut appeler des histoires en racourci, des abrégés de notre vie, et des espèces de confessions générales. . . . Ainsi l'on ne saurait trop les vanter").

The preface of *Le Receuil des portraits* is indicative of a preoccupation with history, its composition and its use, among the members of the salon culture. Painted portraits were also the object of much interest among this court public. During the first half of the century, courtiers began to collect portraits, and each gallery had a certain bias.[95] The three most important—Richelieu's, the Grande Mademoiselle's at St. Fargeau and at Choisy, and Bussy-Rabutin's at his château in Burgundy—illustrate the particular/public dichotomy that I have been delineating. In his "Galerie d'histoire," Richelieu emphasized the actions of illustrious men of the church. In Bussy-Rabutin's gallery, which he constructed later in the century (1666–1682) while in exile after the publication of L'Histoire amoureuse des Gaules, the portraits were grouped in three categories: captains, kings and famous men, and famous women. Although Bussy-Rabutin did include his cousin Sévigné, in general both his and Richelieu's galleries accentuated recognizable, public figures and thus maintained the hierarchies and categories of the traditional historical canon. Montpensier, in contrast, seemed especially aware of the possibilities inherent in the portrait and used it as a vehicle for historical revision. Unlike the owners of the two "public" portrait galleries, Montpensier collected family portraits and sought to present the entire spectrum of her Bourbon ancestors. Her accent was thus on completeness rather on selectivity. She chose not to limit her choices to persons famous in the public sphere. In a sense, her inclusiveness can be seen as reflecting an attraction—common among many seventeenth-century women writers—to the lesser-known, less celebrated, and more personal aspects of history.

The salons influenced both the style of women authors and their outlook on society at large. Within the salon milieu, the participants discussed not only literary matters but also issues of social concern. The précieuses took strong feminist positions, particularly with respect to marriage and women's education. They were especially against forced or arranged marriages, but marriage in general they viewed with disfavor.[96] Somaize gives two especially telling phrases the précieuses used in referring to marriage: "the end of love" ("l'amour fini") and "the abyss of liberty" ("l'abîme de la liberté.").[97] In de Pure's La Prétieuse, imaginary salon participants rail against the institution, which is usually depicted in précieuse rhetoric as a form of slavery. The best position for a woman, if she has married at all, is to be either widowed or separated from her husband. Significantly, this is the case for many of the women writers during the period—for example, Scudéry and Montpensier never married, and Lafayette was separated from her husband.[98] In the précieuse tradition, Montpensier and Motteville carried on a correspondence in 1660 in which they envisioned a utopia where women could be free of this "slavery." Montpensier's words reflect the sentiments of many of her female contemporaries:

> Marriage has made men superior; and this dependence has made
> us be known as the fragile sex, this dependence that the male sex

has subjected us to, often against our will, and for family reasons of which we have often been victims. Let us get out of this slavery; let there be a corner of the world where it can be said that women are their own "masters" [maîtresses] and that they do not have all the faults that are attributed to them.

Ce qui a donné la supériorité aux hommes a été le mariage; et ce qui nous fait nommer le sexe fragile a été cette dépendance, où le sexe nous a assujetties, souvent contre notre volonté, et par des raisons de famille dont nous avons été les victimes. Tirons-nous de l'esclavage; qu'il y ait un coin du monde où l'on puisse dire que les femmes sont maîtresses d'elles-mêmes, et qu'elles n'ont pas tous les défauts qu'on leur attribue. (36:301)[99]

Not all *précieuses* adopt such a radical solution to the problem of marriage. The fictional women of *La Prétieuse,* for example, suggest that couples share power, with the position of "master" going alternately to the husband and to the wife. Another proposal would have couples separate as soon as the first child is born—which would have the advantage of sparing the woman numerous and dangerous pregnancies.[100] In *Le Grand Cyrus,* Scudéry has Sapho, who is also against marriage, retire to the "pays des Sauromates," a utopia similar to Montpensier's ideal.[101] Unmarried, she remains there with her lover, whom she dominates completely. Her dominion is strengthened by the laws of the "pays des Sauromates," which is a matriarchy. Love is not excluded from the *précieuse* ideal, but it is controlled entirely by the woman. In any case, love is rarely a part of marriage. Although such opinions may have often been ridiculed, they nonetheless exerted a strong influence over the minds of the salon participants and often found expression in their literary works.

Equally important in the *précieuse* notion of social reform is education for women. As Maclean remarks, the ideal for the cultivated woman is to be "learned without showing it" ("savantes sans la paraître").[102] Many of the salon women, such as Lafayette, had private tutors and were especially well versed in Latin and Italian.[103] In fact, the century produced some very learned women. Antoinette du Ligier de la Garde, who became Madame Deshoulières, knew Latin, Italian, Spanish, and philosophy. Madame Dacier, born Anne Le Febvre, studied Latin and Greek and translated the Ancients. Marguerite Buffet was an admired grammarian who was unanimously elected to the Académie des Ricovrati of Padua. In her *Eloge des illustres sçavantes, tant anciennes que modernes* (1668), to which I will return, she celebrated other learned women. Jacquette Guillaume, too, in *Les Dames illustres,* immortalized women.[104] Other women, as well, turned to literary pursuits to express their knowledge. Significantly, the vast majority of these women signed their works, for it was not considered completely indecent or scandalous to pick up a pen.[105] Particularly at the end of the century, anthologies and compendia of women writers attest to their relatively great number. In *La Nouvelle Pandore, ou les femmes illustres du siècle de Louis le Grand* (1698), Claude de Vertron inscribes the names of famous intellectual women, including writers, and the prizes they won in the various academies, especially that of Arles, where women could actually gain admittance. Marguerite Buffet's list of women also attests to the significant number of creative women, as does Joseph de la Porte's eighteenth-century anthology, *Histoire littéraire des femmes françaises* (1769).

The salons thus encouraged literary productivity and advocated knowledge for women. But although they were an important part of the intellectual and literary scene, they were not unopposed. Molière and Boileau, among others, attempted to reduce their influence by ridicule.[106] In fact, in the years after Louis XIV took power, the salons—and particularly the *précieuse* phenomenon—did weaken. Albistur and Armogathe term the period beginning in 1660 "the great enclosure [*renfermement*] of the woman."[107] But perhaps the political activism embodied by the *frondeuses* and expressed in the social and intellectual discussions of the salons inspired and was ultimately replaced by another form of expression, primarily a literary one. The same group of women who had formed the nucleus of the salon culture—Montpensier, Lafayette, Villedieu, Scudéry—and the women who had been *frondeuses* turned to novels and memoirs in the age of absolutism. Their works reveal the effect of the salon milieu, where culture was female. As we shall see, these women's novels and memoirs bear the imprint of the salons, and their outlook on history is founded in part upon what under Louis XIV was forced to become an idealistic vision of the supremacy of an essentially female private sphere.

The position of this group of women writers and their contemporaries during the Fronde and in the salons supplied the spirit of historical innovation and inspiration for their literary works in the later part of the century. Having actively participated in the political and social life of the nation, women desired a narrative that would reflect that participation. Because the debate over historiography included an evaluation of the "particular" realm—exactly the sphere of activity filled by women during the Fronde and in the salons—women writers profited from the ideological and methodological disorder to rectify the historical record in their favor. Although it may be argued that male authors such as Retz and Saint-Reál were also actively expanding the boundaries of history, women writers had a larger stake in the development of particular history, for they greatly contributed to this realm that military or patriarchal history rejected. Seventeenth-century women writers promoted a new definition of history and new narrative forms to express this formulation, as they redirected the historian's gaze in order simultaneously to reflect their own participation in history and to glorify it.

WOMEN WRITERS: DEFINING A LITERARY AND HISTORICAL SPACE

When women's memoirs and novels of the second half of the seventeenth century are read together as a literary corpus, a collective female voice emerges, a voice that constitutes an important addition to the polemic about the relative merits of general and particular history. Writers such as Montpensier, Lafayette, and Villedieu consider the narrative of "memorable" events to be incomplete because of the choice of events deemed worthy of recording. Women in the mid-seventeenth century were not the first to question the definition of history and its exclusion of women. Rather, they were adding their literary voices to a line of feminist thinkers drawn to this subject.[108] They were also laying the groundwork for succeeding discussions that continue to this day. Two of their contemporaries, Madeleine de Scudéry and Marguerite Buffet, took up similar questions in works outside of the genres of memoirs and historical novels. An analysis of the revisionist efforts of Scudéry and Buffet will provide a context for the designs of the women memorialists and novelists.

Feminist Inquiries

One seventeenth-century woman writer can be seen as a kind of matriarch for her contemporaries and a forerunner of those who questioned history. Madeleine de Scudéry was one of the most prolific writers of her time, creating, in particular, a model for the voluminous heroic novel. Her immense multivolumed novels such as *Le Grand Cyrus* and *Clélie* have some superficial affiliations with history, for she turned to Greece and Rome for the names of her principal characters and refers to specific events; however, she does not put these works forward as alternative history, as historical novelists do with their own works later in the century. A work on the periphery of Scudéry's corpus deserves particular attention as an illustration of contemporary feminist thought. Her *Les Femmes illustres* is a collection of portrayals of female historical figures, primarily from antiquity. The text consists of a series of *harangues,* or short exposés, in which a female personage takes center stage and speaks of her historical situation. Among the women Scudéry chooses to include are Artémise, Marianne, Cléopatre, Zénobie, Bérénice, Octavie, Agrippine, and Sapho. In all, the voices of forty women are inscribed for posterity. The whole work is designed to alter previous historical accounts by giving prominence to normally silenced women's voices. The historical character of *Les Femmes illustres* is enhanced by Scudéry's inclusion of engraved "médailles" of each female personage, like Mézeray's in his *Histoire de France*. She underscores the creative aspect of her feminist brand of historical writing by admitting, in authorial interventions, that these *harangues* are imaginary, but she attributes this to the fact that traditional historical accounts have failed to incorporate the female point of view. Scudéry constantly emphasizes that she is drawing the speeches from history itself. For example, of Cléopatre's oration to Marc-Antoine, the narrator explains,

> I have at least *founded* the words I put in the mouth of this queen on the *conjectures of History:* and here *in my opinion* is what she could have said to this irritated lover on this occasion.

> Au moins ai-je *fondé* les paroles que je mets en la bouche de cette Reine, sur les *conjectures de l'Histoire:* et voici *selon mon sens,* ce qu'elle put dire en cette occasion à cet Amant irrité. (my emphasis)[109]

The curious mixture of fact and fiction evident here is the principal characteristic of *Les Femmes illustres*. The vocabulary of the passage underscores this amalgamation. "Founded" and "History" give the work objectivity and a factual status, whereas "in my opinion" and "conjectures" reveal the subjective, creative aspects of the author's work. The two become fused, resulting in an addition to history. Moreover, the end of each *harangue* stresses the historicity of the preceding conversation or speech: in a separate section, the narrator reenters to explain the effect that the imagined speech had on past events. For example, following Athenais's speech to Théodose, the narrator states: "This speech was not useless, even though its effect was belated: it left warm feelings in Théodose's soul. . . . Athenais left, it is true. But she came back in glory" ("Ce discours ne fut pas inutile, quoi que l'effet en fût tardif: il laissa des impressions de chaleur en l'âme de Théodose. . . . Athenais partit, il est vrai. Mais elle revint avec gloire" [1:282]). Lucrèce's harangue to Acolatin has a more drastic effect: "The effect of this harangue was Tarquin's flight, his father's banishment, the loss of his kingdom, and the beginning of the Roman republic. It cost Lucrèce's abductor his life and his crown" ("L'effet de cette harangue fut la fuite de Tarquin, le bannissement de son père, la perte de son Royaume, et le commencement de la République Romaine. Il en coûta la vie et la Couronne au ravisseur de Lucrece" [1:217]). Because Scudéry often includes recognizable factual events, the status of the speeches remains in doubt. To make the speeches seem more historically authoritative, Scudéry minimizes the importance of the creative quality of the work. She also uses the "effects" to promote the notion that these "particular" conversations had important consequences for public history.

In addition, as each *harangue* is founded upon what she calls "the conjectures of History," historical narrative itself is challenged. Furetière defines *conjecture* as "reasoning founded upon probability without any proof" ("raisonnement fondé sur des probabilités sans aucune démonstration"). His synonyms of the verb form *conjecturer* are "to judge by chance" ("juger au hasard") and "to guess" ("deviner"). Furetière goes on to warn that "judgments based solely on conjecture must not be taken seriously" ("il ne faut point faire cas de ces jugements qui ne se sont que par conjecture"). As Scudéry uses the term, "the conjectures of History" refers on one level to the author's extrapolations from history. On a second, less explicit level, Scudéry opts for "conjecture" to imply that history as a body of knowledge is actually composed of "conjectures" and that her *harangues* are simply drawn from a historical canon that in itself is invented. The second level is justifiable in light of the skepticism surrounding historiography. In this atmosphere, the feminocentric historical narrative of *Les Femmes illustres* could be as valid as traditional homocentric accounts.

Scudéry's *Les Femmes illustres* is also an integral part of the intellectual climate because it valorizes the woman writer. The climax of the first volume is the portrait of Sapho, the heroine Scudéry chose as her model, even taking her name. In this *harangue,* Sapho attempts to persuade Erinne to become a writer "to show that women are capable of such an enjoyable occupation and that they are wrong to neglect it" ("afin de faire voir que les Dames en sont capables et qu'elles ont tort de négliger, une si agréable occupation" [1:410]). Sapho expounds upon the value of education for women, thus reflecting the conversations of seventeenth-century salon women, whose ideal is to be "learned without showing it." This harangue in fact resembles the conversations and debates of de Pure's fictional *précieuses.*

Sapho points out that the only way for a woman to survive into eternity is by being a writer: "Among all this infinite number of beautiful women who doubtless lived during the centuries preceding our own, we have barely heard of only two or three: and during those same centuries, we can see the glory of many men solidly established by the written works they have left us" ("De tout ce nombre infini de belles femmes, qui ont sans doute vécu dans les siècles qui ont précédé le nôtre, à peine avons-nous ouï parler de deux ou trois seulement: et dans ces mêmes siècles, nous voyons la gloire de plusieurs hommes, solidement établie, par les écrits qu'ils nous ont laissés" [1:426]). The latter part of the remark can be understood in two ways: men survive through their own literary efforts as well as through the efforts of a universalized "they" that includes all men. Because these "written works they have left us" record the past, they can be viewed not only as literary texts but also as works of history. Scudéry encourages her female contemporaries to fill the silence of the past by composing their own literature to memorialize themselves as well as other women. *Les Femmes illustres* thus prefigures the intense literary production of a few decades later.

Approximately twenty years after Scudéry's inspirational example, a less well known woman, Marguerite Buffet, followed in the footsteps of the illustrious Sapho and wrote her own history of "women worthies."[110] *L'Eloge des illustres sçavantes, tant anciennes que modernes* was published as the second half of Buffet's *Nouvelles Observations sur la langue française*, a volume dedicated to Anne d'Autriche. In the dedication, Buffet clearly enunciates the purpose of *L'Eloge:* "I bring the most illustrious women of past centuries back to life in order to join them with the most learned and most virtuous women of your court and of all Europe" ("J'y fais encore revivre les plus illustres Dames des siècles passés pour les joindre aux plus savantes et aux plus vertueuses de votre Cour, et de toute l'Europe").[111]

To fulfill her goal of recording "illustrious learned women" ("illustres savantes"), Buffet makes an interesting departure from the models offered her by *Les Femmes illustres*. In writing of past women, she includes those who were considered illustrious in earlier histories; but in writing the history of her female contemporaries, Buffet elects to limit herself to those women who merit her intriguing title of "learned heroine" ("savante héroïne"). Thus, only contemporary women renowned for their knowledge find a place in her *Eloge*— prominent intellectual figures such as Christine de Suède, Mlle de Scurman, the duchesse de Montausier, the comtesse du Plexis, and Madamae de Bonnevent, to name but a few among Buffet's impressive gallery.

Moreover, Buffet expands her intellectual history by following her descriptions of living learned women with accounts of their illustrious precursors, among them Marie de Gournay, Catherine de Médici, and Marguerite de Valois. In fact, Buffet situates her contemporaries in a female lineage. She calls the duchesse de Montausier, for example, "another Cornelia, the most skillful of all Roman women, and the one who wrote the best" ("une autre Cornélia la plus habile de toutes les Romaines, et celle qui a le mieux écrit" [249]). And Buffet does not search for her exempla only among the noblewomen of the realm; she sets out to prove that women of varying social status can achieve renown, and have done so, by intellectual pursuits. To this end, she follows her description of Christine de Suède with one of Mlle de Scurman "to show you that women's knowledge does not appear only when they are on the throne" ("pour vous faire voir que la science des Dames ne paraît pas seulement dans le Trône" [242]). She hopes to add to the collective memory, not simply reproduce it.

Buffet's choice of "women worthies" has a different emphasis from Scudéry's, for she focuses on women's intellectual qualities. She thus excludes women such as the Amazons, whose status as heroine is due to their resemblance or relationship to men. In defining heroine, Buffet highlights "learned," thus subtly rewriting history by valorizing a quality not normally associated with the women admitted to general history. According to her, women can be remembered for characteristics other than those—such as military prowess—that place them in a category with men, or for reasons other than their public positions at men's sides. Even when Buffet identifies women as heroines in a military sense, she is careful to keep her focus on intellectual as opposed to physical attributes. Describing Christine de Suède, for example, she writes:

> Her first victories over the Germans and other northern peoples were the fruit of her knowledge and her planning. And the many battles her generals have won under her guidance show well that Mars is never as fortunate as when he is guided by Pallas.

> Ses premières victoires sur les Allemands et sur les autres Peuples du Nord les fruits de sa première sagesse et de ses conseils. Et toutes les batailles que les Géneraux ont gagnées sous sa conduite, font bien voir que Mars n'est jamais plus heureux que quand il est conduit par Pallas. (239)

Intellectual pursuits are placed on a par with military prowess. In another example, Buffet writes that the maréchalle de la Mothe gives "as great signs of her wisdom as her whole family has given of its valor in the army" ("d'aussi belles marques de sa sagesse que toute sa famille en a donné de sa valeur dans les armées" [225]). Buffet's reconsideration of what should be worthy of the historical record reflects the period in which she composed her work. No longer in the age of the Fronde, French women had traded amazon weapons for literary materials. Writing had become their principal means of exerting influence and effecting change. Thus Buffet deems the qualities and actions associated with literature "worthy of memory" and equivalent to actions in a more public sphere. She resurrects these "learned ladies" from the abyss in which Molière attempts to bury them.

Women's memoirs and historical novels constitute, in effect, another step in women's revision of history, as seventeenth-century women writers continue the questioning begun by their literary matrilineage. These memorialists and novelists extend their revisionary efforts more deeply into the roots of a gendered history by questioning not only its exclusion of women but also the completeness and truthfulness of its narrative. An examination of their texts reveals a sensitive awareness of the general polemic over history. They openly place their memoirs and novels under the auspices of particular history as they all interpret its meaning and implications in surprisingly similar ways. An analysis of the vocabulary that female memorialists and novelists use to describe their undertakings reveals a consensus among these women about the relationship between their work and history. Although there is obviously some element of play with *H/histoire*, their replication of the discourse of the "crisis of history" points to their deliberate and common effort to place their narratives within the larger framework of history and their century's debate over its epistemology.

Memorialists

Among women writers, memorialists define most directly the relationship between their literary enterprises and history, in part because connections between the two genres already exist. In many cases authors of these memoirs, crossing both literary and historical genre distinctions, conceive of their works as historical undertakings, conscious that their works offer alternative constructs of the past, both in content and in style. The memorialists' use of the terms *particulier* and *public* to describe aspects of their narratives underscores the intentionality of their historical revisions and their specific attraction to and redefinition of the "particular."

Like many of the memorialists, Montpensier makes a continual effort to separate her *Mémoires* from common historical knowledge and place her text in what she presents as the privileged domain of particular history. In the *Mémoires,* she uses the terms "particular" and "public" to distinguish between what she views as two realms of historical discourse. The two adjectives occur frequently in a variety of contexts that, taken together, indicate a "Montpensierian" vision of what constitutes particular and general history and of the advantages each holds for the author.

The public sphere is, as expected, that which is known by everyone: "The state I was in, the way Monsieur [her father] treated me, were circumstances that were publicly known so that all of France was my witness" ("L'état ou j'étais, la manière dont Monsieur me traitait, étaient des circonstances assez publiques pour que toute la France me fût témoin").[112] Montpensier frequently refers to this public domain of history and contrasts it with a domain marked by her personal interpretation. As public events are verifiable by many people, they have a factual status, a parallel she draws when she remarks, for example, "What I told them was a fact, and even public" ("Ce que je leur disais était un fait, et même public" [42:1]). In contrast, in the context of Montpensier's *Mémoires,* "particular" can be synonymous with "specific," "detailed," "private," or "personal," but the emphasis is on "personal." The first sense is evident in the following: "As this affair will be in all the histories of the time, I did not bother to learn the specifics" ("Comme cette affaire sera dans toutes les histoires de ce temps, je ne me mis pas en peine d'en savoir le particulier" [42:377]). From such remarks, it is evident that Montpensier is especially interested in revealing certain specifics that she feels will be eliminated from history. The events belonging to this particular history that she plans to unveil are often qualified further in the *Mémoires* as being personal. Although Montpensier envisions the *Mémoires* as a specific narrative, what counts above all is its quality as a personal vision of events. "The specifics will be in history. . . . Thus I will only say what I saw and did" ("Tout ce détail sera dans l'histoire. . . . Ainsi je n'en dirai que ce que j'ai vu et fait" [42:485–486]).[113] In the Montpensierian vision of historical narrative, public history can be specific and detailed while still omitting the "particularities" she deems important. Public history thus needs to be completed, which Montpensier can do by adding her own valuable, personal perspective on events.

Many other female memorialists define their undertakings in a similar fashion, stressing the need for another perspective on events. The title page and *avertissement* of *Les Mémoires de M.L.D.D.N.*, the duchesse de Nemours, again reveal that the author is particularly attuned to distinctions in historical narrative. The same terms appear as in Montpensier's *Mémoires*, but the contexts in which they are used allow the characteristics of particular history to be expanded. Nemours is more precise as to what constitutes this type of historical narrative. The title page of the first edition of 1709 reads: "The Memoirs of M.L.D.D.N., Containing what happened that was most particular during the Paris war, until the cardinal de Retz's emprisonment, which took place in 1652. With the various characters of the people who took part in this war" ("Mémoires de M.L.D.D.N., Contenant ce qui s'est passé de plus particulier en France pendant la Guerre de Paris, jusqu'à la prison du Cardinal de Retz, arrivée en 1652. Avec les différents caractères des personnes, qui ont eu part à cette Guerre").[114] "Particulier" is associated with "the various characters of . . . people," which suggests that the version of history in the succeeding pages will have a psychological orientation. This perspective links Nemours's text with particular history as delineated in the preface to Montpensier's *Le Recueil des portraits*. Although the title page could have been written by the book's editor, it nonetheless corresponds to Nemours's intentions as expressed in her preface. There, she clearly explains what she intended, as she reflects on the relationship between personalities and events:

> My purpose in giving these memoirs is only to *report simply*, and as much as *I can remember*, what happened, *to my knowledge*, that was most *particular* during the king's minority; for I am not skilled

enough to write about all the *great actions* he has done since with
the dignity that is appropriate. Thus I will talk only about the sad
state that France saw itself reduced to . . . because of the implacable hatred that existed for Cardinal Mazarin. . . . I will make the
secret motives known, and I will report the *different characters* of the
principal actors.

Mon dessein en donnant ces Mémoires n'est que de *rapporter
simplement* et autant que je pourrai *m'en souvenir*, ce qui s'est passé
à ma connaissance de *plus particulier* pendant la Minorité du Roi; car
je ne suis point assez habile pour pouvoir écrire avec toute la dig-
nité qu'il conviendrait, les *grandes actions* qu'il a faites depuis.
Ainsi je ne parlerai que de l'état malheureux où on se vit reduite,
. . . par la haine implacable qu'on y avait pour le Cardinal Mazarin. . . . Je ferai connaître les *motifs secrets*, et je rapporterai les *différents caractères* des principaux Acteurs. (4–5, my emphasis)

As in Montpensier's *Mémoires*, the status of eyewitness is essential to
this particular history. In addition, Nemours contrasts her account
with a narrative of "the great actions," further qualifying "particular": "particular" events are those that are less well known than those
found in most accounts of the Fronde. This contrast is underscored by
her promise to reveal the "secret motives" and the "characters of the
principal actors": the opposition is not just between public and private but between actions and their underlying causes—a distinction
that recalls Saint-Evremond's desire for a narrative that does not stop
at the "precise narrative of events" but includes the passions that determine much of history. In Nemours's text, events are viewed from
behind the scenes, as she recounts history from an interior perspective. Later in her narrative, Nemours reiterates her desire to contribute
"particularities" to the knowledge or the past. When, for example, she
speaks of the moment during the Fronde when Anne d'Autriche
freed the princes, she interrupts herself, saying,

A lot of things happened, . . . but I will not say anything about
them here, as much because others have already written about
them as because I have resolved to report only certain particularities that others could have omitted, which relate only to a few
circumstances of the motives and characters of those whose roles
have already been amply represented.

Il se passa bien des choses, . . . mais je n'en dirai rien ici, tant
parce que d'autres les ont déjà écrites, que parce que j'ai résolu de
ne rapporter seulement que ce qu'ils ont pû omettre de certaines
particularités, qui ne regardent que quelques circonstances des
motifs et des caractères de ceux, dont les rôles ont été déjà ample-
ment représentés. (17–18)

This memorialist expands the connotations of particular from Montpensier's "specific" and "personal" to add "secret," "causal," and "psychological" to the list of possible meanings.

Nemours's explanation of her position vis-à-vis historical events and the narration of them also illuminates the style in which these events are to be depicted. Inherent in the opposition "particular/great actions" is a parallel stylistic opposition, one between "simply" and "with dignity." In writing about particular events "simply," Nemours distinguishes her history from those of historiographers such as Racine, who concentrate on "the great actions" and write "with dignity." Nemours underscores the veracity of her narrative when she states that she aims to "report simply," because in so doing she allies her narrative with Menestrier's category of *histoire simple* and its truthful quality. For historians of *histoire simple* are, to repeat Menestrier's definition, those who "[speak] about things simply . . . with even more of an appearance of truth because there [is] less artifice." However, Menestrier would not place Nemours's text in his category of *histoire simple* because of her inclusion of "le particulier." Nemours goes beyond the simple recitation of events and creates another category of history, one that is as truthful as *histoire simple* but adds "secret motives" and "characters."

Nemours's preface is remarkably reminiscent of that of an earlier female memorialist, Marguerite de Valois, whose *Mémoires* was published earlier in the century (1628) and was very widely read. As the first memorialist, de Valois can be viewed as a model for many women. She modestly distinguishes her *Mémoires* from what she depicts as the nobler realm of history. In dedicating her work to the historian Brantôme, she states,

> I will write my memoirs, to which I will not give a more glorious name, even though they merit the title of history for the truth which is included *plainly* and *without any ornamentation*, because I don't consider myself capable of doing so and don't have the leisure for it at the present time.

> Je tracerai mes mémoires à qui ne je donnerai un plus glorieux nom, bien qu'ils méritassent celui d'histoire pour la vérité qui y est *contenu nuement* et *sans ornement aucun*, ne m'en estimant pas capable et n'en ayant aussi maintenant le loisir. (my emphasis)[115]

Like Montpensier and Nemours, Marguerite de Valois stresses the style of her *Mémoires* and, especially, the fact that they are "without any ornamentation." These female memorialists, in qualifying their narratives as straightforward accounts, are aligning themselves stylistically with the tradition of historians, especially erudite ones, who recount events without the rhetorical flourishes used in the latter half of the seventeenth century, to invest their narratives with the veracity of *histoire simple*. At the same time, the memorialists' accounts are different, as they adopt a "particular" perspective to reveal the actions behind the scenes.

Two other women memorialists use *particulier* in a way that provides equally illuminating and complementary visions of history. Lafayette in the preface to her *Histoire de Madame Henriette d'Angleterre* and Motteville in her *Mémoires pour servir à l'histoire d'Anne d'Autriche* underscore the historical aspects of their literary initiatives, while specifying the nature of the history to be recounted. Again they rely on the term "particular." Lafayette begins by evoking an atmosphere of confidentiality between herself and Henriette d'Angleterre:

> The acquaintance gave me afterward the honor of familiarity with her; so that after she was married, I had "particular" access to her at any time.

> Cette connaissance me donna depuis l'honneur de sa familiarité en sorte que, quand elle fut mariée, j'eus toutes les entrés particulières chez elle.[116]

In this instance, "particular" is associated with "familiarity," giving particular history a somewhat different connotation from those we have already seen. Lafayette is going to write not only a personal history but also a privileged one. She may not know everything, but because of her position she is in Henriette's confidence.

Motteville's comments in her *Mémoires pour servir à l'histoire d'Anne d'Autriche* echo those of Lafayette as well as those of Montpensier and Nemours with respect to intention and vision, with one important difference. She specifically dissociates her work from general history: "I did not have the intention of writing history in a regular fashion; but I did take care to say only the truth" ("Je n'ai pas eu le dessein d'écrire l'histoire régulièrement, mais j'ai pris soin seulement de ne dire que la vérite").[117] Motteville expounds on the weaknesses of existing historical narratives, to glorify her own particular history. Her long introduction is an important contribution to the general polemic over the nature of historiography:

> It will be difficult for those who will write the history of our time not to praise the good sense and the great courage she [Anne d'Autriche] showed during a long regency, when she was reduced to supporting a foreign war and two civil wars. But I thought it *necessary* to *add to the great events* that those writers will not fail to teach posterity, the *particular* side of her life, which they may not be as well informed about as I am, who have studied her with much attention because of my ardor and my tenderness for

her. Obliged not to be contented with what is found in newspapers, and with no other way to express to her the gratitude I feel for all her goodness and to repay her (if that can and should be said) for the *intimacy* with which she honored me, I have mixed into her *history* some of her words, her thoughts, and her actions that deserve to be known by everyone, and that would remain unknown if I had not immediately written them down.

Il sera difficile à ceux qui écriront l'Histoire de notre temps, de ne pas louer le bon sens et le grand courage qu'elle a fait paraître dans une longue Régence, où elle a été réduite à soutenir une Guerre étrangère et deux Guerres civiles. Mais j'ai cru qu'il était *nécessaire* de *joindre aux grands Evénements*, qu'ils ne manqueront pas d'apprendre à la postérité, *le Particulier* de sa vie, dont ils ne sont pas peut-être si bien instruits que moi, qui l'ai étudiée avec beaucoup d'application, par le zèle et la tendresse que j'avais pour elle. Obligée de ne pas me contenter de ce qu'on met dans les Gazettes, et hors d'état de lui témoigner autrement la reconnaissance que j'ai pour toutes ses bontés et de la payer (si cela se peut et se doit dire) de la *familiarité* dont elle a bien voulu m'honorer, j'ai mêlé, dans son *Histoire,* quelques-unes de ses paroles, de ses Pensées, et de ses Actions, qui méritent d'être sues de tout le monde, et qu'on ignorerait si je ne les avais écrites sur le champ. (Preface, my emphasis)

As in Nemours's preface, the "great events" included in history are just one part of the picture. Motteville uses them as a framework for her narrative but concentrates on going beyond their superficial portrayal. Historians "will not fail to teach posterity" about these "great events" but, Motteville's comment implies, "the particular" will be excluded. In contrast, she will include the queen's "thoughts" and hopes to reveal the personality behind the actions. Motteville is like Lafayette in associating "particular" with a privileged narrator, a narrator familiar with her subject and therefore able to present an interiorized point of view. To Motteville this point of view is not simply an addition, but "necessary."

Motteville goes one step beyond Montpensier, Nemours, and Lafayette by glorifying the particular history that her *Mémoires* recounts:

It is these particular aspects that those who will write general history will not know, or will not find worthy of inclusion. Yet it is these particular aspects, in which one is not watchful and cautious, that betray the secrets of our inclinations and reveal our character. . . . This is why people are more curious to know this side of things than to know what happens in front of everyone, where we usually want to appear what we are not and where we are always on our guard.

C'est ce particulier que ceux qui écriront l'histoire générale ne sauront point, ou ne trouveront pas mériter d'y être mis. Cependant c'est ce particulier, dans lequel on ne s'étudie pas, qui trahit le secret de nos inclinations, et marque notre caractère. . . . C'est pourquoi on a plus de curiosité de le savoir que ce qui se passe devant tout le monde, où nous voulons la plupart du temps paraître ce que nous ne sommes pas et où nous nous tenons toujours sur nos gardes. (4:312)

Motteville gives more truth value to particular history than to official history, which she characterizes as merely a mask. In unveiling the particular side of experience, an author tells the real story, one that is more natural and therefore more truthful and also pleasing. It satisfies the curiosity of the public in the same way Montpensier's *Le Recueil des portraits* does—by concentrating on the individual, the "character."

The memoirs that are overtly linked with particular history appear to have been composed primarily during the first decades of Louis XIV's reign.[118] By the end of the century, memorialists such as Hortense and Marie Mancini stress that they hope to reveal their own lives, not necessarily the "particularities" of the public realm.[119] However, the precedent set by the earlier generation is kept alive by at least one memorialist at the end of the century, Madame de Caylus, who describes in her *Souvenirs* what she refers to as "the particular things of the court that I saw close up" ("des choses particulières d'une cour que j'ai vue de près").[120] The placing of memoirs under the aegis of particular history also seems to be done almost exclusively by female writers. Male contemporaries such as Retz, La Rochefoucauld, and Lenet do not justify their literary initiatives or pique the reader's interest in this way. Mlle l'Héritier's *avertissement* to her 1709 edition of the duchesse de Nemours's *Mémoires* contrasts this work with a more general concept of the genre:

> Most of those who have written memoirs were brought to do so from a desire either to write their apologia or to teach posterity the part they played in great and important affairs. Neither of these motives engaged the illustrious person whose memoirs we present here. She wanted only to depict the truth.

> La plupart de ceux qui ont écrit des Mémoires, y ont été portés ou par le dessein de faire leur Apologie, ou par l'envie d'apprendre à la Postérité la part qu'ils ont eue dans de grandes et importantes Affaires. Ce n'est ni l'un ni l'autre de ces motifs, qui ont engagé à écrire l'illustre Personne dont on donne ici les Mémoires. Elle n'a uniquement pensé qu'à peindre la vérité.[121]

La Rochefoucauld's and Retz's memoirs can be ascribed to l'Héritier's two primary motives, respectively. Women, in contrast, develop particular history because it corresponds to their experiences and to what they want to say. Not until the eighteenth century does a man, Saint-Simon, follow in their footsteps. Saint-Simon is consistently praised for revealing "the secret motivations" of history. But his positioning of himself with respect to particular history is very different from the positioning of his female precursors. In the foreword of his *Mémoires* (1743), where he describes historical writing in order to situate his own effort, he takes up the rhetoric of the previous century's debate and states:

> To be useful, a narrative of events must unveil their causes, their effects, and their relationships to each other. . . . It must unveil the interests, the vices, the virtues, the passions, the hatreds, the friendships, and all the other motivations, both primary and accessory, of the intrigues, plots, and public and particular actions.

> Pour être utile, il faut que le récit des faits découvre leurs origines, leurs causes, leurs suites et leurs liaisons les uns aux autres . . . les intérêts, les vices, les vertus, les passions, les haines, les amitiés, et tous les autres ressorts, tant principaux qu'incidents, des intrigues, des cabales et des actions publiques et particulières.[122]

But whereas his ideal history is the same as that of the female memorialists, his conception of the author is not:

> The person who writes the history of her/his time . . . takes care not to reveal that s/he has done so. For what would one not have to fear from so many powerful people. . . . A writer would have to lose her/his mind even to let people suspect s/he is writing. Her/his work must ripen under the surest lock and key.

> Celui qui écrit l'histoire de son temps . . . se garde bien de la montrer. Que n'aurait-on point à craindre de tant de gens puissants. . . . Il faudrait donc qu'un écrivain eût perdu le sens pour laisser soupconner seulement qu'il écrit. Son ouvrage doit mûrir sous la clé et les plus sûres serrures, passer ainsi à ses héritiers. (15)

Unlike the female memorialists, Saint-Simon does not associate his own life and knowledge with particular history. As a historian outside the events he recounts, Saint-Simon is less implicated than a Montpensier or a Nemours. In addition, the court he describes belongs primarily to the past. He is not depicting his own contemporaries for future readers. On the contrary, he discourages that, saying that one cannot be truthful about the present for fear of repercussions. Thus, although Saint-Simon's final product often resembles the women's memoirs composed during the preceding century, he is not consciously adding to the history of his own time. He does not feel the same impulse to profit from the instability of historiography to write his own experiences. It can be argued that Saint-Simon follows the lead of his female precursors, but his stance is far less "compromising," or politically and ideologically charged.

Whereas most male memorialists do not resemble their female counterparts, many prominent women novelists use much the same rhetoric as the female memorialists to characterize their works. These women advocate and express a similar conception of historical narration, as they join memorialists to create a representation of reality that not only supplements, but also rivals, the traditional representations.

Nouvelles historiques

As we have seen, the historical novel was viewed in the seventeenth century as the domain par excellence of particular history. When we examine the historical terminology in authorial prefaces and elsewhere, it becomes evident that writers of fiction are as aware as memorialists of the debate about the forms of historical narrative. Lafayette and Villedieu, for example, play with the term "H/histoire" (history/story) with the desire to be seen not only as fictionalizing history but also as writing history the same way the memorialists do.

Lafayette, who like most novelists in the mid-seventeenth century does not preface her works with lengthy critical discussions, explicitly draws a parallel between her novel La Princesse de Clèves and memoirs in a letter written to Lescheraine: "It is a perfect imitation of the court and of the way one lives there. There is nothing novelistic and contrived: thus it is not a novel: it is really memoirs and this was, I was told, the title of the book, but it was changed" ("C'est une parfaite imitation de la Cour et de la manière dont on y vit. Il n'y a rien de romanesque et de grimpé: aussi n'est-ce pas un roman: c'est proprement des mémoires et c'était, à ce que l'on m'a dit, le titre du livre, mais on l'a changé").[123] Thus, like the memorialists, Lafayette recounts a story that is another facet of history. By denying that the style and content can be considered "novelistic and contrived," Lafayette-novelist joins Lafayette-memorialist and qualifies her work as another version of histoire simple. She affirms the novel's historical nature by referring to it as memoirs.[124]

Marie-Catherine-Hortense Desjardins, Mme de Villedieu, overtly challenges history from the opening pages of many of her works. The prefaces of her historical novels are miniature critical treatises in which she defines her contribution to this new literary genre, specifically with respect to history. She establishes a parallel between what she terms the "general or public history" of her sources and the "gallant history" and the "particularities" she extrapolates from them. For example, she characterizes her Portrait des faiblesses humaines as "truths . . . drawn from public and famous Histories" ("les vérités

. . . tirées d'Histoires publiques et fameuses").[125] Similarly, in the preface to *Les Annales galantes*, she forcefully states, "I . . . thus declare that the *Annales galantes* are historical truths. . . . They are faithful elements of general History" ("Je . . . déclare donc, que les *Annales galantes* sont des Vérités Historiques. . . . Ce sont des traits fidèles de l'Histoire Générale").[126] Thus Villedieu does not sever her story from history but, rather, presents it as one aspect of history. There is no question of "imitation of the court and of the way one lives there" in her proceeding, for Villedieu does not acknowledge any distance between her narrative and the reality already found in the past. Her creations are "truths" that issue directly from historical events themselves.

Villedieu accentuates both the truthful and the creative element of this gallant, particular history much as Scudéry does before her. Of one story in the collection, she remarks, "The foundation is almost completely historical, and the fable with which it is ornamented has a plausible tint, completely drawn from thoughts on history itself" ("Le fond est presque tout historique, et la Fable dont il est orné, a des couleurs vraisemblables, et toutes prises des *réflexions de l'Histoire même*" [my emphasis]).[127] As with Scudéry's "historical conjectures," these "thoughts on history," although not verifiable, are not to be considered as separate from history but, rather, as another historical narrative that has been hidden. History is given priority over fiction— "the fable with which it is ornamented"—revealing Villedieu's desire, like Scudéry's, to have her work appear to be not an imagined history, but history itself.

Villedieu consistently elevates her form of history above the exteriorized counterpart embodied by official history. She most clearly enunciates the need for the revisionist history put forward by her novels in the *Épistre au roi* of *Les Amours des grands hommes:*

> Great men have been conveyed to posterity only as terrible figures; authors imagined they were elevating them above the common man when they stripped them of all natural feelings: they show us insensitive philosophers, and conquerors come before us only with weapons in their hands. As for me, Sire, who am persuaded that love is as old as the world, I believed that I could discern it in incidents where it would seem to have had the smallest role. I have not been disappointed in this opinion; secret chronicles have been more faithful than general histories.

> Les grands Hommes n'ont été traduits à la postérité que sous des figures terribles; Les Auteurs se sont imaginés les élever au dessus de l'homme, quand ils les ont dépouillés de tous les sentiments de la Nature: ils nous représentent les Philosophes insensibles, et les Conquérants ne se montrent à nous que les Armes à la main. Quant à moi, Sire, qui suis persuadée que l'Amour est

aussi vieux que le monde, j'ai cru pouvoir le démêler dans les incidents, où il semble avoir le moins de part. Je n'ai pas été deçue
dans cette opinion, les Chroniques secrètes ont été plus fidèles
que les Histoires générales.[128]

Like Nemours, Villedieu stresses her intention to humanize history
by accentuating personalities, "natural feelings." This perspective results in a narrative that she valorizes as more "faithful" than that of
official historians and equally well founded historically. This passage
also resonates with the same reasoning that we saw in the preface to
Montpensier's *Le Recueil des portraits*. Villedieu goes beyond the conventional, superficial portrayal of "great men" with "weapons in their
hands" to unveil an intrinsic part of general history: the interior arena
of human experience. She posits her history as derived from a legitimate, albeit more "particular," source: "secret chronicles." Whether
or not such sources actually exist, what is striking is Villedieu's valorization of the same interior perspective on history as that valorized
by the women writers who were her contemporaries.

By the end of the century, prefaces such as Villedieu's had become commonplace and their rhetoric stylized and predictable.[129]
Caumont de la Force, for example, begins her *Histoire secrète de Catherine de Bourbon* (1703) with a justification, saying that "the best authors
neglected to report to us everything that could give us particular
knowledge" ("les meilleurs Auteurs ont négligé de nous rapporter
tout ce qui pouvait en donner une connaissance particulière")—thus
the need for her addition.[130] But because Villedieu was the first to
compose such polemical prefaces, hers were far from stereotypical.
Given the precise time when she was writing—specifically, the 1670s
—her comments may have been read in the context of the debate over
history, rather than as a commonplace of the novel. Her frequent use
of the same arguments as those used by the critics of general history
reveals her desire to enter the debate.

◻   ◻   ◻

The preceding pages reveal the common effort made by women
writers, whether of memoirs or novels, to place their works in the
realm of historical narrative while at the same time specifying that
their kind of history is different. In each case, this alternative history
or the actions it encompasses is qualified with the adjective "particular" as women appropriate the category of particular history and expand and give form to its characteristics. Whereas particular history is
usually identified as the account of a town or as a synonym for biography, the female memorialists and novelists I have cited associate it

with a more interiorized perspective, in keeping with the theoretical pronouncements of Saint-Réal and Saint-Evremond. The women writers call upon all the connotations of the term "particular" to delineate the narrative they present, be it the account of a woman's own life or a historical novel. Memorialists and novelists thus participate in the debate about history, they all take the same side, and, most important, they all share the same terminology.

The seventeenth-century women writers' efforts to portray another facet of human experience were recognized by their eighteenth-century successors. Two influential women in the late eighteenth century, the marquise Du Deffand and Germaine de Staël, reinforce the association between memoirs or novels and history, and even view their predecessors' works as improvements on history. Du Deffand, in her famous correspondence with Horace Walpole, denounces conventional histories and makes clear her preference for narratives that correspond to the one delineated by her seventeenth-century precursors. Of Le Vassor's *Vie de Louis XIII*, Du Deffand writes,

> This author pleases me; . . . his style is in line with that of the *Memoirs of Mademoiselle* [de Montpensier], and I prefer this way rather than that of grand speeches. . . . I have much respect for your taste; but are there not a lot of wars in *The History of Malta*? Can one disentangle in that book the intrigues and ploys? These are what I like to have in histories . . . and what show me that in everyday events one does not discern truth at all, one does not see the underpinnings.

> Cet auteur me plaît; . . . son style est dans le goût des *Mémoires de Mademoiselle*, et j'aime mieux cette manière que celle des beaux discours. . . . J'ai beaucoup de respect pour votre goût; mais n'y a-t-il point bien des guerres dans *L'Histoire de Malte*? Y démêle-t-on les intrigues, les manèges? C'est ce que j'aime dans les histoires, . . . et qui me fait voir que dans les choses qui se passent journellement on n'en démêle point la vérité, on ne voit point le dessous des cartes.[131]

Staël echoes Du Deffand's desire for a narrative that goes beneath the surface. In her *Essai sur les fictions*, Staël condemns general history for its inability to speak to anyone lower than kings. In history, Staël states, "Morality can exist only en masse. . . . Its lessons are not applicable to individuals, but only to people in general" ("Cette moralité toutefois ne peut exister qu'en masse. . . . Ce n'est point aux individus, mais aux peuples que ses leçons sont constamment applicables").[132] Staël calls for an alternative perspective that would reveal "private destinies"/"destinées privées," offering accounts useful to individuals. Later, in her preface to *Delphine*, Staël reiterates her position on the inadequacy of general history:

> History informs us only of the general characteristics of events but it cannot enable us to penetrate personal feelings that, by influencing the will of some, determined the fate of all. Discoveries of this sort are inexhaustible.

> L'Histoire ne nous apprend que les grands traits manifestés par la force des circonstances, mais elle ne peut nous faire pénétrer dans les impressions intimes qui, en influant sur la volonté de quelques-uns, ont disposé du sort de tous. Les découvertes en ce genre sont inépuisables.[133]

To resolve this dilemma, Staël offers the novel, stating that novels should "enable us to penetrate" below the surface of events and thus complete history: "This is how the history of mankind must be represented in novels; this is how fictions must explain to us, by our virtues and feelings, the mysteries of our fate" ("C'est ainsi que l'histoire de l'homme doit être représentée dans les romans; c'est ainsi que les fictions doivent nous expliquer, par nos vertus et nos sentiments, les mystères de notre sort" [3]). She credits a woman's novel, *La Princesse de Clèves*, with being the first work to fulfill her vision of the necessary supplement to history: "Madame de LaFayette is the first who, in *La Princesse de Clèves*, knew how to join the touching language of passionate affections to the depiction of those brilliant customs of chivalry" ("Madame de la Fayette est la première qui, dans *La Princesse de Clèves*, ait su réunir à la peinture de ces moeurs brillantes de la chevalerie le langage touchant des affections passionnées" [4]). In Staël's opinion, the novel as a genre is superior to history because it contains "more practical morality than history" ("plus de moralité pratique que l'histoire").[134] Novels are the accounts of individual lives which can serve as examples for everyone. But although Staël attributes this pedagogical function to the novel, she does not exclude other possible means of achieving the same purpose. For example, "Memoirs could achieve this purpose if famous men and public events were not, as they are in history, the only subjects" ("Les mémoires attiendraient ce but, si, de même que dans l'histoire, les hommes célèbres, les événements publics, n'étaient pas seuls le sujet").[135]

The commentaries of Du Deffand and Staël reveal their predilection, typical among women, for a perspective that is not inherent in conventional historical narratives but that can be supplied by alternative accounts, namely, memoirs and novels. Their remarks echo and reinforce the course taken by Montpensier and Lafayette, whose works both Du Deffand and Staël single out for praise.

In the remaining chapters, I analyze four texts by seventeenth-century French women: Montpensier's *Mémoires*, Lafayette's *Histoire de Madame Henriette d'Angleterre* and *La Princesse de Clèves*, and Villedieu's *Les Désordres de l'amour*. My analysis reveals the common desire of these writers to profit from a specific historical moment to revise a history from which women have been consistently excluded. When one views these four works as forms of history—a possibility the authors themselves suggest—the four literary undertakings become political acts. In their works, Montpensier, Lafayette, and Villedieu underscore women's association with particular history as they concurrently rework its definition and implications and mold it into a subversive female vehicle of expression.

CHAPTER TWO

From Military to Literary Frondeuse: Montpensier's Feminization of History

Je ne sais ce que c'est que d'être héroïne: je suis d'une naissance à ne jamais rien faire que de grand et d'élevé. On appellera cela comme on voudra; pour moi, j'appelle cela suivre mon inclination et aller mon chemin; je suis née à n'en pas prendre d'autres.

MONTPENSIER, *MÉMOIRES*[1]

In a recent interview, Marguerite Duras articulated an intriguing relationship between literature and politics: "For me, to be political . . . is to write. . . . It's always writing. I am incapable of distinguishing between politics and what one calls the novel" ("Pour moi, faire de la politique . . . c'est écrire. . . . C'est toujours de l'écriture. Je ne parviens pas à faire la différence entre politique et ce qu'on appelle roman").[2] Here Duras makes the case for literature as a political act, conflating the spheres of action and writing—a political move in and of itself. In addition, she enters the politics of literary criticism by distancing herself as author from the critic, the "one" who attaches the generic appellation "novel" to her works. Duras thus denounces the validity of terms like "novel" as she extends the influence of her literary activity beyond the realm of literature. Her works cannot be contained within canonical generic categories.

In equating literature and politics and calling into question the penchant of literary critics to categorize works as well as spheres of action, Duras is attempting to liberate the public from a literary tunnel vision created when texts are measured only according to preset canonical categories and definitions. Duras's challenge, surprisingly, echoes one penned 250 years earlier by the duchesse de Montpensier, the celebrated *frondeuse*, who also endows words with political significance. In a letter to her father, later published as *Le Manifeste de Mademoiselle*, Montpensier writes:

> My sex doesn't give me the freedom to accomplish deeds worthy of my origins during this time when noble souls are in demand, and the reign of the Amazons is abolished. . . . I have as a weapon only the word, which attests to my desire [to act on the political stage].

Mon sexe m'ôte la liberté de faire des actions dignes de mon origine dans le temps qui demande le secours des âmes généreuses,
et le règne des Amazones est Aboli. . . . Je n'ai pour toutes armes
que la parole, qui témoigne mon désir.[3]

In equating words with weapons, Montpensier is proposing an approach to her literary works that, like Duras's, conflates writing and
politics.

Montpensier's principal work, her voluminous *Mémoires*, is a
perfect illustration of the political importance of words as well as
a challenge to the politics of literary criticism. Montpensier creates a
text that, like many women's memoirs, has been relegated to the margins of literary history, primarily because her text eludes existing
generic distinctions. Denied status as history, literature, or autobiography, Montpensier's *Mémoires* inhabits a critical void. But as shall
become apparent, Montpensier intentionally creates an elusive text
in order, like Duras, to challenge such generic distinctions and, especially, to construct a new literary and historical space within the
genre of history. Although Montpensier is concerned with textualiz-
ing herself and her experience, an analysis of her *Mémoires* unveils an
intertext—specifically, a particular theory of history—that orients her
narrative and impels her to write.[4] In the process of transcribing her
experience, she revises both the content and the form of history,
weaving her political and personal achievements into an account that
both celebrates the inscription of women into history and changes the
very fabric of history itself.

A REBELLIOUS PUBLIC FIGURE

In literary history and history during the past three centuries, Montpensier's name, which is also—and more significantly—her mother's
name, connotes controversy and eccentricity. In the majority of the
extant portraits, La Grande Mademoiselle, as she was called in the
seventeenth century, is most frequently portrayed as Minerva or as an
Amazon. Literary critics reinforce the myths created about her, concentrating on the warrior image as it is present in the *Mémoires*. In the
eighteenth century, after identifying her as a "literary patron and . . .
author," Genlis goes on to stress her military accomplishments as an
"Amazon": "During the Fronde, she played a famous role, which was
not one of a woman or of a royal princess; she was an Amazon and
a rebel against royal authority" ("Elle joua, dans les guerres de la
Fronde, un rôle célèbre, qui ne fut celui ni d'une femme ni d'une princesse de sang; on la vit à la fois amazone, et rebelle à l'autorité ro-

yale").[5] Genlis's remarks point to Montpensier's exceptional position. The critic posits a dichotomy between, on the one hand, "woman" and "princess" and, on the other hand, the roles Montpensier whole-heartedly espoused, "Amazon" and "rebel against royal authority." For this reason, numerous biographers and historians have been attracted to the life story of La Grande Mademoiselle and have produced a plethora of biographies. They concentrate mainly on her heroic feats during the Fronde.[6]

Anne-Marie-Louise-Henriette d'Orléans, duchesse de Montpensier, by Pierre Bourguignon, 1671 (Courtesy of Musées Nationaux)

Montpensier's life (1627–1693) spanned one of the most volatile and fascinating periods in French history, and her lineage made her one of the most influential women in the realm. As the daughter of Gaston d'Orléans, the brother of Louis XIII, Anne-Marie-Louise was the granddaughter of Henri IV and first cousin to Louis XIV, eleven years her junior.[7] Her royal rank was enhanced and strengthened by the huge fortune left to her by her mother, Marie de Montpensier, which made her the most attractive marriage alliance in France. For a time she was even destined to marry Louis XIV. She was raised at court, where her exceptional rank and position were impressed upon her. She spent her adolescence primarily at the Tuileries Palace, next to the Louvre. As her mother had died giving birth to her, her aunt, Anne d'Autriche, carefully monitored her upbringing and played the role of surrogate parent. In her early teens, the princess saw power pass from male to female hands upon the death of Louis XIII and Anne d'Autriche's assumption of the regency.

When the Fronde erupted, Montpensier first took on the role of mediator between the *frondeurs* and Anne d'Autriche's regency. She accompanied the court to Bordeaux, for example, and was sent back to Paris by Mazarin to inform her father of the regency's victory over the rebels. But as the war continued, her affiliation changed. When the princes were imprisoned, she officially joined Condé's party and worked for Mazarin's destruction. She was particularly successful in replacing her wavering father at the head of eager anti-Mazarin troops, twice repelling the prime minister's forces. In 1652 she led her troops to Orléans and rescued the city for Condé's party. Later that same year she was instrumental in helping Condé to enter Paris successfully. As his troops battled at the Porte Saint-Antoine, Montpensier climbed to the top of the Bastille and ordered the cannons turned upon her cousin's royal army, an act that killed any chances of an alliance between La Grande Mademoiselle and Louis XIV. We will return to these important actions.

Obviously such participation did not ingratiate Montpensier with her aunt. When the rebellions were suppressed, Montpensier paid a heavy price. She was exiled for more than ten years to her domain of St. Fargeau, a nearly ruined château in the Burgundian woods. After renovating it, Montepensier called upon her friends who were also disgraced to join her there, thus reconstituting a kind of court. Surrounded by Mmes de Frontenac and de Fiesque, among others, Montepensier channeled her energies into literary pursuits. She initiated one of the most popular seventeenth-century salon games, the literary portrait.[8] At her own expense, she had the best examples of these portraits published as *Divers Portraits* in 1659. The authors included some of the most recognizable court figures—Sévigné, La Rochefoucauld, Lafayette, and Villedieu. The Parisian publisher Barbin later produced an augmented version entitled *Le Receuil des portraits*, which was dedicated to Montpensier and widely circulated. In addition to portraits, Montpensier was attracted to the newest literary genre of the day, the novel. At St. Fargeau, she composed *La Princesse de Paphlagonie*, a novel based on the life of her friend the comtesse de Fiesque. A volume of short stories, *Les Divertissements de la Princesse Aurélie*, attributed to the duchess's secretary Segrais, mirrors the literary activity at St. Fargeau.[9] A collection of the fictional stories recounted in Montpensier's salon milieu, it is modeled after Marguerite de Navarre's *Heptameron* and Boccaccio's *Decameron*. In *Les Divertissements*, Montpensier and her friends, disguised by pseudonyms gather and proceed to tell stories. Like the volume of portraits, *Les Divertissements* underscores Montpensier's desire to translate reality into narrative, to inscribe her own milieu. Both works possess historical resonances in that they are first and foremost *à clé* portrayals of a specific period and constitute a particular contemporary history.[10] During Montpensier's exile at St. Fargeau, her literary efforts culminated in her magnum opus, her *Mémoires*, which she worked on intermittently for the rest of her life.

Although La Grande Mademoiselle remained active at St. Fargeau and continued to govern her principality of Dombes, she nonetheless longed to be reintegrated into the court. Finally in 1661 she was pardoned and allowed return to Paris, where she took up residence in the Luxembourg Palace and regained her central place at court. After rejecting numerous marriage proposals, among them one by the king of Portugal, Montpensier chose for her husband the comte de Lauzun, but Louis XIV refused to accept the union because he considered Lauzun too lowly for his influential cousin. Lauzun and Montpensier were both briefly exiled. Historians speculate that they were eventually married, but this has never been proven conclusively. When Lauzun turned out to be a disappointment, Montpensier rejected him and returned to her creative activities, namely, writing her memoirs and constructing her architectural masterpiece, Choisy, a château situated on the outskirts of Paris. These two pursuits occupied her until her death in 1693.

MONTPENSIER'S DISRUPTIVE TEXT: GENERIC ALIENATION

La Grande Mademoiselle was thus at the center of the social and political scene, and her particular history, her personal story, therefore overtly intersects general history. It is precisely the juncture between the two that she attempts to transmit through her *Mémoires*. It covers the period 1627–1686 and includes what Montpensier considers "worthy of being written" ("dignes d'être écrit" [41:25]).[11] She imposes a specific way of viewing the past in an effort to redefine what should be considered "the great events" and the "memorable" ones—thus, the terms of history.

How can Montpensier's text be characterized? If the number of pages allotted to an event reflects its importance to the author, then her authorial bias is clearly evident. In general, she consecrates two-thirds of her narrative of more than 1,600 pages (in the Petitot edition) to the events in which she played a pivotal role, both at court and away from its constraints: negotiations for alliances for which her marriage was to be the primary catalyst, the Fronde, her principality of Dombes and her governance of it, and her life at St. Fargeau. However, in the last four hundred pages, corresponding to her years in exile for refusing to marry the king of Portugal, the narrative becomes more introspective, devoted less to her role in events and more to her inner life, a trait Lejeune calls characteristic of autobiography.[12] Given the fact that Montpensier recounts almost exclusively those public events to which she was witness, this eventual inward turn of the narrative corresponding to her time in exile is hardly surprising. Of primary importance in these final pages are the affair with Lauzun and her creative enterprises, notably the construction of Choisy.

Montpensier frames the account of her personal activities with references to well-known events of general history, most frequently the deaths or births of notable historical figures such as Louis XIII, Henriette d'Angleterre, Richelieu, Mazarin, Anne d'Autriche, Colbert, and Louis XIV, but also references, for example, to the civil war in England, to Louis XIV's coronation, to the condemnation of Fouquet (Louis XIV's finance minister), and to the king's military exploits. Using these recognizable markers as well as general references to holidays, she instills a sense of temporality in her narrative, although dates themselves appear very rarely. This verifiable, albeit loose, chronological framework serves to legitimate Montpensier's personal account by grounding it in general history. But such references to historical events are usually asides and are left undeveloped.

Certain public events, however, have an exemplary status and are thus exempted from Montpensier's general preference for a more personal narration of the past: the Fronde (350 pages) and Louis XIV's marriage (96 pages) are the principal ones. I will return to these exceptional occurrences and to their purpose and significance. In addition to the inclusion of specific public events, various recurrent themes echo from beginning to end; especially evident are the problem of marriage, family interests (above all, Montpensier's relationship with her father), and her concern with her social status at court. Overall the *Mémoires* thus reflects the concerns and preoccupations of its author—events that affected her directly as well as those that interested her outside her own life—although not to the complete exclusion of "the great events."

The *Mémoires* can be characterized as particular history not only in terms of content but also stylistically. The focus is narrower and more interiorized than that of general histories or of many memoirs of her day. In comparison with most contemporary accounts, her *Mémoires*, like many women's memoirs during the same period, contains more detailed depictions of court personages and happenings at court. In fact, editors often turn to women's accounts, especially Montpensier's and Motteville's, to supplement narratives that were written from a more exteriorized perspective.[13] Descriptions of places and even of meals, as well as detailed portraits of numerous people, are intrinsic to Montpensier's work and help convey her vision of what historical texts should be. None of her male equivalents—La Rochefoucauld, Retz, Saint-Simon—describes places and daily life as avidly as she does. By evoking feasts and costumes and by describing customs, she creates an almost visual portrait of her time. Her contribution to history focuses on completing the picture, giving "les particularités"—the details or specifics—of human lives as Montpensier observed them.

Because it brings together personal activities and the events that have been engraved in the collective historical memory, Montpensier's text is unclassifiable for critics such as Duras's "one." The work's style, especially its authorial perspective on the various events recounted, and its content are determined by a woman who occupied a public position because of her birth and a particular position because of her sex and who sought to recount history from this unconventional stance. Since the publication of Montpensier's *Mémoires* in 1718, critical reaction has been virulent and condemnatory. In *Le Siècle de Louis XIV*, Voltaire adopted a critical stance that has plagued it ever since and that continues today to inhibit evaluation of the work. According to Voltaire, "Her memoirs are more those of a woman preoccupied with herself than those of a princess who witnessed important events, but there are some interesting things in it."[14] By characterizing the content as autobiographical to the exclusion of "the great events" of history, he belittles the historical value of the work. La Porte comes to a similar conclusion: "The six volumes of memoirs that she wrote . . . are nothing more than her life, recounted in the smallest detail" (1:431).[15] Voltaire, La Porte, and the other critics who subscribe to such an interpretation judge the work by a set of values that dictates what constitutes "great events" and historical narrative in general.

La Porte concludes that Montpensier intentionally avoids the rigor of a historical narrative in favor of a less precise and more personal account, to the detriment of the *Mémoires:* "Maybe it [the *Mémoires*] would have been more interesting if she had only just wanted to trouble herself to keep a bit of order in what she was writing. . . . A reader has to pay exceptional attention [*une attention singulière*] to follow the narration of events recounted in this fashion" (1:437). Given the connotations of "exceptional" ("singulier")—"that which is alone, distanced, cannot be compared" ("qui est seul, qui est à part, hors de comparaison" [Furetière])—La Porte can be interpreted as criticizing Montpensier because her text makes extraordinary demands on the reader. The *Mémoires* does not conform to expectations for narrative order. La Porte implicitly suggests that Montpensier's account is too personal to be viewed as history and that she composed her text for herself, not necessarily for others.

More recent critics echo the earlier judgments. Jean Garapon, for example, calls the *Mémoires* "simultaneously a novel and the refusal of a novel." [16] He specifically locates the difference between the better-known *Mémoires* of Retz and those of Montpensier in the different relationship each author has with history. In contrast to Retz, who "wants to be first a historian following his natural vocation, given the extent of his political experience" (184), Montpensier—a "novelistic princess"—is unaware of history (185–186). "Her memorialistic enterprise is situated in the main line of a typically feminine and princely culture, a worldly culture stemming from the art of conversation, nourished by novels and the theatre. . . . She does not at all seek to tell us the narrative of her public career" (186). Thus Garapon views Montpensier's *Mémoires* as a step toward the genre of autobiography and a huge leap away from history. In his view, her only purpose is to recount "an intimate I." [17]

Yet, in contrast to the prevailing view, other critics consider the work to be history and ignore or even delete the personal narrative thread. The publication history of the *Mémoires* provides the best example of this critical approach, for an effort was made to transform the account into a narrative that conformed more to what was expected for history. The Réserve of the Bibliothèque Nationale has a version that bears no date and is but a fragment. The catalogue of the Bibliothèque Nationale describes this edition, most likely the first, in the following manner: "Missing the title, the beginning, and the end. Very old notation on manuscript: 'The publication of these memoirs was stopped and suppressed. This was the only volume printed, which is only one-fourth of the work; it is very rare.' " The editor of the 1879 edition of Saint-Simon's *Mémoires* refers in a footnote to a 1718 version of Montpensier's work. He remarks, "As early as 1718, the *Mémoires* of Mademoiselle was printed, but the Regent and the Keeper of the Seals of Agenson had this edition suppressed. (unedited correspondence of the Marquise de la Cour, vol. vi, fol. 192 v.) It reappeared only in 1735, with the corrections and suppressions that continued to disfigure it for a long time. Saint-Simon cites this edition. . . . He had a copy of the *Mémoires* of Mademoiselle in his library." [18]

Whereas many memoirs that treat the Fronde, including those of Retz, were censored in the eighteenth century because the regent felt they might incite Fronde-like activity, [19] Montpensier's text was disfigured for further motives. The first edition of the work, the 1727 Amsterdam edition published in six volumes, omits much of the text, especially the introduction and other similar moments when the authorial voice, as we shall see, is especially strong and personal. The 1735 edition mentioned by Saint-Simon's editor and the 1728 and 1730 editions do likewise. Gabrielle Verdier enumerates a range of changes wrought by eighteenth-century editors. For example, they suppressed passages considered too private, inserted motivations for various actions, and transposed passages written in direct discourse to indirect, which was considered less personal.[20] Later editions are equally inattentive and unfaithful to the original text.[21] These editors all tried to organize the text, adding chapters and dividing it into chronological sections, whereas the possible autograph manuscript (B.N. 6698 fr.) contains no such divisions. In this process the editorial footnotes multiply, as editors carefully inserted more dates and expanded the scope of the *Mémoires* by adding historical background and references to other contemporary accounts. These editors, joined by many critics today, thus insist that Montpensier's text can be useful as a historical document if one ignores the extraneous "autobiographical" content.

As a result of the generic strangeness of Montpensier's *Mémoires*, critics and readers have approached the text as either autobiography or history but never as an attempt to reformulate the genre of history itself. I will argue that Montpensier intentionally creates an unclassifiable text in which historical narrative and autobiography coexist and form an alternative vision of the past.[22] As White remarks, histories that do not conform to the accepted rules of narrative are not necessarily "imperfect histories" but should be viewed "as particular products of possible conceptions of historical reality."[23] An examination of Montpensier's text will serve to reveal her "conception of historical reality" and her development of a form for its presentation. In contrast to Fumaroli's assessment of "this hybrid genre," Montpensier not only embraces the role of public author but also creates a text that is very "compromising."

THE AUTHORIAL STRATEGIES OF A SELF-CONSCIOUS *HISTORIENNE*

One of the principal distinguishing characteristics of Montpensier's *Mémoires* is the authorial discourse that runs through the text.[24] This author openly addresses questions of intent and comments upon her text, describing the nature of her narrative and establishing the framework in which the work should be read. An analysis of this discourse reveals her intention to evade conventional generic categorizations and to create, instead, a personal literary space, equal to yet distanced from general history, against which she openly measures her account. The authorial discourse announces the fusion of autobiography and history, with a consciously female signature.

In the opening paragraphs of the *Mémoires*, the author adopts the complementary stances of autobiographer and historian that characterizes the narrative as a whole. It is these opening lines, in which Montpensier describes the genesis of her *Mémoires* and states her two-fold purpose to write of the self and of history, that early editors omitted.[25] The inclusion of the paragraphs restores full authorial command and self-consciousness to the undertaking. The following passage from the opening conveys the reasoning behind this memorialist's project, and her intention to write a particular version of history:

> Since I retired to my home, I have agreeably experienced the fact that the memory of everything that has happened in one's life occupies a person fairly pleasurably, so that one does not count this time spent in retirement [in exile] as one of the least agreeable of periods. Besides being a state conducive to putting the events of one's life in order, retirement gives one the spare time necessary to put this past onto paper: so that the ease I have in remembering everything I have seen, and even what has happened to me, today makes me, at the request of a few people whom I love, take on a task I would never have thought I could resolve to do. I will thus report here everything I noticed, from my childhood to the present day, without observing any order other than that of time, as precisely as I can. I hope, thanks to the good memory God has given me, that none of the things I knew will escape me; and my natural curiosity has led me to discover some fairly particular things so that I can promise that reading this will not be boring.

> Depuis que je suis retirée chez moi, j'éprouve avec douceur que le souvenir de tout ce qui s'est passé dans la vie occupe assez agréablement pour ne pas compter le temps de la retraite pour un des moins agréables que l'on passe. Outre que c'est un état très propre à se le représenter dans son ordre, l'on y trouve le loisir nécessaire pour le mettre par écrit: de sorte que la facilité que je sens de me ressouvenir de tout ce que j'ai vu, et même de ce qui m'est arrivé, me fait prendre aujourd'hui, à la prière de quelques personnes que j'aime, une peine à laquelle je n'aurais jamais cru pouvoir me résoudre. Je rapporterai donc ici tout ce que j'ai pu remarquer depuis mon enfance jusqu'à cette heure, sans y observer d'autre ordre que celui des temps, le plus exactement qu'il me sera possible. J'espère de l'heureuse mémoire que Dieu m'a donnée, qu'il ne m'échappera guère de choses de celles que j'ai sues; et ma curiosité naturelle m'en a fait découvrir d'assez particulières pour me pouvoir promettre que la lecture n'en sera pas ennuyeuse. (40: 367–368)

These lines reveal the duality of purpose at the core of the *Mémoires*. Unlike the self-effacing omniscient historian in Lafayette's *Mémoires de la cour de France*, Montpensier's narrator personally determines and orders the historical narration she is beginning. She deliberately centers her account on the "I": "the ease I have in remembering," "everything I have seen," "what has happened to me," "the things I knew." But unlike many seventeenth-century memorialists, especially those writing of the Fronde, this author does not project a desire for self-justification but, rather, for self-description. She proposes to give an expanded version of the self-portraits so popular when she began to compose her memoirs. Throughout the *Mémoires*, Montpensier includes personality traits such as the following:

> I like to say the truth; thus I describe my faults and my good qualities with the same good faith as if another were writing.

> J'aime à dire la vérité; ainsi je dépeins mes défauts et mes bonnes qualités avec la même bonne foi qu'un autre le pourrait faire. (42:488)

> □ □ □

> Thus I am a person who is not bothered by anything, and who is above unimportant things.

> Aussi suis-je une créature qui ne m'incommode de rien, et fort au-dessus des bagatelles. (42:45)

Such remarks could easily find their place in Montpensier's volume of literary portraits. The autobiographical character of the text is enhanced by the fact that she begins her *Mémoires* with her childhood, a proceeding that Lejeune identifies as one of the defining traits of autobiography.[26] But although the introduction does confer an autobiographical, subjective tone on the *Mémoires*, it does not exclude a second and equally important purpose: to recount history. The duchess endows her "I" with the status of observer, eyewitness, and reporter: "I will thus report here everything I noticed."

In contrast, in the opening lines of his memoirs, Retz excludes the more objectified stance of historian. He limits himself to "the story of my life" and describes his project as self-reflective and self-descriptive:

> Madame, whatever repugnance I may feel in giving you the story of my life, which has been stirred up by so many different adventures, I nevertheless obey you, as you commanded me, even if it costs me my reputation. The whims of fortune have bestowed on me many faults; I doubt that it is wise to lift the veil that hides

some of them. However, I will inform you of the smallest details frankly and straightforwardly, from the moment I began to know my state, and I will not conceal from you any of the actions I took at any time of my life.

Madame, quelque répugnance que je puisse avoir à vous donner l'histoire de ma vie, qui a été agitée de tant d'aventures différentes, néanmoins, comme vous me l'avez commandé, je vous obéis, même aux dépens de ma réputation. Le caprice de la fortune m'a fait honneur de beaucoup de fautes; et je doute qu'il soit judicieux de lever le voile qui en cache une partie. Je vais cependant vous instruire nuement et sans détour des plus petites particularités, depuis le moment que j'ai commencé à connaître mon état; et je ne vous cèlerai aucunes des démarches que j'ai faites en tous les temps de ma vie.[27]

Retz's introduction refers entirely to himself. Even the "smallest details" he proposes to recount pertain to his life, as opposed to Montpensier's promising to include "everything I noticed . . . some fairly particular things," that is, the events to which she was a witness or of which she has particular knowledge. She does not privilege either one of her two purposes; both the personal and the general coexist in the *Mémoires*.

Montpensier's personal rank confers a privileged status on her historical narrative. In the introduction, she promises to include events she qualifies as "fairly particular," thus distinguishing her account from historical documents (both other memoirs and histories) and joining Lafayette and Motteville, who, as we have seen, also capitalize on their privileged position to recount "particularities." Here "particular" connotes "personal" and also "detailed." Because of her "natural curiosity," Montpensier can include "the smallest details" that La Porte remarked. The initial statement of intent also reveals her effort to write a structured account. The narrative is planned, as is indicated by her preoccupation with order ("putting the past of one's life in order," "without observing any order other than that of time") and with her desire to include everything ("that none of the things I knew will escape me"). Montpensier announces her intention to conform partly to a historical model in which, as in Mézeray's history, events are recorded in their chronological sequence. She later stresses that she is well acquainted with conventional historical accounts, proudly stating, "I have read the history of France, and almost all histories in French" ("J'ai lu l'histoire de France, et quasi toutes celles qui sont en français" [42:143]).

Yet in her opening paragraphs, Montpensier also specifies her intention to subvert this implied model by including "particular things." This purpose occurs as a refrain throughout the subsequent volumes. The author vacillates between conventional categories of history, refusing to embrace a single purpose and choosing instead to develop the potential of the seemingly inherent dichotomy between a narrative of personal experience and one of general events. That she conceives of her work as a historical account is further evident in her inclusion of explanations and details such as the following, which could figure in the more conventional general histories: "Even though the name Fronde only developed from a trifle, I must put its origin here" ("Quoique le mot de Fronde ne soit venu que sur une bagatelle, il faut que je mette ici son origine" [41:31]). Furthermore, she openly characterizes many of her personal experiences as worthy of the historian's pen. Lamenting her inability to recall all the details of a certain conversation, Montpensier explains that she had not intended to become a historian at that moment: "If I had thought at that time that I would one day find myself writing about my adventures and if I had even thought that I would have as many as I have since had, and as worthy of being written, I would have remembered those remarks, but that was the last thing on my mind at the time" ("Si j'eusse eu en pensée dans ce temps-là que je me trouverais un jour en dessein d'écrire mes aventures, et si j'eusse cru même qu'il m'en fût arrivé autant que j'en ai eu depuis et aussi dignes d'être écrites, j'aurais bien retenu ces propos, et c'était à quoi je songeais le moins dans ce temps-la" [41:25]). In describing her actions as "worthy of being written" she echoes Furetière's specification that the events deserving of the historical record are those "worthy of memory." As Patricia Cholakian has underscored, Montpensier sees herself as recording not only her personal "aventures" but also the history of her ancestral house—"my house" ("ma maison"), as she terms it.[28]

Throughout the *Mémoires*, Montpensier measures her narrative against a standard history and carefully dissociates her text from such an account. Instead, she allies her text with personal memoirs, specifically those of women. She states that her own initiative is authorized by the *Mémoires* of her grandmother, Marguerite de Valois: "When Mme de Fouguerolles's life was published, I found that this pastime had amused me: I had read Queen Marguerite's *Mémoires;* all this, along with the proposition made to me by the comtesse de Fiesque, Madame de Frontenac, and her husband that I write my memoirs, encouraged me to begin this account" ("Quand la Vie de madame de Fouguerolles fut imprimée, je trouvai que cette occupation m'avait divertie: j'avais lu des Mémoires de la reine Marguerite: tout cela, joint à la proposition que la comtesse de Fiesque, madame de Frontenac et son mari me firent d'écrire des Mémoires, m'engagea à commencer ceux-ci" [41:383]).

Elsewhere Montpensier distinguishes between the accounts by such female exempla and most histories. She also views personal memoirs as a specifically French phenomenon. Speaking of Spain, she writes:

> I heard of a certain event that happened in Spain at about the same time, which possibly will not be in the history of that country. The people of that nation are not as curious as the French, and thus do not record the most minute details: there are not even personal memoirs in Spain as there are in France.

> J'ai ouï conter *une particularité* qui arriva en Espagne à peu près dans le même temps, qui ne sera peut-être pas dans l'histoire de ce pay-là. Cette nation n'est pas si curieuse que la française d'écrire jusqu'aux moindres circonstances: il n'y a pas même de *Mémoires particuliers* en Espagne comme en France. (42:431–432, my emphasis)

By indirectly associating women with particular memoirs and the genre with France, she is like Huet who, in the preface to *Zaïde*, associated the novel with women's position in French society.

Montpensier sets the limits of her particular history through the authorial discourse: she does not intend to record all events. As she openly declares regarding one incident, "As all the histories and the memoirs of many people recount everything that happened, . . . I will say nothing more" ("Comme toutes les histoires et les Mémoires de force gens qui écrivent disent tout ce qui se passa, . . . je n'en dirai pas davantage" [41:30]). Similar interjections appear almost every time the memorialist refers to an event that was already publicly known. She thus makes a conscious effort to avoid repeating what was common knowledge. She avoids describing Louis XIII's death because "this is not a subject that must be part of my memoirs: this will be better recorded in the histories of the time" ("ce n'est pas une matière qui doive faire partie de mes Mémoires: cela se verra mieux dans les histoires du temps" [40:426]). Such remarks indicate her precise notion of what constitutes general history, as she anticipates which of the events she has witnessed will be included in the official record of her age. About Louis XIV's finance minister, Fouquet, imprisoned for embezzlement, she writes,

> This was such an important and long affair that had so many consequences, and in which so many people were involved, that it is not possible that personal memoirs and historians will not speak about it; thus I will not venture to say more.

> Ça a été une si grande et si longue affaire qui a eu tant de suite, et tant de gens y étaient intéressés, qu'il ne se peut faire que les Mémoires particuliers et les historiens n'en parlent; ainsi je ne m'aviserai pas d'en dire davantage. (43:20)

Certain events do not need to be included or expanded upon in her memoirs because Montpensier believes they will receive adequate treatment by official historians. She thus defines her own role in opposition to that of official historians.

This authorial limitation is not a complete rejection of the role of historian but a conscious reorientation of the narrative focus, to highlight personal experience and perspective. Montpensier's conception of personal experience as an important form of history is in direct opposition to that of many other memorialists, who remark that they judiciously exclude personal aspects except when they illuminate "the great events." A case in point is Saint-Simon who, although his account is often autobiographical, does not openly equate the autobiographical with history. He remarks, "[There are] many other events that I have neglected to write about because they concern only myself and do not elucidate worldly affairs" ("[Il y a] bien d'autres occasions que j'ai négligé d'écrire, parce qu'elles ne regardaient que moi, sans connexion d'éclaircissement ou de curiosité sur les affaires ou le cours du monde").[29] La Grande Mademoiselle chooses to recount in detail those affairs, such as her acts during the Fronde, which she feels will not merit inclusion in other accounts even though they illuminate the official record. As a principal court figure, she produces a narrative that has many affinities with official histories because the same events form their framework. Her purpose is thus twofold: she writes of herself and of historical events. As she never completely resolves the opposition between the two, Montpensier refuses absolute assimilation into either category, preferring her personally constructed space.

This dual stance of autobiographer and historian accounts for the complex notion of a reading public inscribed in the *Mémoires*. On the one hand, she sees this public as composed uniquely of her contemporaries.[30] On the other hand, the *Mémoires* addresses a second public, a hypothetical one existing in the future. She expects the contemporary readership to fill in the details, and in the authorial discourse she clearly instructs them to do so:

> Not long ago that box was discovered which provoked what happened at Val-de-Grace, about which people have already heard too much.

> Il n'y avait pas longtemps que l'on avait découvert cette cassette qui donna sujet à ce qui se passa au Val-de-Grace, dont on n'a que trop ouï parler. (40:377)

> ☐   ☐   ☐

> The next day he went to the parliament to have registered against him that declaration whose subject is known without my explaining it here.

[Il] alla le lendemain au parlement faire enregistrer contre lui la
déclaration dont on sait le sujet sans que je l'explique ici. (40:414)

These deliberate narrative ellipses are related to Montpensier's stated
purpose of recounting aspects of the history of her time that general
histories will not include. She underscores her desire to avoid repeating facts that are already included in other accounts or held in the
minds of her readers. Instead, what draws this contemporary public
to the *Mémoires* is its "particular" (in the sense of personal) or autobiographical content, that is, its privileged ability to shed light on affairs
and reveal heretofore unmentioned details because it filters events
through the person of Montpensier herself. But her hypothetical future readers need to be instructed, hence her explanation of the origin
of the word "Fronde" or her description of a tax obviously known to
her contemporaries (40:439). This is a historical document written
both to complement and to clarify general histories.

Her contemporaries and her future public share one characteristic as readers—the desire to be entertained as well as instructed.
Montpensier continually underscores her intention to please both of
these publics. Above all, her narration must avoid being "boring," an
adjective that frequently appears in the authorial discourse. She constructs her account on this principle of pleasing in addition to instructing. As we have seen, the text is prefaced with the promise that
"reading it will not be boring," a remark echoed later: "If I were to
start writing down the details of this ceremony, I would say too much
and I would bore myself" ("'Si je voulais embarquer à faire le détail de
cette cérémonie, j'en dirais trop et je me deviendrais ennuyeuse à
moi-même" [43:97]). The desire to avoid repetition can also be ascribed to her intent to entertain.

Associated with Montpensier's desire to please her readers is a
concurrent, and often opposing, desire to please herself and to enjoy
the act of literary creation. Although she often establishes a "reading
contract," to use Lejeune's term for an autobiographical contract between a writer and a reader,[31] she also occasionally breaks it and turns
the dialogue introspectively upon herself, as is evident in the following passage: "My head is so full of events that I would like to say this
will make me forget many that would delight readers and would not
give me as much pleasure to write" ("J'ai la tête si remplie d'affaires,
que j'ai envie de dire que cela m'en fera oublier beaucoup qui ré-
jouirait les lecteurs, et qui ne me feraient pas tant de plaisir à écrire"
[42:425]). "I would like to say" implies awareness of a prospective
reader, as Montpensier justifies for "readers" her choice of events.
The last words of the passage, however, reveal the same autobiographical emphasis as her introductory declaration of purpose when
she states that her account will revolve around the "I."

With the fourth volume and its gradual shift toward the self, the refrain "I am writing only for myself" (43:135) is used to justify deviation from an implied model of history: "As I am writing only for myself, accuracy seems less necessary to me" ("Comme je n'écris que pour moi, l'exactitude m'en paraît moins nécessaire" [42:418]). There is an interesting parallel between these remarks and the change in content, as Montpensier turns from the events of the Fronde to her affair with Lauzun. Yet, although the *Mémoires* at times takes the form of a private journal, as critics frequently perceive it, it is important to note that the purpose of writing for herself does not predominate over that of composing a historical account for a public, as shall become even more apparent when I analyze the content of the *Mémoires*. Writing for herself is but one of the memorialist's narrative strategies and can be interpreted not as a "refusal of exchange"— Beaujour's term for the self-portrait—but as a refusal of one recognizable model of historical narrative.[32]

In the authorial discourse, Montpensier underscores for the reader the difference between that recognizable model and her own account. She always justifies her deviation from the model, as in the following: "I think I learned this during a trip I made to Blois since writing the preceding passage: As I am having fun writing these memoirs only for myself and because maybe they will not ever be seen by anyone, at least during my lifetime, I will not bother to correct them" ("Je crois avoir appris ceci en un voyage que je fis à Blois depuis que j'ai écrit ce qui est ci-devant: comme je ne m'amuse à ces Mémoires que pour moi, et qu'ils ne seront peut-être jamais vus de qui que ce soit, au moins durant ma vie, je ne m'attacherai point à les corriger" [41:117–118]). Montpensier clearly intends an audience that has specific expectations for historical narratives, even if this public will not necessarily exist "during [her] lifetime." If she were truly writing only for herself, she would have no reason for including such interjections. And by using "maybe," she leaves open the possibility that her *Mémoires* may indeed become public. She thus feels the need to account for the existence of variants in her narrative, as here when she inserts information she gained after an event to supplement her own earlier account. The *Mémoires* is thus not a strict reflection of the past but one that is filtered through the present moment of composition.

Lack of strict chronological order is one of the major differences Montpensier underscores when comparing her work with a prototype.[33] Throughout the *Mémoires*, disorder is always associated with the autobiographical aspect of her undertaking. At one point she states, "I might occasionally not situate events in their period or in sequence; as I already said, I am writing only for myself" ("Je pourrai quelquefois ne mettre pas les événements dans leurs temps et dans leur ordre, comme j'ai déjà remarqué, je n'écris que pour moi" [43:134–135]), thus directly contradicting her initial statement that her intent is "[not to] observe an order other than that of time." Throughout her text, Montpensier in fact often determines the sequence subjectively: "As there are some circumstances which are necessary, or which I value too much to let them escape, I am writing about most events out of their context, as they come to me, according to how concerned I am about them" ("Comme il y a des enchaînements qui sont nécessaires, ou qui me tiennent trop au coeur pour pouvoir les laisser échapper, cela fait que j'écris la plupart des affaires hors de leur place, à mesure qu'elles me viennent, et qu'elles m'occupent plus vivement" [43:372–373]).[34] This reconstruction of the past is thus avowedly subjective, dependent on the caprices of personal memory and desire. But at the same time, she often does inscribe events in an orderly fashion and adheres to a model she alludes to throughout by frequently introducing events with the words "it is necessary to" ("il faut") and "I must" ("je dois"). The model she has in mind dictates what must be included, what is "worthy of memory." For example, of one person Montpensier remarks, "I must not omit this story, because it was the grounds for a matter that was talked about at court and in society" ("Je ne dois pas omettre le récit, puis que ça a été le fondement d'une affaire qui a fait assez parler à la cour et dans le monde" [41:5]). Elsewhere, she uses "it is necessary" to insert another story: "It is necessary to leave Saint-Germain for a while to speak about Mme d'Epéron, and then I will return to the court" ("Il faut laisser quelque temps Saint-Germain pour parler de madame d'Epéron, et puis je reviendrai à la cour" [41:34]). In such instances, her referential model includes her desire to add specifics that only she may know. She feels the necessity to insert "the grounds for a matter" known to the public and to add a particular story of Mme d'Epéron in order to complete the public's knowledge. Montpensier thus derives her model from her knowledge of historical narrative and transforms this general model by incorporating her personal vision of what history should be.

The personal not only interrupts the order of the narrative, but it also occasionally serves as a filter for the inclusion or exclusion of events. Montpensier admits the effect of this personal vision, which at times inhibits narration: "This memory brings back too much pain for me to be able to say more" ("Ce souvenir me renouvelle trop de douleur pour que j'en puisse dire davantage" [40:411–412]). Speaking of a certain court intrigue, she states,

> There were many changes and intrigues, about which I will not say anything, not because I do not remember, as it has not been very long since this happened; but because there were too many people whom I care about who would not appear as advantageously here as they will elsewhere; and where I feel my friends were at fault, I prefer to say nothing rather than blame them.

> Il y eut beaucoup de changements et d'intrigues, desquelles je ne dirai rien, non pas faute de m'en souvenir, puisqu'il y a si peu de temps que cela s'est passé: mais c'est qu'il y avait trop de gens que j'aime qui ne trouveraient pas leur place aussi avantageusement en ce lieu qu'ils le feront ailleurs; et où il me semblera que mes amis auront manqué, j'aime mieux n'en dire rien que de les blâmer. (41:135)

Thus, despite her promise to include the "particularities" of her existence, the *Mémoires* does not tell the whole story. The reader, as addressee of this open discourse, becomes part of the memorialist's creative process, as s/he is forced to draw on her/his own knowledge of the events Montpensier refuses to develop. Her frank discourse placates the reader who seeks the whole truthful story: as s/he is informed of an ellipsis, s/he is implicitly invited to complete it.

Montpensier is acutely aware that the inclusion of autobiographical elements may affect the validity she wishes to create for her history. To ensure historical accuracy despite the inclusion of the personal, she relies on a convention common to both memorialists and historians in seventeenth-century France: the account of the eyewitness is to be valued over all others. She uses her discourse to promote herself as this faithful and trustworthy observer of historical events. Remarks such as the following constitute one of the refrains of the *Mémoires*:

> I will not say anything about the way this was done, because I did not have any knowledge of it.

> Je ne dirai rien de la manière dont cela se fit, pour n'en avoir eu aucune connaissance (40:373)

> ☐ ☐ ☐

> I will not amuse myself by describing in detail what I did not see at all. To say what one has heard said would not always be the truth; that is why I leave out what others will write.

> Je ne m'amuserai pas à décrire en détail ce que je n'ai point vu. Dire ce qu'on entend dire ce ne serait pas toujours la vérité: c'est pourquoi je supprime ce que d'autres écriront. (41:410)

Montpensier thus portrays herself as a serious historian who conforms to an accepted model of historical narrative, in this instance to generate the essential quality of truth for her account. By inserting a maxim—"To say what one has heard"—she recalls this model and places herself in agreement with a general public that views the eyewitness's account as the surest. Concurrently, she validates her personal experience as a historical subject worthy of a reader's attention.

The polarities evident in Montpensier's discourse are, like the discourse itself, one of the most remarkable features of this text and thus should be not resolved but comprehended. The inherent tension between her models (both literary and historical) and the historical vision she wishes to transmit translates into a complex historical narrative. In commenting on her own text, she calls attention to her deviation from conventional history and locates this deviation in her transgression of a number of conventional boundaries—specifically, those separating the self and history, two spheres usually opposed as private and public. Montpensier calls into question any account of the past that remains imprisoned in such dichotomies, as she puts forward a different narrative constructed according to an alternative theory of history.

The theory that governs Montpensier's historical revision, as implied in the narrator's discourse, becomes explicit when one analyzes the style and content of the *Mémoires*. The "particularities" that intentionally characterize the *Mémoires* are most apparent when her narrative is compared with contemporary accounts of the same incidents. Two events to which she accords a principal place in the *Mémoires*, the Fronde (especially the battles at Orléans and at the Porte Saint-Antoine in Paris) and Louis XIV's marriage at Saint-Jean-de-Luz, are especially illuminating in this respect. Both these events are part of the public historical record and therefore merit inclusion in other contemporary accounts. In addition, the two occasions illustrate Montpensier's two authorial stances in the *Mémoires*—active participant in the case of the Fronde, and observer at Saint-Jean-de-Luz. As we shall see, each event is especially well suited to Montpensier's attack on a history she considers to be homocentric and thus incomplete.

THE FRONDE: WOMEN AS HISTORICAL AGENTS

In selecting those experiences judged "worthy of being written," Montpensier accords the place of honor to her participation in the riotous years of the Fronde. For four hundred pages, she recounts the civil war's inception, takes the reader into the back rooms of the princely party, describes the various participants with the fervor of an artist, and traces an itinerary of the principal confrontations. As observer and participant, Montpensier records for posterity what she deems an essential component of the past, concentrating on the moments she experienced firsthand, notably the conflicts at Bordeaux and Orléans and Condé's entry into Paris through the Porte Saint-Antoine.

Given Montpensier's explicit intention to avoid events that will be recorded elsewhere, her decision to devote more than one quarter of her *Mémoires* to the Fronde appears contradictory at first glance.

Her desire to record the events of the Fronde can be attributed to a variety of motives. First, her own actions at Orléans and during the siege of Paris constitute what she refers to as her "triumphs" (41:26) and are thus highlights in her personal story. But this memorialist is drawn to the Fronde for more than personal reasons. She correctly anticipated what would be allowed in the official historical record. The Fronde presented seventeenth-century historians with an ideological dilemma and raises fundamental questions even today about the nature and purpose of historiography. There has been and continues to be a systematic suppression of this rebellion.

In the political climate following the Fronde, Louis XIV sought to erase most of this civil war from the annals of French history, retaining only those elements that would augment his own power and authority.[35] As Ranum has remarked, in a humanist climate in which history served primarily a pedagogical function, a negative example such as this aristocratic uprising had little place. In fact, official historians turned their efforts to praising Louis XIV and to obliterating the Fronde.[36] Only one official history was commissioned by Colbert: Priolo's *Histoire des dernières guerres,* composed first in Latin and then, in 1662, translated into French. Priolo's account has a strong royalist slant dictated by Colbert, emphasizing Mazarin's triumph over dissent and ridiculing nobles of the princely party.[37] Even Montpensier's funeral eulogy conforms to Louis XIV's desires. Père Anselme, her eulogist, refers to the Fronde only obliquely and only to express what he portrays as the duchess's horror at her own rebellious actions:

> I go back to that tumultous and stormy time when a poisoned atmosphere of division was spread throughout this realm. I see a young woman who goes beyond the timidity of her sex and, with male self-confidence, defies water, iron, and fire because a thoughtless zeal made her mistake the bad advice of political advisors for good. I blame her, Messieurs, and heaven forbid that I pretend to justify behavior of which she herself disapproved.

> Je remonte vers ces temps de tumulte et de tempête, où un air empoisonné de faction, s'était répandu dans ce Royaume. J'y vois une fille, qui s'élève au-dessus de la timidité de son sexe, et qui avec une assurance mâle, brave l'eau, le fer, le feu; parce qu'un zèle inconsidéré lui fait prendre pour un bien le mal où l'engagent des conseillers politiques. Je la blâme, Messieurs, et à Dieu ne plaise que je prétende justifier une conduite qu'elle-même a désapprouvée.[38]

He goes on to attribute true contrition to Louis's rebellious cousin, stating that after the Fronde Montpensier tried to atone for her faults "in a voluntary exile, by abundant tears of sadness and repentance, by sincere and persevering submission" ("dans une retraite volontaire, par des larmes abondantes de douleur et de repentir, par une soumission sincère et persévérante").[39]

The erasure of the Fronde is evident if one turns to Furetière's *Dictionnaire*. When Furetière composed his definition of *fronde*, the first connotation most likely to spring to mind was the civil rebellion that had wreaked havoc only forty years previously. Yet he follows the lead of the historians of his time and virtually empties the term of its dangerous political significance. He devotes his definition mainly to describing in detail *fronde* as a military or hunting instrument: "A rope instrument used to throw stones with more force. . . . Mothers fed their children only the game that was killed with a sling" ("Instrument de corde qui sert à jeter des pierres avec plus de violence. . . . Les mères ne donnaient à manger à leurs enfants que du gibier qu'ils avaient abattu avec leur *fronde*"). One sentence serves to ascribe historical and political significance to *fronde:* "Was also a league or a party against the minister of France in 1648" ("A été aussi une ligue ou un parti contre le Ministère de France en l'année 1648").

Furetière's ellipses are especially telling. First he reduces the uprising to one year instead of the actual four. More important, he designates only "the minister" as the party objected to, notably excluding both the regent and her son. In fact, even when Furetière turns to the verbal and adjectival forms of the noun, he eliminates all royal associations, confines the revolt to the parliament, and says it opposed only Mazarin, thus supporting the royal effort to suppress an embarrassing and disturbing past:

> Fronder, often said since the Fronde to mean to contradict, to combat, to refute.

> S'est dit fort communément depuis le parti de la Fronde, pour signifier, contredire, combattre, refuter.

□   □   □

> Frondeur [3d definition] is also said of those who formed and followed the Fronde party in France against the government. This word came into use in 1649 during which time the advisors of the parliament who were against Mazarin during the princes' absence were called Frondeurs.

> Se dit aussi de ceux qui ont formé et suivi le parti de la Fronde en France contre le gouvernement. Ce mot est venu en usage en l'année 1649 auquel temps on appela Frondeurs, les Conseillers du Parlement qui opinaient contre le Ministère en l'absence des Princes.

Yet, despite Furetière's attempt to aid in the suppression by using the past tense—"was," "said"—the Fronde remained a presence in the minds of its participants, as betrayed by Furetière's final slippage into the present tense—"is also said"—as well as by the proliferation of memoirs composed by the Fronde's principal participants.

The silencing of the Fronde is not only a political phenomenon of the seventeenth century. This short civil war also provides a perfect example of historians' judgments about what is "worthy of memory." Nearly 350 years after the uprising, historians are still attempting to piece together the intricate puzzle of characters and events and to form a coherent representation of the widespread unrest. The Fronde's complexity is mind-boggling, as Mazarin humorously noted during the disorders: "I tell you, if among so many intrigues, so many relationships, and so much disloyalty, one does not go crazy, it's great luck" ("Je vous avoue que, si parmi tant d'intrigues, tant de rapports et tant d'infidélités on ne devient pas fou, c'est un grand bonheur").[40] Mazarin's astute commentary isolates exactly what it is about the Fronde that creates a disturbing dilemma for historians. This war, perhaps more than any other, was a public war waged on the "particular" level of intrigue and personalities. As a result, to record and analyze it fully, a historian is forced to deal with sources and events that often lie outside the conventional realm of history. One nineteenth-century historian, for example, prefaces his article on women's activity during the Fronde by saying that he has uncovered "completely new aspects which at first glance do not seem at all to belong to history."[41] The Fronde is not only a series of battles in the military sense but also, and more important for our purposes, the subject since that time of a series of disputes over the implicit ideology that governs historiography. If the Fronde has continued to draw scholars during the centuries, it is because of the conflict over what should or should not be included in the explanation of the war—thus, a conflict over the nature of history itself.

An understanding of the Fronde's historiographical fate is essential for comprehending Montpensier's insistence on events of the realm of male history. Until very recently, historians of the Fronde could be fairly neatly divided into two camps: those, such as Kossmann and Moote, who reconstruct primarily the public events—for example, military skirmishes, political negotiations about spheres of power, and the role of the parliament—and those, such as Ch.-L. Livet, who are drawn to the personal intrigues and alliances. Not surprisingly, the differences in these approaches are strongly gender-marked. Historians in the first category either exclude female participation altogether or briefly mention the principal figures of Longueville, Montpensier, and the princesse de Condé but leave their actions obscured. Thus, even women's actions in the public sphere do not always merit inclusion in the official record. In contrast, historians drawn to unveiling the intricate patterns of political intrigue tend to focus their accounts on these women, yet they rarely incorporate these events into the larger picture. Such depictions usually take the form of popularized biographies with a distinct penchant for the novelistic.[42] Seventeenth-century memoirs are often the foundation of these accounts, whereas memoirs receive only passing acknowledgment from the historians of the "official" accounts.

As historians have become more aware of the arbitrariness of such dichotomies as public/private, a new wave of historiography on the Fronde has emerged in which the two previous approaches are combined. Concomitant with the rise of a more social perspective on the political events of the Fronde is a reevaluation of memoirs, among other documents such as letters and the *mazarinades,* as a valid source for the historian.[43] Works such as Christian Jouhaud's *Mazarinades: La Fronde des mots,* Lorris's *La Fronde,* and Méthivier's *La Fronde* have opened the way for a more complete vision of this civil war, a vision that takes into account women's roles and highlights the intrigues and machinations behind recognized political events.[44]

To appreciate Montpensier's revisionary spirit, one must see her *Mémoires* as one struggle in the ideological war over historiography for which the Fronde is a perfect battleground. Montpensier's *Mémoires* can be seen as an effort to fill in this intentional void in history and to offer an account that she judges will be excluded from the collective memory. Contrary to many of her contemporaries, such as La Rochefoucauld, she does not offer her account to justify herself but, rather, to glorify the exploits of Condé's party. She makes no attempt to apologize, a fact that perhaps incited the first editors of her *Mémoires* to delete almost all mention of the civil strife. La Grand Mademoiselle's account is in fact a political act of restitution as she ensures that her own acts and those of her party will be known by posterity. Through her narrative stance and choice of events, she counterbalances perspectives such as Priolo's and provides an alternative historical exemplum, as she comments upon the ideology of historiography.

In general, Montpensier's narrative recounts the actions of the court and of the princely party and depicts a France drawn to the interests of Condé and the *frondeurs.* This is not the chronological account of an impartial observer but, rather, the reflections of a devoted member of the opposition. Montpensier mentions many of the skirmishes and battles but describes in detail only those she can use for political or personal commentary. When narrating the siege of Bellegarde, for example, she glorifies the spirit of devotion among the many supporters of the princely party:

> The siege of Bellegarde lasted a relatively long time, because of the governor's resistance and the number of illustrious people. . . .

They were in perfect agreement about their goal of serving M. le prince. The resistance was such that they displayed a black flag on the wall; one knows well enough what that means without my having to explain it; it would seem as if I would like to pride myself on being eloquent, which I do not pretend to be; I want only to say what I know simply, and to make it as intelligible as I can.

Le siège de Bellegarde dura assez longtemps, par la résistance du gouverneur et de quantité de personnes de condition. . . . Ils s'accordaient néanmoins parfaitement dans le dessein qu'ils avaient de servir M. le prince. La résistance fut telle qu'ils arborèrent un drapeau noir sur la muraille; l'on sait assez ce que cela veut dire, sans que je m'amuse à m'expliquer là-dessus; il semblerait que je voudrais me piquer d'éloquence: à quoi je ne prétends pas; je veux seulement dire ce que je sais simplement, et le rendre le plus intelligible qu'il m'est possible. (41:85–86)

She limits her account to the psychological component of warfare, excluding aspects, such as precise military maneuvers, that might appear in other accounts. Her brief references to battles such as that at Bellegarde are more an effort to draw such events back into the minds of her prospective readers than a desire to describe completely every confrontation. "One knows well enough"—if Montpensier simply brings the names of the places and participants to light again. Although these events may have been erased from the official record, she knows that they have remained intact in the minds of many in her hypothetical public.

As she explains here, Montpensier focuses her account on what she knows, the ambiance of the Fronde years, but she reinforces the veracity of this possibly subjective stance by emphasizing her desire to be the faithful historian who relates "simply" and clearly, without adding eloquence or unnecessary flourishes. Montpensier's description of herself as historian corresponds perfectly to Menestrier's definition of *histoire simple*. She equates her narrative with his " plain and faithful narrative" related "simply . . . with even more of an appearance of truth because there [is] less artifice" Yet the content of her *Mémoires* corresponds more to Menestrier's category of *histoire raisonnée*, whose authors, "not content to write down and represent events, . . . look for the most secret motivations and, going back to their causes, examine the motives." Montpensier situates her account between Menestrier's two rigid categories and infuses her *histoire raisonnée* with the legitimacy ascribed to the simple and faithful historian.

In keeping with the definition of *histoire raisonnée*, Montpensier includes details and often entire events that others fail to mention. She thus personalizes her narrative in an effort to avoid what "one knows well enough." When she evokes the important occurrences at Bordeaux, for example, she includes a description of the city and its citizens.[45] She also uses her personal experiences at Bordeaux to suggest the general attitude of the city toward her future adversaries, Mazarin and Anne d'Autriche. Her actions later in the Fronde color her portrayal of Bordeaux as it was before she and her father embraced the cause of the *frondeurs*. In fact, at Bordeaux Montpensier actually served as an emissary for Mazarin, who sent her back to Paris to report to her father on the negotiations. But in her account, Montpensier downplays Mazarin's hold over the city in order to diminish his authority. She relates an exchange she had with Mazarin while they were watching the naval fleet pass:

> The Cardinal Mazarin said to me, "At least the Bordelais see that if we had wanted to harm them we could have, with such a great naval fleet." As for me, . . . I did not find [this spectacle] to be so great, and I saw this exhibition only as providing a new reason for the enemies of Cardinal Mazarin to mock him, seeing him so triumphant about so little.

> M. le cardinal Mazarin me disait: "Au moins les Bordelais voient que si l'on avait voulu leur faire du mal l'on le pouvait, avec une si belle armée navale." Pour moi, . . . je ne trouvai pas celui-là beau, et je ne jugeai cette promenade propre qu'à donner une nouvelle matière aux ennemies de M. le cardinal Mazarin de se moquer de le voir triompher de si peu de chose. (41:109)

She also undermines Anne d'Autriche: "During the ten days that the court stayed there, no one went to the queen's chambers, and when she passed through the streets no one cared: I don't know if she was particularly pleased to hear that I had a lot of visitors, and that no one budged from my house, whereas so few people went to hers" ("Pendant les dix jours que la cour y séjourna, personne n'allait chez la Reine, et quand elle passait dans les rues on ne s'en souciait guère: je ne sais si elle avait fort agréable d'entendre dire que ma cour était grosse, et que tout le monde ne bougeait de chez moi pendant qu'il en allait si peu chez elle" [41:109]). Montpensier's privileged position within the court and her direct access to the participants on both sides allow her to include details such as Mazarin's proud remark in order to portray well-known events in a more personal light. As in her description of the battle of Bellegarde, she situates the action entirely on the psychological level, using psychological precision to resurrect the intrigues of the Fronde, the essential level of action omitted by historians.

In addition to reorienting the historical perspective, Montpensier narrates in detail the two battles in which she herself played a pivotal role: Orléans and the siege of Paris at the Porte Saint-Antoine. These are Montpensier's moments of glory, when she incarnates the Amazon and assumes her father's position at the head of his army.

Her description of these two battles does not simply fulfill the auto-biographical purpose of the *Mémoires*. It also illustrates her theory of history.

The account of these battles occupies a major portion of the second part of the *Mémoires* (41:165–215 and 255–305). In comparing her past with a hypothetical historical prototype, Montpensier accurately predicts that these actions will be eliminated. In fact, the battle at Orléans is accorded little or no space in any general histories of the Fronde, and even in the other personal memoirs of the period it is allotted only a few lines. The battle in Paris figures better, but Montpensier's own role is frequently obscured. By describing these events at length, she fulfills her desire to complete official history. At the same time she adopts an alternative perspective to challenge further the historical prototype. These revisions are especially apparent when her account is contrasted with those of two of her contemporary memorialists, Retz and La Rochefoucauld. On the same side as the princess, Retz and La Rochefoucauld were fully aware of her actions and their significance. Their versions of these events, however, diverge strikingly from hers, and the variations amount to more than simply a difference in personal perspective and opinion.

La Rochefoucauld does not so much as allude to the battle at Orléans. Retz at least treats this incident, although he allots it only two pages. But even in describing the beginning of the adventure, Montpensier's conscription, he has a different perspective and interpretation from her. Retz, who was against sending Gaston d'Orléans to the provincial city, uses the account first to advance his own opinion. After mentioning the generals' request for the duke's presence at Orléans, Retz negates the importance of the maneuver by countering the officers' opinion:

> Messieurs de Beaufort and de Nemours . . . wrote to Monsieur [Montpensier's father] that there was a very strong faction in favor of the court in the town [Orléans] and that his presence at [Orléans] was very necessary. You can easily see that it was even more so in Paris. Monsieur did not hesitate for a moment, and everyone, without exception, was of the same opinion.

> MM. de Beaufort et de Nemours . . . écrivirent à Monsieur qu'il y avait dans la ville une faction très puissante pour la cour, et que sa présence y était très nécessaire. Vous croyez facilement qu'elle l'était encore beaucoup plus à Paris. Monsieur ne balança un moment, et tout le monde, sans exception fut d'un même avis.[46]

In this way Retz effectively diminishes the importance of Montpensier's enterprise and sets a negative tone for the rest of his account. He calls upon his inscribed reader to confirm his opinion "easily," agreeing with "everyone, without exception" who, in Retz's opinion, regarded Monsieur's presence at Orléans as futile and unnecessary. When Retz turns to Montpensier herself, his attitude becomes one of mockery:

> Mademoiselle offered to go: Monsieur granted her [permission], but with great difficulty, for reasons of propriety, but even more because of his lack of confidence in her leadership.

> Mademoiselle s'offrit d'y aller: ce que Monsieur ne lui accorda qu'avec beaucoup de peine, par la raison de la bienséance, mais encore plus par celle du peu de confiance qu'il avait en sa conduite. (801)

In Retz's version, Montpensier takes the lead only through personal initiative and goes against the expectations associated with the more influential public sphere. Retz removes her from the decision-making process and alienates her from "everyone." She "offered to go," she was not chosen, nor was she part of any unanimous decision. Even her father has little "confidence in her leadership." In taking the position of leader, Montpensier defies society's rules of "propriety" further separating herself from the better-intentioned and more logical public of which Retz is a member.

When Retz turns to the duchess's actual exploits, he continues to denigrate her authority as leader. In reporting a conversation he had with Monsieur, he depicts Montpensier as subservient to those who accompanied her: "I remember he said to me, the day she left: 'This exploit would be very ridiculous, if it were not backed by the good sense of Mme de Fiesque and Mme de Frontenac.' These two women indeed accompanied her, as well as M. de Rohan, and Messieurs de Croissi and de Bermont, members of parliament" ("Je me souviens qu'il me dit, le jour qu'elle prit congé de lui: 'Cette chevalerie serait bien ridicule, si le bon sens de Mmes de Fiesque et de Frontenac ne la soutenait.' Ces deux dames allèrent effectivement avec elle, aussi bien que M. de Rohan, et MM. de Croissi et de Bermont, conseillers du Parlement" [801]). Montpensier herself is portrayed as a figurehead devoid of personal judgment, in need of support and guidance, and is saved from the ridiculous only by the group that surrounds her.

In a fascinating reversal, Montpensier begins the account of her adventure by stressing that her actions were in accordance with her father's as well as other people's wishes. In place of Retz's public that condemns her actions is a parallel group that lauds and supports her efforts. She is Monsieur's logical replacement:

> M. de Beaufort [a general] . . . came to see me and said: "If Monsieur doesn't want to go, then you must." . . . Everyone came to say to me: "Surely you will go to Orléans." M. de Chavigny said

to me: "This is the best action you could take for yourself, and [it] will help M. le prince significantly." . . . The comte de Tavannes . . . came in and murmured to me: "We are overjoyed, it is you who are coming to Orléans."

M. de Beaufort . . . me vint voir et me dit: "Si Monsieur n'y veut pas aller, il faut que ce soit vous." . . . Tout le monde me venait dire: "Vous irez assurément à Orléans." M. de Chavigny . . . me dit: "Voici la plus belle action du monde à faire pour vous, et qui obligera sensiblement M. le Prince." . . . Le comte de Tavannes . . . entra, et me dit tout bas: "Nous sommes trop heureux, c'est vous qui venez à Orléans." (41:165–166)

By enumerating a variety of voices, Montpensier increases her prestige. Unlike Retz's anonymous "you" and "everyone," many of her acquiescent voices have specific names that connote authority, for they are the outstanding *frondeurs* leaders. This influential group accepts her unanimously as their chief. In addition, her use of direct discourse endows the scene with greater verisimilitude and life. Montpensier goes on to portray her appointment to head the army as perfectly natural, not even referring to the demands of "propriety." In her version, she does not ask to trespass such boundaries, she is begged to do so, and thus her capacity to command the troops is never called into question. "M. de Rohan arrived and brought me that order which I received, as I always received Monsieur's commands, with much joy in obeying him. . . . I asked the comte and comtesse de Fiesque to accompany me, and Mme de Frontenac" ("M. de Rohan arriva, m'apporta cet ordre; ce que je reçus, comme j'ai toujours fait les commandements de Monsieur, avec beaucoup de joie de lui obéir. . . . Je priai le comte et la comtesse de Fiesque de m'y accompagner, et madame de Frontenac" [41:165–166]). Montpensier portrays herself as the unanimous choice of all the male authority figures. Although the personal element is not excluded—this is to be "the best action [she] could take for [herself]"—it does not constitute the foundation of her initiative. The stimulus for her actions comes instead from the public sphere. Montpensier's command of the troops "will help M. le prince significantly." She receives an "order," Monsieur's "commands," just as any general would. As Montpensier assumes the focal position of the narrative, all others are placed in positions inferior to hers. She chooses those who are to accompany her and does not confer authority on her enterprise by alluding to the "members of parliament," as Retz does. She has no need for such external confirmation because, as a leader who is approved and chosen by a select and influential public and is seen as completely natural for the task, she herself embodies all the necessary legitimizing authority.

This *frondeuse*'s account is further distinguished from Retz's by her inclusion of "particularities," namely, the personalities of those involved. For instance, Montpensier accepts her father's order because she is the dutiful daughter who always has "much joy in obeying him." By turning her perspective inward, she continues to demonstrate that character traits and motivations play an essential role in public affairs. In discussing her appointment as leader, she depicts her father's character and provides a commentary on his general behavior or, more precisely, on his lack of initiative. Montpensier views his refusal to go to Orléans as revelatory of his personality:

All the conversations one had with him, when he was dissatisfied with the people who wanted to make him act, always ended by [his] wishing to be left in peace at Blois and by [his commenting about] the happiness of people who were not involved in any-thing. . . . This did not please me in the least; I judged by [these comments] that as time passed, this business would go nowhere and everyone would be reduced . . . to [remaining in] her/his own place; this does not suit people of our position.

Toutes les conversations que l'on avait avec lui, lorsqu'il n'était pas satisfait des gens qui le voulaient faire agir, finissaient tou-jours par des souhaits d'être en repos à Blois et par le bonheur des gens qui ne se mêlent de rien. . . . Cela ne me plaisait point; je jugeais par là qu'à la suite du temps cette affaire irait à rien et qu'on se verrait réduit . . . chacun chez soi: ce qui ne convient guère aux gens de notre qualité. (41:165)

Montpensier's own actions are motivated by her father's indecision. This explanation of the attack on Orléans reveals the complex per-sonal exchanges and relations that constitute an essential but little-known factor in the battle. As she describes the anti-exemplum her father provides for "people of [their] position," her explanation takes on a pedagogical quality.

In her account of the actual battle at Orléans, Montpensier pre-sents herself as the exemplum and thus the antithesis of her father. Even Retz, in his succinct and factual description, begrudgingly ac-knowledges her exceptional actions: "Patru said . . . that the walls of Jericho had fallen to the sound of trumpets, while those of Orléans opened to the sound of violins. . . . In the end, all this absurdity was a success due to Mademoiselle's strength, which was in fact very great" ("Patru disait . . . que les murailles de Jérico étaient tombés au son des trompettes, celles d'Orléans s'ouvriraient au son des vio-lons. . . . Enfin tout ce ridicule réussit par la vigueur de Mademoi-selle qui fut effectivement très grande" [801–802]). Although Retz recognizes Montpensier's "strength," he nonetheless portrays the conquest of Orléans as a relatively simple affair that succeeded despite "all this absurdity." As in his description of Montpensier's conscription, Retz quickly takes the power out of her hands to attribute it to male legitimate and conventional authority in the persons of Beaufort and Nemours, who "came to join her [and] decided with her" ("la vinrent joindre [et] résolurent avec elle" [802]). The generals usurp the position of subject, and Montpensier is relegated to mere object.

Montpensier's own account is naturally much more detailed and expansive than Retz's because of her own central position in the events. She devotes more than twenty pages to the conquest of Orléans. The details she includes are designed above all to augment her authority. For instance, she refers to the pleasure the generals had upon receiving her: "Upon arriving at Toury, I found M. de Nemours, M. Clinchamp, and many other officers, who displayed great joy at seeing me, even more than if it had been Monsieur" ("Arrivée à Toury, j'y trouvai messieurs de Nemours, Clinchamp et quantité d'autres officiers, qui me témoignèrent avoir grande joie de me voir, et même plus que si c'eût été Monsieur" [41:170]). Montpensier easily assumes her rightful position as orchestrator of the battle: "M. de Nemours said to me . . . that one would no longer do anything without my orders" ("M. de Nemours me dit . . . que l'on ne ferait plus rien sans mes ordres" [41:170]). Throughout the passage, she re-emphasizes her power, and her ability to command becomes a constant refrain:

> I controlled the city as if they had begged me to do it.

> Je commandai dans la ville comme s'ils m'en avaient suppliée. (41:191)

> □   □   □

> Everyday they sent word about everything, upon which I ordered as I pleased.

> Ils envoyaient tous les jours me rendre compte de toutes choses sur quoi j'ordonnais ce qui me plaisait. (41:201)

> □   □   □

> Tavannes . . . said, "Wherever Mademoiselle is, the orders one has that are not from her no longer exist; only hers are to be obeyed."

> Tavannes . . . dit "Là où est Mademoiselle, les ordres que l'on a, qui ne sont pas d'elle, ne subsistent plus; l'on ne doit reconnaître que les siens. (41:224)

In this complete reversal of Retz's text, the princess takes command and never relinquishes it. Montpensier not only emphasizes her position of authority with respect to the troops, but she also becomes monarch of the people. The conquest of Orléans is her personal victory achieved by the "strength" Retz mentioned and, in Montpensier's version, by her capacity to inspire those around her: "The ferrymen . . . came to offer me their services. I accepted with pleasure; I made good speeches to them, such as are suitable to these kinds of people to encourage them to do what one wants them to do. . . . Everyone who was with me feared I was endangering myself too much. . . . I forced them to be silent" ("Les bateliers . . . me vinrent offrir leur service. Je l'acceptai volontiers; je leur tins de beaux discours, et tels qu'ils conviennent à ces sortes de gens pour les animer à faire ce que l'on désire d'eux. . . . Tous ceux qui étaient avec moi craignaient que je ne m'exposasse trop. . . . Je leur imposai silence" (41:177–178]). The duchess attributes her political prowess in part to what she depicts as her understanding of "these kinds of people." She emphasizes this psychological advantage throughout her account of Orléans, as she focuses on these more personal military strategies. She portrays her entry into Orléans as a self-sacrificing crusade to save the people: "When those of my rank endanger themselves, this greatly animates the people. . . . I was [the savior] of that poor city" ("Quand on voit les personnes de ma qualité s'exposer, cela anime terriblement les peuples. . . . Je fus [le salut] de cette pauvre ville" [41:170, 191]). She is a public figure who commands and whose presence and rank are recognized by her subordinates, "the people." Her entry at Orléans succeeds more by the effect of her person than by any specific actions.

Having entered Orléans, Montpensier goes on to describe her moment of triumph, her official assumption of the position of matriarch: "Two men took hold of me and placed me on a wooden chair. . . . After passing through the streets, carried in triumph . . . I asked them to put me down. . . . I stopped to wait for the women, who arrived a moment later as muddy as I was, and equally delighted" ("Deux hommes me prirent, et me mirent sur une chaise de bois. . . . Après avoir passé quelques rues, portée en triomphe . . . je les priais de me mettre à terre. . . . Je m'arrêtai pour attendre les dames, qui arriverèrent un moment après crottées aussi bien que moi, et fort aises aussi" [41:180]). Of special interest here is Montpensier's reference to the women who followed her through the mud. She makes no mention of the generals or of the troops, to portray a feminocentric victory. In fact, her *Mémoires* is the only account to include these women.

Montpensier's particular history of this public event, with its explanatory details and psychological motivations, counters traditional historical narrative as represented by Retz's account by offering an alternative perspective and enlarging the cast of actors. This memorialist is impelled to write in order to complete other accounts and, more important, to revise history according to the principle she seeks to illustrate, a principle that is illustrated especially well by Montpensier herself and by her contingent of women at Orléans. Her account of the battle of Orléans inscribes women who assume nonconventional roles into the public record. The battle provides the duchess with the occasion both to exemplify women's capabilities and to provide a feminist pedagogy. She includes the names of all those who accompanied her, names that have been excluded from history on the grounds that women's actions in such a male realm can be neither influential nor important. Montpensier even boasts openly about her military prowess to increase her authority in this sphere. For example, she puts forth a general maxim—"one who is master of the countryside is master of the country where one is. The small towns are good only for sustaining the troops" ("qui est le maître de la campagne est maître du pays où l'on est. Les petites villes ne sont bonnes que pour contribuer à la subsistance des armées" [41:172])—that has the effect of placing her on a par with any military leader. As the head of her army, Montpensier illustrates the moral she derives from her narrative of the episode:

> Ordinarily women speak badly about war: I assure you that in this circumstance as in any other, good sense governs everything, and when one has that there is no woman who would not command armies well.

> Les demoiselles parlent pour l'ordinaire mal de la guerre: je vous assure qu'en cela comme en toute autre circonstance le bon sens règle tout, et que quand on en a, il n'y a dame qui ne commandât bien des armées. (41:191)

Her *Mémoires* is proof that a woman can speak about war as well as participate in it. Moreover, Montpensier's interiorized narrative illustrates her intention to "speak . . . about" it in such a way as to add another dimension to the historical record.

Montpensier justifies women who assume public roles from which they are normally excluded because of the stringent demands of *bienséance*/propriety. She glorifies her actions by, for example, strategically inserting a congratulatory letter from her father: "My daughter, You can imagine the joy I took in the action you have just accomplished: you saved Orléans for me, and secured Paris; this is a public joy, and everyone says your deed is worthy of the granddaughter of

Henri the Great" ("Ma fille, Vous pouvez penser la joie que j'ai eue de l'action que vous venez de faire: vous m'avez sauvé Orléans, et assuré Paris; c'est une joie publique, et tout le monde dit que votre action est digne de la petite-fille de Henri-le-Grand" [41:195]). The princess is thus placed in a royal, paternalistic line headed by her grandfather, Henri IV. In addition, she describes a letter of congratulations her father wrote to the women who accompanied her:

> Monsieur had written to them, after my entry into Orléans, to compliment them on their bravery in climbing the ladder to follow me; and at the top of the letter he had written: to mesdames the countesses brigadiers in my daughter's army [which is] against Mazarin. Ever since, all the officers of our troops greatly revered them.

> Monsieur leur avait écrit, après mon entrée à Orléans, des compliments sur leur bravoure d'avoir monté à l'échelle en me suivant; et au-dessus de la lettre il y avait mis: A mesdames les comtesses maréchales de camp dans l'armée de ma fille contre le Mazarin. Depuis ce temps-là tous les officiers de nos troupes les honoraient fort. (41:221)

The battle at Orléans provides Montpensier with the occasion to covertly undermine societal gender boundaries and to offer an example of women who transgress society's expectations. The uniqueness of her acts at Orléans inspires her to develop her lengthy exposition of this event. In fact, she depicts herself as a worthy example for the entire royal line. Following her victory at Orléans, there is some discussion as to who should be registered officially as the governor of the city, and she records this debate because of its extraordinary exemplarity:

> As I had displayed my power to the city, it was necessary to register [this act] with the administrators of the city. When it was first mentioned to that group, some of them raised difficulties, [saying that] as the marquis de Sourdis was empowered by the king, Monsieur could govern him but could not transfer this power to someone else, and that there was no precedent, a son of France had never acted this way within his rights. I conferred with the ministers of the parliament of Paris who were with me; to them I said it seemed to me that, given my state at Orléans, nothing should be impossible for me, and that when there was not a single example of such a thing, I would be very happy to create one for the future; that it was glorious to be [an example] of a thing as beneficial as this and that it would be an example in the future for all the sons of France who would be able to follow it on those

occasions when there had been only the king who would have done it. As the thing was not unjust, they were of my opinion.

Comme j'avais montré mon pouvoir à la ville, il le fallait enregistrer au présidial. D'abord que l'on en parla à cette compagnie, quelques-uns en firent difficulté, sur ce que M. le marquis de Sourdis étant pourvu par le Roi, Monsieur pouvait lui commander, et non pas donner ce pouvoir à un autre, et qu'il n'y avait point d'exemple que jamais fils de France en eût usé de cette manière dans son apanage. J'en conférai avec les conseillers du parlement de Paris qui étaient avec moi; à qui je dis qu'il me semblait qu'en l'état où j'étais à Orléans, rien ne me devait être impossible, et que quand il n'y aurait point d'exemple de chose pareille, je serais bien aise d'en faire un pour l'avenir; qu'il y avait de la gloire de l'être d'une chose avantageuse comme celle-là, et que c'en serait un à l'avenir pour tous les fils de France de pouvoir commettre en des occasions où il n'y avait eu que le Roi que l'eût fait. Comme la chose n'était pas injuste, ils furent de mon avis. (41:208–209)

In this remarkable passage, Montpensier begins by underscoring the exceptional nature of her position and actions and posits herself as a new model to be followed, a new universal standard to serve not only women but also the sons of France, a point she makes twice. Montpensier thus places herself not only within, but also above, the male lineage. She will lead the way for "the future." Moreover, in this instance she actually replaces the king at the apex of power. The king's singular authority is diminished as she assumes the position where previously "there had been only the king."

The preceding passage displays more than self-aggrandizement, although this is obviously present. Montpensier is preoccupied with setting herself up as a universal example not only for her contemporaries but also for the future, a point she stresses. She thus not only writes her own story but also rewrites history, for if the goal of history is to provide examples, her own story is indeed history because of the exceptional experiences she offers as models—models with an inherent element of subversion.

□ □ □

With the narration of her second crucial battle, the siege of Paris at the Porte Saint-Antoine, Montpensier continues to rescript history by offering herself as exemplum. In her lengthy account, she describes how, inspired by her victory at Orléans and filled with the sense that "nothing should be impossible for [her]," she once again took command of Monsieur's troops and triumphed over her royal cousin. The princess's exploits in this instance are the ingredients of legend, and many of her contemporaries indeed refer to her actions in their own accounts of the Fronde. Retz, for example, succinctly writes about what he calls "this famous battle":

> Mademoiselle, who had done everything she could to oblige Monsieur to go to the Porte Saint-Antoine and have it opened for M. le prince, decided to go herself. She entered the Bastille [and] had the cannon fired upon the troops of the maréchal de la Ferté. . . . Next she harangued the guard at the Porte Saint-Antoine. The gate was opened, and M. le prince entered with his army, which was more covered with glory than wounds, even though there were many of these. This famous battle took place July 2.

> Mlle, qui avait fait tous ses efforts pour obliger Monsieur à aller dans la rue Saint-Antoine pour faire ouvrir la porte à M. le prince, prit le parti d'y aller elle-même. Elle entra dans la Bastille . . . fit tirer le canon sur les troupes du maréchal de la Ferté. . . . Elle harangue ensuite le garde qui était à la porte Saint-Antoine. Elle s'ouvrit, et M. le prince y entra avec son armée, plus couverte de gloire que de blessures, quoiqu'elle en fût chargée. Ce combat si fameux arriva le 2 de juillet. (688)

Retz limits his account of the battle to a mere enumeration of the actions of the major participants, as he himself remained in seclusion and away from the center of action. As in his description of Orléans, his narrative stays on the level of major events and does not delve into the complex personalities involved.

La Rochefoucauld's version of the day's events in his *Mémoires* is scarcely more detailed, despite the fact that he was a brave combatant and was even wounded. Interestingly, La Rochefoucauld's positioning of La Grande Mademoiselle varies from Retz's:

> In short, everything was badly prepared for receiving M. le prince and his troops when Mademoiselle, making an impression on the mind of her father Monsieur, brought him out of the lethargy in which the cardinal de Retz was keeping him. She took his orders to the town hall in order to have the bourgeoisie take up arms; at the same time, she ordered the governor of the Bastille to fire the cannon on the king's troops.

> Enfin, tout y était mal disposé pour y recevoir M. le prince et ses troupes, lorsque Mlle, faisant un effort sur l'esprit de Monsieur son père, le tira de la léthargie où le tenait le cardinal de Retz. Elle alla porter ses ordres à la Maison de Ville pour faire prendre les armes aux bourgeois; en même temps, elle commanda au gouverneur de la Bastille de faire tirer le canon sur les troupes du Roi.[47]

First, La Rochefoucauld designates Montpensier as simply the inter-mediary between Monsieur and city hall, the dutiful daughter con-veying her father's orders. When he reports her actions at the Bastille, however, he grants her a more independent status: "She ordered." La Rouchefoucauld adds a qualification that Retz, perhaps intentionally, avoids. Whereas Retz states that Montpensier "had the cannon fired upon the troops of the maréchal de la Ferté," La Rochefoucauld speci-fies that these are "the king's troops," a variation that reveals more fully the rebelliousness of her act.

Like Retz, La Rochefoucauld does not enrich his account with specific details or even with the names of more than the immediately recognizable figures. He ends his narrative, as Retz does, by stressing the importance of that particular day: "That day can pass for one of the most glorious in the prince's life. His merit and his leadership never had a greater part in victory" ("Cette journée peut passer pour l'une des plus glorieuses de la vie de M. le prince. Jamais sa valeur et sa conduite n'ont eu plus de part à la victoire.").[48] In his final assess-ment, the ultimate glory goes to M. le prince; Montpensier is com-pletely displaced.

Montpensier greatly amplifies her version of this very public event by including the "particularities" she regards as essential in de-picting the event. As in her account of the battle of Orléans, she seeks to convey ambiance as well as motivations. Once again, the person-alities of those involved emerge. She attributes her decision to enter the battle to her father's insensitivity and indecisiveness:

> I urged him [Monsieur] to the point of saying, "Unless [you] have a treaty with the court sewn up, I don't understand how you can be so calm; would you indeed have one so that [you would] sacri-fice the prince to Cardinal Mazarin?" He didn't answer at all; everything I said lasted an hour, during which time all the friends we had could have been killed. . . . This seemed to me a great harshness.

> Je le pressai jusques à lui dire: "A moins que d'avoir un traité fait avec la cour en poche, je ne comprends pas comment vous pouvez être si tranquille; mais en auriez-vous un pour sacrifier M. le prince au cardinal Mazarin?" Il ne répondit point; tout ce que j'ai dit dura une heure, pendant laquelle tout ce qu'on avait d'amis pouvait être tué. . . . Cela me paraissait une grande du-reté. (41:256)

Montpensier comes to the aid of her friends in order to counter her father's "great harshness." Later she includes a brief conversation with M. le prince, where again the princely party is depicted as a group of friends:

The prince came to see me; he was in a piteous state: he had two inches of dust on his face, his hair was all tangled; his cape and his shirt were covered with blood. . . . He said to me: "You see a man in despair. I have lost all my friends: MM. de Nemours and de la Rochefoucauld and Clinchamp are mortally wounded." I assured him that they were in better condition than he thought.

M. le prince m'y vint voir; il était dans un état pitoyable: il avait deux doigts de poussière sur le visage, ses cheveux tout mêlés; son collet et sa chemise étaient pleins de sang. . . . Il me dit: "Vous voyez un homme au désespoir, j'ai perdu tous mes amis: messieurs de Nemours, de la Rochefoucauld et Clinchamp sont blessés à mort." Je l'assurai qu'ils étaient en meilleur état qu'il ne les croyait. (41:262).

This emotional scene and the ones that follow have the effect of humanizing and thus demystifying the battle:

On Tixeranderie Street I came upon the most piteous sight to be seen: it was M. de la Rochefoucauld, who had had a bullet go in the corner of one eye and out the other. His son held him by one hand and Gourville by the other.

Je trouvai dans la rue de la Tixeranderie la plus pitoyable spectacle qui se puisse regarder: c'était M. le duc de la Rochefoucauld qui avait un coup de mousquet qui entrait par un coin de l'oeil et sortait par l'autre. Son fils le tenait par une main et Gourville par l'autre. (41:260–261)

□   □   □

At the beginning of Saint Antoine Street I found Guitaut on horseback, without a hat, completely unbuttoned, who was being helped by a man.

Je trouvai, à l'entrée de la rue Saint-Antoine, Guitaut à cheval, sans chapeau, tout déboutonné, qu'un homme aidait. (41:261)

The duchess also makes a special effort to include the names of the women who accompanied her: "Madame de Nemours, and the comtesses de Fiesque, mother and daughter" (41:257). In fact, no detail is too insignificant for the pen of this historian. In numerous asides she mentions the fate of all those around her (41:273). No other memorialist paints a more complete and human picture of the Fronde.

Even when she turns to minutely describing her own exceptional actions, Montpensier continues to humanize this event in an effort to go beyond a hypothetical historical account. As before, she focuses on herself, the eyewitness and central character, to guarantee the veracity of her detailed narrative. As at Orléans, she is a natural and totally accepted leader. From the moment she enters the streets, the townspeople of Paris regard her as their commander-in-chief: "All the townspeople were gathered in the streets and asked me as I passed by, 'What shall we do? You have only to command, we are ready to follow your orders'" ("Tous les bourgeois étaient attroupés dans les rues, qui me demandaient en passant: 'Que ferons-nous? Vous n'avez qu'à commander, nous sommes tous prêts à suivre vos ordres'" [41: 257]). She has no need of the authority conferred on her as the supposed emissary of her father. In her account, the details of her assault on her cousin from the ramparts of the Bastille figure prominently: "I went to the Bastille, . . . I walked along the towers for a while, and I had the cannon loaded. . . . I looked through a telescope and saw many people on the Charonne heights, . . . which led me to believe that that was the king, and I have since learned that I was not mistaken" ("Je m'en allai à la Bastille, . . . je me promenai longtemps sur les tours, et je fis charger le canon. . . . Je regardai avec une lunette d'approche, je vis beaucoup de monde sur la hauteur de Charonne, . . . ce qui me fit juger que c'était le Roi, et j'ai appris depuis que je ne m'étais point trompée" [41:270]). The divergent registers in this passage are especially striking. In one and the same sentence Montpensier calmly walks around the towers and orders the cannon to be loaded, thus creating a curious ambiance for her ambitious deed. The nonchalant tone would seem to be entirely inappropriate for one who identifies her target as "the king"—not "the king's troops," as La Rochefoucauld specified, but simply "the king." The reader is left to fill in the rest and reach her/his own conclusion. To aid in this process and turn the event to her advantage, Montpensier records that following the victory she was hailed as "our liberator" by the troops. In her opinion, "There are no decent people who would not have said the same thing if they had been there" ("Il n'y a point d'honnêtes gens qui ne m'eussent tenu le même discours s'ils y eussent été" [41:271]).

As with the battle at Orléans, Montpensier considers her heroic acts to be exempla appropriate and necessary for inclusion in history. She qualifies her deeds as "extraordinary" (41:295) and stresses that she has acted "in a manner so out of the ordinary, and which possibly had never happened to a person of my status" ("d'une manière si peu ordinaire, et qui n'est peut-être jamais arrivée à une personne de ma condition" [41:273]). "Status" refers less to her noble rank—after all, she was but one of many nobles in the Fronde—than to her sex. The true exemplarity of her action resides in the fact that, as a woman, she played a pivotal role in a crucial battle.

In general, Montpensier's account of the years of the Fronde, as exemplified by her descriptions of the battles at Orléans and Paris, reveals the central motivations that underlie her entire composition of the *Mémoires*. Her Fronde is conducted not only on a level of action but also on a literary level, as she battles against the stereotypes associated with women's place as well as against the ideology governing construction of the historical record. Montpensier carries what Jouhaud has termed "La Fronde des mots" to a metahistorical level, as she includes the specifics that she believes òthers will exclude.[49] She feminizes this "Fronde against history" by offering herself as the ultimate and universal historical exemplum. By recounting these events as she saw them, she is able to construct another version of public history. She compounds her revision by including the motivations and thoughts of her compatriots, thus developing a *histoire raisonnée* of these events that her particular involvement has made possible.

The *Mémoires* can be termed a feminocentric historical narrative not only because of its protagonist but also because Montpensier consciously incorporates into history women's experiences in both the public and particular spheres.[50] Throughout the text, she lists the names of all the female participants in a given event—in battles of the Fronde, at her salon at St. Fargeau, and at court (41:136; 41:313; 42:52; 42:276). All the women of her entourage find their place, not just those with the most illustrious names. Montpensier completes history by incorporating and valorizing women's experience. By placing women at the center of her narrative, she changes the angle from which all events are considered. Her perspective determines the account of public events. War, for example, is not simply a political exercise but also has emotional and human effects:

All these deaths caused much unhappiness and grief at court. . . . Mme de Seneçay and Mme the comtesse de Fiesque were to be pitied most in this misfortune; the children they lost were fine people.

Toutes ces morts causèrent beaucoup de déplaisir et de chagrin à la cour. . . . Madame de Seneçay et madame la comtesse de Fiesque étaient les plus à plaindre dans ce malheur; les enfants qu'elles perdaient étaient d'honnêtes gens. (40:462)

□   □   □

I didn't sleep at all, my mind was on all those poor dead people.

Je ne dormis point toute la nuit, j'eus tous ces pauvres morts dans la tête. (41:273)

The *Mémoires* is in fact a detailed account of the position and occupations of aristocratic women in mid–seventeenth-century France, as Montpensier constructs her narrative in keeping with her belief that women, in both their public and their particular roles, will be excluded from history. In addition to the central narrative of her own life, various feminocentric intercalated histories illustrate individual facets of female experience, for example, marriage and education. Occasionally, Montpensier even disrupts chronological continuity to include digressions of particular importance. For example, she interrupts her narrative and goes back to a moment seventeen years earlier to insert her stepmother's adventures (41:92) that, in fact, resembles those of Villedieu's novelistic heroine Henriette-Sylvie de Molière, as Madame disguises herself in male garb to escape from Nancy unnoticed to join Monsieur. Montpensier includes such digressions whenever possible. In contrast, she never departs from her narrative to include the personal adventures of a male figure. In fact, aside from members of the royal family, potential marriage partners, and her own generals during the Fronde, men rarely figure in the *Mémoires*. They are replaced by their female counterparts as Montpensier offers alternative female models. She inserts into her narrative the actions of a vast number of her female peers—as we have seen in her account of the Fronde—and especially of those in her entourage and those who wield political power: Mme de Longueville and the princesse Palatine figure prominently in Montpensier's account of the Fronde, and England's civil strife is described by references to Henriette d'Angleterre. The political turmoil in Portugal, too, is associated with its queen: "She was the one who organized and led the revolt" ("C'était elle qui l'avait fait et conduit la révolte" [43:28]).

A particular *historienne*, Montpensier unveils women's roles behind the scenes, frequently revealing their associations with well-known enterprises. Her vision of the past corresponds to that of Lenglet Dufresnoy, who called for a reevaluation of the importance of women by a different type of historical narrative. References to influential political manipulations by women abound in the *Mémoires:*

> The king sent one of his people to Chantilly to remain with Madame the princess [Henriette d'Angleterre]; he had heard that she had intrigues and was forming leagues.

> Le roi envoya un de ses ordinaires à Chantilly pour demeurer auprès de Madame la princesse; il avait su qu'elle avait des intrigues et qu'elle faisait des ligues. (41:85)

□ □ □

> [Henriette d'Angleterre] drew the king's respect because she had merit and because she negotiated business between her brother [Charles II of England] and the king. Thus the trip she was going to take was as necessary for the king's interests as it was for Madame's personal pleasure.

Elle s'attirait la considération du Roi parce qu'elle avait du mérite, et qu'elle négociait les affaires avec son frère et le Roi. De sort que le voyage qu'elle allait faire était aussi nécessaire pour les intérêts du Roi que pour le plaisir particulier de Madame. (43:178)

"The king's interests" often intersect women's "intrigues," "leagues," and "business," transforming such events from the "personal pleasure" of the female participant to the level of state interests. This kind of explanation is precisely what more conventional histories of the period lack, especially those pertaining to the Fronde. Montpensier underscores the intersection of the particular and political realms and advances an alternative version of political history.

The retracing and, often, the elimination of the boundaries between particular and specifically political experience is especially evident in Montpensier's discussion of marriage. This institution is the major point of intersection between the particular and the political in the *Mémoires*. According to Hipp, marriage in the *Mémoires* is only Montpensier's personal "quasi-obsessive dream . . . that comes back page after page with annoying regularity."[51] However, Montpensier's interest in marriage, like her interest in the Fronde, cannot be attributed solely to her personal participation. As we shall see, marriage, like the Fronde, provides a battleground for the war over historiography. The social institution in which women of Montpensier's class are normally depicted as political pawns provides her with fertile ground for a feminist commentary. More than a personal obsession, the theme of marriage in the *Mémoires* affords Montpensier the opportunity to rescript women's roles in this public, political, and personal arena.

SAINT-JEAN-DE-LUZ: A PARTICULAR VIEW OF POLITICS

Although descriptions of marriage pervade the *Mémoires*, there is one ceremony in particular that offers Montpensier an unparalleled opportunity to revise the official historical record: the marriage of Louis XIV to Marie-Thérèse, the infanta of Spain. As Charnes remarks, "The marriages of kings are not forgotten in history" (122). Montpensier's lengthy inclusion of the events surrounding this marriage is especially intriguing, given her stated intention of not lingering over occasions that will figure in official history. Why does she devote a relatively large share of her *Mémoires*, more than one hundred pages, to an event that merits a place in most of the memoirs and histories of the time?

If one compares her account to that of the royal historian Mézeray, striking differences in perspective become apparent.[52] Mézeray's *Abrégé chronologique* provides a good basis for comparison because it enjoyed immense popularity among the court public, the same public

Montpensier inscribes in her *Mémoires*. In his three-page account, Mézeray places the emphasis on the political ramifications of the union, especially the resulting peace treaty between France and Spain: "But this burgeoning attraction [of Louis XIV for the duchesse de Savoie] had to give way to politics, which always decides the marriages of kings. That of the young monarch with the infanta [of Spain] having already been decided, the preliminary [articles] of the peace [treaty], which was to be the fruit of this alliance, were quickly drawn up" ("Mais il fallut que cette inclination naissante cédât à la politique, qui décide toujours du mariage des rois. Celui du jeune monarque avec l'infante ayant été arrêté, on ne tarda pas à dresser les préliminaires de la paix, qui devait être le fruit de cette alliance" [765]). In Mézeray's description, the motivation behind the union is the abstraction, "politics." Even the agents are reduced (in French) to the impersonal "one." Specific persons and personalities are subsumed within an all-engulfing power of the nation. Mézeray discusses the articles of this treaty at length and includes specific dates that mark the steps in the year-long negotiations and plans for the wedding. His account is factual, concise, and chronologically exact.

Mézeray incorporates three digressions into his account of the marriage: a reference to the love affair between Louis XIV and Marie Mancini and an enumeration of Louis's other amorous conquests, an explanation of the reconciliation between Louis XIV and the prince de Condé, and a list of the king's actions during the year of negotiations. Because Mézeray adopts the authorial stance of a distanced historical narrator, he records these events from an external perspective, not expounding on motives or intimately describing the participants. For instance, although the various love affairs of Louis XIV provide a long digression, what receives most attention is the superficial qualities of his mistresses and the political effects of these liaisons, especially the one with Marie Mancini. Mézeray attributes the end of the affair with her to "the subtle politics of the cardinal [Mazarin], which prevented the king from putting [Mazarin's] niece on the throne" ("fine politique du cardinal, qui l'empêcha de mettre sa nièce sur le trône" [766]).[53]

Mézeray is primarily interested in keeping the focus on Louis XIV, and he emphasizes Louis's public persona rather than the personal attributes and events that could be recorded by a privileged narrator. In this respect the *Abrégé* takes on the qualities of a historical chronicle, as is evident in the following account of Louis's principal actions:

> While waiting for the infanta to be brought to the border, the king traveled around the southern provinces of his realm, where he accomplished three things that he had planned to do for a while; one was to build a citadel at Marseille. . . . Another was to

make the Protestants of Languedoc obey . . . and the last was to seize Orange. . . . Next this monarch went to Aix, where the peace was publicly declared for the first time. From there, advancing towards the Pyrénées, he passed through Avignon, where he exercised all the actions of sovereignty.

En attendant que l'infante fût amenée sur la frontière, le roi se promenait dans les provinces méridionales de son royaume, où il exécuta trois choses qu'il s'était proposées depuis longtemps; l'une fut de bâtir une citadelle à Marseille. . . . L'autre de réduire à l'obéissance les protestants du Langueduc . . . et la dernière, de s'emparer d'Orange. . . . Ensuite ce monarque se rendit à Aix, où la paix fut premièrement publiée. De là, s'avançant vers les Pyrénées, il passa à Avignon, où il exerça tous les actes de la souveraineté. (766)

Louis, referred to by his official title of "the king" and "this monarch," is depicted uniquely with respect to these roles. The historian's declaratory sentences create a public persona for the monarch but do not divulge the inner workings of "politics."

To describe the marriage, Mézeray uses much the same style:

The day when the two kings were to meet having arrived, they went to the Ile de la Conférence, where they embraced each other with all the visible signs of a perfect reconciliation. June 3d, Don Louis de Haro, to whom the very Christian king had sent his procurator to marry the infanta, fulfilled this duty in the Fontarabie cathedral, and the next day the marquis de Créqui was sent from Saint-Jean-de-Luz to take the king's presents to the young queen. On the sixth day of the same month, the king of Spain led her to the Ile de la Conférence. . . . June 9 at Saint-Jean-de-Luz . . . the king himself married the infanta all over again.

Le jour étant venu auquel l'entrevue des deux rois devait se faire, ils passèrent l'Ile de la Conférence, où ils s'embrassèrent avec toutes les marques apparentes d'une parfaite réconciliation. Le troisième de juin, don Louis de Haro, à qui le Roi très chrétien avait envoyé sa procuration pour épouser l'infante, s'acquitta de cette commission dans l'église cathédrale de Fontarabie, et le lendemain le marquis de Créqui fut dépêché de Saint-Jean-de-Luz pour porter à la jeune reine les présents du roi. Le sixième du même mois, le roi d'Espagne la conduisit à l'Ile de la Conférence . . . le 9 de juin à Saint-Jean-de-Luz . . . le roi en personne épousa tout de nouveau l'infante. (766–767)

Mézeray's report is concise and factual, with an emphasis on chronological accuracy, as he records all the steps in the marriage process.

The focus is on action, and only a few members of the immense entourage are specifically mentioned. Even when Mézeray turns to the elaborate marriage ceremony, only the two kings, the infanta, and the bishop are subjects, with the royal figures referred to uniquely by their official titles. Mézeray's description of the ceremony as a whole remains superficial, depersonalized, and properly laudatory: "Nothing was more beautiful than this sight, where the husband and wife, who appeared made for each other, shone brilliantly" ("Rien n'était plus beau que ce spectacle, où l'on voyait briller ces deux époux, qui paraissaient faits l'un pour l'autre" [767]). The marriage ceremony at Saint-Jean-de-Luz, which Mézeray seems to use above all as a pretense for his long portrait of Louis XIV, is so stylized that it gives little indication of the king's true character, even though—in keeping with the rules of portraiture as practiced in *Le Recueil des portraits*—the description includes both physical attributes and Louis's personality:

> The king, in the prime of his youth, presented himself with a majesty, a bearing, a stature, an air of greatness that attracted everyone's attention. . . . He had a beautiful face, brown hair, naturally curly. . . . His slightly tan complexion gave him a masculine look, which, combined with a free and easy bearing, made him, without exception, the most attractive [man] of his realm. . . . As concerns his mind, it was sound, easy, natural.

> Le roi, dans la fleur de sa jeunesse, s'y faisait voir avec une majesté, un port, une taille, un air de grandeur qui attiraient les yeux d'un chacun. Il avait la tête belle, les cheveux châtain brun, naturellement bouclés. . . . Son teint un peu brun lui donnait un air mâle, qui, joint à une contenance libre et dégagée, le rendait, sans contredit, le mieux fait de tout son royaume. . . . A l'égard de l'esprit, il l'avait juste, aisé, naturel. (767)

Mézeray presents an abbreviated portrait of Marie-Thérèse, limiting his description to her physical appearance. Like Louis, she is a persona more than a person:

> The young queen was a striking blond. . . . Her complexion, a mixture of lilies and roses, dazzled through the liveliness of its colors. Her limpid blue eyes lent a certain charm to her whole person. . . . Such was the queen that heaven gave to France, and who was received everywhere she went by thousands of acclamations. As she brought peace to the realm, the people exhibited great joy.

> La jeune reine était une blonde éclatante. . . . Son teint, mêlé de lis et de roses, éblouissait par la vivacité de ses couleurs. Ses yeux bleus et mourants donnaient je ne sais quel charme à toute sa per-

sonne. . . . Telle était la reine que le ciel donnait à la France, et qui fut reçue dans tous les lieux de son passage, avec mille et mille acclamations. Comme elle apportait en même temps la paix dans le royaume, les peuples en témoignèrent une extrême joie. (767)

By depicting Marie-Thérèse as a gift "that heaven gave to France," as the physical incarnation of "peace to the realm," Mézeray incorporates her into the military and political system that determines his entire narrative of the event. In his depiction of the marriage, participants and actions enhance Louis's political power and public approbation. Realm, king, and queen are raised to abstract representations of the state.

Montpensier, on the other hand, chooses to recount the event on another level. From the beginning, her authorial discourse is marked with a desire to distinguish this account of the event from all others. As in other situations, she reiterates her intention to transmit a personalized version: "I will say only what I saw and did" ("Je n'en dirai que ce que j'ai vu et fait" [43:486]).

In her historical revision, Montpensier emphasizes intricate, courtly details. Minute descriptions, in-depth portrayals of the participants, and Montpensier's own experience as eyewitness come together as she meets her objective of writing an alternative history. The result is a much expanded version of Mézeray's public history. Of Montpensier's approximately one hundred pages, sixty are devoted to the movement of the court during the eight months preceding the marriage and to the various preparations leading up to the treaty and the actual ceremony. In the remaining forty pages, she describes the festivities once the court has arrived at Saint-Jean-de-Luz. The description of the court's wanderings reads like a travel brochure of southern France, as Montpensier evokes the atmosphere and the people of each region. Each city—Bordeaux, Toulouse, Montpellier, Nîmes, Avignon, Arles, Fontarabie, Salon, Marseille, and Saint-Jean-de-Luz—as well as the châteaux in which Montpensier was lodged is carefully distinguished and characterized by minute descriptions of places. For example, Montpensier carefully recalls a visit to the gardens of the château of Nérac inspired by "the *Mémoires* of Queen Marguerite and the stories she told about what had happened to her during the long sojourn she made there" ("les *Mémoires* de la reine Marguerite; et les histoires qu'elle a contées lui être arrivées pendant le long séjour qu'elle y fit" [42:430]). In another instance she depicts Toulouse as the most animated city of the trip (42:430). The Pont du Gard merits a detailed account because it is "very interesting" ("fort curieux"). To render her account as specific as possible, Montpensier even records information received from guides or from books (42:478).

In addition to presenting this travelogue, Montpensier extends her descriptive powers to the interior arena of the court. Unlike Mézeray, she elaborates on each step of the marriage agreement. Because she was present at every one of them, a privileged position she constantly underscores, she has the capacity to include what only an eyewitness can. She depicts the room where the agreement was signed on the Ile de la Conférence with the detail of a Le Brun: "There were two doors: one on the French side and one on the Spanish, to reach two rooms richly furnished, with very beautiful tapestries. . . . [On their side,] the Spaniards had Persian rugs with gold and silver backgrounds on the floor. . . . Ours were of scarlet velvet, brocaded with a wide braid of gold and silver" ("Il y avait deux portes: l'une du côté de France, et l'autre du côté d'Espagne, pour entrer dans deux chambres magnifiquement meublés, avec de très belles tapisseries. . . . Les Espagnols avaient par terre, de leur côté, des tapis de Perse à fond d'or et d'argent. . . . Les nôtres étaient d'un velours cramoisi, chamarrés d'un gros galon d'or et d'argent" [42:486–487]). In all, this one description fills two pages, as Montpensier creates an exact portrait for posterity.

Continuing to fill in the lacunae of a purely factual account, Montpensier reports on the entire ceremony held at Fontarabie, to which Mézeray only alluded. She accentuates her own exceptional position as an incognito observer (42:493) and includes every aspect of the dress of the principal participants as well as of the church itself (42:495–496).[54] She even refers to the food present at the reception following the ceremony. Whenever possible, she underscores differences between the customs of the two countries, as in the following: "The infanta did not give her hand to Don Louis, and he didn't give her a ring, as is done everywhere" ("L'Infante ne donna pas la main à don Louis, et il ne lui donna point de bague, comme l'on fait partout" [42:498]). During the ceremony at Fontarabie, the duchess, like Mézeray, refers to the king's gifts. But, characteristically, she goes on to describe the contents of what she terms "a fairly large chest constructed of aloe wood, decorated with gold" ("un assez grand coffre de calambour, garni d'or" [42:493]), containing "all the most beautiful things except the crown jewels, because they never leave the realm and queens cannot own them" ("tout ce que l'on avait de plus beau à la réserve des pierreries de la couronne parce qu'elles ne sortent jamais du royaume, et que les Reines ne peuvent les avoir en propre" [42:493]). Such explanatory descriptions reveal that her narrative is destined for the edification as well as the enjoyment of a reading public.

Her account of the ceremony at Saint-Jean-de-Luz includes descriptions of the couple as Mézeray's does, but her perspective varies significantly from his. First, she describes the personalities involved and not simply their political personae. After the ceremony, "the king seemed to be in the best possible mood: he was laughing and jumping around, and went to talk to the queen with signs of tenderness and friendship that were a pleasure to see" ("Le Roi parut de la plus belle humeur de monde: il riait et sautait, et allait entretenir la Reine avec des marques de tendresse et d'amitié qui faisaient plaisir à voir" [42:516]). For her "particularization" of history, Montpensier concentrates on individuals rather than the state and does not depict the events to create the impression of an abstract and glorious political realm. To emphasize what can be termed the personalization of an official event, she extends the circle of participants beyond the royal couple privileged by Mézeray to include the entire entourage. The names of many of the participants appear in what seem to be extensive lists. For example, Montpensier gives the name of everyone in the two royal carriages on the way to the ceremony (42:504–505) as well as the name of everyone present at the signing of the accord (42: 507). The narrative spotlight, normally focused on Louis XIV and the infanta, illuminates all the members of the court, in striking contrast to Mézeray's sole focus on the newly married monarchs. Such procedures displace the king from the center and underscore Montpensier's belief that official history must include a host of details and people.

Like Montpensier's account of the battle at Orléans, this "particularization" is also a feminization, as she mentions women's participation and expounds upon this aspect of politics—marriage—that necessarily involves women. She always names the women in her own company (42:422, 425, 441, 459) and puts the queen's activities on a par with the king's, as she narrates from the vantage point of a woman in Anne d'Autriche's inner circle: "Everyone who came from Saint-Sébastien gave the queen long reports about the infanta and, as she was greatly pleased to hear good things said about her, everyone paid [the queen] their respects and showed great impatience to see [the infanta]" ("Toutes les personnes qui venaient de Saint-Sébastien faisaient de grandes relations à la Reine sur la personne de l'Infante, et comme elle prenait un grand plaisir à entendre dire du bien, chacun lui faisait sa cour, et lui marquait de grandes impatiences de la voir" [42:489]). This marriage is the queen's personal political coup. Montpensier effectively transfers the political power from Mazarin, to whom most historians attribute the marriage negotiations, to Anne d'Autriche, who "takes pleasure" in hearing the court speak well of the infanta because of her own decisive involvement in the affair.

Montpensier's preoccupation with marriage, evident throughout the *Mémoires*, translates into an obsession about delimiting and defining a political space for women in general and for herself specifically. Marriage provides such a space, but only if, while its political function is emphasized, women are portrayed as initiators of and not as pawns in such ventures. This is precisely the possibility Montpensier seeks to promote. In the *Mémoires*, marriage is a means of political elevation or mediation governed primarly by women. Love and personal needs are overwhelmed by political ramifications, as the female role within marriage becomes a bona fide political position.[55] Montpensier uses her own opinions on marriage and her own numerous marriage negotiations to underscore the alliance between marriage and politics and the possibility of women's controlling their own fate: "As one will see, from everything I have written in these memoirs, I had no desire to marry, unless it was to find the glory that would accord with my birth and with the correct ambition it was supposed to give me" ("L'on verra, par tout ce que j'ai écrit dans ces Mémoires, que je n'ai eu aucune envie de me marier, à moins que de trouver des grandeurs qui fussent conformes à ma naissance, et à la juste ambition qu'elle me devait donner" [42:439]). After the death of Henriette d'Angleterre, the wife of the king's brother Philippe, Louis XIV offers this political position to Montpensier: "'My cousin, here is a vacant position: would you like to fill it?'" ("'Ma cousine, voilà une place vacante: la voulez-vous remplir?'" [43:194]). Marriage allows access to political positions such as Henriette d'Angleterre's, which, as we have seen, Montpensier endows with great influence. Throughout the *Mémoires*, she emphasizes her own political importance because of her marriageability: "As I was not supposed to mix my aversion [to a specific marriage] with such a great advantage for the state, I did not know how to separate one from the other" ("Comme je ne devais pas mêler mon aversion à un si grand avantage pour l'Etat, je ne savais comment démêler l'un de l'autre" [41:27]).

This conception of marriage as a political tool is not, of course, unique to Montpensier or to women in general, but it carries added significance when the narrative voice is female, when marriage is granted a central position in the historical narrative, and when it becomes a principal bargaining tool controlled by women. For Montpensier, women pull the strings of public marionette figures, often using marriage, as in the following example: "The duchesse de Bouillon died while I was at Saint Cloud. She had married her daughter to the prince d'Harcourt a year and a half before. . . . In creating this alliance with the House of Lorraine, she hoped to have that family support her own interests and maintain her principality" ("Madame la duchesse de Bouillon mourut pendant que j'étais à Saint-Cloud. Elle avait marié sa fille avec le prince d'Harcourt il y avait un an et demi. . . . Elle espérait que par l'alliance à la maison de Lorraine elle attacherait toute sa famille aux intérêts de la sienne, et qu'ils maintiendraient sa principauté" [42:183–184]).

Accompanying Montpensier's revision of political history is a vein of sociopolitical commentary that focuses on society's *bienséance* with respect to women. From her position at the top of the court hierarchy, Montpensier openly moralizes, criticizes, and reflects on issues such as women's right to govern and head armies and their role in marriage decisions and in society at large. Drawing upon the conventional association of history with pedagogy, she offers alternative maxims in what can be viewed in many respects as history in the service of a feminist pedagogy. These maxims, distinguished in the narrative by the present tense, instruct women to develop their own powers and initiatives. Instead of acting as marriage pawns, for example, women should make every effort to reason and act: "I have always believed that from the time one reaches the age of reason, one should use [reason] in this situation [marriage], for it is the most important one in life because it is the foundation of one's peace of mind" ("J'ai toujours cru que depuis que l'on avait l'âge de raison l'on devait l'employer en cette rencontre [marriage] comme la plus importante de la vie, parce qu'il y va de tout son repos" [41:62]). Such maxims are drawn from Montpensier's own experience, and her person guarantees the possibility of their realization. By endowing women with "reason," this memorialist places them in a different sphere of influence that openly defies conventional expectations.

Occasionally these traditional expectations that constitute *bienséance* are enunciated together with Montpensier's revision, as she challenges the conception of women's place held by society:

> He [M. Le Bon, a parlementarian who wanted to become her advisor] said to me: "You know your own business too well; it is not women's role to be involved in business. People of your condition must play, amuse themselves, and never hear their business spoken of." . . . This did not please me in the least. . . . I like to be in charge of the people who are dependent upon me, and I want everything reported to me.

> Il me dit: "Vous savez trop vos affaires; ce n'est pas le métier des dames de s'en mêler. Il faut que les personnes de votre qualité jouent, se divertissent, et n'entendent jamais parler de leurs affaires." . . . Cela ne me plut pas du tout. . . . J'aime à commander aux gens qui dépendent de moi, et je veux que l'on me rende compte de tout. (42:6)

Montpensier's own experience as related in the *Mémoires* subverts expectations associated with aristocratic court women. Even when she describes inner court life, she does not accentuate the games that supposedly are women's occupation. Instead, she specifically includes those of her peers who are examples of self-determination, and she often adopts such figures as her own models: "I have always heard that the Infanta Isabelle, sovereign of the Netherlands, watched over all affairs, even the smallest ones, as did the grand duchess of Tuscany of the House of Lorraine, both women as famous for their merit, their ability, and their virtue as for their birth: I will be very pleased to imitate them" ("J'ai toujours ouï dire que l'infante Isabelle, souveraine des Pays-Bas, voyait toutes les affaires, jusques aux plus petites, aussi bien que la grande duchesse de Toscane de la maison de Lorraine, toutes deux aussi illustres par leur mérite, leur capacité et leur vertu que par leur naissance: je serai fort aise de les imiter" [41:386]).

In other instances, Montpensier introduces these alternative maxims more subtly, letting the entire narrative promote them. For example, after her detailed description of the battle at Orléans, where, as we saw, she focused primarily on women's participation in the military sphere, she interjects the following conversation she had with one of the officers:

> He said that he had just driven back a group of the enemy that had appeared; but in reality he had just negotiated with one of Cardinal Mazarin's men. Then he threw himself on the ground, saying, "I'm dying; I was going to have myself bled, but when I learned you were bringing some women to me, I went to see if I could not catch a courier with a lot of letters, to have something to amuse them with; for what will they do in the army?" The duchesse de Sully was on horseback with me, [as were] the comtesses de Fiesque and de Frontenac, and Madame d'Olonne.

> Il dit qu'il venait de pousser un parti des ennemis qui avait paru; mais en effet il venait de négocier avec un homme du cardinal Mazarin. Après il se jeta à terre, disant: "Je me meurs; je m'allais faire saigner: mais comme j'ai su que vous m'ameniez des dames, je suis allé voir si je n'attraperais point quelque courrier qui fût chargé de lettres, afin d'avoir de quoi les divertir; car que feront-elles à l'armée?" Madame la duchesse de Sully était à cheval avec moi, les comtesses de Fiesque et de Frontenac, et madame d'Olonne [aussi]. (41:245)

The comedy is created by the interplay of conventional and revisionist maxims of female behavior. Montpensier lists the women—specifying that they are "on horseback," as opposed to in carriages—whom the officer seeks to amuse, for they are the same ones who accompanied her in storming Orléans. The officer's own military deed pales in comparison, as he "had just negotiated with" instead of "driven back . . . the enemy," as the duchess and her women had done.

In Montpensier's account, even Louis XIV is aware of what we would call her feminist position. She recounts that during the marriage negotiations between herself and the king of Portugal, Louis XIV appealed to her feminist consciousness in trying to persuade her to accept:

> [He told me that] I would be the master in that country, where money was abundant; that I would govern everything, that I would introduce freedom for women, who were kept like slaves,

and who didn't see anyone; that if they were found speaking to a man, or if they looked out the windows, they gained the reputation of being worthless; that they were miserable; that I would determine everything as I saw fit.

[He told me that] je serais la maîtresse dans ce pays-là, où l'argent était abondant; que je régirais tout; que j'y introduirais la liberté des femmes, qui étaient détenues comme des esclaves, et qui ne voient personne; que si on les trouvait parler à un homme, ou qu'elles regardassent par les fenêtres, elles attiraient la réputation de ne valoir rien; qu'elles étaient misérables; que je réglerais tout de la manière que je le voudrais. (43:52)

The various maxims and the narrative as a whole reveal Montpensier guided by the desire to be what her cousin proposed: a political matriarch. The ultimate reversal of political and sexual hierarchies is the utopian vision that pervades the *Mémoires*. Although it is never actually realized, this utopian dream becomes a literary reality through the *Mémoires*, as Montpensier uses writing to create an alternative female order with herself as matriarch.[56]

"LA P/PRINCESSE DE MONTPENSIER": CREATION OF A HISTORICAL PERSONA

In *Le Portrait du roi*, Marin analyses Louis XIV's appropriation of historical discourse, in both its verbal and its visual form, to promote a conception of absolute kingship.[57] Literature and visual art join forces to present this monarch, who incarnates the divine essence of every king throughout history. Under Louis XIV, officially sanctioned historical narrative is placed in the service of this divine, patriarchal essence.[58] Louis XIV, the quintessential omnipotent *Roi*, is the only historical actor of importance.[59] In a two-step process, history becomes the account of Louis XIV's person and actions, which are then transformed into a universal model for posterity.

In her *Mémoires*, Montpensier appropriates this paradigm—in which one person creates history and is the source of the historical narrative—and feminizes it. Because she conceives of herself as being "of a lineage to never do anything except what is great and lofty" ("d'une naissance à ne jamais rien faire que de grand et d'élevé" [41: 340]), her personal narrative is in and of itself a version of official history. The autobiographical content possesses added significance when it is viewed within the general authorial strategy of the *Mémoires*. In her text, the duchess not only recounts her particular story, but she also subjectively constructs a utopian "Portrait de la Princesse" to rival the portrait of her cousin Louis XIV. She goes one step further and portrays herself as a monarch in her own right, thus reinforcing the usurpation she establishes through literary means by placing herself at the center of her history. In Montpensier's textual translation of her past, she in fact transforms historical reality, and the result is a subversive form of political commentary.

Using the literary medium of the *Mémoires*, Montpensier consistently establishes for her persona a position of elevation and grandeur and makes the persona worthy of such a position. She focuses her account on the actions that project this persona or contribute to its creation. In writing this specific role for herself, she carefully elevates her status. Her possible marriage alliances, for example, are all carefully recorded in her narrative because they reflect this aggrandizement. In the *Mémoires*, every head of state is at one time or another passed in review as a possible husband for her. Louis XIV, for example, acquires Montpensier's endearment of "my little husband" ("mon petit mari" [40:401]) at birth. In addition, she recounts her accomplishments in the military world, where she briefly attained an almost mythical status, meriting the parallel Henriette de France (queen of England) draws between her and Joan of Arc, a parallel she strategically inserts into her text: "When the queen of England learned that I had conquered Orléans, she said she was not surprised that I had saved Orléans from the hands of my enemies, as the maid of Orléans had done before" ("Lorsque la reine d'Angleterre sut que j'étais entrée à Orléans, elle dit qu'elle ne s'étonnait pas que j'eusse sauvé Orléans des mains de mes ennemis comme avait autrefois fait la pucelle d'Orléans" [41:233]).

But the account of such actions is only the first step in Montpensier's design of creating a powerful historical persona within her text. Less overtly, she uses the overall content of the *Mémoires* to present this ideal persona by creating a self who crosses the boundaries of gender and propriety to radiate the essence of a female monarch within the context of the homocentric court of Louis XIV. *Princesse* and *Roi* become parallel constructs in the *Mémoires*, as the physical incarnation of each wields considerable political influence and evokes respect and love from the people. The princess herself is consistently applauded and obeyed:

The people of Paris have always loved me.

Le peuple de Paris m'a toujours beaucoup aimée. (41:29)

□   □   □

Monsieur had deemed it necessary to send me credentials for the exclusive right to govern as he would himself, so that the officers in the army would obey me.

Monsieur avait jugé nécessaire de m'envoyer un plein pouvoir pour commander dans tout son apanage comme lui-même, et pour que les officiers de l'armée m'obéissent. (41:204)

The power she holds as the subject of her narrative is reinforced and expanded as Montpensier consistently places herself at the center of the political arena.

In many instances, she overtly upsets the conventional political hierarchy. The example of her replacing her father at the head of the troops in the battle of Orléans immediately comes to mind. But her affront to the political structure extends beyond her real father to the nation's pater, Louis XIV. As in her *Divers Portraits* (1659), where Louis is not given his habitual primacy, in her *Mémoires* Montpensier writes herself above her monarch-cousin.[60] This is strikingly clear when she describes her principality of Dombes and the visit there of Louis XIV. At Dombes, she appears to have the same rapport with the people that Louis XIV has. At one point in the narrative she even has the people draw a parallel between the two "monarchs": " 'She knows well that we treat her as we do the king himself'" (" 'Elle sait bien que nous en usons pour elle comme pour la personne du Roi'" [42:197]). Then, upon the occasion of Louis's visit, the parallelism is replaced with Montpensier's own regal superiority:

I love honors. Thus my parliament went to salute the king as one body, dressed in red robes. The officers did not get down on their knees, and the first president addressed the king in everyone's name, for they were not his subjects.

J'aime l'honneur. Mon parlement alla donc saluer le Roi en corps et en robes rouges. Les officiers ne se mirent point à genoux, et le premier président parla au Roi au nom de tous, comme n'étant point ses sujets. (42:385)

□   □   □

My subjects wanted to see me.

Mes sujets désiraient me voir. (42:391)

□   □   □

After dinner, my parliament came to address me wearing red robes. I had not wanted them to come to Lyon [dressed] in this way, for fear that someone from the court would be at my house and would argue with me, [saying] I was very pleased to see myself spoken to like the queen and to have people on bended knee before me.

Après mon dîner, mon parlement vint me haranguer en robes rouges. Je n'avais pas voulu qu'ils y vinssent à Lyon de cette sorte, de peur qu'il ne se trouvât quelqu'un de la cour chez moi, et que l'on ne me fît la guerre que j'étais bien aise de me voir haranguer comme la Reine, et que l'on mît un genou en terre devant moi. (42:394)

These two scenes together make Montpensier's usurpation explicit. Louis remains a stranger to this realm, meriting not even a "bended knee." The use of the possessive adjective—"*my* parliament" and "*my* subjects"—carries the separation a degree further. To underscore her transgression, Montpensier imagines the reaction of a hypothetical "someone from the court," who would argue with her if s/he were to witness this bold substitution.

Montpensier's description is so explicit that her intentions cannot be misunderstood: "I forgot to say that at Dombes, one prayed publicly only for me and not for the king" ("J'oubliais de dire qu'à Dombes on n'y priait Dieu dans les prières publiques que pour moi et non pour le Roi" [42:396]). Throughout the *Mémoires*, by highlighting certain events, she presents herself as overriding royal authority. The ultimate height she seeks to attain in her narrative as a whole is represented by the account of her actions at Dombes, her own principality. The political implications of this account come together in the commentary that Montpensier makes indirectly by reporting the words of one of her officers at Dombes: "After having praised me highly, he said that if I had lived during the time of those who wrote the Salic law, or if they had been able to predict that France would have a princess such as myself, they would never have written it, or at least they would have abolished it for me" ("Après m'avoir fort louée, il me dit que si j'eusse été du temps de ceux qui avaient fait la loi salique, ou qu'ils eussent pu prévoir que la France eût eu une princesse telle que moi, on ne l'aurait jamais faite, ou que du moins on l'aurait supprimée en ma faveur" [42:354]). The use of the subjunctive in addition to "if" in this passage creates a utopian space that corresponds to Montpensier's own conception of her rightful rank and power, a conception that, after Louis's assumption of the throne, can be realized only in literature and no longer in actions.

In addition to reporting the actions and events that elevate her person, Montpensier devotes much of the *Mémoires* to descriptions of places where she accomplishes the same purpose. The interiorized optic of this "particular" *Historienne* has a specific function. In the *Mémoires*, she establishes an alternative court for her persona, a court associated to an exceptional degree with locations where women have power: the various salons she foregrounds; St. Fargeau, her place of exile after the Fronde; and Choisy, the château she had built during the last decade of her life. La Grande Mademoiselle in fact recounts history from her particular perspective by giving detailed descriptions of these various feminocentric locales. She spends pages of the *Mémoires* describing the historicization of St. Fargeau and Choisy that she achieved by installing immense portrait galleries of her ancestors, especially women, in this way creating a historical *cadre* for her female gatherings.[61] She delights in these descriptions of interior spaces because they present the feminocentric historical vision of women as matriarchs that she wishes to represent throughout her *Mémoires*. Joined by many of her female contemporaries, Montpensier dominates these interior spaces described in the *Mémoires*.

Montpensier attributes the inspiration for her text and for the creation of some of the feminocentric spaces she writes about to female influence. Of St. Fargeau, for example, she remarks, "In showing my rooms to everyone who came to see me, I had as much satisfaction with my work as my grandmother the queen [Marie de Médicis] could have had when she showed the Luxembourg Palace" ("Je montrais mon appartement à tous ceux qui me venaient voir, avec autant de complaisance pour mon oeuvre qu'aurait pu faire la Reine my grande-mère lorsqu'elle montrait le Luxembourg" [41:414]). She accentuates her own creative powers when she turns to Choisy, the space she established during the last ten years of her life: "I love this house as my own work; I made it all myself" ("J'aime cette maison comme mon ouvrage: je l'ai toute faite" [43:418]). (Interestingly, when Montpensier commissioned Choisy in 1682, she appropriated not only the land but also the town, whose name was changed from Choisy-sur-Seine to Choisy-Mademoiselle to glorify its new inhabitant.)[62] Her châteaux are therefore like her *Mémoires*. These locales, like the text, underscore women's exertion of power from particular spaces—from the interior spaces of the châteaux and from the textual spaces of *mémoires particuliers*. In her narrative Montpensier foregrounds female material creations to prove that women can appropriate their own space and exert influence. St. Fargeau and Choisy are female equivalents of Louis XIV's Versailles, as Montpensier recounts history from a utopian, matriarchal point of view and, in so doing, rivals the propagandistic effort of her cousin.[63]

□ □ □

In Pierre Bourguignon's famous 1671 portrait of La Grande Mademoiselle, Anne-Marie-Louise-Henriette d'Orléans, duchesse de Montpensier, is represented as Minerva/Athena, wearing the loose-flowing robes of antiquity while concurrently sporting the plumed helmet of an amazon warrior.[64] The left side of the portrait, emphasized by Montpensier's gaze in that direction, accentuates the military motif with two weapons: a shield at her feet with a man's agonized face in its center representing Gorgon, surrounded by rays of light, and a lance that Montpensier holds triumphantly. On the right another man's face appears, as Montpensier's left arm encircles a portrait of her father. This curious mise-en-scène, which in reality is a triple portrait, is possibly Montpensier's personal fabrication, for it represents pictorially the same self-image she depicts in her *Mémoires*. Like the *Mémoires*, the portrait is a feminocentric historical depiction glorifying the princess. In both the memoirs and the portrait, this woman dwarfs the figures representing the patriarchal structure—literally her father, whose portrait she holds, and figuratively the king, who can be seen subversively represented in the defeated face surrounded by sun's rays on the shield at her feet. As in the *Mémoires*, the conventional hierarchical structure is overturned in an artistic utopia, with matriarch substituted for patriarch.

The choice of amazon garb for this matriarch is crucial for, as we have seen in the *Mémoires*, Montpensier associates herself with the tradition of the *femmes fortes*, especially in her description of the Fronde. But in the *Mémoires* the military *frondeuse* undergoes a change and substitutes the pen for other weapons, "la parole" for "toutes armes," in Montpensier's own words. The transition from *femmes fortes* to *femme de lettres* was necessary once the glories of the Fronde were relegated to the recesses of the past. Montpensier transfers her desire to disrupt to a textual, specifically historical ground, reviving and paying tribute to the period when women transgressed sex-role boundaries. As we shall see, this effort allies her with many of her contemporaries, who express a similar conception of history in their literary creations. These literary *frondeuses* rewrite the historical medium in surprisingly similar ways.

Histoire de Madame Henriette d' Angleterre: *Passion, Politics, and Plausibility*

Si femmes eussent les livres fait
Je sais de vrai qu'autrement fût de fait.
CHRISTINE DE PIZAN, *EPISTRE AU DIEU D'AMOUR*[1]

ortense Mancini begins her *Mémoires* by acknowledging the expected relationship between women and society in seventeenth-century France. She states, "I know that the glory [fame, praise] of a woman consists of not provoking people to talk about her" ("Je sais que la gloire d'une femme consiste à ne faire point parler d'elle").[2] This remark is especially suggestive and curious given its textual context, for the very act of writing her *Mémoires* places Mancini at odds with the maxim she enunciates. As Louis XIV's mistress and Mazarin's flamboyant niece and principal heiress, she certainly flouted this maxim by consistently keeping her actions on the public's tongue. She then magnified the transgression when she took up the pen to enter the literary public sphere, where she would inevitably be talked about again. Thus, she compounds her dangerous public exposure, so against a woman's *gloire*, by inviting the public to discuss not only her past actions but also her present act of authorship. According to the logic of the maxim, the act of putting one's life on paper is arguably more controversial for a woman than any deed, however scandalous, she may have done. Writing one's life makes it an eternal object for public consumption and discourse, for a written life is not erased when one's contemporaries die but is, rather, perpetuated by the future reading public.

With her *Mémoires*, Mancini intentionally upsets the contemporary expectations she refers to in her text as well as the expectations of a twentieth-century public living in the shadow of the nineteenth-century ambience of pseudonyms and myriad works by anonymous women. Perhaps even more surprising to twentieth-century readers than Mancini's open acknowledgment of her work is the fact that she destined it to be published during her lifetime. This forces us to reconsider the position of the seventeenth-century woman writer in terms other than those bequeathed to us by the nineteenth century.

Whereas one sector of society may have been saying that a woman must never provoke discussion of herself, another sector did not dissuade her from acknowledging her literary creations.

The majority of women writers in seventeenth-century France signed their literary productions, with one very important exception: Marie-Madeleine Pioche de la Vergne, comtesse de Lafayette. Adjudged by posterity the most illustrious among her female contemporaries, Lafayette embodies the often contradictory, ambivalent attitude of her society toward women's publication of texts and self.[3] On the one hand, Lafayette refused to attach her name to her novels, thus conforming to our own stereotypical expectations of a modest literary woman who secretly produced masterpieces but attempted to ensure that no one could discuss her with certainty. But, on the other hand, Lafayette did not always remain an anonymous creative figure, nor did she necessarily wish to. Her works were circulated in the salon milieu, where her name was associated with them. Correspondence form this time proves that she never denied her authorship of *Zaïde* and *La Princesse de Montpensier*, even though she did not sign these novels. She did sign a portrait of Sévigné which she wrote for Montpensier's collection.[4] This is much less compromising—because it was part of a collective salon game—than acknowledging her authorship of a work that has escaped critical attention, the *Histoire de Madame Henriette d'Angleterre*.

Although not published until 1720, Lafayette's *Histoire* most likely circulated in manuscript, for a surprising total of eight complete copies of it exist.[5] Although she never finished the main body of the text, her preparation of the manuscript, to which she added both a lengthy preface explicitly discussing her authorship and an account of Madame's death, reveals that she envisaged the work for a public of both her contemporaries and future readers. The *Histoire* is in fact a collaborative female effort intended to provoke discussion not only about Lafayette's subject, Henriette d'Angleterre, but also about Lafayette herself and her other literary works as well as about the general role of women in society and in history as cultural record.

Even though Lafayette is relatively open about her authorship here, this text raises even more questions than her anonymous fictions. Why was Lafayette drawn to Henriette d'Angleterre as a subject, and why did she more openly associate herself with this work than with any other of her literary endeavors? Did Lafayette have a specific purpose in mind that impelled her to write more openly about herself? How did she envisage this work? Was it just "a pleasant story" ("une jolie histoire"), as she says Henriette herself considered it? Or were Lafayette's intentions more serious, as the tone and content of her preface and of her account of Madame's death would imply?

The enigmatic *Histoire* does not provide easy answers. Even the title contains the ambiguity that, as shall become apparent, pervades the whole work. Unlike Motteville's *Mémoires pour servir à l'histoire d'Anne d'Autriche*, which is the only other example of a nonfictional biography written by a woman in seventeenth-century France, this work carries the title to which, as we have seen, a number of definitions are attributed.[6] On the one hand, given Henriette's position as the wife of Louis XIV's brother, Philippe d'Orléans, a narrative about her could contain "the great events" of general history. On the other hand, the title also resembles the titles of many novels and thus could simply reflect another connotation of *histoire* in Furetière's definition of it:

> Is also said of novels, of fictional but plausible narratives. . . . Is also said of a short account of some adventure in some way pleasant or extraordinary which happened to someone, especially who is somewhat known to us.

> Se dit aussi des Romans, des narrations fabuleuses, mais vraisemblables. . . . Se dit aussi d'un petit récit de quelque aventure qui a quelque chose de plaisant ou d'extraordinaire qui est arrivé à quelque personne, et surtout quand elle est un peu de notre connaissance.

An English translation of the *Histoire de Madame Henriette d'Angleterre* that appeared in 1722, just two years after publication of the work in France, clearly illustrates the complex status of Lafayette's biographical memoirs.[7] On the title page, the translator, Ann Floyd, highlights the fictional connotations of the French term *histoire* and seeks to entice prospective readers with the seductive title *Fatal Gallantry: Or, the Secret History of Henrietta Princess of England*. In her dedication, Floyd continues to appeal to a public eager for novels, stating that she wishes "to divert the English Ladies with these Historical Gallantries." Curiously, after the dedication Floyd switches strategies and presents a second title page, where she translates *Histoire* as "history"—*The History of the Princess Henrietta of England*—choosing to complement the first title and thus take both connotations of the French term into account. The first French edition also accentuates the duality of the work in order to interest concurrently a public drawn more to novels and a public seeking historical knowledge. The title page of this edition, which includes Lafayette's name, designates Michel Charles le Cène in Amsterdam as the publisher. Hipp, however, notes that the Dutch place of publication has been contested since the eighteenth century and that the work may in fact have been published in France.[8] According to her hypothesis, the editor marked Amsterdam because most scandalous or subversive works, fiction as well as nonfiction, were printed in Holland. In addition, the *Histoire* was published without the *approbation* and *privilège* that constituted official authorization. "Amsterdam" and the lack of official protection allowed the text to be read either as a secret and possibly controversial history or as an illicit novel. As we shall see, the content of this auto/biography does not elucidate this semantic confusion. Lafayette deliberately constructs a complex narrative that plays with the double register of the term *histoire*.

The dual nature of Lafayette's narrative can be explained in part by the compositional history of the text. As Lafayette records in the preface, Henriette chose her as scribe because of their strong friendship. The principal text was composed intermittently between 1665 and 1669 and covers primarily the early years of Henriette's life at court, with occasionally strong novelistic overtones. Lafayette abruptly interrupted this narration in 1670 when Henriette suddenly died. Probably not long after Henriette's death, Lafayette added the short section entitled "Relation de la Mort de Madame" in which she minutely recounts her friend's painful death. It is possible that she composed these pages in 1673, at a time when, she wrote to Madame de Sévigné, she was rereading all Madame's letters and was "full of her" ("toute pleine d'elle").[9] Approximately ten years later, in 1684, Lafayette took up her pen to complete the principal text and the *Relation* with a preface but refused to pursue the original project and continue the narration of Henriette's adventures. The resulting fragmented text is thus, in reality, three historical texts: the main auto/biography of Henriette, Lafayette's preface, and the eyewitness account of Henriette's death. In each part of the text Lafayette adopts a different narrative stance, and the content varies considerably. In the enigmatic *Histoire de Madame Henriette d'Angleterre*, Lafayette in fact combines the genres of memoirs, the novel, and history to produce a text whose multigeneric quality makes it utterly unclassifiable.[10] Her refusal to conform to generic expectations is an essential quality of the text. An analysis of each section of the *Histoire* will reveal that nonconformity—generic and other—is at the heart of Lafayette's literary and historical undertakings, as she creates a text designed to question the gendered composition of history as well as to reflect on her novelistic works.

STRATEGIES OF AUTHORITY

When Lafayette went back to the unfinished *Histoire* in 1684 and added a preface, she did more than simply conclude the narrative and package it for public consumption. She uses the preface to prepare the prospective reader for the account that follows. Furthermore, she carefully constructs the final addition to her literary auto/biography to establish her own authority as historian and suggest the interpretive strategies needed for comprehending the principal text that recounts Henriette's short life.

Lafayette wrote the preface most obviously to explain the unusual genesis of the work. But curiously, Henriette does not make her entrance until almost halfway through the introduction. In fact, the opening paragraph reads like a general history recounted by an impartial narrator who greatly resembles the narrative voice in the introduction to *La Princesse de Clèves*. Henriette's mother is succinctly introduced:

> Henriette de France, the widow of Charles the First, king of England, having been obliged by her misfortunes to withdraw to France, had chosen the convent of Saint-Marie de Chaillot for her place of retreat. She was attracted to it by its beauty and, even more, by her friendship with Mother Angélique, the superior of that house. When very young, this lady had come to the court as a maid of honor to Anne d'Autriche, the wife of Louis XIII.

> Henriette de France, veuve de Charles I, roi d'Angleterre, avait été obligée par ses malheurs de se retirer en France, et avait choisi pour sa retraite ordinaire le couvent de Sainte-Marie de Chaillot. Elle y était attirée par la beauté du lieu, et plus encore par l'amitié qu'elle avait pour la Mère Angélique, supérieure de cette maison. Cette personne était venue fort jeune à la Cour, fille d'honneur d'Anne d'Autriche, femme de Louis XIII.[11]

Lafayette's choice of an introduction is puzzling. First, she begins with Henriette de France, who does not play an active role in the narrative and, in fact, appears in the main text only very briefly. By introducing this queen, Henriette d'Angleterre's mother, Lafayette seems to be assuming readers who are either her own contemporaries or are well enough versed in French history to know the relationship between her titular protagonist and the figure who opens the narrative. She also leaves it to this knowledgeable, seemingly contemporary reader to remember the nature of the queen's "misfortunes," specifically, the civil war that led to the beheading of her husband. But at the same time that she presumes an enlightened public, Lafayette also adopts the position of a historian for a future public who has not lived the events evoked so generally and has not known the characters. She identifies Charles I as the king of England, explains that Henriette sought refuge in France, and names Anne d'Autriche as the wife of Louis XIII, all facts that it would be entirely superfluous to name for Lafayette's own contemporaries.

The mystery of this opening is compounded by the next paragraph, where Lafayette does not develop the events surrounding the two well-known queens previously mentioned but, instead, develops those surrounding Mother Angélique, whom she has referred to as Anne d'Autriche's former maid of honor. In a surprising twist, Lafayette turns to Mother Angélique not to evoke her piety as head of the convent where Henriette de France sought refuge but, rather, to recount the story of her love affair with the king: "This prince, whose passions were very innocent, had fallen in love with her; and she had responded to his passion by the most tender friendship and fidelity in return for the trust with which he honored her, such that she merited all the advantages that the cardinal de Richelieu had made her envisage" ("Ce prince, dont les passions étaient pleines d'innocence, en était devenu amoureux, et elle avait répondu à sa passion par une amitié fort tendre et par une si grande fidelité pour la confiance dont il l'honorait, qu'elle avait été à l'épreuve de tous les avantages que le cardinal de Richelieu lui avait fait envisager" [20]). This paragraph constitutes a dramatic shift from the preceding one. The focus has passed from the public world of Henriette's "misfortunes" and exile to the particular realm of passion, albeit innocent. This change in perspective is accompanied by a shift from the specific to the universal. In the first paragraph, Lafayette carefully identifies each actor not only by name but also by that person's relation to the other characters. However, when she turns to the interior realm of passion, the names suddenly disappear, replaced by generic pronouns and substantives: "this prince," "her," "she," "he." Only the mention of the cardinal de Richelieu grounds this story in the same court as the one invoked in the first paragraph. From an identifiable historical realm, one passes to a vague territory that bears many resemblances to the novel. One could substitute for the pronouns the names of either historical or novelistic characters. The author thus fuses the two genres she practiced in her oeuvre as a whole.

Lafayette goes on to recount Richelieu's termination of the affair and Mother Angélique's retreat to the Chaillot convent: "When this minister saw that he could not win her over, he believed, with some appearance of truth, that she was governed by the bishop of Limoges, her uncle, who was attached to the queen's interests by Madame de Senecey. For this reason, he resolved to ruin her and force her to leave the court" ("Comme ce ministre vit qu'il ne la pouvait gagner, il crut, avec quelque apparence, qu'elle était gouvernée par l'évêque de Limoges, son oncle, attaché à la Reine par Madame de Senecey. Dans cette vue, il résolut de la perdre et de l'obliger à se retirer de la Cour" [20]). Lafayette strategically mixes proper names and generic pronouns, thus identifying the story with one woman while implicitly suggesting that Mother Angélique's experience could be that of any maid of honor. In describing how Richelieu achieved his goal of causing the downfall of the young woman he could not govern, she returns to her elliptical mode, addressed primarily to knowledgeable contemporaries who can fill in the gaps: "Things completely opposed to the truth" ("Des choses entièrement opposées à la vérité" [20]) led Mother Angélique to consider herself disgraced and to end the love story in a way that brings to mind Lafayette's novels: "She imagined that she would soon be abandoned and rushed off to the nuns of Saint-Marie. The king made every effort to take her away from there. . . but she resisted everything and took the veil when, in time, she was allowed to" ("Elle s'imagina qu'on l'allait abandonner et se jeta dans les Filles de Sainte-Marie. Le Roi fit tous ses efforts pour l'en tirer . . . mais elle résista à tout et se fit religieuse quand le temps le lui put permettre" [20]).

As this is the preface to the biography of a person who has not yet even been introduced, Lafayette rather artificially builds upon these lines to link the episode of Mother Angélique with the supposed main purpose of the preface, that is, to introduce Henriette d'Angleterre: "The king remained good friends with her and placed his confidence in her; thus, even though she was a nun, she was regarded with great consideration, and she deserved to be. I married her brother a few years before she professed; and as I often went to her cloister, I saw the young princesse d'Angleterre" ("Le Roi conserva pour elle beaucoup d'amitié et lui donna sa confiance: ainsi, quoique religieuse, elle était très considérée, et elle le méritait. J'épousai son frère quelques années avant sa profession; et comme j'allais souvent dans son cloître, j'y vis la jeune princesse d'Angleterre" [20]). After relating herself to Mother Angélique and telling how she met the princess, Lafayette then goes on to explain the genesis of the main text and establish her narrative authority.

If Lafayette devotes so much of her preface to Mother Angélique's story—which is only slightly related to that of the two principal narrators—it is because the story, and specifically Lafayette's retelling of it, illustrates fundamental characteristics of Lafayette's primary text. As we shall see, the account Lafayette composes as Henriette's scribe is, like the beginning of the preface, destined for two publics, one known and one hypothetical. In addition, just as Mother Angélique's story is recounted in two registers—that of the impartial historian and that of the knowledgeable, privileged author who is Mother Angélique's sister-in-law—so, too, as we shall see, is Henriette's story. In the preface, Lafayette provides a double register in the content and in the perspective on events. She shifts from a public narrative to an interiorized one, using the first to authorize the second. And she privileges the interior realm of gallantry by allotting it more space. In fact, one has the impression that the first half of the preface exists only to tell Mother Angélique's story, first with the authoritative stance of the distanced, general historian and then with the authoritative stance of the insider eyewitness who knows the whole truth. This combination of factual history and an interiorized history that has affiliations with the novel—a parallel enhanced by Lafayette's use of generic pronouns—will be echoed by the main text. It will prove to be an essential aspect of Lafayette's purpose in writing.

Lafayette continues to stress the coexistence of different narrative registers as she describes how the narrative took shape. She explains that, when Madame's "lover,"[12] the comte du Guiche, was exiled, the princess called upon her to record "some fairly extraordinary circumstances of his passion for her" ("quelques circonstances assez extraordinaires de sa passion pour elle"):

> Do you not believe, she said to me, that if all the things that have happened to me, and many other affairs connected to them, were written, this would make a pleasant story? You write well, she added; write, I will furnish you with good memoirs.

> Ne trouvez-vous pas, me dit-elle, que, si tout ce qui m'est arrivé et les choses qui y ont relation était écrit, cela composerait une jolie histoire? Vous écrivez bien, ajouta-t-elle; écrivez, je vous fournirai de bons Mémoires. (21)

Henriette's conception of the project seems to reflect the more novelistic ambience that surfaces in the description of Mother Angélique's aborted affair with Louis XIII. Henriette appears to intend her story to be modeled on the historical novel, describing it as "pleasant" and stating that it will contain "particular things" (21) usually excluded from general history and that it has as its inspiration Guiche's "passion for her."

But the "pleasant story" will have two authors, and Henriette's coauthor expresses another purpose in the preface. Although emphasizing that the content will be "particular," Lafayette associates this insider's narrative more with the genre of history than with that of the novel. She consistently uses the term *Histoire* to designate the narrative: "We made the plan for our *Histoire*. . . . She remembered the project of this *Histoire*. . . . Those who will read this *Histoire*" ("Nous fîmes ce plan de notre Histoire. . . . Elle se souvint du projet de cette Histoire. . . . Ceux qui liront cette Histoire" [21]). Lafayette's intention to write history surfaces in her obsession, evident throughout the preface, with her own authority and with the truth of the joint narrative. She establishes her position as the most privileged of historians because, like Motteville, she can combine the qualities of author, narrator, eyewitness, historian, and informed friend. She uses the preface to list her credentials as a "particular" historian. As Henriette's friend, Lafayette had "the honor of familiarity with her" and "'particular' access to her at any time" (20). Madame also told her "particular things" unknown to others: "I was not in her confidence for some happenings, but when they were done and almost made public, she took pleasure in telling me about them." ("Je n'avais aucune part à sa confidence sur de certaines affaires; mais, quand elles étaient passées, et, presque rendues publiques, elle prenait plaisir à me les raconter" [20]). Lafayette also points out that she was present at Henriette's death, even mentioning it twice: "I had the honor of being with her when this fatal misfortune happened" ("J'avais l'honneur d'être auprès d'elle lorsque cet accident funeste arriva" [21]); "her death, which I witnessed" ("sa mort, dont je fus témoin" [22]). Lafayette thus distinguishes both herself as narrator and her account from general history by pointing to her special relationship with the princess. More than simply an eyewitness, Lafayette is the "familiar" confidant. The terms she uses to characterize her relationship with Henriette—"familiarity", "'particular' access"—are mirrored by the adjective that qualifies the content of this history: "particular things" ("des choses particulières").

Conscious that a "particular" account could be considered biased and therefore unworthy of being called history, Lafayette takes great care in the preface to establish the credibility of her *Histoire,* an effort that would be unnecessary if she considered it simply "a pleasant story." Lafayette insists that the succeeding narrative is faithful to the princess's own words: "For some time, when I would find her alone, she would recount to me some particulars that I did not know. . . . In 1669, . . . she told the rest of the things. . . . I began to write them down again; in the morning I would show her what I had written from what she had told me the evening before; she was very pleased" ("Pendant quelque temps, lorsque je la trouvais seule, elle me contait des choses particulières que j'ignorais. . . . En 1669 . . . elle me conta la suite des choses. . . . Je me remis à les écrire; je lui montrais le matin ce que j'avais fais sur ce qu'elle m'avait dit le soir; elle en était très contente" [21]). Lafayette thus transcribed the princess's words. Henriette d'Angleterre serves as guarantor of her own biography. Lafayette minimizes her own role to close the distance between narrator and scribe and thus lessens the possibility for subjective interpretation. In addition, passages of the text have added truth value because Henriette wrote them herself: "She was so interested in what I was writing that, during a two-day journey I took to Paris, she herself wrote what I have marked as being in her hand, and which I still have" ("Elle prit tant de goût à ce que j'écrivais, que, pendant un voyage de deux jours que je fis à Paris, elle écrivit elle-même ce que j'ai marqué pour être de sa main, et que j'ai encore" [21]).

When Lafayette does evoke her own role, her implicit concern to ensure a trustworthy account resurfaces. The only description she gives of the actual writing experience focuses on the notion of truth: "In my work it was fairly difficult to phrase the truth in certain places in a way that would make it known but not offend or displease the princess. She would often tease me about those places which gave me the most trouble" ("C'était un ouvrage assez difficile que de tourner la vérité, en de certains endroits, d'une manière qui la fît connaître, et qui ne fût pas néanmoins offensante ni désagréable à la Princesse. Elle badinait avec moi sur les endroits qui me donnaient le plus de peine" [21]). Again, the different agendas of the coauthors appear. Lafayette speaks of her own difficulties and trouble and contrasts herself with the princess, who "teased" her and made light of her effort to be simultaneously a diplomatic historian and a truthful one.

Lafayette's person confers authority on the resulting text. She inserts autobiographical references to show that she is as much a part of the creative process as the princess and can be relied upon for veracity. Lafayette in fact uses two maneuvers to project the narrative as historical truth, maneuvers that can seem contradictory. First, as we have seen, she stresses her fidelity to Henriette's oral story, placing in the background her own position as intermediary. Second, in the passage quoted above, her own role is in the forefront, as she writes of her effort to "phrase the truth," an act that clearly involves her own interpretive and literary skills. It is as though Lafayette wishes to cover all the bases. If the public does not trust Henriette, they can put their confidence in Lafayette, who is obviously concerned with truth. As Lafayette was constantly with her friend—a fact she stresses by naming specific places and dates—many of the experiences included in the narrative were in fact shared, and in this respect Lafayette is writing her own autobiography. In openly identifying herself in the preface by naming her relationship to Mother Angélique, Lafayette calls upon the reading public to verify her close relationship to the princess, and she reminds them of her creative abilities and literary reputation when she inscribes Henriette's words, "You write well." The illustrious novelist counts on her own contemporaries—whom she includes when, for example, she refers to the "duchesse de Savoie, who reigns today" ("duchesse de Savoie, aujourd'hui régnante")—to verify the narrative more readily and fill in any ellipses more easily.

Lafayette ends her preface on an autobiographical note, depicting her emotions upon the death of her friend:

> I felt all the sadness one can feel on seeing the kindest princess who ever was, and who had honored me with her favors, expire.

This loss is the sort for which one is never consoled, the sort that leaves a bitterness that continues the rest of one's life. The death of this princess did not leave me either the intention or the inclination to continue this history, and I wrote only the circumstances of her death, which I witnessed.

Je sentis tout ce que l'on peut sentir de plus douloureux en voyant expirer la plus aimable princesse qui fût jamais, et qui m'avait honorée de ses bonnes grâces. Cette perte est de celles dont on ne se console jamais, et qui laissent une amertume répandue dans tout le reste de la vie.

La mort de cette princesse ne me laissa ni le dessein ni le goût de continuer cette Histoire, et j'écrivis seulement les circonstances de sa mort, dont je fus témoin. (21–22)

Through writing herself into the preface of this coauthored text, Lafayette directs the reader to remember that she is as much a part of the narrative as the woman whose story it is. She indicates the lines of a reader's interpretive strategy for the succeeding narrative of the princess's life—an indication that complicates rather than simplifies the reader's task, as it enriches the narrative with further implications. Even though Henriette may have considered her literary enterprise a "game" ("jeu"), to use Hipp's interpretation, Lafayette reminds us in the preface that she, too, is an implicit part of the story.[13] The novelist who "writes well" recognizes the power of literature and may have had other intentions.

A WOMEN'S *H*/*HISTOIRE*

When one turns to the main text, it becomes clear that Lafayette's role in the creation of this *Histoire* is even larger than the preface would have us believe, for Henriette does not appear until almost one-fourth of the way into the narrative. The narrative voice, one of the most striking characteristics of this text, underscores that this is much more than the careful transcription of a princess's words. The complicated narrator allows one to glimpse Lafayette's own artistic maneuvers and manipulations. In a surprising departure from the expectations established in the preface, the narrative begins not with the collective voice of Henriette and Lafayette but with that of an unidentifiable, omniscient narrator who takes the position of an official historian to set the scene: "The peace treaty was concluded between France and Spain; the king's marriage was accomplished after many difficulties; and Cardinal Mazarin, glorious from having brought peace to France, seemed to have nothing more to do than enjoy the great fortune to which his good luck had raised him" ("La paix était faite entre la France et l'Espagne; le mariage du Roi était achevé après beaucoup de difficultés; et le cardinal Mazarin, tout glorieux d'avoir donné la paix à la France, semblait n'avoir plus qu'à jouir de cette grande fortune où son bonheur l'avait élevé" [22]). This person, or rather this nonperson, appears distanced from events about which s/he, as neuter/neutral subject, is speaking and is thus, at least superficially, more objective than a first-person participant.[14] Although this voice continues sporadically throughout the narrative, it is often replaced by other narrative voices that take alternative stances, complicating and compromising this initial position of omniscient historian or storyteller. The all-powerful and all-knowing narrator who resembles Louis XIV's historians is first undermined by a note of uncertainty in the form of "perhaps": "The king, at his majority, had found him [Mazarin] in possession of this authority and had had neither the force nor perhaps even the desire to take it from him" ("Le Roi, à sa majorité, lui avait trouvé cette autorité entre les mains et n'avait eu ni la force ni peut-être même l'envie de la lui ôter" [22]). This speculation has the effect, on the one hand, of rendering the narrator less trustworthy than a hypothetical official historian who does not need to guess. Racine, Pellisson, and Louis's other historians remain faithful to the stance of the omniscient historian and do not admit uncertainty. But, on the other hand, "perhaps" draws the narrator's presence back into the text, lessening the distance between the events and the voice that recounts them, making the narrator seem more involved in the events because s/he is willing to hypothesize about their causes. This maneuver thus also stresses authenticity by projecting the narrator as a possible eyewitness.

The contamination of the omniscient narrator's voice continues with the introduction of both a "we" and an "I." An unidentified "I" enters to comment on the composition of the narrative: "In describing the royal household, it seems that I should start with the one who is its head; but he cannot be described except by his actions; and those we saw up to the time of which we have just spoken were so different from those we have seen since, that they could hardly serve to make him known" ("Il semble qu'en voulant décrire la maison royale je devrais commencer par celui qui en est le chef; mais on ne saurait le dépeindre que par ses actions; et celles que nous avons vues jusqu'au temps dont nous venons de parler étaient si éloignées de celles que nous avons vues depuis, qu'elles ne pourraient guère servir à le faire connaître" [26]). This "I" is that of a conscientious historian who explains the creation of her/his narrative and justifies a deviation from the precepts governing the composition of general history. "In describing . . . I should . . . but" reveals the narrator's awareness of conventions and her/his willingness to transgress the rules. This "I" is accompanied by a "we" who is equally associated with the narrative voice: "But to explain better the state of the court after the death of Cardinal Mazarin and the rest of the things of which we are to speak, it is necessary to describe in a few words the persons in the royal household" ("Mais, pour faire mieux comprendre l'état de la Cour après la mort du cardinal Mazarin, et la suite des choses dont nous avons à parler, il faut dépeindre en peu de mots les personnes de la maison royale" [24]). The "I" is related to this "we" through the events recounted. Both "I" and "we" are witnesses: "we have seen." This "we" shares the narrative spotlight with "I," and both are participants, not just scribes or distanced historians.

Just before Henriette makes her entrance, the narrator again enters to explain her/his choices in constructing the narrative and to comment on its evolution: "The remainder of the distinguished people who were at court play too small a part in what we have to say to oblige me to speak about them, and we will mention only those who will be involved as the narrative progresses" ("Le reste des belles personnes qui étaient à la Cour ont trop peu de part à ce que nous avons à dire pour m'obliger d'en parler; et nous ferons seulement mention de celles qui s'y trouveront mêlées, selon que la suite nous y engagera" [32–33]). Again the responsibility for the narrative is split between a single person—"to oblige me"—and the collective "we." In light of Lafayette's preface, the reader identifies the "I" with Lafayette and the "we" with her and her friend, an interpretation that attributes the upper hand in the composition of the narrative to the scribe, as she is often separate from the "we."

But Lafayette does not allow this simplified personification of the narrative voice to stand unquestioned. Throughout the main text, she never identifies herself overtly with the "I" as she did in the preface. As we have seen, the "I" is occasionally the anonymous official historian who is concerned about the rules of the genre of history. The identity and function of this narrator are further obscured when the person this "I" designates ceases to be an abstraction and becomes an identifiable person, although, surprisingly, not Lafayette. Toward the end of the account, "I" can be associated with Henriette as she directly addresses her scribe: "He sent for Montalais to ask her to tell him the truth; you will learn the details from her. I will just tell you that the maréchal . . . could not disguise his nature for long, and his fear made him send his son to Holland, who would not have been sent away if he had held firm" ("Il envoya prier Montalais de lui dire la vérité; vous saurez ce détail d'elle. Je vous dirai seulement que le maréchal . . . ne put longtemps se démentir, et son effroi lui fit envoyer son fils en Hollande, qui n'aurait pas été chassé s'il eût tenu bon" [78]). This is perhaps the passage to which Lafayette referred in the preface as the one written by Madame herself (21). These lines, albeit clearly out of context, serve only to muddle further the "I," who now becomes Henriette instead of either Lafayette or an omniscient historian.

Like the "I," the "we" cannot be easily identified. Given the co-operative effort that generated this text, it would seem logical to assume that "we" is the dual voice of the scribe Lafayette and the princesse Henriette. On occasion, however, both of these persons are eliminated from the voice, as the "we" is objectified and Henriette is referred to in the third person, as in the following: "The court paid their compliments to the princesse d'Angleterre, whom we shall henceforth call Madame" ("Toute la Cour rendit ses devoirs à madame la princesse d'Angleterre, que nous appellerons dorénavant Madame" [38]). Lafayette is similarly detached from the narrative. This distancing is compounded when her portrait is inserted:

> Mademoiselle de La Trémoille and Madame de La Fayette were of this number. The first pleased her by her goodness. . . . The other was agreeable to her because of her [Lafayette's] good fortune, for although she was not thought to be without merit, this merit was so serious in appearance that it would not have seemed likely to please a princess as young as Madame. Nevertheless, she had been agreeable to her, and she had been so touched by the merit and mind of Madame that she must have then pleased her by the affection she had for her.[15]

> Mademoiselle de La Trémoille et madame de La Fayette étaient de ce nombre. La première lui plaisait par sa bonté. . . . L'autre lui avait été agréable par son bonheur; car, bien qu'on lui trouvât du mérite, c'était une sorte de mérite si sérieux en apparence, qu'il ne semblait pas qu'il dût plaire à une princesse aussi jeune que Madame. Cependant elle lui avait été agréable et elle avait été si touchée du mérite et de l'esprit de Madame, qu'elle lui dût plaire dans la suite par l'attachement qu'elle eut pour elle. (38–39)

In this description of the author, aided by the information given in the preface, the reader can distinguish the disguised voices of Henriette and Lafayette as they exchange compliments and speak of their friendship. In these instances, however, the narrator is neither the author nor the protagonist, as the preface might have us believe. Instead, the use of the third person creates an omniscient presence in the text and endows the narrative with the objectivity of a historical account, while concurrently connecting this narrative with Lafayette's novels, which are recounted by equally omniscient narrators. The elusive narrative voice thus reveals an effort to upset the expectations established in the preface. There is a deliberate merging of genres as Lafayette's and Henriette's complex narrator fluctuates between various stances, appearing as autobiographer and historical participant or disappearing within the rhetoric of the detached and objective historian. In refusing the unequivocal position of a first-person memorialist such as Montpensier, a first-person scribe such as Motteville, or the impersonal chronicler, Henriette and Lafayette invite the public to compare their narrative with what it is not and to suspend expectations in order to experience an alternative narrative form with its own inner logic.

The content of the principal text illustrates the same deliberate merging of genres as does the narrative voice. The main text, like the preface, opens with an overview of the historical situation and with an introduction to the main characters. Because the account begins with 1659, the year before Henriette arrived at court, the princess herself does not yet figure in the cast of characters, a strategy that connects the account more to general history than to either memoirs or the "pleasant story" envisioned by Henriette. To set the scene, Lafayette chooses to focus on the transitional moment when Mazarin passed the reins of government to Louis XIV.[16] She first elevates Mazarin with a panegyric on his absolute authority, especially by attributing the end of the Fronde to this "cardinal's star" ("etoile du Cardinal" [23]): "This same star of the cardinal . . . had stifled all the remaining dissension and cabals in France; the general peace had ended all foreign wars" ("Cette même étoile du Cardinal . . . avait étouffé dans la France tous les restes de cabale et de dissension; la paix générale avait fini toutes les guerres étrangères" [23]). This description reflects the same state of felicity Racine evokes in the opening paragraph of his history of Louis XIV. Lafayette thus externally conforms to her contemporaries' expectations for official history. She continues painting the background by recounting Louis XIV's authoritative seizing of power, describing his contemporaries' surprise that "he wanted to repossess both the authority of the king and the functions of the prime minister" ("il voulut reprendre à la fois et l'autorité du Roi et les fonctions de premier ministre" [24]). This historian then turns to the configurations of personalities under the new monarch. What follows is a portrait gallery, the content and implications of which I will return to later.

Having set the scene with the names and descriptions of recognizable personalities, Lafayette introduces her principal subject, the princesse d'Angleterre. She mentions Henriette's marriage to Monsieur, referring to the princess in the third person to retain the authoritative tone of official history and reinforce the position of the distanced narrator: "The first important thing that happened after the death of the cardinal was the marriage of Monsieur to the princesse d'Angleterre" ("La première chose considérable qui se fit après la mort du Cardinal, ce fut le mariage de Monsieur avec la princesse d'Angleterre" [33]). In recounting the early years of Madame's activities as one of the court's principal figures, Lafayette includes references to well-known events to support the narrative's historical authenticity. In introducing Henriette, for example, she evokes England's civil war that led to the princess's and her mother's exile in France. She also devotes a detailed aside to Fouquet's disgrace, beginning with the sumptuous party he gave at his château of Vaux-le-Vicomte and following him to Dampierre and then Nantes, where he was eventually arrested. By mentioning the precise locations of the court peregrinations, here and throughout the narrative, Lafayette grounds her story in a precise and verifiable historical reality. She augments this truth by including the names of all the historical figures at court. Lafayette describes Madame's entire entourage, from her brother-in-law Louis XIV to her lady in waiting Montalais. Lafayette implicitly calls upon the public to recognize these figures and their various relationships, as well as châteaux such as Vaux-le-Vicomte and Fontainebleau and an occasional "great event," to confirm the truth value of the account.

Lafayette is concerned with veracity for the reading public because she conceives of her project as history. This public, as in the preface, consists of both her contemporaries and hypothetical future readers interested in the court under Louis XIV. Lafayette's narrator creates a bond with contemporaries by including them in the account, as when she speaks of England's civil disorder: "The history of *our* century is filled with the great revolutions of that kingdom" ("L'Histoire de *notre* siècle est remplie des grandes révolutions de ce royaume" [34, my emphasis]). This use of "our" and the present tense creates a bond with the contemporary reader, whom Lafayette invites to verify the content of Madame's story. Concomitantly, Lafayette seeks to instruct a public who was not a part of these historical events. In bringing moments such as the Fouquet affair back into the minds of her contemporaries, she also informs the future about these happenings. To be more comprehensible to readers in the centuries to come, she often identifies participants, a procedure that would be unnecessary if the narrative were destined only for a seventeenth-century public. For example, she introduces Louis XIV's well-known mistress La Vallière as "a maid of honor to Madame, very pretty, very sweet, and very naïve" ("une fille de Madame, fort jolie, fort douce et fort naïve" [41]).

Like any worthy historian, Lafayette aims both to please and to instruct the public. She reinforces the pedagogical function of her history by drawing general maxims from the events recounted. These general truths are enunciated in the present tense. For example, Lafayette states that "only truth can get people out of a bad situation" ("la vérité seule tire les gens d'affaire" [78]). Many maxims are drawn from gallant experiences. For example, "It is difficult to mistreat a pleasant confidant when the lover is absent" ("Il est difficile de maltraiter un confident aimable quand l'amant est absent" [63]), and "It is hardly in each other's presence that people in love find expedients no longer to see each other" ("Ce n'est guère en présence que les gens qui s'aiment trouvent ces sortes d'expédients" [55]). The narrative is not only Henriette's personal biography but also a history from which everyone can learn.

But whereas, on the one hand, Lafayette seeks to persuade her readers that this account is history, on the other hand she undermines their expectations for general history with her principal subject matter and her portrayals of the historical actors. As the maxims suggest, Lafayette focuses almost exclusively on the love intrigues at court, especially on Madame's and Louis XIV's love interests. In addition to Henriette and Louis, who are involved with each other, the primary characters are the other two men vying for Madame's attention, the comte de Guiche and Vardes, and Louis's mistresses, especially La Vallière. The whole narrative evolves around these characters' amorous conquests. The first situation described in detail is Louis's passion for Mazarin's niece Marie Mancini. The first quarter of the narrative recounts this affair and Mazarin's objection to it. Mazarin "knew that the queen could not hear of this marriage proposition without horror and that its execution would have been very dangerous for him" ("savait que la Reine ne pouvait entrendre sans horreur la proposition de ce mariage, et que l'exécution en eût été très hasardeuse pour lui" [30]). Lafayette focuses on the emotions and reasoning behind the situation, which was eventually resolved by Louis's marriage to the infanta of Spain and Marie's forced alliance with the Italian connétable Colonne. With novelistic flourishes, she depicts the lovers' final separation:

> The king was afflicted as much as a lover can be upon losing his mistress; but Mademoiselle de Mancini, who was not content with the impulses of his heart and would have liked him to show his love by authoritative actions, reproached him upon seeing him shed tears as she got into the carriage, "that he was crying and he was the master." These reproaches did not compel him to want to be the master; he let her leave.

> Le Roi en fut aussi affligé que le peut être un amant à qui l'on ôte sa maîtresse; mais Mademoiselle de Mancini, qui ne se contentait pas des mouvements de son coeur, et qui aurait voulu qu'il eût témoigné son amour par des actions d'autorité, lui reprocha, en lui voyant répandre des larmes lorsqu'elle monta en carrosse, "qu'il pleurait et qu'il était le maître." Ces reproches ne l'obligèrent pas à le vouloir être; il la laissa partir. (30)

This scene was well known by Lafayette's contemporaries and in fact found its way into a host of memoirs. Thus, despite its novelistic tone, contemporaries would have recognized it as historically accurate. Lafayette continues to follow Marie after Louis's marriage. She, too, was married and was forced to join her husband in Italy. Lafayette accentuates the miserable state of the rejected mistress:

> At the first place where she spent the night after leaving Paris, she was so crushed by her pain and so overcome by the extreme violence she had done to herself, that she thought of staying there. Finally she continued on her way, and she went to Italy, with the consolation of no longer being the subject of a king whose wife she had expected to be.

> Au premier lieu où elle coucha en sortant de Paris, elle se trouva si pressée de sa douleur et si accablée de l'extrême violence qu'elle s'était faite, qu'elle pensa y demeurer. Enfin elle continua son chemin, et s'en alla en Italie, avec la consolation de n'être plus sujette d'un Roi dont elle avait cru devoir être la femme. (33)

Marie's story presents a corollary to that of Mother Angélique, for both women were opposed by strong ministers because they could not be governed. As we have seen, when Richelieu "saw that he could not win [Mother Angélique] over, he . . . resolved to ruin her" (20). Similarly, Lafayette writes that Mazarin feared the control Marie exercised:

> At first the cardinal was not opposed to this passion; he thought it could conform to his interests; but when he afterward saw that his niece gave him no account of her conversations with the king, and that she took all the influence over his mind that was possible for her/him, he began to fear that she took too much, and he wanted to diminish this attachment.[17]

> Le Cardinal ne s'opposa pas d'abord à cette passion; il crut qu'elle ne pouvait être que conforme à ses intérêts; mais, comme il vit dans la suite que sa nièce ne lui rendait aucun compte de ses conversations avec le Roi, et qu'elle prenait sur son esprit tout le crédit qui lui était possible, il commença à craindre qu'elle n'y en prît trop et voulut apporter quelque diminution à cet attachement. (29)

In both cases, the ministers fear losing their influence to women, whom Lafayette endows with strong political power. Passion is taken seriously and is portrayed as an integral, determining factor in politics.

This interiorized depiction of the court world and its politics continues throughout the princess's story. From Marie Mancini, Louis turns first to her sister Hortense, then to Henriette. When the queen mother fears Henriette's influence—"she thought Madame took the king completely from her" ("il lui parut que Madame lui ôtait absolument le Roi" [40])—Henriette and Louis decide he should pretend to be attracted to someone else. They choose Louise de La Vallière, with whom the king then falls madly in love. The narrator describes in detail their relationship, which also resembles that of Mother Angélique and Louis XIII. La Vallière even enters a convent when she believes she has lost Louis's favor (52). The account of this royal relationship is interwoven with descriptions of Madame's own affairs, first with the comte de Guiche and then with his friend Vardes. Most of the narrative consists of the complex interplay among all these characters as they vie for one another's favor and attention. They play tricks on each other to win the game of power and intrigue. For example, Mazarin's niece Hortense, the comtesse de Soissons, becomes jealous of La Vallière and tries to overcome her by informing the queen of the affair between La Vallière and the king:

> The comtesse de Soissons did not doubt La Vallière's hatred of her; and, vexed to see the king in her power, she and the marquis de Vardes resolved to tell the queen that the king was in love with her. They believed that the queen . . . would compel Monsieur and Madame to send La Vallière from the Tuileries Palace, and that the king, not knowing where to put her, would send her to the comtesse de Soissons, where she would have her entirely in her power; they also hoped that . . . the queen would compel the king to break off with La Vallière and that, having left her, he would attach himself to someone else of whom they might be the masters.

> La comtesse de Soissons ne doutait pas de la haine que La Vallière avait pour elle; et, ennuyée de voir le Roi entre ses mains, le Marquis de Vardes et elle résolurent de faire savoir à la Reine que le Roi en était amoureux. Ils crurent que la Reine . . . obligerait Monsieur et Madame à chasser La Vallière des Tuileries, et que le Roi ne sachant où la mettre la mettrait chez la comtesse de Soissons, qui par là s'en trouverait la maîtresse; et ils espéraient encore que . . . la reine obligerait le Roi à rompre avec La Vallière, et que, lorsqu'il l'aurait quittée, il s'attacherait à quelque autre dont ils seraient peut-être les maîtres. (54)

The primary focus is on the motivations and emotions of these characters, and their desire to become "mistresses" and "masters," that is, rulers in the game of passion politics. Hortense and Vardes write a letter to the queen, have it translated into Spanish, and deliver it to her as though it came from Spain. In a typically complex chain of events, the king receives the letter, is furious, and ends up attributing its authorship to the innocent Madame de Navailles, who is disgraced. The letter's real authors, however, remain bound together. Because Vardes had confided in the comte de Guiche, "this made such a strong tie between them that they could not break it without folly" ("cela faisait une telle liaison entre eux qu'ils ne pouvaient rompre sans folie" [59]). When Vardes discovers that Montalais, one of Madame's ladies in waiting, has learned of the affair, "this gave him considerations for her for which the public could not guess the cause " ("cela lui donnait des égards pour elle dont le public ne pouvait deviner la cause" [59]). In fact, Henriette's story is designed to accentuate these underlying emotions and the subterranean web of intrigue whose surface cannot be accurately read by anyone who does not comprehend all the intricate maneuverings among the principal court players. Lafayette increases the importance of this subterranean sphere of activity by associating all the important names, including the king's, with this arena of power struggles, emotions, and plots. In fact, she gives the impression that all court activity revolves around such machinations. Not only do these intrigues influence politics, but they also completely constitute the political realm. Montalais, for example, attempts to construct "an intrigue that would govern the state" ("une intrigue qui gouvernerait l'Etat" [51]). All political actions other than these gallant incidents are excluded, as Lafayette remarks, for example, that "the adventure of La Mothe was the most important thing that happened at Saint-Germain" ("l'aventure de La Mothe fut ce qui se passa de plus considérable à Saint-Germain" [61]).

Lafayette's decision to privilege the "particular" realm of passion politics is a conscious one. In her *Mémoires de la cour de France*, this author shows she is perfectly capable of discussing conventional, public politics, including war and political negotiations. In the *Histoire*, however, she chooses to depict a world that functions according to the same laws and personal interests as the milieus of her novelistic works. Because of the "particular" nature of this H/*histoire* and the ambiguous identity of the narrator, Henriette's narrative is very similar to that in a historical novel. In fact, Lafayette's descriptive rhetoric in the *Histoire de Madame* reinforces the deliberate conflation of history and fiction. The entire opening in which the scene is set parallels that of *La Princesse de Clèves*. Like the princess, Henriette does not make her appearance until well into the narrative, and the terms in which she is then described echo the description of her fictional counterpart: she possesses "an extraordinary charm" ("un agrément extraordinaire" [34]). In addition, "As she grew, her beauty also increased, and thus when the king's marriage was concluded, hers with Monsieur was resolved. There was no one at the court to whom she could be compared" ("En croissant, sa beauté augmenta aussi; en sorte que, quand le mariage du Roi fut achevé, celui de Monsieur et d'elle fut résolu. Il n'y avait rien à la Cour qu'on pût lui comparer" [35]).

This narrative is strewn with novelistic commonplaces of the period, both linguistic formulations and events. For example, letters are constantly compromising their senders and receivers. The comte de Guiche, Henriette's lover, disguises himself as a woman to be near her (51); the two accidentally meet at a masked ball (76); and his life is spared because of his attachment to Henriette's portrait: "He exposed himself to great dangers in the war against the Muscovites and even received a shot in the stomach that no doubt would have killed him, had not Madame's portrait, which he always wore in a very thick box, received the ball, and been completely shattered" ("Il s'exposa à de grands périls dans la guerre contre les Moscovites et y reçut même un coup dans l'estomac qui l'eût tué sans doute, sans un portrait de Madame qu'il portait dans une fort grosse boîte qui reçut le coup et qui en fut toute brisée" [67]). To describe such extraordinary events, Lafayette often resorts to hyperbolic discourse that echoes the rhetoric of her novels:

the blackest stratagem that could ever be imagined.

la pièce la plus noire qu'on puisse s'imaginer. (69)

□   □   □

These chimeras, or others like them, made them make the craziest and most hazardous resolution that has ever been made.

Ces chimères, ou d'autres pareilles, leur firent prendre la plus folle résolution et la plus hasardeuse qui ait jamais été prise. (54)

□   □   □

They saw the comte de Guiche go into Madame's apartment. Madame de La Basinière informed the queen mother through Artigny; and the queen mother, behaving in a way that cannot be pardoned in a person of her virtue and goodness, wanted Madame de La Basinière to inform Monsieur. Thus this prince was told what would have been kept hidden from any other husband.

Elles virent entrer le comte de Guiche dans l'appartement de Madame. Madame de La Basinière en avertit la Reine mère par Artigny; et la Reine mère, par une conduite qui ne se peut pardonner à une personne de sa vertu et de sa bonté, voulut que madame de La Basinière en avertît Monsieur. Ainsi l'on dit à ce prince ce que l'on aurait caché à tout autre mari. (57)

Such passages sound familiar because they mirror the style of Lafayette's better-known fictional works and of works by other novelists of the period, such as Villedieu. As we shall see, the spirit of the last example resurfaces in Lafayette's chef-d'oeuvre, *La Princesse de Clèves*. But although such events often find a place in the novel, in the *Histoire de Madame Henriette d'Angleterre* Lafayette intends them to be viewed as historically verifiable and accurate. Because the characters involved are well known, Lafayette's contemporaries could no doubt recognize them and verify their stories. The vision of the world she presents reflects that of the preface, where she makes an effort to guarantee the truth of the *Histoire*. She makes it easy for a reader to accept Mother Angélique's novelistic story, which in turn makes the acceptance of similar incidents in Lafayette's and Henriette's main text more likely. History and a novel are both composed in the same "particular" way.

Lafayette offers as history an alternative depiction of the world, a "particular" vision founded on passion and human relationships. She seeks to unveil the interconnections among the court figures and the motivations governing their behavior. In what can be considered this "ensemble cast," no single person dominates the historical scene. Louis XIV, the focal point in official history, leaves the center to melt into the cast of general characters. His actions and concerns are no different from theirs. Henriette, the protagonist according to the title and the preface, is equally displaced as the central focus. By refusing to privilege any one person, Lafayette universalizes the history she develops and puts it forward as a general portrayal of the past. This account becomes an alternative general history in which an interiorized perspective replaces the superficial, exteriorized perspective that would conform to generic expectations. Lafayette reinforces this universalization by frequently inserting an abstract and unidentifiable "one" as the subject, both in the maxims and in references to specific events: "One returned to Paris" ("On revint à Paris" [61]), "One thought only of entertainment at Fontainebleau" ("L'on ne songea qu'à se divertir à Fontainebleau" [71]). This imprecision gives the impression that anyone could be involved in this more interiorized version of the past, dominated by gallantry, and that in fact everyone was.

The universal character of this history as well as its multigeneric quality is especially evident in the opening pages devoted to the overview of the court. Henriette's H/*histoire* begins with a portrait gallery, which, as we have seen, Lafayette introduces as a necessary part of the narrative: "It is necessary to describe briefly the persons of the royal household, the ministers who could hope to have some part in governing the state, and the women who could aspire to be in the king's good graces" ("Il faut dépeindre en peu de mots les personnes de la maison royale, les ministres qui pouvaient prétendre au gouvernement de l'Etat et les dames qui pouvaient aspirer aux bonnes grâces du Roi" [24]). Lafayette stresses her desire to include a depiction of the whole court to advance the particular history of Henriette as an alternative perspective on general history. She emphasizes the medium chosen for this end: in the original 1720 edition as well as in many succeeding editions, the portraits that follow are set off within the text, each headed by the name of the personage described, precisely as in Montpensier's volume of portraits. As she later does in *La Princesse de Clèves*, Lafayette associates her narrative with what was viewed as the female genre of literary portraiture. Remarkably, as in Montpensier's *Divers Portraits* and the portrait gallery at the beginning of *La Princesse de Clèves*, the king is displaced. Lafayette begins with Anne d'Autriche, who, in Lafayette's words, "held the first place in the royal household" ("tenait la première place dans la maison royale" [25]). The unflattering portrait that follows criticizes Anne for not exercising much political influence: "She had thought only of leading a quiet life, of occupying herself with exercises of devotion, and had shown fairly substantial indifference to everything"("Elle n'avait pensé qu'à mener une vie douce, à s'occuper à ses exercices de dévotion, et avait témoigné une assez grande indifférence pour toutes choses" [25]). In the next portrait, the young queen, Marie-Thérèse, does not fare better. She is considered a disappointment because she has traded the politically "ambitious plans so talked about" ("desseins ambitieux dont on avait tant parlé" [25]) for "a violent passion for the king" ("une violente passion pour le Roi" [25]), which consumes her entirely. The third portrait is of Louis's brother, Philippe d'Orléans, who is completely distanced from political activities. Lafayette accentuates his effeminate qualities and succinctly states that "he had no part in affairs" ("il n'avait nulle part aux affaires" [26]).

Only after describing these figureheads does Lafayette turn to Louis XIV, the supposed center of official history, and then she does so only to withdraw from her obligation to depict him at all. As we have already seen, Lafayette recognizes that Louis should not only figure in the list but also be at the top: "In describing the royal household, it seems that I should start with the one who is its head" (26). This historian explains her deviation from convention by saying that his actions during the period she is evoking, that is, the beginning years of his reign, "were so different from those we have seen since, that they could hardly serve to make him known" (26). The present time of narration, only four years later, affects the portrayal of the king in the past, although it does not prevent the author from describing and criticizing the past of everyone else. Moreover, in enigmatic words the narrator warns the reader that s/he must construct her/his own portrait of the king from the narrative: "He can be judged by what we have to say; he will doubtless be found one of the greatest kings who ever was, and one of the finest men of his kingdom" ("On en pourra juger par ce que nous avons à dire; on le trouvera sans doute un des plus grands rois que aient jamais été, un des plus honnêtes hommes de son royaume" [26]). This nonportrait remains confusing. On the one hand, Lafayette says she cannot include the king's portrait because he can be described only by actions that, at that time in the past, were not up to royal par. On the other hand, Lafayette instructs the reader to judge the king "by what we have to say" throughout the narrative. One presumes that the actions included will be the same unworthy ones that precluded the composition of Louis's portrait. Yet Lafayette covers her tracks by pronouncing in advance what the reader's interpretation will be: "He will be found one of the greatest kings." These authorial maneuvers are designed to deflect potential criticism and even censorship, which the author has reason to fear, given her portrayal of Louis XIV.

Continuing the visit to this literary portrait gallery, one next finds the royal ministers. Lafayette concentrates on their characters, focusing especially on Fouquet, who embodies the spirit behind the politics of this court: "This surintendant . . . made use of state finances to acquire money and involved them in his intrigues, and his designs were boundless not only in public affairs but also in gallantry" ("Ce surintendant . . . se servait des finances pour les acquérir et pour les embarquer dans ses intrigues, dont les desseins étaient infinis pour les affaires aussi bien que pour la galanterie" [27]). Fouquet, like the other characters, inhabits equally the arenas of politics and gallantry. Lafayette underscores the combining of these two spheres by immediately turning from the brief descriptions of the ministers to the portraits of female court figures, who conventionally can be found only in the gallant realm. The introduction to this set of women's portraits conveys an important double meaning: "It remains for us to speak of the women who were the most important in the court and who could aspire to be in the king's good graces" ("Il nous reste à parler des dames qui étaient alors le plus avant à la Cour et qui pouvaient aspirer aux bonnes grâces du Roi" [27]). On the one hand, the qualification "who were the most important in the court" can simply be interpreted to mean that the women to be described were the most influential among the women. Yet "the most important" can also be a subtle acknowledgment that these women were the principal members of the court cast of both women and men, an interpretation that the rest of the narrative—dominated by women's interests— seems to confirm. In the portrait gallery, the longest description is reserved for Marie Mancini, Louis's mistress. This depiction becomes a lengthy aside that recounts the affair from beginning to end, while remaining framed by three other portraits, those of the comtesse de Soissons, of Madame d'Armagnac, and of Mademoiselle de Tonnay-Charante. These four women's portraits, especially Marie Mancini's, usurp the narrative space that would conventionally belong to Louis XIV. Instead, these lesser-known women and the type of passion politics they represent completely overwhelm the preceding portraits.

Through this allotment of textual space, Lafayette subtly indicates, as she did in the preface, that her vision of history will focus on the lesser-known participants who exert the political power that, in Lafayette's account, the traditional actors of history—the queen, the king, and the queen mother—are usually incapable of assuming.

Lafayette uses Marie's portrait to further diminish Louis's authority as she includes a series of the actions that she has previously characterized as unworthy of history. She justifies the aside within Marie's portrait, saying it is to "show just how far this passion had led [Louis]" ("faire comprendre jusqu'où cette passion l'avait mené" [29]). In fact, Lafayette reveals that Louis was "led" in the sense of both guided and dominated. Marie maintains power until she is overwhelmed by Mazarin and the queen mother. First, Lafayette remarks that "it may be said that she forced the king to love her" ("l'on peut dire qu'elle contraignit le Roi à l'aimer" [29]). Louis, who is "entirely abandoned to his passion" ("entièrement abandonné à sa passion" [29]), remains blind to the power struggle between Mazarin and the latter's niece. He is portrayed as powerless: "Finally she [Marie] so distanced from the king's mind those who could destroy her, and became such an absolute mistress of it, [that he] asked the cardinal for permission to marry her" ("Enfin elle éloignait si bien de l'esprit du Roi tous ceux qui pouvaient lui nuire, et s'en rendit maîtresse si absolue, [qu'il] demanda au Cardinal la permission de l'épouser" [29–30]). When the cardinal refuses and exiles Marie from the court, "the king was afflicted as much as a lover can be upon losing his mistress" (30), but he does not attempt to exert his own power to overturn Mazarin's decision. Louis becomes like other unfaithful, duplicitous lovers, and even though Lafayette reports that he said he "would never consent to his Spanish marriage" ("ne consentirait jamais au mariage d'Espagne" [30]) and that he "promised her [Marie] the same fidelity always" ("lui promit toujours la même fidélité" [30]), he abandons her.

Throughout the *Histoire*, Louis continues to seem no different from the rest of the court figures. Lafayette includes only his amorous exploits and his involvement in the intrigues of others, as she unseats him from his conventional position at the apex of power and situates him on the same plane as everyone else. Louis is, in fact, involved in all the court intrigues in his role as gallant lover and seems incapable of keeping his sentiments in check. After Marie, he has a series of emotional relationships, seemingly to the exclusion of any other activity. Throughout the account, the king passes from one affair to another. First, "he became very attached to her [Henriette] and showed her extreme kindness" ("il s'attacha fort à elle et lui témoigna une complaisance extrême" [39]). Then he chooses three women to replace her, and "he began to act like a lover not only to one of the three . . . but to all three together" ("il commença non seulement à faire l'amoureux d'une des trois . . . mais de toutes les trois ensemble"

[42]). Finally he decides on La Vallière, and when she deceives Louis by confiding in someone against his orders, he is devastated. An emotional and hardly omnipotent king "tearfully" ("les larmes aux yeux" [53]) forgives her. In a complex series of events, he is then duped by the comtesse de Soissons (60–61). Louis remains Henriette's confidant throughout and thus is an integral factor in all her personal affairs. Like the other characters, Louis sends, receives, and reads letters that tell about the undercurrents of the court. Characterizing the head of the nation this way is a form of subversion. Not only is Louis displaced in the narrative but also, when he finds a place, it is in the interior, gallant arena of the court.

The primary political agents in this history are the women who instigate sexual and other politics, not the king, who seems, instead, to submit to their governance. Henriette and all the women around her replace Louis as the focal point of this history. The *Histoire* emphasizes women's roles in the machinations behind political affairs. The downfall of Fouquet, for example, is attributed to the duchesse de Chevreuse, "who had always kept some of the great influence she had over the queen mother, [and] undertook to use it to convince her to ruin Monsieur Fouquet" ("qui avait toujours conservé quelque chose de ce grand crédit qu'elle avait eu sur la Reine mère, [et] entreprit de la porter à perdre M. Fouquet" [44]). Like Chevreuse, the comtesse de Soissons attempts to dishonor the comte de Guiche. Her personal motivations intersect with public history as she accuses him of trying to turn Dunkerque over to the English (77). All women, even those conventionally excluded from official accounts, are allotted more textual space than government ministers.

The author who shapes the narrative and authorizes this representation of the court is, of course, also a woman, and her personal experiences and concerns appear in a veiled form throughout the auto/biography. With the help of the preface, many of Lafayette's contemporaries, or those familiar with court configurations and friendships in the mid-seventeenth century, could recognize this self-inscription, designed to authenticate the narrative as well as to comment occasionally on the events. For example, the one well-known public affair described at length is the downfall of Fouquet. The choice of this event can be explained by the fact that Lafayette was a close friend of many of Fouquet's allies, especially Sévigné and Scudéry. She was even invited to the feast that Fouquet gave at Vaux-le-Vicomte. Seemingly gratuitously, Lafayette decides to include a discussion of the women who found themselves associated with Fouquet after his arrest:

> More letters of gallantry than papers of importance were found in
> M. Fouquet's boxes, and, as some of them were from women who
> had never been suspected of having any commerce with him,

this made people say that there were some from all the most reputable women in France. The only one who was found guilty was Meneville.

L'on trouva dans les cassettes de M. Fouquet plus de lettres de galanterie que de papiers d'importance; et, comme il s'y en rencontra de quelques femmes qu'on n'avait jamais soupçonnées d'avoir de commerce avec lui, ce fondement donna lieu de dire qu'il y en avait de toutes les plus honnêtes femmes de France. La seule qui fut convaincue, ce fut Meneville. (46)

Lafayette's desire to describe this event at length can be interpreted as an effort to exonerate her friend Sévigné, whose letters were among those found.[18] Her remarks thus constitute a contemporary commentary on the affair.

The intimate circle to which Lafayette belongs surfaces throughout and provides an additional source beyond Henriette herself for this historical narrative. Although many of these autobiographical moments can be recognized only by contemporaries, or through research, one of them especially is easily pinpointed because of Lafayette's preface. Lafayette describes the circulation of one of the numerous sets of letters by referring to her sister-in-law, Mother Angélique:

They [Malicorne and Corbinelli] prevailed upon Mother [Angélique] de La Fayette, the superior of Chaillot, to speak to Madame about these letters. . . . All this business to get the letters returned made it necessary for Madame and Vardes to see one another, and Mother de La Fayette, *believing that nothing was involved besides returning these letters*, gave her consent for Vardes to come secretly to one of the parlors at Chaillot to speak with Madame.

Ils firent donc parler de ces lettres à Madame par la Mère de La Fayette, supérieure de Chaillot. . . . Tout ce commerce pour faire rendre les lettres fit trouver à Vardes et à Madame une nécessité de se voir; et la Mère de La Fayette, *croyant qu'il ne s'agissait que de rendre des lettres*, consentit que Vardes vînt secrètement à un parloir de Chaillot parler à Madame. (64–65, my emphasis)

Lafayette could have easily heard this inside story from Mother Angélique, all the more so because, in describing the nun's thoughts, she gives the impression of having consulted her. Such passages implicate the author in the narrative, as she subtly incorporates her own life, friends, and relatives in her tale. In the process, Lafayette further substantiates the story she is telling, for it becomes her story as well as Henriette's. The intimate details and commentaries are grounded in Lafayette's personal authority and experience.

THE *RELATION*: PERSONAL HISTORY

In the final section of the text, the account of Henriette's death, Lafayette further uses autobiography to generate historical authority. In fact, here the autobiographical aspect dominates, as she adds her own personalized version of her friend's death to the historical record. She begins the *Relation* using the same tone and narrative positioning seen at the beginning of the preface and of the main narrative. The omniscient historian takes over to set the scene and offer this as an authoritative, carefully constructed version of history:

> Madame had returned from England, with all the glory and pleasure that can be given by a voyage undertaken out of friendship and followed by a good result in business. . . . It was known . . . that the negotiations in which she was involved were on the verge of being concluded; she saw herself at the age of twenty-six the tie between the two greatest kings of this century; she had in her hands a treaty on which depended the destiny of part of Europe; the pleasure and the esteem that business gives were joined in her by all the charms that youth and beauty give. . . . She was in the happiest state she had ever been in when death . . . ended such a great life and deprived France of the kindest princess who will ever live.

> Madame était revenue d'Angleterre, avec toute la gloire et le plaisir que peut donner un voyage causé par l'amitié et suivi d'un bon succès dans les affaires. . . . On savait . . . que la négotiation dont elle se mêlait était sur le point de se conclure; elle se voyait à vingt-six ans le lien des plus grands rois de ce siècle; elle avait entre les mains un traité d'où dépendait le sort d'une partie de l'Europe; le plaisir et la considération que donnent les affaires se joignant en elle aux agréments que donnent la jeunesse et la beauté. . . . Enfin elle était dans la plus agréable situation où elle se fût jamais trouvée, lorsqu'une mort . . . termina une si belle vie et priva la France de la plus aimable princesse qui vivra jamais. (79–80)

This introduction is more than a portrait of the principal subject. Lafayette depicts Henriette acting in a political situation and elevates her to the essential role of mediator. Not only is the princess a participant in political negotiations, but she is also the pivotal force and holds "in her hands . . . the destiny of part of Europe."[19] Lafayette highlights Henriette's political prowess, then turns to a detailed description of the fateful events that put an end to "the kindest princess."

One of the most striking characteristics of the *Relation* is Lafayette's extreme attention to chronology. Immediately after the introduction, she specifies the date of the tragedy as she begins detailing the circumstances of Henriette's death:

> On the 24th day of June in the year 1670, eight days after her return from England, she and Monsieur went to Saint-Cloud. The first day she was there, she complained of a stitch in her side and a pain in her stomach, to which she was subject. . . . She bathed [in the river] on Friday, and on Saturday she felt so ill that she did not bathe at all. I arrived at Saint-Cloud on Saturday at ten at night. . . . The next day, Sunday June 29, she got up early.

> Le 24 juin de l'année 1670, huit jours après son retour d'Angleterre, Monsieur et elle allèrent à Saint-Cloud. Le premier jour qu'elle y alla, elle se plaignit d'un mal de côté et d'une douleur dans l'estomac, à laquelle elle était sujette. . . . Elle se baigna le vendredi, et le samedi elle s'en trouva si mal qu'elle ne se baigna point. J'arrivai à Saint-Cloud le samedi à dix heures du soir. . . . Le lendemain, dimanche 29 juin, elle se leva de bonne heure. (80)

The rest of the events take place on this Sunday, and in enumerating them, Lafayette precisely delineates each hour. It is as though Lafayette, witness and historian, kept a notebook to mark the decline of her friend by the hour. For example, three pages into the narrative, she announces, "Everything I have just said happened in less than half an hour" ("Tout ce que je viens de dire s'était passé en moins d'une demi-heure" [82]. Various other temporal precisions follow:

> It was not more than three hours since she first fell sick.

> Il n'y avait pas plus de trois heures qu'elle se trouvait mal. (85)

□   □   □

> M. Vallot returned to Versailles around 9:30.

> M. Vallot's s'en retourna à Versailles sur les neuf heures et demie. (85)

□   □   □

> Two whole hours were spent waiting for this remedy to take effect.

> On fut deux heures entières sur l'attente de ce remède. (86)

□   □   □

> She expired at 2:30 in the morning, and nine hours after having first been taken ill.

Elle expira à deux heures et demie du matin, et neuf heures après
avoir commencé a se trouver mal. (91)

Such precision relates the *Relation* to official history, where chronology is of the utmost importance.

But Lafayette does not merely assume the position of an eyewitness historian capable of relaying the facts. She adds an autobiographical content that transforms the narrative from public to
particular (in the sense of detailed and personal) history. As historian
and privileged friend, she places herself in the center of the narrative
and consistently underscores her exceptional position vis-à-vis the
events and their participants. Lafayette is singled out by Madame,
Monsieur, and even Louis XIV and most frequently prefaces their remarks with the words, "[he/she] did me the honor of" ("[il/elle] me fit
l'honneur"), thus underscoring her privileged status. Lafayette is be-
side the princess throughout the whole ordeal and records her own
reactions to every detail of Henriette's decline and suffering:

> She then went to see Mademoiselle painted, an excellent English
> painter was drawing her portrait, and she began to talk to Mme
> d'Epérnon and me about her trip to England and her brother the
> king. . . . After dinner, she lay down on pillows. . . . She had
> put me next to her, so that her head was almost on top of me.
> During her sleep, she changed so considerably . . . [that] I
> thought her mind must have contributed a lot to the beauty of her
> face, since it made her so pleasing when she was awake. . . . I
> was nevertheless wrong to make this reflection, since I had seen
> her sleep several times, and I had never seen her less charming
> [than when she was awake].

> Ella alla ensuite voir peindre Mademoiselle, dont un excellent
> peintre anglais faisait le portrait, et elle se mit à parler à Madame
> d'Epérnon et à moi de son voyage d'Angleterre et du Roi son
> frère. . . . Après le dîner elle se coucha sur des carreaux. . . . Elle
> m'avait fait mettre auprès d'elle, en sort que sa tête était quasi
> sur moi. . . . Pendant son sommeil elle changea si considérable-
> ment . . . [que] je pensais qu'il fallait que son esprit contribuât
> fort à parer son visage, puisqu'il la rendait si agréable lorsqu'elle
> était éveillée. . . . J'avais tort néanmoins de faire cette réflexion,
> car je l'avais vue dormir plusieurs fois, et je ne l'avais pas vue
> moins aimable. (80–81)

Lafayette thus filters the event through her own experience, both at
the time of the events and earlier, and uses the experience to provide
specifics. In an extraordinary moment of self-revelation she gives the
narrator her own name, creating a verifiable and recognizable referent
for the "je": "After the king had left, I was near her bed. She said to
me, 'Madame de La Fayette, my nose is already pinched in'" ("Lors-

que le Roi se fut retiré, j'étais auprès de son lit; elle me dit: 'Madame de La Fayette, mon nez s'est déjà retiré.'" [88]).

Lafayette's personal reflections are often combined with commentary on the princess's personality, which she is justified in adding because of her close relationship to Henriette: "She still complained, and I observed that she had tears in her eyes. I was surprised and touched, for I knew her to be the most patient person in the world" ("Elle se plaignait toujours, et je remarquai qu'elle avait les larmes aux yeux. J'en fus étonnée et attendrie, car je la connaissais pour la personne du monde la plus patiente" [82]). More than "the circumstances of her death," this history gives an insider's view and recounts the past by concentrating on the characters of its participants. As is often the case with Montpensier and other female memorialists, the particularities included to distinguish the account from others take the form of personality traits and personal reactions.

Lafayette uses her interiorized perspective to add insight and to comment upon the politics surrounding Henriette's death. She thus separates her narrative yet again from a mere reporting of facts, a type of account exemplified in this text by the letters at the end of the volume. These letters, written by court officials, record only the circumstances of Henriette's death. The English and French officials were especially concerned to avoid a political scandal that would endanger the peace recently established between the two countries. Many contemporaries believed Henriette had been poisoned by a glass of water containing chicory. Most of the letters mention this drink, which the princess herself at one point believed had poisoned her. The English ambassador, Monsieur Montaigu, wrote to Charles II's secretary to explain Henriette's death, and focused on this event:

> Madame, at Saint-Cloud on the 29th of this month, with a great deal of company, at 5:00 p.m. asked for a glass of chicory that had been prescribed for her to drink, because she had been indisposed for two or three days after bathing. She had no sooner drunk it, when she cried out that she was dead.

> Madame, étant à Saint-Cloud, le 29 du courant, avec beaucoup de compagnie, demanda sur les cinq heures du soir, un verre d'eau de chicorée qu'on lui avait ordonné de boire, parce qu'elle s'était trouvée indisposée pendant deux ou trois jours après s'être baignée. Elle ne l'eut pas plus tôt bu qu'elle s'écria qu'elle était morte. (91–92)

Like the authors of the rest of the letters, Montaigu includes this episode only to undermine its importance later by stating that the doctors, after performing an autopsy, were convinced that Henriette died of a stomach disorder and had not been poisoned.

Lafayette adds her own opinion about the affair, an opinion that carries added validity and weight because of her personal and privileged stance. Her whole *Relation* is designed to eliminate the dangerous notion of a deliberate poisoning. As we have seen, she begins by remarking that Henriette was not well before she went swimming. Montaigu, in contrast, attributes Henriette's illness to the swimming. When Lafayette recounts the circumstances surrounding the dubious drink, she adds precise details and persons to eliminate the suspicion of foul play: "Madame left Boisfranc and came to Madame de Meckelbourg. While she was talking to her, Madame de Gamaches brought her, *as well as myself*, a glass of chicory water that she had asked for some time before. Madame de Gourdon, her lady in waiting, gave it to her" ("Madame quitta Boisfranc et vint à Madame de Meckelbourg. Comme elle parlait à elle, Madame de Gamaches lui apporta, *aussi bien qu'à moi*, un verre d'eau de chicorée qu'elle avait demandé il y avait déjà quelque temps; Madame de Gourdon, sa dame d'atours, le lui présenta" [81, my emphasis]). This is a very different scene from the one described by Montaigu. Lafayette replaces his disembodied "one" with specific names of Henriette's ladies in waiting. And instead of being ordered to drink, she asks to do so. The drink is presented to her by her faithful friends, not by an impersonal "one." Lafayette herself partakes of the same beverage. By including such details and especially her own role, this historian presents a much more convincing case than the official ministers.

Lafayette strengthens her opinion by reporting Henriette's own thoughts: "The ambassador asked her if she was poisoned. . . . I know well that she told him that the king her brother must not be told of it . . . and that he especially should not think of vengeance; that the king was not guilty in the least" ("Ensuite l'ambassadeur lui demanda si elle était empoisonnée. . . . Je sais bien qu'elle lui dit qu'il n'en fallait rien mander au Roi son frère . . . et qu'il fallait surtout qu'il ne songeât à en tirer vengeance; que le Roi n'en était point coupable" [89]). Although Henriette's discourse is unclear, Lafayette uses it to exonerate her from the accusation that she provoked a political crisis. Through her own "particular" vantage point and account of events, this author thus makes a historical statement of political importance. Her *Histoire* is designed to serve as an official account as well as to expand the frontiers of general history to include personal experience. She in fact highlights personal experience and underscores the need for it in comprehending the public realm.

□ □ □

The *Histoire de Madame Henriette d'Angleterre* illustrates the strong interdependence between the developing genres of personal memoirs and novels and the close connection between these genres and history. Throughout the *Histoire,* Lafayette adopts a variety of stances to question the distinctions among these three genres. She chooses to amalgamate personal memoirs and the novel in order to usurp the power of official history. The text reveals an implicit agenda, one that runs as an undercurrent in all Lafayette's works: to combat the confining definition and perspective of official history by offering an alternative representation of reality. She recognizes that traditional representations of reality have been constructed as if men's experiences were the norm and, in her own period, as if one male monarch were the only historical subject of value.[20] Lafayette attempts to overturn the conventions by offering women's experience, and specifically that of Henriette and herself, as normative. Even Louis XIV is swept into this other reality. By multiplying the participants as she enlarges the perspective on events, Lafayette undermines Louis's belief that one person can stand for universal history. In this "particular" universal history, women are included as agents instead of passive, silent observers. Their participation in history increases further as Lafayette illustrates, with herself as example, that they can not only act in history, they can also write its narrative. By identifying herself as the narrative voice, Lafayette ensures that women's potential as historical writers is recognized and that their perspectives are valued.

Lafayette's open acknowledgment of her authorship of this specific *Histoire* also serves as a signal to readers of her historically grounded novels. Her overt preoccupation with history and its forms in the *Histoire* compels us to reexamine the historical character of her novels, especially given the affinities Lafayette herself creates with the novel as she narrates Henriette's *Histoire*. By openly identifying herself in this text, Lafayette reveals that she is a historian who is familiar with the narrative strategies of conventional history. She admits that she has a particular perspective on reality, which she uses to rewrite history. Lafayette encourages us to go back and reread the historical foundation within her novels, as she did obliquely when she said of *La Princesse de Clèves* that it is a work "that has to be read more than once" ("qu'il faut même relire plus d'une fois").[21] Because *vraisemblance*, the primary criterion for the novel, is derived from history and its representation, Lafayette, with her alternative, particular history, can be viewed as advancing a new basis for the concept of plausibility. The fictional, *vraisemblable* narrative generated by history in the novel is the same as the authentic history recounted by Henriette and Lafayette in the *Histoire*.[22] Both reflect a particular view of historical reality and derive their definition of plausibility from this representation. Far from being the simple "game" that Hipp considers the *Histoire*, Lafayette's personally acknowledged literary creation is a bold statement of opposition to conventional history and to the hierarchical structures of male power that seek to control its production.

CHAPTER FOUR

An Injudicious Historian: Villedieu's Désordres

Quand on choisit un siècle qui n'est pas si éloigné qu'on n'en sache quelque chose de particulier, ni si proche, qu'on sache trop tout ce qui s'est passé; et qui le soit pourtant assez, pour y pouvoir supposer les événements qu'un Historien a pu vraisemblablement ignorer, et n'a pas même dû dire: il y a lieu de faire de bien plus belles choses.
MADELEINE DE SCUDÉRY, *DE LA MANIÈRE D'INVENTER UNE FABLE*[1]

In his *Dictionnaire* of 1697, Pierre Bayle laments the existence of what he considers a controversial literary genre—the historical novel—and attributes its creation to one of the most prolific women writers of the latter half of the seventeenth century, Marie-Catherine-Hortense Desjardins, or Madame de Villedieu:

> It is deplorable that Mlle Desjardins opened the door to a liberty that is more and more abused each day; that of attributing her inventions and her gallant intrigues to the greatest men of past centuries and mixing them with events that have some foundation in history. This mixture of truth and fiction is spreading to an infinite number of new books, ruins the taste of young people, and makes it so that one does not dare believe what really is to be believed.

> Il est facheux que Mlle Desjardins ait ouvert la porte à une licence, dont on abuse tous les jours de plus en plus; c'est celle de prêter ses inventions, et ses Intrigues Galantes, aux plus grands hommes des derniers siècles, et de les mêler avec des faits qui ont quelque fondement dans l'Histoire. Ce mélange de la vérité et de la fable se répand dans une infinité de Livres nouveaux, perd le goût des jeunes gens, et fait que l'on n'ose croire ce qui au fond est croyable.[2]

Bayle is objecting to the creative strategy of the historical novel, whereby the history of "the greatest men" is contaminated with "gallant intrigues." From his critical perspective, Villedieu's literary undertaking, like that of similar *H/historiens,* is not only "deplorable" but also threatening to "young people" and, especially, to the notion of historical truth.

Implicit in Bayle's remark is the recognition that Villedieu, perhaps more than any of her contemporaries, profited from the critical standard of *vraisemblance* to confuse "fact" and fiction and, in the process, to undermine historical "fact." Bayle's choice of Villedieu, however, as the object of his critical tirade could appear surprising to a twentieth-century public that, except for a very small group of specialists, has never heard of her and has certainly never read any of her works. Literary history usually attributes the development of the historical novel in France to Lafayette and her 1662 work, *La Princesse de Montpensier,* or alternatively to Saint-Réal, who, according to critical cliché, was truly serious in attempting to combine history and fiction, a seriousness to which his *Don Carlos* attests.[3] Villedieu is remembered less for her numerous literary works than for what has come to be known as a life-style legendary for its licentiousness and immorality. Until very recently, no one bothered to look at the works of "that pleasant fool," as Dulong characterizes her.[4] Instead of delving into her immense literary corpus, critics have been only too happy to accept the word of Tallemant des Réaux, whose *Historiettes* includes a scathing report of Villedieu at the beginning of her career in Paris. He begins by begrudgingly acknowledging that his contemporaries do not necessarily share his opinion: "They placed her above Mlle de Scudéry and all the rest of the females" ("Ils l'ont mise au-dessus de Mlle de Scudéry et de tout le reste des femelles") because of her obvious literary talents.[5] But then he concentrates on her public persona and depicts her as a libertine. He comments, for example, about her public recitations of poetry: "I have never seen anything less modest; she made me lower my eyes more than a hundred times" ("Je n'ai jamais rien vu de moins modeste; elle m'a fait baisser les yeux plus de cent fois" [2:901]). He devotes much of his diatribe literally to discrediting her name. After having a public affair with a Monsieur de Villedieu, Desjardins assumed his name when he died even though he had refused to marry her, and she continued to sign her works with this stolen name.[6] Villedieu's self-formation and self-publication are unacceptable to Tallemant, who labels her the "greatest liar in the world" ("la plus grande menteuse au monde") and the "most scatterbrained" ("plus grande étourdie" [2:902]). La Porte later follows Tallemant's lead and confounds Villedieu's life and literary efforts, privileging the former. According to him, Villedieu "from early on gave proof of her mind and her propensity for gallantry . . . but, despite her literary occupations, her tendencies led her always toward gallantry" ("donna de bonne heure des preuves de son esprit et de son penchant á la galanterie . . . mais malgré ses occupations littéraires, son penchant l'entraînait toujours vers la galanterie" [2:1–2]).

Thus, until very recently, everything about Villedieu except her biography was consigned to oblivion. This is the ultimate example of the deliberate excising of a female writer from literary history. Recently the renewed interest in the development of the French novel has resurrected Villedieu from her critical tomb.[7] But it has primarily been the efforts of feminist critics that have led to a serious reappraisal of her works and of the place her "liberty" and "inventions" hold in literary history.[8] Villedieu merits this renewed interest because she was one of the most influential writers of her time.

Villedieu's literary corpus is vast and diverse.[9] She began by writing poetry. In 1659, her first successful poem, entitled "Pleasure" ("Jouissance"), was published, to the horror of some conservative members of the public.[10] She contributed to Montpensier's literary portrait galleries and, in fact, remained closely involved with the princess throughout their lives. Villedieu even dedicated her works *Manlius* and *Lisandre* to Montpensier. In 1661 she followed the lead of Scudéry and published the first volumes of a heroic novel, *Alcidamie*, which, like the works of her illustrious predecessor, was viewed as a roman à clé. Leaving *Alcidamie* unfinished, Villedieu turned her talents to the theatre, a bold move into a domain that was recognized to be male. Her plays met with some success, especially her tragicomedy, *Le Favory*, which Molière's troupe presented in 1665. Having succeeded as a playwright, Villedieu shifted her creative energies to the fashionable genre of the historical novel. Between 1667 and 1675, she produced an astounding total of at least twelve novels (two others were published posthumously and may also have been composed during this frenetic time of literary productivity). Interspersed among her novelistic undertakings are also a volume of fables, an epistolary novel, and one of the first pseudomemoirs in French literature, *Mémoires de la vie de Henriette-Sylvie de Molière* (1672).

This immense productivity can be partly explained by the fact that, unlike many of the women writing at the time, Villedieu was not of noble extraction and actually earned her living by writing. Louis XIV did grant her a pension in 1676, an honor shared by only one other woman writer, Scudéry. And, like Scudéry, Villedieu was named to the Ricovrati Academy in Padua. Along with Mme Deshoulières, she was even proposed for admission to the French Academy. Although nothing came of this proposal, it illustrates how seriously Villedieu was taken and how admired and recognized a literary figure she was. As an integral member of the literary circles of her day, Villedieu was well aware of the tastes and trends of the public she sought to please.[11] The duchesse de Nemours, who, as we have seen, was also an author, was Villedieu's principal patron. Villedieu was part of the circle of former *frondeuses*, women like Chevreuse, Montbazon, Nemours, and Montpensier. Her works bear the imprint of this female milieu and, especially, of these women's concern with literature and history.

Villedieu questions history more directly than any other novelist among her contemporaries. Using the prefaces of her many novels, she associates her works with the general polemic over history. As we saw in Chapter 1, Villedieu is like other memorialists and novelists in identifying her literary endeavors as a form of history. She stresses not only the historical foundation of her works but also the historicity of her own inventions, which she terms "historical truths" ("des Vérités Historiques").[12] But although Villedieu's discourse resembles that of her contemporaries, it is more polemical.

In her prefaces, Villedieu discounts the creativity of her literary enterprise and openly adopts the authorial stance of revisionist historian. In the preface to *Les Annales galantes*, for example, she justifies her proposed histories:

> I admit that I have added a few ornaments to the simplicity of history. The majesty of historical subjects does not permit the judicious historian to elaborate on incidents that are purely gallant. . . . In my Annals I have dispensed with this austerity.

> J'avoue que j'ai ajouté quelques ornements à la simplicité de l'Histoire. La Majesté des matières historiques ne permet pas à l'Historien judicieux de s'étendre sur les Incidents purement Galants. . . . J'ai dispensé mes Annales de cette austérité.[13]

This author is one who "adds" to the narration of the past, through a process not merely of imagination but also of interpretation. As an "injudicious" historian, Villedieu goes beyond the "simplicity of history." Using a tone of sarcastic, forced respect, the novelist seemingly elevates general history above her own gallant history by referring to the "majesty" of "historical subjects." This phrase also contains a provocative undercurrent. Villedieu is concurrently reiterating the rule that the official, judicious historian must keep within certain boundaries and specifically must maintain the "Majesty" in history. Thus, she implicitly recognizes and criticizes the fact that official, especially royal, historians do not recount the whole story. This point is strengthened when she says that if the words she imagines when composing her history "are not those they [the historically verifiable characters] said, they are those they should have said. . . . As long as Historians will make them mute, I will believe I can make them speak in my way" ("ne sont ceux qu'ils ont prononcés, ce sont ceux qu'ils auraient dû prononcer. . . . Tant que les Historiens les rendront muets je croirai pouvoir les faire parler à ma mode" [preface, *Les Annales galantes*]. Villedieu uses historians' volontary silence to authorize her poetic license.

What at first glance appears merely an effort to manipulate the reader is, in reality, a probing evaluation of history that joins the rhetoric of history's seventeenth-century theorists and commentators. In the critical discourse of the prefaces, Villedieu advances the view that, as an "injudicious" historian, she goes beyond the surface of official history to complete the lacunae of that recognizable narrative with an alternative history devised from an interiorized perspective. Her authorial discourse on the need for an interiorization of historical narrative echoes the terminology we have already seen in critics such as Saint-Evremond and Saint-Réal, who advocate narratives that go beyond the superficial recounting of events. Villedieu, like the theorists to whom she is adding her voice, anticipates a critical reaction against her rewritten narrative of the past, revealing her sensitivity to the general polemic: "I do not doubt that scholars will revolt against this metamorphosis, and I believe I already hear them say I am violating the respect due to sacred antiquity. But I do not know if they will find as many examples to support their censure, as I have to authorize my liberty" ("Je ne doute pas que les Savants ne se révoltent contre cette métamorphose, et je crois déjà les entendre dire, que je viole le respect dû à la sacrée Antiquité. Mais je ne sais s'ils trouveraient autant d'exemples pour soutenir leur censure, que j'en ai pour autoriser ma licence" [preface, *Les Annales galantes*]). Villedieu's defense of her "metamorphosis" reveals an awareness of the implications of her literary and historical endeavors. By juxtaposing general history and a narrative composed from an interiorized perspective, she inscribes her work into the polemic about what constitutes a "proper" historical account. Inherent in her literary enterprise is an appeal for a change in the general history she uses as her source.[14]

Villedieu's prefatory reflections on history, its inclusions and exclusions, culminate in the last novel published during her lifetime, *Les Désordres de l'amour* (1675). The *Désordres* was very popular and was even translated into English as early as 1677.[15] This work does not contain a preface, for Villedieu incorporates her historical and theoretical politics into the fabric of her novel to provide an illustration of the way these politics function. She provokes Bayle's criticism by creating a dialectic between the general history upon which her history is based and the particular history she extrapolates and projects as her fiction. This fiction is designed to appear historical and to fill in the gaps between the events of general history. In no previous work does Villedieu combine general history and her "metamorphosed" history as intricately or as self-consciously.[16] By structurally and thematically intertwining the two, she creates a text with which she continues the debate over the merits of these two approaches to representing the past, advancing her opinion on the epistemological crisis.

The structure and themes of *Les Désordres* reveal that Villedieu's approach to the genre of the historical novel is fundamentally different from that of many of her contemporaries, especially her better-known colleague, Lafayette. These differences underscore Villedieu's desire to comment on the merits of official versus particular history. Whereas Lafayette, as we will see, uses history to enhance fictional events and cast them in a different interpretive light, Villedieu draws all the elements of her novel, including the principal love intrigues, from the domain of general, public history, almost nullifying the boundaries between history and fiction. For example, Lafayette uses history in *La Princesse de Clèves* to lend plausibility to an entirely fictional love affair between Nemours and the princess; Villedieu, in contrast, embellishes events already mentioned in history or in memoirs, such as Mme de Sauve's seduction of the roi de Navarre, and places these affairs at the heart of the most sacred public and political sphere, war. Villedieu does not depart from her principal source, Mézeray, to recount her fiction but, rather, imagines her story between the lines of history, thus confirming her pronouncement in the preface to *Les Annales galantes* that these are "historical truths. . . . They are faithful elements of general History" ("des Vérités Historiques. . . . Ce sont des traits fidèls de l'Histoire générale"). The entire cast of characters, for example, with one exception in the third part of the novel, is historically founded, and all events, including the majority of the amorous liaisons, are verifiable history. Villedieu's fiction is thus generated more directly from history than are the majority of the period's historical novels.

The *Désordres* consists of three stories divided into four parts, the last two parts constituting one longer story. Like Lafayette and Saint-Réal, Villedieu situates her fiction in the sixteenth century, choosing Henri III's reign and the beginning of Henri IV's. Unlike both the novelists to whom she is most frequently compared, however, Villedieu places much emphasis on the political strife of the time, specifically on the civil disorder of the Ligue. She follows Mézeray's account and is especially precise about the various battles.[17] Other sources include Brantôme's *Mémoires* (for the characters of the various personages) and Marguerite de Valois's *Mémoires* (especially for the first story and Mme de Sauve's character). Unlike Saint-Réal, who in *Don Carlos* (1672) lists at least twenty sources and even notes his references throughout the text, Villedieu establishes her history without a documentary aura. By including precise dates and the names of battles and characters, she expects her readers to recognize the historical references, especially because the vast majority are drawn from the historical work most familiar to and popular among her contemporaries.[18]

Villedieu is strikingly faithful to her sources. As Cuénin remarks, all the principal characters play the roles history attributes to them.[19] For example, according to Mézeray, the male protagonist in the last two stories, Givry, actually did try to die in the battle of Laon because of an unhappy love affair.[20] But although it is essential to recognize Villedieu's rigorous fidelity, especially because through such faithfulness she pushes the genre closer to history than any of her contemporaries does, her changes and choices are equally important. For whereas everything in the novel is historically plausible, not everything is historically verifiable. To examine closely the dialectic Villedieu establishes between particular and public history, it is necessary to pinpoint some of her novelistic inventions and omissions with respect to the authoritative account of history.

Villedieu's choice of characters reveals her desire for historical accuracy. Only two members of the large cast are actually fictitious—the marquis de Termes in the second story and Mme de Maugiron in the last two—but one of them, the marquis de Termes, remains plausible because a real maréchal de Termes actually existed at the time. Villedieu attributes this fictitious son to him. The real maréchal de Termes did will his possessions to a nephew, but not to Bellegarde, as Villedieu's marquis de Termes does. Villedieu is thus simply inventing between the lines of history. Mme de Maugiron is also invented, but with less concern for historical reality. In addition, Villedieu takes liberties with the various locations in which she situates the action. She frequently mentions, for example, the châteaux of Saint-Germain and Champigny to lend more credibility to her text. As history does not mention the location of many negotiations and, especially, of court intrigues, Villedieu can reposition them without sacrificing historical veracity.

The process used for these place names is in fact the one used for the text as a whole. Villedieu develops the footnotes of history, adding to them by including what was possibly left out. This process changes the focus and character of the depiction of the past. Whereas in Mézeray, the king, his ministers, and other members of the royal household determine history, especially the political history of battles upon which Villedieu focuses, in the *Désordres* the king all but disappears. As Arthur Flannigan notes, Henri III remains mute or entirely effaced. Henri IV is the only vocal king, and then he speaks only to help Givry with his love affair because he is sympathetic to his friend's amorous plight as he, too, is entangled in a love affair. When Givry dies for love of Mlle de Guise, the king again becomes active, but only to reprimand Mlle de Guise for weakening his troops.[21] As in Lafayette's *Histoire de Madame Henriette d'Angleterre,* the figure of the monarch, embodied here by both Henri III and Henri IV, is absorbed into the world of gallant politics.

The king and his influence are replaced by his subjects, often minor, whom for the most part Mézeray mentions only briefly. These subjects most frequently prove to be the female characters, to whom

Villedieu grants voice and the power to determine the well-known events of history. As shall become clear when I turn to a close analysis of the stories, the female sphere dominates what at the time was normally seen as the male political world. Whereas Lafayette also privileges women in the *Histoire de Madame Henriette d'Angleterre* and *La Princesse de Clèves*, she hardly mentions the political realm of war and intrigues such as those of the Ligue. Villedieu, in contrast, delineates public history and inserts women into the crevices of the history to create a more provocative and more obvious dialectic between general history and this plausible story that could constitute particular history. For example, she invents the strategies (supported by Catherine de Médicis) and dialogue of Mme de Sauve, who appears as the king's mistress only in Marguerite de Valois's *Mémoires*. De Sauve becomes the primary source of division between the duc de Guise and the roi de Navarre. Although this division is historically accurate and Mézeray even identifies it as something Catherine wished for, de Sauve supposedly had no real part in it. In the *Désordres*, Villedieu has Catherine de Médicis identify de Sauve as the central figure: "The queen mother loved this woman, and judged her to be necessary for her plans. She made efforts to appease the king's anger and, talking to him about the division of the two princes as a thing useful for the tranquility of the state, she claimed that Mme de Sauve deserved more recompense than punishment" ("La Reine Mère aimait cette femme, et la jugeait nécessaire à ses desseins. Elle fit des efforts pour apaiser la colère du Roi, et lui parlant de la division des deux princes comme d'une chose utile à la tranquillité de l'Etat, elle prétendait que Mme de Sauve en méritait plus de récompense que de punitions" [33]). In the second story, the marquise de Termes helps the queen avoid being overthrown (93), a threat that exists in Mézeray but, again, without mention of a minor character such as the marquise. The last two stories present Mlle de Guise as the force that weakens the king's army by destroying one of the primary generals, Givry. Villedieu uses these women to undermine the official narrative by inventing the motivations and causes of publicly known events. She rearranges history to prove that the interior arena of sentiments, such as love, jealousy, and the desire for power, irrationally rules the supposedly rational world of past events. A particular *Historienne*, Villedieu transforms her strictly official account to explain history according to her belief that passions always play a role. In the first story, amorous deceptions split powerful allies and lead to war (61). In the second, such intrigues are at the foundation of the Ligue (117), and in the third and fourth they directly affect the king's military strategies (145, 162). In fact, in the last example, personal interests override affairs of state (140, 145). In no other novel is the dialectic between intrigue and politics (as conventionally defined) so strong. Even

Saint-Réal, who posits emotions and characters as the foundation of history in *De l'usage de l'histoire*, does not translate this theory so concretely into his two novels. In *Don Carlos*, the psychological component dominates, and the exterior political world is barely evoked. In *La Conjuration des Espagnols contre la république de Venise* (1674), his second and last novel, he abandons the world of passion to concentrate uniquely on that of politics.

Villedieu uses the preponderance of general history in the *Désordres* to comment more forcefully on the relationship between history and the "particularities" she both draws from history and imaginatively adds to the record. This commentary is clearest in the work's guiding maxim, with which the first story ends:

> Love is the motivating force behind all the passions of the soul. . . . If one carefully examines the secret motives of the revolutions that happen in monarchies, one will always find it guilty or an accomplice in all of them.

> L'amour est le ressort de toutes les passions de l'âme. . . . Si on examine soigneusement les motifs secrets des révolutions qui arrivent dans les monarchies, on le trouverait toujours coupable ou complice de toutes. (66)

In this strong, universalist vision, the interior court arena is the only source of the events of the public, political realm. Love is "always" part of "all" public affairs. The explicitness with which Villedieu states her intention to concentrate on love as related to "revolutions" and "monarchies" distinguishes her from Lafayette and Saint-Réal, who do not overtly express their intent to demonstrate the political ramifications of love.

The juxtaposition of the two historical perspectives is especially striking in the opening paragraphs of the account of the first story, devoted to Mme de Sauve and Henri III. Villedieu establishes her historical context in a way that both contrasts with and resembles Lafayette's portrait gallery at the beginning of *La Princesse de Clèves*, while at the same time revealing her own brand of historical revision:

> The glorious beginnings of Henri III's reign promised a similar continuation. This was a charming prince, who before he was eighteen had won two battles, and who by an apprenticeship to royalty was supposed to know how to govern a people wisely.
> He was impatiently awaited with these hopes. . . . The queen his mother went ahead of him. . . . She presented the duc d'Alençon, his brother, to him . . . and the roi de Navarre his brother-in-law, both of whom during his absence had made an

attempt against his authority. . . . He generously pardoned their fault. . . .

Maxim I

But love, this tyrant of the most illustrious souls . . .
Makes its chimeras shine in the new king's eyes . . .

In the past the king had fervently loved the princesse de Condé. . . . This proposition [to marry her] did not please the queen: she wanted a princess less knowledgeable about affairs for the king's wife.

Les glorieux commencements du règne de Henri III promettaient des suites semblables. C'était un prince charmant par sa personne, qui avant dix-huit ans avait gagné deux batailles, et qui par un apprentissage de royauté devait savoir l'art de gouverner sagement un peuple.
   Il était impatiemment attendu sur ces espérances. . . . La Reine sa mère fut devant de lui. . . . Elle lui présenta le Duc d'Alençon, son frère . . . et le Roi de Navarre son beau-frère, qui pendant son absence avaient attenté quelque chose contre son autorité. . . . Il leur pardonna généreusement cette faute . . .

Maxime I

Mais l'Amour, ce tiran des plus illustres âmes . . .
Aux yeux du nouveau Roi fait briller ses chimères . . .

Le Roi avait autrefois ardemment aimé la Princesse de Condé. . . . Cette proposition ne plaisait pas à la reine; elle voulait pour femme du Roi une princesse moins stilée à la connaissance des affaires. (3–6)

In the first three pages leading up to the maxim, Villedieu foregrounds official history. A comparison with her source, Mézeray, reveals that she excludes almost all references to Henri's character, concentrating instead on his military battles and royal actions, or his ability to govern.[22] She preserves and advances the aura of kingship. These opening paragraphs are almost wholly devoted to men and their political relationships, in sharp contrast to what we will find in the opening of *La Princesse de Clèves*. Villedieu thus chooses an introduction that has all the qualities of her official source.
   This narration of history is then abruptly interrupted by the maxim, which introduces a second textual level. The king is inserted into the interior court arena and consequently loses his official attributes and essence of kingliness. Henri becomes demystified and humanized, as he falls prey to "love, this tyrant." From this point on,

the level of particular events overwhelms that of official history, which becomes the backdrop for the interiorized vision of the past. Characters' actions in political negotiations and even in "this civil war, which for many years tore apart the very soul of this realm" ("cette guerre intestine, qui pendant plusieurs années a déchiré les entrailles de ce royaume" [65]) are not excluded, but the accent is placed on the "chimeras" of love. Accompanying this change of emphasis from official to particular history is a transition from the male-dominated realm of war to the female-centered space of the court. All the men, the "most illustrious souls," with whom the novel opens move from battles and governing to a world where such events are guided by "love, this tyrant" and where women often "make the law" ("[font] la loi" [15]). The opening paragraphs implicitly mark this transition to female rule. The queen at first serves only to introduce the male figures, but after the maxim she takes her position as the one to be pleased. Her desires for her son's marriage are the foremost consideration in the affair.

The characteristics evident in this introduction—the shift from public, recognizable history to the "particular" realm of the court, the predominance of love, and the positioning of women in the forefront—mark Villedieu's entire text. The constant interplay between the two facets of history that is evident in the content is paralleled by the narrative voice, which is a strong presence and emphasizes the dialectic between public and particular history. Unlike Saint-Réal's third-person narrator in *Don Carlos,* who distances himself from the account by always using the past tense, Villedieu's narrator enters frequently to comment on the characters and their actions in the present tense and occasionally in the first person. Such narratorial interventions, often in the form of maxims, are, in fact, the primary distinguishing characteristic of this text. Villedieu begins each story with a general maxim and inserts a total of nine long maxims in verse. Also embedded throughout the novel are numerous reflections made by the narrator, usually a single line in the present tense and frequently including a prose maxim.[23] For example, in the first story the narrator remarks of one character's speech, "The person who was saying this should have made it suspect, but love and its effects are determined rarely by reason" ("La personne qui faisait ce discours devait le rendre suspect, mais l'amour et ses effets, se règlent rarement par la raison" [32]). Here the narrator first comments on the text, then offers a general maxim that could easily be included in La Rochefoucauld's volumes.

The preceding example is typical of Villedieu's maxims. Each one is a comment on the "disorders of love," and at their core there is often an opposition between unpredictable, yet powerful love and ineffectual reason. Villedieu is out to prove that reason, the supposed foundation of historical narrative, did not actually exist in these past events, even in military battles. Tyrannical love rules everything and everyone unpredictably, subtly, and without regard for rank or position. This is clearly expressed in the work's second poetic maxim:

But is there a real and lasting happiness
In what is centered on love?
Everything is subject to the perils of a reversal;
Its most just and plausible hope
Is born, is destroyed and is reborn in one day.
Its sweetness passes like a dream,
Its promises are only seductive lies;
And yet, oh sad blindness!
What we know to be the greatest on earth,
What in our eyes is its most beautiful ornament,
Laws, honor, peace, war
Everything is subject to its enchantment.

Mais est-il un bonheur effectif et durable,
Dans ce qui roule sur l'Amour?
Tout s'y trouve sujet aux périls d'un retour;
Son espoir le plus juste et le plus vraisemblable;
Naît, se détruit, et renaît dans un jour.
Ses douceurs passent comme un songe,
Ses promesses ne sont qu'un séduisant mensonge;
Et toutefois, ô triste aveuglement!
Ce que nous connaissons de plus grand sur la terre,
Ce qui fait à nos yeux son plus bel ornement,
Les lois, l'honneur, la paix, la guerre,
Tout se trouve sujet à son enchantement. (43)

This maxim is not only a reflection on the instability of love. It is also, implicitly, a commentary on narratives that attempt to impose order on a world that "is centered on love." Villedieu contrasts the fragile and fluctuating images of a world ruled by love with the static, comprehensible, and explanatory representation of the past as given in the general narratives of "reasonable" historians. Villedieu shows in her historical examples that sentiments rule even what is "the greatest on earth" and create a cyclical, volatile world that "is born, is destroyed and is reborn in one day." As this maxim explains, reality as determined by love is always in "peril" of becoming clouded or of disappearing "like a dream." The rhyming words that Villedieu chooses to describe a world ruled by love and its implications—"dream, lie, blindness, enchantment"—negate any possibility of "reasonable" and concrete representations. The official representation of "what we know to be the greatest on earth, . . . laws, honor, peace, war"—that is, history—is "subject to [love's] enchantment"; thus, any effort to carve history in stone can only be partial or even deceptive.

Throughout the *Désordres*, Villedieu affirms this alternative representation of reality in which the interior arena of human events undermines "what we know," that is, the standard, general depiction of "laws, honor, peace, war," the tenets of official history. Villedieu's narratorial maxims guide the reader to question the history s/he recognizes in Villedieu's text and accept this author's answer as to the "real" truth of events—the particular history of personal intrigues. Villedieu in fact substitutes passionate and personal politics for conventional politics in her account of well-known people and events, and puts forth her representation of the past as universal history. She creates an entire ideology for the writing and interpreting of history. In her approach, all important events can be explained by the particular caprices of love, which—personified in the maxims—becomes the only agent, replacing all others, including the king. And because these maxims precede the historical text upon which they comment, the reader is led to interpret the history according to the maxim, replacing all agency with love.[24]

Through the maxims and other narratorial interventions, the narrator presents her/himself as the ordering force in an otherwise chaotic state.[25] S/he creates a bond with the reader, asking her/him to verify the general truths drawn from the historical exempla. This narrator is not the distanced historian who comments on the past but is part of the collective "us" ("nous") to which s/he refers in the text, a "nous" that is composed of a specific group of contemporaries. Speaking of the château of Saint-Germain-en-Laye, for example, the narrator comments that "the court was then at Saint-Germain which, since King François I had had built the château that is still seen there, has been one of the most beautiful country houses of our kings" ("La Cour était alors à Saint-Germain, qui depuis que le Roi François I y avait fait bâtir le château qu'on y voit encore, était une des plus belles maisons de plaisance qu'eussent nos Rois" [43]). In the maxims, love imposes itself upon an "us." The narrator is thus part of the experience, the eyewitness who can be trusted to unveil the truth. At one point, the narrator even openly calls upon this personal experience to lend authority to the account. After railing against love's powerful grip and its ability to arouse "all the other passions of the soul" ("toutes les autres passions de l'âme"), the narrator remarks: "I do not doubt that at this point more than one reader is saying ironically that I have not always spoken this way, but that is exactly what I am relying on in saying so many bad things about it [love], and it is from experience that I consider myself authorized to depict it in such dark colors" ("Je ne doute point qu'en cet endroit plus d'un lecteur ne dise d'un ton ironique que je n'en ai pas toujours parlé de cette sorte, mais c'est sur cela même que je me fonde pour en dire autant de mal, et c'est pour en avoir fait une parfaite expérience que je me trouve auto-risée à le peindre avec de si noires couleurs" [118]). This, which could refer to Villedieu herself, identifies the narrator as a public figure who has spoken out before and is familiar to readers. This is someone who has reflected upon passions and events and has come to a new con-clusion through experience. This narrator, through honest complicity with readers, hopes to draw them into agreeing with this new per-spective, according to which the interior realm prevails and thus must be revealed and accounted for in any historical narrative.

The remark just quoted appears at the end of the second story. The narrator in fact enters after each historical exemplum, that is, after the first, second, and fourth stories, in each instance comment-ing with a pedagogical exegesis upon the history recounted. As Flan-nigan has noted, Villedieu thus valorizes herself as a historian, as someone who is able to give coherence to history.[26] This voice that oc-casionally draws upon personal experience or comments on the act of composing the narrative supplements the one that begins the stories with general, impersonal maxims. Having indicated with the maxim how the account should be interpreted, the more personalized nar-rator reiterates the lesson in case it has not been properly assimilated. Villedieu thus frames her narratives with pedagogical tools to elevate the "particular" history she is recounting to the level of a universal history capable of illuminating and instructing, which is also the goal of the best general histories.

Not surprisingly, the concluding commentaries also illustrate how the passion politics that have just been played out affected the well-known events familiar to readers. For example, after the first story, the narrator explains that amorous rivalry "laid the first founda-tions of that internal war [the Ligue], which for many years tore apart the insides of this realm. . . . [The war] was born in the year 1577 . . . and had its source in the love intrigues that I have just written about" ("jetta les premiers fondements de cette guerre intestine, qui pendant plusieurs années a déchiré les entrailles de ce royaume. . . . [Cette guerre] prit naissance dès l'année 1577 . . . [et] eut sa source dans les intrigues d'amour que je viens d'écrire" [65]. The second story serves to prove that "that same love which in the first part of this work, produced the seeds of the Ligue, in this part created a secret obstacle to the general peace of the realm, and cost us a stretch of land that could be reconquered only at the price of much blood and much toil" ("ce même amour qui dans la première partie de cet ouvrage a produit les semences de la Ligue, met dans celle-ci un obstacle secret à la paix générale du royaume, et nous a coûté une étendue de terre qui ne pourrait être reconquise qu'au prix de beaucoup de sang et de beau-coup de travaux" [117]). Likewise, after the third and fourth parts, the professorial narrator supplants the official explanations for war with motivations taken from the particular realm:

> Givry was the most accomplished of all the men of his century. At the age of twenty-six he was showered with honors, favored with the good graces of his king, and on the verge of obtaining all the dignity a gentleman can achieve. An amorous despair destroyed these hopes and robbed the kingdom of one of its greatest ornaments.

> Givry était le plus accompli de tous les hommes de son siècle. Il se trouvait à vingt-six ans comblé d'honneur, favorisé des bonnes graces de son Roi, et en passe d'obtenir toutes les dignités où un gentilhomme peut monter. Un désespoir amoureux fit avorter ces espérances, et priva le royaume d'un de ses plus beaux ornements. (208)

The narrator echoes the king, who laments Givry's loss in the final paragraph of the story: "He complained grievously to Mlle de Guise: 'You killed Givry, Mlle, and you have weakened my troops more by this stroke of your cruelty than the duc du Maine did by all the effort of his weapons'" ("Il s'en plaignit douloureusement à Mademoiselle de Guise. 'Vous m'avez tué Givry, Mademoiselle, lui dit-il, et vous avez plus affaibli mes troupes par ce trait de votre cruauté que le Duc du Maine par tout l'effort de ses armes'" [207]). As each concluding commentary makes clear, particular history, which here consists of Mlle de Guise's "cruelty," dominates public history, which here is the verifiable actions of the duc du Maine during the Ligue. Each story not only "enables [Villedieu] to join the gallantries of [her] subject with the important truths of general history" ("[lui] sert à joindre aux galanteries de [son] sujet les vérités importantes de l'histoire générale" [66]), as Villedieu explains the use of her stories, but also, and more importantly, enables her to devalue the well-known narrative by revealing the supposedly real motivations for it. Viewed within the context of the debate over history, Villedieu's *Désordres* advocates the more interiorized perspective excluded by Louis's historiographers. By advancing the view that love is to be found behind all "the revolutions that happen in monarchies," the novelist juxtaposes particular and public history and clearly identifies historical truth with the former.

Villedieu's position is a daring affront to conventional history, an affront that, given history's function under Louis XIV, takes on considerable political significance. Flannigan views the change of focus from battles to love intrigues in Villedieu's depiction of the past as a feminization and consequently, in his view, a depoliticization of history: "[Villedieu] sees herself merely as redescribing the historical reality in a different (and I would specify feminine) mode and speech. It is, to be sure, a kind of de-politicized speech, the purpose of which is to fill in the lacunae of the official document."[27] Although I would agree that Villedieu is "redescribing" history, I believe she does so with political intentions. By identifying particular history as the foundation of the political events of general history, Villedieu in effect politicizes her version of history. She replaces, not just redescribes, general history. In so doing, she joins many of her female contemporaries, and in this respect her narrative can be seen as a type of feminization. In addition, she reverses traditional hierarchies and reveals the female presence in all historical events. Particular history does not become the female domain par excellence, as Flannigan suggests. Rather, it becomes true, universal history, affecting men and women, politics and passion, equally. It is this realm, from which women are not excluded as they are from war, that official historians ignore and that Villedieu uses for her "metamorphosis" and her commentary.

THEATRICAL ILLUSIONS: PRIVILEGING THE PARTICULAR

The general commentary on history that Villedieu develops in the overall construction of her text is embedded in each of the three stories in different but complementary ways. Villedieu covertly develops her "politicized speech" by thematically inscribing the polemics of the debate over official and particular history. The first story, devoted to Mme de Sauve and the origins of the civil war, explores the classical *être/paraître* (to be/to appear) opposition, with Villedieu substituting the two perspectives on history for the elements usually contrasted. In a complex plot constructed to valorize her interiorized perspective, characters take on a variety of roles and appearances that are ultimately discovered to be a deforming and misleading surface. Each person is deceived by the superficial reflections of others. Reality as it appears is but a system of mirrors whose unstable reflections Villedieu reveals.

The principal character, Mme de Sauve, incarnates the duplicity of the *être/paraître* thematic as a whole as she systematically seduces each of the male figures, including the monarchs Henri III and the roi de Navarre, with her art. Of this devious person, one character remarks, "The solidarity of love pleases her less than its brilliance, and because she is incapable of a sincere commitment, she does not know how to distinguish what creates it from a passing love" ("La solidarité de l'amour lui plaît moins que son éclat, et comme elle est incapable d'un sincère engagement, elle ne sait pas distinguer ce qui le fait, d'avec un amour de passage" [19]). This description illustrates the two poles of the plot: the characters try to go behind appearances to find truth, represented here as love that is "sincere" and based on "solidarity," that is, founded upon a stable state of *être*. The characters' efforts are constantly subverted by figures such as Mme de Sauve, who are more interested in the surface of reality, in their own "brilliance." The dilemma of each character is to "distinguish" reality from appearance, true from false roles. Villedieu reveals truth as residing beneath the surface of general events (which is the *paraître*) in the interior, courtly sphere of human experience (which can be equated with the *être*).

One scene illustrates to an exceptional degree the opposition between *être* and *paraître* as Villedieu thematically inscribes it in *Les Désordres*. Angry that Mme de Sauve has managed to conquer the heart and mind of the king, whom they had hoped to seduce, the two principal female characters, Mlle d'Elbeuf and Mlle de Chateauneuf, decide to take revenge upon this court coquette. They are joined by de Sauve's jilted lover, the duc de Guise, and the reine de Navarre, who is against de Sauve because she feels that the coquette persuaded Catherine de Médicis to banish one of her friends from court.[28] The conspirators engage the roi de Navarre to pretend to love de Sauve: "They decided that the roi de Navarre would pretend to love Mme de Sauve, that he would try to get her to prefer him to all the other lovers, and after succeeding, he would display public signs of contempt and make her the laughing stock of the whole court" ("Il fut arrêté entr'eux que le Roi de Navarre feindrait d'aimer Mme de Sauve, qu'il tâcherait d'en obtenir une préférence sur tous les autres amants et qu'après l'avoir obtenue, il lui donnerait des marques publiques de mépris, et la rendrait la risée de toute la Cour" [15]). For the final public scene of revenge, the schemers decide to present a ballet of Apollo and Daphne for which the cast of characters is carefully established— with the roi de Navarre as Apollo and Mme de Sauve as Clitie, the favorite mistress who, in the myth, is ultimately rejected: "They hoped to compel the roi de Navarre to show this contempt strongly; and to say to Mme de Sauve after the ballet, that the fiction was the truth" ("On prétendait obliger le Roi de Navarre à marquer fortement ce mépris; et à dire à Mme de Sauve, après le Ballet, que cette fable était une vérité" [22]). This scene is designed to underscore the fusion of *être* and *paraître* as the characters first create a fiction to reveal the truth. The ballet they construct depends on a resemblance between surface and reality.

When the ballet of Apollo and Daphne is enacted, however, there is an ironic reversal of what the conspirators planned, resulting in a state of utter chaos. The roi de Navarre has secretly fallen in love with de Sauve and thus subverts his role in favor of another truth:

> The duc de Guise . . . saw the roi de Navarre do the opposite of what had been proposed.

This monarch began with excuses to Mme de Sauve, that the parts were badly distributed; he then told her that her beauty was powerful enough to reverse ancient and modern orders and, following her every time he was supposed to shun her, he created so much confusion in the order of the ballet that no one knew what it was supposed to represent.

Le Duc de Guise . . . vit le Roi de Navarre faire le contraire de ce qu'on lui avait proposé.

Ce monarque commença par des excuses à Madame de Sauve, de ce que les personnages étaient si mal disposés; il lui dit ensuite que sa beauté était assez puissante pour renverser les ordres anciens et les modernes, et la suivant toutes les fois qu'il devait la fuir, il mit tant de confusion dans l'ordre du ballet qu'on ne sut ce qu'il devait représenter. (24)

The ballet epitomizes the thematic opposition between *être* and *paraître* and the way in which an explanation of events is constantly displaced onto another level of signification. In this scene, *paraître* only too clearly corresponds to *être*, but the ballet proves to be incomprehensible—"no one knew what it was supposed to represent." To restore the "order of the ballet" amidst "so much confusion," the astute observer must read below the surface. Although the ballet does represent reality, no one can interpret it properly without knowing of the king's secret love for de Sauve. Villedieu thus reveals that a public, superficial reading of events cannot disclose the truth. She effectively underscores the superficiality of the official history she uses to construct her novel and valorizes the particular history she reveals. A worthy historian such as Villedieu is one who discloses underlying motives beneath the unstable and confused exterior.

The implications of Villedieu's ballet of Apollo and Daphne go beyond a general commentary on the merits of the two perspectives on history. This ballet is politically provocative, as Villedieu subverts the authority ascribed to official history as it existed specifically during the reign of Louis XIV. She chooses to stage textually a ballet whose principal character, the Sun King Apollo, evokes obvious connotations for her readers. Her public was surrounded by artistic reminders (such as the central fountain at Versailles) that Louis personified "Le Roi Soleil."[29] In Villedieu's production, the Sun King Apollo, symbol of the ruler who is the focus of official history in seventeenth-century France, himself undermines this official narrative and "created so much confusion in the order of the ballet that no one knew what it was supposed to represent." Apollo, the raison d'être of official history, is portrayed in the particular realm of affairs, abandoning his public role as husband to the reine de Navarre for the private one as Mme de Sauve's lover. Apollo himself becomes part of the paradigm of particular history and destroys the official order—

metaphorically represented by the ballet his wife designed—that he is supposed to uphold.

The potentially subversive parallel between the roi de Navarre and Louis XIV is further enhanced by the fact that in reality Louis XIV lived out this theatrical representation. He actually danced the role of Apollo in a ballet that Villedieu may have attended.[30] Villedieu's decision to use a ballet to reveal the superficiality of official discourse is especially significant, given her monarch's frequent use of this medium to reinforce the image of an all-powerful deity that his royal historiographers were creating. Such theatrical representations have the same premise as the general histories devoted to the military exploits of the king—that what is "great" and "public" is true history. The novelist uses her interpretive history to undermine this premise.

This first story also serves to valorize the strong narrator in the *Désordres*, who is capable of leading the reader through this maze of mirrors, reflections, and appearances because s/he knows the inside story, the "particularities" of this *H/histoire*. The need for such an interpreter of events is subtly made evident after the ballet scene, when the reine de Navarre scolds Monsieur for his reliance on appearances and his resulting interpretive blindness:

> "What!" continued the reine de Navarre, "You still believe that this love [between the roi de Navarre and Mme de Sauve] is not real, . . . weren't you a witness to the ballet yesterday and what happened to show that it is true?"
>
> Monsieur had neither seen nor known anything about what had happened; he was part of the ballet, and because of the character he represented, he had to be behind the theatre.

> "Quoi!" poursuivit la Reine de Navarre, "la Vous en êtes encore à croire cet amour une feinte, et vous ne fûtes pas témoin hier au ballet de ce qu'on fit pour marquer que c'est une vérité?"
>
> Monsieur n'avait ni rien vu ni rien su de ce qui s'était passé; il était du ballet, et le personnage qu'il y représentait l'obligeait à être derrière le théâtre. (29)

Even those who participate in events often lack the distance to be able to distinguish the true story, the truth, from the theatre. The narrator in *Les Désordres*, however, is a capable historian who can explain the various machinations behind the theatre of official history. S/he possesses the insight to interpret appearances and leads the reader in the correct direction by making remarks such as "the monarch believed himself to be happier than he actually was" ("le monarque se crut plus heureux que dans la vérité il ne l'était" [15]); by calling Mme de Sauve "the coquettish lady" ("la dame coquette" [39]); and by disclosing the truth to the reader: "[Mme de Sauve] sighed, she let flow some tears of frustration that she made pass for tears of love" ("elle soupira, elle laissa couler quelques larmes de dépit, qu'elle fit passer pour des larmes d'amour" [40]). Thus, as in the maxims, this "injudicious" historian guides the reader to a more valid interpretation of the past, one derived from the particular realm.

INTERPRETIVE ABILITIES: THE GENDER GAP

The second story in the *Désordres de l'amour* illustrates the same valorization of the particular realm for interpreting history. The story of Bellegarde and the marquise de Termes has traditionally sparked critical interest only because it contains a wife's declaration (*aveu*) to her husband that she loves another man, a novelistic invention that has been seen as prefiguring Lafayette's heroine's own act of avowal.[31] But this story is of interest for more reasons than its importance in explaining a specific moment in literary history. Within the context of Villedieu's text as a whole, the second story is another step in the author's critique of general history and constitutes a "disordering" of the hierarchies and expectations associated with this kind of history. This is a complex story of people who are minor characters in official history, but here their story upstages the king's. The historical givens are remarkably close to Mézeray, as they are all wars and political negotiations and all characters but one are verifiable. The story proves that love and politics can often have disastrous consequences, and in this case the fusion is responsible for the loss of a part of France.

Briefly, the marquis de Termes, the fictional son of the real maréchal de Termes, marries a wealthy woman from the provinces and falls madly in love with his new wife. She, however, does not share his sentiments and falls into a deadly state of melancholy. In the much discussed confession, the marquise reveals that she is really in love with the marquis's nephew, Bellegarde. Unlike Monsieur de Clèves in Lafayette's novel, the marquis accepts his fate and very cooperatively takes steps to have the marriage annulled. Before this can be accomplished, he is killed at Jarnac, a real battle that occurred at precisely the time when Villedieu situates it. Before his untimely death, however, the marquis made his nephew his legitimate heir, but only on the condition that Bellegarde marry the widowed marquise. Villedieu's fidelity to historical fact is evident here, for although Bellegarde was not the real maréchal's nephew or heir, he did marry the widow, Marguerite de Saluces.[32]

What would appear to be a happily arranged fairy tale turns to disaster. The heirs of the defunct marquis contest the will, and the widow's father questions the propriety of the new alliance. The lovers flee to Savoie and marry, but Catherine de Médicis, the queen mother, who bears an old grudge against Bellegarde, persuades her son, the king, that the will is false and that the marriage is therefore illegitimate. Bellegarde is exiled and politically disgraced and blames his wife. The supposedly perfect couple grow to hate each other, and both seek revenge for their disappointment. The marquise goes to Catherine de Médicis and complains of her husband's treatment. To Bellegarde's fury, Catherine and Henri II both side with the marquise. Catherine applies to the pope for an edict reinforcing the marriage, an act that Bellegarde knows will enslave him forever. The marquis attempts to ingratiate himself with the king and queen mother by exhibiting bravery in the king's battles and is even promoted to maréchal. But this is not enough to keep him in favor, especially because his wife revealed his attempt to overthrow the queen mother, another event that Villedieu draws from history, although Bellegarde is not specifically mentioned as the culprit (92). In a final act of desperation, the new maréchal decides to create a love affair for his wife in order to show Catherine de Médicis that she is not the innocent, mistreated wife Catherine believes her to be and that he himself is to be pitied. This scene, which has much in common with the ballet scene in the first story, again is aimed at juxtaposing *être* and *paraître*. But in this instance, Villedieu identifies one person with the ability to reveal truth, and the specificity of her choice is an important stage of her overall commentary on history.

The maréchal believes that in this instance he is the master creator of appearances: "He only hoped for a gallantry from his wife, and he resolved to take refuge in an appearance, if he could not obtain a truth" ("Il n'en espérait plus que d'une galanterie de sa femme, et il résolut de se retrancher sur une apparence, s'il ne pouvait parvenir à une vérité" [106]). For his scheme, Bellegarde seizes upon an unknowing Bussi d'Amboise, who is attracted to Bellegarde's wife for her beauty. With the help of Mme de Bellegarde's childhood governess, Bellegarde works to convince Bussi that his wife is secretly in love with him. Bellegarde and the governess even invent a correspondence between Bussi and the maréchalle:

> They [Bellegarde and the governess] made great difficulties for him [Bussi] at first, to involve him more, and then imperceptibly softened them. They took his letters, and assured him they had had them read. They invented a few lines of a response, and they added that, if he would be quiet and be content with this just until the papal dispensation arrived, the silence would be justly rewarded. . . . Bussi's letters could always be good for something, and the maréchal judged that it would be useful to assemble the greatest number he could.

> On lui fit d'abord de grandes difficultés, afin de l'engager davantage, et puis insensiblement on les adoucit. On prit de ses lettres, qu'on assura qu'on avait fait lire. On y supposa quelques

lignes de réponse et on y ajouta que, si jusques à l'arrivée de la dispense, il voulait se taire et se contenter de cela, ce silence serait dignement récompensé. . . . Les lettres de Bussi pouvaient toujours être bonnes à quelque chose, et le maréchal jugeait à propos d'en assembler le plus grand nombre qu'il pourrait. (105)

Soon this feigned literary love affair proves to be unsatisfactory for the aspiring lover Bussi, who wants to talk to the maréchalle directly. Desperate, the maréchal continues his theatrical creations and decides to substitute one of the ladies in waiting of the duchesse de Nemours for his wife. Because this "Piedmont woman" ("Piémontoise") resembles his wife, he believes Bussi can be tricked: "The maréchal hoped to put the Piedmont woman in the place of his wife and then give so much false information to Bussi, that he would believe he could dispense with discretion and would publicize the favor he thought he had obtained" ("Le maréchal espéra de pouvoir supposer la Piémontoise à la place de sa femme, et ensuite de donner sous main tant de faux avis à Bussi, qu'il se croirait dispensé d'être discret, et publierait la faveur qu'il penserait avoir obtenue" [107]). Bellegarde counts on the publicizing of the affair, which would put public opinion on his side and enable him to regain favor with Henri II and Catherine de Médicis.

But the maréchalle prevails. As the narrator remarks, "It was written in the stars that Madame de Bellegarde would unravel all her husband's intrigues, and her guardian angel [natural talent] helped her on this occasion, as on many others" ("Il était écrit dans les astres que Madame de Bellegarde démêlerait toutes les intrigues de son mari, et son génie familier l'assista dans cette occasion comme en plusieurs autres" [107–108]).[33] She manages to intercept her husband's letter of instructions to the Piedmont woman, uncovers the affair, and goes to the designated meeting place herself to meet Bussi and clarify the situation. The maréchalle explains to Bussi that she had never been interested in having an affair with him, saying, "You were fooled if you were made to use another language" ("On vous a trompé, si on vous a fait tenir un autre langage" [110]). Bussi thus realizes that he has been tricked by false discourse—the letters as well as Bellegarde's own oral encouragements. The narrator emphasizes this notion of deceitful, empty discourse. Bussi laments that "people said encouraging things to me on your behalf; I was given letters that I thought were in your handwriting, people convinced me that you were coming here to give yourself up to my amorous transports" ("on m'a tenu de votre part des discours obligeants; on m'a donné des lettres que j'ai crues de votre main; on m'a persuadé que vous veniez ici vous livrer seule à mes transports" [111]). Bussi has been unable to read beneath the surface of discourse and actions and has thus completely misrepresented reality to himself.

The maréchal also turns out to be an incompetent reader who is seduced by appearances. When the Piedmont woman arrives at the meeting place and discovers the maréchalle she is supposed to replace, she informs the maréchal, who misreads the now-foiled scene he had concocted: "On the contrary, he believed that the maréchalle loved Bussi, and that love rendered the false summons true. . . . He ran to play the part that he had wanted to play for a long time" ("Il crut au contraire que la maréchalle aimait Bussi, et que l'amour rendait la fausse assignation véritable. . . . Il courut faire le personnage que depuis longtemps il avait envie de jouer" [112]). Bellegarde continues his theatre by adopting the role of a *voyeur* as he runs to spy on his wife. The maréchal is a clandestine witness to the maréchalle's truthful explanation to Bussi:

> Do not persist in a plan that can give you only unhappiness and confusion. The follies I did for Monsieur de Bellegarde may have persuaded the public that I would be capable of others for someone else, but that was a caprice of fortune. . . . I am naturally virtuous enough never to enter into another gallantry.

> Ne vous opiniâtrez point dans un dessein qui ne peut vous donner que du chagrin et de la confusion. Les folies que j'ai faites pour Monsieur de Bellegarde ont peut-être persuadé le public que j'en serais capable pour quelqu'autre, mais ce fut un caprice d'étoile. . . . Je suis naturellement assez vertueuse pour ne faire jamais d'autre galanterie. (113)

The maréchal misinterprets the true discourse and believes he is witnessing a theatrical performance:

> He thought that, despite his orders, she had been advised of his arrival and that before this she had said things that were just the opposite of these. "Your subtlety is useless, Madame," he said, revealing himself, "you were warned too late, and we heard what you said before you believed you had witnesses to your conversation."

> Il crut que, malgré ses ordres, elle avait été avertie de son arrivée, et qu'elle avait tenu auparavant des discours contraires à ceux-là. "Votre finesse est inutile, Madame," dit-il en se montrant, "vous avez été avertie trop tard, et nous avons entendu ce que vous disiez avant que vous crussiez avoir des témoins de votre entretien." (114)

Bellegarde refuses to believe the reality he sees and imagines instead a previous conversation that never existed. The maréchalle, however, reveals the truth to him; and Bellegarde, covered with disgrace and reproaches from the king and queen mother, flees to Piedmont. Out of anger, he conquers the marquis de Saluces's territory from France for Piedmont, with grave political consequences: "This great parcel of land passed into the power of the duc de Savoie, who still owns it" ("Ce beau morceau passa depuis sous la puissance du Duc de Savoie, qui le possède encore" [117]).

This example of love's political effects thus illustrates once again that "what appears is almost never the truth" ("ce qui paraît n'est presque jamais la vérité" (*La Princesse de Clèves*, 56) and that true interpretation is to be found below the surface of theatrical appearances. In this exemplum, a woman proves to be the one who possesses truth. The two male figures, Bussi and Bellegarde, remain trapped in the artificiality of superficial discourse, enlightened only by a woman. Villedieu thus valorizes the maréchalle as the correct interpreter of events because she adopts a "particular" perspective and, like the ingenious but injudicious "particular" historian, does not remain on the surface of events. The maréchalle becomes emblematic of the historian Villedieu, endowed with genius or "natural talent" that guides her "on this occasion, as on many others."

WRITING THE SCENARIO OF HISTORY

The "natural talent" attributed to the principal female character in the second story is embodied by the dominant Mlle de Guise in the third and fourth parts, which constitute one story.[34] In her account of Mlle de Guise and Givry, Villedieu magnifies the political effects of love as she comments upon the equally disordering power of the written word, for the loss of one of the king's favorite generals is caused by a woman's writing and by the recipient's inability to interpret it except according to his own desires and false hopes.[35]

The historical events are again drawn from the period of the Ligue and focus on the Guise family's opposition to the crown. Givry, the protagonist, was raised with the Guise family and then, after the assassination of the duc de Guise and his brother at Blois, allies himself with Henri II. At court, Givry falls in love with Mme de Maugiron, who writes him love letters that Givry carries with him wherever he goes. His box of letters is seized in battle by the Guise faction but is returned to him. He opens it to find Mme de Maugiron's letters, but with passionate commentaries written on them in an unknown hand. Givry's friend the duc de Bellegarde (the nephew of the Bellegarde in the previous story) identifies the handwriting as that of Mlle de Guise. Seduced by the writing and by the idea that he might be loved by a great princess, Givry abandons Mme de Maugiron to try his chances with Mlle de Guise. When Bellegarde reprimands him, Givry explains that he is guided by ambition more than love:

> I admit . . . that I am in love with Mme de Maugiron and that I would not give up this passion for some verses whose purpose I do not know, but if Mlle de Guise considered them an honor, Mme de Maugiron won't prevent me from being sensitive to them. I am young, I have ambition, and Mlle de Guise is one of the most beautiful princesses in the world. I would be thought a fool if, being able to have a love intrigue with her, I missed the chance.

> J'avoue . . . que je suis amoureux de Madame de Maugiron, et que je ne renoncerais pas de cette passion pour des vers dont j'ignore le dessein, mais si Mademoiselle de Guise les avait considerés comme une faveur, Madame de Maugiron ne m'empêcherait pas d'y être sensible. Je suis jeune, j'ai de l'ambition, et Mademoiselle de Guise est une des plus belles princesses du monde. On me traiterait d'insensé si, pouvant avoir une intrigue d'amour avec elle, j'en manquais l'occasion. (131)

Thus believing he can put love in the service of his ambition, Givry sets out to conquer Mlle de Guise. But the two cannot be reconciled, for Givry is an officer in the king's army and Mlle de Guise is in the opposing Ligue faction. Givry falsely believes he can separate the public from the particular, duty from sentiment. He explains to Bellegarde, "If I am forced to maintain on general occasions the character of an enemy of the Ligue, on particular occasions I could take that of a faithful servant of the Guise family" ("Si je suis forcé à soutenir dans les occasions générales le caractère d'un ennemi de la Ligue, je pourrais dans les particulières prendre celui d'un fidèle serviteur de la maison de Guise" [140]). But this equilibrium proves impossible to maintain, and Givry tips the scale in favor of the "particular." He is more and more overcome by love for the beautiful princess. During one battle he allows the Ligue's troops to pass unharmed and, when the Guise family is under siege, Givry permits wheat to cross the lines to nourish them and their troops, thus prolonging the war. Givry's actions are excused by the new king, Henri IV, who understands Givry's predicament because he himself has just fallen madly in love with Gabrielle d'Estrées. He gives Givry many opportunities to serve the Guise family, but to no avail. Mlle de Guise remains unmoved.

Givry's misfortunes are compounded by the fact that Mlle de Guise finds herself attracted to Bellegarde, who has written a passionate letter to her and signed it with his friend's name. The daring letter infuriates Mlle de Guise, who reminds a confused Givry of their difference in social status. In the end, Mlle de Guise rejects both Bellegarde and Givry. Givry quickly seeks death in the next battle, and the king blames an unremorseful Mlle de Guise for weakening his troops by depriving him of one of his best generals. Only the faithful Mme de Maugiron laments her weak lover's death.

This story is designed to show that the particular and the public realms have their own laws and that the interior realm always prevails over the public. Givry's grave mistake is in believing that he can interpret the particular domain of love by using the public one of ambition. Mlle de Guise's confidant berates him for being incapable of distinguishing the two spheres: "Did you view her [Mlle de Guise] as a rebel town that you had resolved to take by force?" ("La regardiez-vous comme une ville rebelle que vous auriez résolu de prendre d'assaut?" [204]).[36] As the maxims reiterate throughout, love is not guided by reason; thus, Givry's "attack" was doomed to failure.

Givry loses not only because he tries to combine the two worlds and make them function only according to public law but also, and primarily, because he is incapable of functioning in the "particular" world embodied by Mlle de Guise. Like Bellegarde in the previous historical exemplum, Givry is a faulty interpreter of the external sign— in this case, the written word. The source of his misfortunes is in fact Mme de Maugiron's letters and the commentaries written on them by Mlle de Guise. Givry's quest throughout the story is to discover whether or not Mlle de Guise's passionate words have any foundation in reality. In the process he convinces himself that they do and is thus seduced by an illusionary appearance. Nor is Givry capable of manipulating the written word in his own right. When he does write a letter to Mlle de Guise, just before his death, it never reaches its destination.

The female characters are again elevated as the interpreters of the sign, able to read beneath the surface. Mme de Maugiron warns Givry that he is mistaken in his assumptions, but he rejects her warnings. Mlle de Guise, although she believes Bellegarde's letter to be written by Givry, is nonetheless free of the seductive trap and is attracted to the missive's real writer, Bellegarde. She thus, albeit unknowingly, correctly interprets the letter. She is not only the dominant interpreter but also the controlling manipulator of the sign. Villedieu places the emphasis on her as a writer, not on the content of the writing. As one character explains, the commentaries that eventually led to such political disorder were written only as an addition to a politicized female writing contest: "Mlle de Guise . . . said only . . . that she wanted to show the ladies of the court that those [verses] of the Ligue surpassed theirs in delicacy of sentiment and finesse of spirit" ("Mlle de Guise . . . dit seulement . . . qu'elle voulait faire voir aux dames de la Cour que celles de la Lique les surpassaient en délicatesse de coeur et en finesse d'esprit" [136]). The princess, like

Villedieu herself, thus destines her work for publication. Villedieu strengthens the tie between herself as author of the *Désordres* and the disordering Mlle de Guise by identifying the princess's commentaries as maxims. These four maxims resemble those of the narrator in the previous two stories, both in content and in form. Much of the emphasis in the princess's maxims is placed on the volatile, misleading appearance of love, as in the following:

Sensitive delicacy always follows
Sincere tenderness step by step;
To love passionately, it is necessary
To feel delicately
Everything that comes from the loved one;
But one often falls into error;
And the one who thinks of going to the supreme degree
Of heart's delicacy,
If one judged oneself harshly,
Will find that these are the caprices of temperament.

La sensible délicatesse
Suit toujours pas à pas la sincère tendresse;
Il faut, pour aimer ardemment,
Ressentir délicatement
Tout ce qui part de ce qu'on aime;
Mais on tombe souvent, sur cela, dans l'erreur;
Et telle croit aller jusqu'au degré suprême
Des délicatesses du coeur,
Qui, si l'on se jugeait sévèrement soi-même,
Trouverait que ce sont des caprices d'humeur. (125)

The fusion between Mlle de Guise and Villedieu is made complete by the fact that this maxim carries the number VI and is thus sequentially linked to the maxims in the preceding stories.

Through Mlle de Guise and her textual maxims, Villedieu valorizes the female writer and endows her textual production with political power.[37] She specifies that this power lies not in the traditional writing of a Madame de Maugiron but in the act of commentary, be it on the text of another writer or on history's narrative. In this final story, Villedieu highlights the written text as a subversive political tool capable of affecting public history—a tool she associates with a specific gender.

□   □   □

When all three stories of the *Désordres de l'amour* are read together in the light of Villedieu's theoretical prefaces where she comments on history and fiction, what could be seen as mere commonplaces of the novel—especially theatrical scenes and letters—can be interpreted as literary inventions designed to contribute to the seventeenth-century quarrel over history. Inherent in Villedieu's literary enterprise is an appeal to revise the general history she uses as her source. These theatrical scenes and letters underscore the premise that one cannot correctly interpret reality using only a public perspective that remains trapped by surfaces that are reflected from one mirror to another. Villedieu identifies truth with the particular perspective, thus taking a clear position in the debate between official and particular history. In *Les Désordres*, she effectively transfers the debate to a narrative space and identifies women and their literary enterprises as the keys to historical enlightenment.

As Miller has justly remarked, by intermeshing love and affairs of state, Villedieu instructs us "to reconsider the dominant definitions and valorizations of masculinity as the privileged source of social value and the proper measure of historicity."[38] Villedieu deliberately provokes Bayle's critical fire by undermining the authority of the official history of "the greatest men," principally of Louis XIV. Bayle's virulent attack on Villedieu's creative strategy is not only a call for a "new science of history," as Showalter has interpreted his remark, but also, and specifically, a tirade against the new formulation of history advocated by Villedieu.[39] Bayle's criticism that "one does not dare believe what really is to be believed" because "gallant intrigues" are associated with the official history of "the greatest men" is an effort to reverse the subversion of historical truth and return to a definition of historical narrative determined by these "plus grands hommes." By going beyond the "Majesty of historical subjects," this novelist calls into question the dominant definition of history, as she puts forward an alternative narrative that fuses the particular and the public but privileges the particular. Villedieu's commentary on history is an attempt to replace the empty, superficial discourse of "judicious" historians with a "metamorphosed" narrative designed to illuminate the recesses of the past.

Lafayette H/historienne
Rescripting Plausibility

L'on parla ensuite de la Princesse de Clèves, car le moyen de n'en pas parler?

VALINCOUR[1]

W hen *La Princesse de Clèves* was published in March 1678, a virulent literary battle arose between those who praised it as a masterpiece of the nascent genre of the *nouvelle historique* and those who condemned it for subverting *vraisemblance*, or plausibility, the primary criterion of the new genre.[2] Chief among the novel's detractors was Jean-Baptiste Trousset de Valincour, an established member of the literary scene, who succeeded Racine both in the French Academy and as historiographer to Louis XIV. Valincour's *Lettres à Madame la Marquise de *** sur le sujet de la Princesse de Clèves* was hailed by de la Motte, his contemporary, as "the model of reasonable criticism" ("le modèle d'une critique raisonnable").[3] In the 370 pages of his "reasonable criticism," Valincour focuses much of his attack on what he considers the unreasonable behavior of the novel's female protagonist, whom he denounces as "an incomprehensible woman. . . . She is the most coquettish prude and the most prudish coquette one has ever seen" ("une femme incompréhensible. . . . C'est la prude la plus coquette et la coquette la plus prude que l'on ait jamais vue" [272–273]).

Throughout Valincour's *Lettres*, the principal verbs are *devoir* and *falloir*—"should" and "must"—as this *honnête homme* attempts to rectify a deviant fiction. The adjectives "unnatural" and "extraordinary" are conflated with "implausible" ("invraisemblable") in this literary trial.[4] At one point, Valincour's fictional expert exclaims in exasperation, "In these short works, extraordinary fictions are unacceptable to the reader because he is not prepared for them, he is expecting only a simple, natural story that he can believe without going against his better judgment" ("C'est dans ces petits ouvrages où les fictions extraordinaires sont insupportables au lecteur parce qu'il n'y est pas préparé, qu'il n'attend qu'une histoire simple et naturelle, à laquelle il puisse ajouter quelque sorte de créance, sans faire tort à son jugement" [116]). Lafayette's "extraordinary" fiction was judged a clear transgression of the "horizon of expectations" associated with the historical novel.

The immense gulf between Lafayette's masterpiece and "a simple, natural story" is attested to by the strength and dimension of the quarrel the novel provoked. Valincour's meticulous attack on the novel's style and content was soon followed by a massive work, *Conversations sur la critique de la Princesse de Clèves*, attributed to the Abbé de Charnes, that refuted the charges advanced by the academician and sought to redeem the novel as a masterpiece of the new genre. Charnes, although unable to boast Valincour's official credentials, frequented Lafayette's salon and thus was an integral member of worldly society.[5]

The quarrel was not limited to these two detailed critical works. Donneau de Visé's newspaper, *Le Mercure Galant*, served as a forum for public opinion, provoking controversy around the novel. Before *La Princesse de Clèves* was even published, the *Mercure Galant* called attention to the princess's declaration to her husband by publishing another story, "La Vertu malheureuse," which featured a strangely similar situation. As Maurice Laugaa remarks, "This can be viewed as a veritable preconditioning of the public."[6] After the appearance of *La Princesse de Clèves*, the *Mercure Galant* asked its readers their opinion of the princess's declaration; the answers occupied three issues of the *Mercure*'s *Extraordinaire*, as readers argued about the plausibility and propriety of the princess's action. In addition, in May of 1678 the *Mercure Galant* published a review of the novel in the form of a letter by a certain "Géomètre de Guyenne," attributed to Fontenelle.[7] No other seventeenth-century work of fiction could boast such immediate and detailed critical attention.

Throughout the seventeenth-century debate, not only the plausibility and propriety of the princess's actions but also the related issue of the combination of history and fiction proved to be problematic. In his *Lettres*, Valincour reproaches Lafayette for having strayed from her task of storyteller to adopt the seemingly neutral role of historian:

> I cannot conceive of a purpose for Mme de Tournon's story, that of Anne Boleyn, and many other elements of French history that are scattered throughout.

> Je ne puis concevoir de quoi servent ici l'histoire de Madame de Tournon, celle d'Anne de Boulen, et plusieurs autres traits de l'histoire de France qui y sont répandus. (22–23)

□   □   □

> From the court of a French king, one is suddenly thrown into the realm of Amadis.

> De la Cour d'un Roi de France, l'on est tout d'un coup jetté dans le Royaume des Amadis. (88–89)[8]

Valincour, like other critics, does not seem to recognize the utility of the history to the "main" story. In his concluding condemnation of this history, he exclaims, "There is no truth in the entire work, except for a few passages from French history which, in my opinion, should not be there at all" ("Il n'y a rien de véritable dans tout l'ouvrage, que quelques endroits de l'histoire de France, qui, à mon sens, devraient n'y être point" [88]). But within the logic of the genre to which Lafayette's novel belongs, Valincour's condemnation makes no sense. As we have seen, the *nouvelle historique* was supposed to use history to guarantee the plausibility of the fiction.

Valincour is not an anachronistic anomaly in the history of the critical reception of *La Princesse de Clèves*. To this day, critical evaluation of history in the novel has barely strayed from the lines he established. To reevaluate the purpose and content of history in *La Princesse de Clèves*, it is necessary to take an approach different from current critical interpretations of the use and composition of history in Lafayette's novel. The first of these views history as a separate entity, of interest only in that it crosses paths with the fictional story, an event many critics consider a rare occurrence. To Charles Dédéyan, among others, the purpose of the history is to provide a "framework for the fiction."[9] J. W. Scott's effort to justify the numerous internal narratives, although illuminating, has the similar disadvantage of viewing *Histoire* and *histoire* as separate entities.[10] And Bruce Morrissette, echoing seventeenth-century critics, denies the relevance of history to the "main" story: "The *Princesse* is not without its faults, chief among which is the inclusion of historical anecdotes which have little bearing on the main story, but its superior elegance and charm are instantly apparent."[11]

A second myth about history in *La Princesse de Clèves* has been given currency by those who recognize and praise her erudition and effort but reproach her for infidelity to her sources. According to this interpretive tradition, Lafayette's history is not to be taken too seriously. Thus H. Chamard and G. Rudler, scrupulously identifying these numerous sources, praise Lafayette for her erudite attention to official histories yet lament the fact that, among other faults, Lafayette is negligent with respect to chronology and does not accurately portray the atmosphere of a Renaissance court.[12] Roger Francillon, among others, dismisses the novel's history because of such inconsistencies. He summarizes his evaluation by stating that "it is better if the reader does not know the dates and details of French history."[13] Claudette Sarlet comes to the conclusion that "the scarcity of chronological references is proof of Lafayette's indifference to [the historical] character of her work."[14]

A third tactic of those dealing with history in *La Princesse de Clèves* is to absolve Lafayette of all intentionality and attribute the use of history to the necessary literary convention of *vraisemblance*. Critics often believe they are complimenting Lafayette by negating the history in her work to stress, instead, the work's timeless quality. Antoine Adam, for example, forgives Lafayette her use of history, which he qualifies as "repulsive" ("rebutant"), "conventional," and "unbearable" ("insupportable"), with the explanation that Lafayette "is only conforming to the laws of the genre she chose."[15] In such an interpretation, the novel's historical content is an embarrassing mistake that would never have spoiled such a great work if the author had been writing at a different time.

Thus, the 250-year critical reaction to Lafayette's masterpiece creates an intriguing paradox. After reading the documentation of the seventeenth-century quarrel, one has the impression that the novelist made no effort whatsoever to create a *vraisemblable* text. The "few passages from French history . . . should not be there at all" because they fail to make this exceptional fiction believable. Yet, after reading modern critics, one is drawn to believe that the historical content, however faulty, is present only to meet the essential seventeenth-century criterion of *vraisemblance*. This paradox is further complicated by Lafayette's own implicit attitude toward her use of history and its relationship to the fiction. In a letter to a friend, she hailed *La Princesse de Clèves* as "a perfect imitation of the court and of the way one lives there" ("une parfaite imitation de la cour et de la manière dont on y vit"), thus defending her fiction's plausibility.[16] When she composed *La Princesse de Clèves* she was very much aware of the critical norm of *vraisemblance*. In fact, critics had based their definition of this new genre on her previous novel, *La Princesse de Montpensier*.

Among Lafayette's historical novels, *La Princesse de Clèves* stands out as the one with the most meticulously constructed history. There is a very lengthy historical introduction, and four of the five internal narratives, traditionally viewed as digressions, are historically verifiable. All the characters are real except the princess, and all the principal events are also historically accurate. Lafayette's principal source is Brantôme's *Mémoires*, which includes *Les Dames illustres* and *Les Dames galantes*. She also consulted an interpretation of Brantôme's works by Jean Le Laboureur in his *Mémoires de Michel de Castelnau*. Furthermore, Lafayette turned to two well-known histories of the time, Pierre Matthieu's *Histoire de France* (1631) and Mézeray's complete *Histoire de France*, as well as the latter's *Abrégé*. Less important sources include the *Histoire de la maison royale de France et des grands officiers de la couronne* (1674) and *Le Palais de l'Honneur* (1663), both by P. Anselme; Godefroy's *Cérémonial Français* (1649); and, for Anne Boleyn's history, a translation of *De origine ac progressu schismatis anglitiani* by Nicolas Sanders. Chamard and Rudler, who have uncovered the majority of these historical sources, state that Lafayette "gathered information with excessive care."[17] Yet, despite the novelist's effort and her own assertions of plausibility, this history failed to make the fictional plot seem plausible to her contemporaries.

The paradox created when critical interpretation of the novel is juxtaposed against the author's extensive consultation of sources underscores Lafayette's complex narrative strategy. I would suggest that Lafayette in fact uses history to subvert the rules governing the historical novel. By superficially following the laws of the genre and founding her fiction on historical fact, she intentionally creates an "extraordinary" and "unnatural" fiction to undermine, internally, the basic requirement of the genre—*vraisemblance*. She creates a complex dialectic between the historical "background" and the fiction to make her heroine's actions plausible within the economy of the text, thus proposing an alternative to her society's concept of plausible female behavior, which her contemporaries then recognized and censured. *La Princesse de Clèves*, in addition to being a fictional masterpiece, is a conscious attempt to rewrite history to promote an alternative view of the past and of plausible conduct for women in the present.[18] One can reveal the feminist notion of *vraisemblance* advanced in her novel by making what Miller has termed "a diacritical gesture, . . . refus[ing] a politics of reading that depends on the fiction of a neutral (neuter) economy of textual production and reception."[19] When Lafayette's specific strategies are identified, it becomes clear that she recognized the gendered, patriarchal nature of textual production and sought to undermine its pervasive and exclusionary power.

RESCRIPTING HISTORY

To perceive Lafayette's strategies, one must recognize that the history in *La Princesse de Clèves* is an important subtext, constructed with the same care and intentionality as the psychological drama of the princess and essential for interpreting the princess's actions.[20] The historical text merits critical attention as a literary invention designed by its author to possess meaning in itself as well as to serve a variety of uses through its relationship to the fictional story. When this subtext is compared with Lafayette's sources, it becomes apparent that besides consulting histories, she analyzed them. For her complex dialectic between history and fiction to function, Lafayette had to rewrite the history of her many sources, juxtaposing them and choosing certain details and events.

The primary choices she made among the historical works available to her reveal a partiality for certain kinds of history. Her two principal sources, Brantôme and Mézeray, have interesting points in common that can help us understand her effort to compose a distinctive history. We have already seen Mézeray's inclusion of the lesser-known aspects of history and, especially, of the lives of the women of the realm. Likewise, Brantôme sees the same kind of reconsideration as an aspect of his historical undertaking. The editor of the 1665 edition of his *Mémoires* cites the inclusion of "some particularities of the history of his time which are not found elsewhere" ("des particularités de l'Histoire de son temps qui ne se trouvent point autre part") as a drawing card for readers.[21] Brantôme himself stresses that, with his *Vies des dames illustres de France*, he is filling a void in historiography. For example, he introduces his chapter on Catherine de Médicis with the following remarks:

> I have been surprised a hundred times by the fact that the many good writers we have seen in our own century in France have not been inspired to compose a volume dedicated to the life and acts of the queen mother, Catherine de Médicis, for she has performed many worthy deeds and has cut their work out for them, if ever a queen did.

> Je me suis cent fois étonné, et émerveillé de tant de bons Ecrivains que nous avons vus de notre temps en la France, qu'ils n'aient été curieux de faire quelque beau recueil de la vie, et gestes de la Reine Mère, Catherine de Médicis, puis qu'elle en a produit d'amples matières, et taillé bien de la besogne, si jamais Reine tailla. (31)

La Princesse de Clèves is thus founded upon two histories that their respective authors characterize as exceptional because they include women. An analysis of the lengthy introduction of *La Princesse de Clèves* and of the book's internal narratives reveals that Lafayette carries the tendencies of her principal sources one step further, constructing a narrative that not only includes but also foregrounds women. She alters history according to a certain vision that lies outside of the horizon of expectations of her contemporaries.

Setting the Scene: Feminocentric History

The long portrayal of the court with which *La Princesse de Clèves* opens provides us with an ideal opportunity to analyze Lafayette's rewriting of history for her fiction. This is the moment in the novel when she most fully dons the robe of historian and creates the atmosphere for her work by depicting the court of Henri II in detail. This is also one of the least appreciated and understood aspects of the novel. The complex network of historical characters presented in these opening paragraphs proved to be a stumbling block for her contemporaries as well as for later readers. Modern-day students breathe a sigh of relief upon reaching "There appeared a beauty at the court" ("Il parut alors une beauté à la Cour") and then skip pages to unearth the "real" story from the historical "digressions." Lafayette's contemporaries had a similar reaction to the initial thirty-six pages (in the original edition) of the novel. They sensed a rupture between this historical opening and the fiction because, to them, this switch in narrative strategy was incomprehensible.

During the seventeenth-century quarrel, detractors and defenders of the novel felt impelled to account for the content of the introduction and to determine its function in the work. Fontenelle, who otherwise praises and defends *La Princesse de Clèves*, speaks of what to him is the author's intentional deception of the reader:

> The remarks that M. de Clèves makes to Mlle de Chartres when he is about to marry her are so beautiful I still remember that during my second reading, I could not wait to reach that point, and I could not help but be ill-disposed toward the description of Henri II's court, and all those proposed and rejected marriages, that pushed so far away the remarks that charmed me. Many people were taken in by this framework. They thought that all the portraits of the characters and all the various intrigues that are explained were a necessary part of the work and were related to what was to follow; but I realized from the beginning that the author wanted only to give us an overview of the history of that time.

> Les plaintes que fait Monsieur de Clèves à Mademoiselle de Chartres, lorsqu'il est sur le point de l'épouser, sont si belles, qu'il me souvient encore qu'à ma seconde lecture je brûlais d'impatience d'en être là, et que je ne pouvais m'empêcher de vouloir un peu de mal à ce plan de la cour de Henri II, et à tous ces mariages proposés et rompus, qui reculaient si loin ces plaintes qui me charmaient. Bien des gens ont été pris à ce plan. Ils croyaient que tous les personnages dont on y fait le portrait, et tous les divers intérêts qu'on y explique, dussent entrer dans le corps de l'ouvrage, et se lier nécessairement avec ce qui suivait; mais je m'aperçus bien d'abord que l'auteur n'avait eu dessein que de nous donner une vue ramassée de l'histoire de ce temps-là.[22]

Fontenelle views the opening, with "all those proposed and rejected marriages," "all the portraits of the characters," and "all the various intrigues," as an uninteresting and insignificant deterrent to a reader's enjoyment of the fiction. To him, the overwhelming accumulation of marriages, portraits, and intrigues is the principal component of "an overview of . . . history" that he perceives as devoid of function and meaning for the fictional story. Whereas other readers think mistakenly that all these descriptions are "a necessary part of the work and [are] related to" the fictional story, he believes he is more astute in recognizing that this introduction is a separate "overview." He congratulates himself for not having been tricked and for understanding that the historical introduction serves no essential purpose in relation to the "real story."

Valincour's reaction to this introductory portrait is harsher than Fontenelle's: "But while reading that long description of the court at the beginning, I thought I was going to read the history of France, and I forgot the princesse de Clèves, whose name I had never seen except in the title" ("Mais en lisant cette longue description de la Cour, qui est au commencement, je crus que j'allais lire l'histoire de France et j'oubliai la Princesse de Clèves, dont je n'avais jamais vu le nom qu'au titre du livre" [6]). As no real princesse de Clèves ever existed, Valincour finds it impossible to situate the supposed subject of the novel within the purely historical opening. The basis of his criticism is thus the same as Fontenelle's: the historical introduction is extraneous to the rest of the work and simply delays the reader's enjoyment of the main story.

Charnes, as usual, disagrees with Valincour, although the phrasing of his defense of the introduction is curiously ambiguous. His fictional addressee defends the introduction, saying it is "a marvellous decoration that gave me a good idea of the events that were to occur" ("une magnifique décoration qui m'a fait concevoir une grande idée des actions qui se devaient représenter" [31–32]). In Charnes's view, the introduction is important for the fiction because it "gives a good idea of the events" that follow. Moreover, by using the term "decoration," Charnes undermines his claim that the history is useful to the fictional story because he separates history from the fiction it allegedly enhances.

In fact, Charnes finds it easier to praise the introduction as well-written history than to see it as an integral and necessary part of the fiction:

This portrait of Henri II's court is only to highlight the portrait of M. de Nemours, who must appear there advantageously for the purposes of the story. Those thirty-six pages that seemed so long to him [Valincour] were boring only to him. If only our history were written in this manner! I'm sure that those thirty-six pages cost the author more than thirty-six hours, and those who are knowledgeable in the matter recognized this. This is the summary of many volumes that the author had to study. These different portraits of people who resemble each other in terms of merit, aristocratic birth, and many other illustrious qualities, and which must nonetheless be varied, are masterpieces; and I am not afraid to say that they come close to those of the best authors of antiquity, and that in the future they can serve as models for the best historians.

Ce portrait de la Cour de Henri II n'est que pour relever et mettre
en son jour le portrait de Monsieur de Nemours, qui y doit
paraître avec tant d'avantage pour les fins de cette histoire. Ces
trente-six pages qui lui ont semblé si longues n'ont ennuyé que
lui. Plût-à-Dieu! que nous eussions notre histoire écrite de cette
manière! Je suis assuré que ces trente-six pages ont coûté plus de
trente-six heures à l'Auteur, et ceux qui s'y connaissent s'en sont
bien aperçus. C'est le précis de plusieurs volumes, qu'il lui a fallu
étudier. Ces portraits différents de personnes qui se ressemblent
par la valeur, par la haute naissance, et par tant de grandes qualités, et qu'il faut néanmoins varier, sont des chef-d'oeuvres; et je
ne crains pas de dire qu'ils approchent de ceux des meilleurs Auteurs de l'antiquité, et qu'à l'avenir ils pourront servir de modèle
aux meilleurs Historiens. (33)

In identifying the introduction's purpose as merely a means of presenting Nemours, Charnes in effect further reduces the introduction's
usefulness and importance to the novel as a whole. But then, unable
to account for the introduction in terms of the fiction, he switches to
praising it as worthy historical narrative. The labor entailed in composing such a history is the painstaking, time-consuming work of a
historian rather than the imaginative task of an author of fiction. To
Charnes the introduction is thus a microhistory, yet one that is distinguished from conventional historical narrative. For like Fontenelle,
Charnes identifies the key traits of this historical presentation as the
"different portraits" and even labels the whole introduction a "portrait of Henri II's court." In Charnes's view, therefore, the introduction provides an example of what to him is a preferred type of history
—particular history. By hoping that these historical portraits, representative of an alternative approach to history, "can serve as models
for the best historians," he accentuates the tie between the introduction and history, as well as Lafayette's deviation from the norms of
conventional historical narration.

The critical uproar aroused by the introduction attests to the fact
that Lafayette transgresses the accepted conventions of the novel by
prefacing her fiction with a historical introduction that is much longer
and more complex than those of other novelists of the period.[23] As
their remarks indicate, the critics, in particular Valincour and Fontenelle, refuse to see that the introduction is a transformation and not
simply a transcription of Lafayette's historical sources. Nevertheless,
by identifying particularities in Lafayette's narrative, Charnes and
Fontenelle do make an effort to appreciate this historical composition.

The introduction in fact differs from Lafayette's sources in both
style and content. As Charnes and Fontenelle remark, the introduction is composed of a series of portraits carefully constructed and
juxtaposed to depict the atmosphere of the court of Henri II. The

twenty-seven portraits that figure in this sixteenth-century Who's Who, however, do not conform to our expectations of historical narrative or to a familiar definition of what constitutes "proper" history. The static nature of the portrait in general—what Brooks has termed its metaphorical quality—would seem to exclude this discursive mode from history.[24] But Lafayette's choice of the portrait is far from gratuitous. In adopting the portrait for her historical medium, Lafayette inscribes her narrative into a tradition of women's writing. Lafayette's introduction resembles Montpensier's portrait volumes. Moreover, Lafayette does not develop a narrative thread to accompany the descriptions. She includes only one brief reference to the religious strife and no references whatsoever to the specific wars with which her sources abound. This choice and the imprecision, in conventional historical terms, of the novel's opening can be interpreted in part as Lafayette's desire to accentuate the discourse rather than the content and therefore pay homage to what in the seventeenth century was considered to be the female genre of portraiture. In choosing the portrait, Lafayette distinguishes herself from official historians and joins the ranks of her female contemporaries. Like Montpensier and other memorialists, Lafayette highlights personalities—and, in that way, she privileges the internal dynamics of the court and creates her historical atmosphere. Causality and historical progression are presented as resulting from the interplay between specific persons.

The events Lafayette does choose to include transmit a very specific historical vision that is sustained throughout the novel and that is, in effect, an alternative to the vision transmitted by her sources. As Fontenelle remarked, the novel contains an overwhelming number of references to love intrigues, marriages, and plans for marriages. In this realm of what I will term politicized gallantry, activities related to love are the principal occupation and preoccupation.[25] Each portrait recounts the exploits and personal attributes of the characters in this "particular" battlefield. This transformation of her sources is evident from the first paragraph, which sets the tone for the entire historical introduction:

> Magnificence and gallantry have never appeared in France with such brilliance as during the last years of the reign of Henri II. This prince was gallant, handsome, and in love; even though his passion for Diane de Poitiers, the duchesse de Valentinois, had begun more than twenty years before, it was no less strong, and his expression of it was no less brilliant.

> La magnificence et la galanterie n'ont jamais paru en France avec tant d'éclat que dans les dernières années du règne de Henri second. Ce prince était galant, bien fait et amoureux; quoique sa passion pour Diane de Poitiers, duchesse de Valentinois, eût

commencé il y avait plus de vingt ans, elle n'en était pas moins violente, et il n'en donnait pas des témoignages moins éclatants.[26]

The reign of Henri II is associated with substantives evoking the interior court milieu ("magnificence," "gallantry"). Then Henri II himself is characterized in terms of courtly values ("gallant, handsome, and in love"). The third term of this opening paragraph, a distinguishing action of the king's, continues the tendency to limit the composition of history to its courtly essence. Henri II's love for Diane de Poitiers is as "brilliant" as his whole reign, with the adjective echoing the earlier noun. Thus the first three characterizing elements—the milieu as a whole, the king, and the first recorded event—all reveal the author's effort to depict a courtly world, one where gallantry is the overriding preoccupation and the major attribute of each participant.

The originality of this perspective is evident when this first paragraph is compared with Mézeray's opening description of the court of Henri II. Like Lafayette, Mézeray begins with a portrait, but his lengthy description is centered solely on the king:

> A great and generous king was succeeded by a good and valiant prince, Henri, his only son, who seemed to possess his father's qualities combined with those of Louis XII. He had all the illustrious virtues of the one, even though to a lesser degree, and the affection of the other for his people. His virtues having already been tested in various events, . . . the nobility expected honor, victories, and rewards from him; the populace [expected] peace, abundance, and exemption from taxes.

> A un grand et généreux Roi succéda un bon et vaillant Prince, Henri son fils unique, qui semblait être composé des qualités de son père et de celles de Louis XII mêlées ensemble. Il avait toutes les illustres vertus de l'un, quoi qu'en un degré moins éclatant, et la tendresse de l'autre envers les peuples: Ses vertus ayant été prouvées déjà en diverses affaires, . . . la Noblesse en attendait de l'honneur, des triomphes et des récompenses, et les peuples la tranquillité, l'abondance, et la décharge des impôts.[27]

Here the description of the king situates him within the patriarchal lineage. Diane de Poitiers is not mentioned until the end of the detailed portrayal, and even then she is not amorously associated with the king. Mézeray's introduction presents the focal point, the king, and the public constitution of his government, in contrast to Lafayette's introduction, subsuming the monarch within the less official realm of gallantry.

The particular history Lafayette evokes through her choice of events is strengthened by her approach within the individual portraits. She consistently includes the characteristics that associate a court figure with this gallant and selective world:

> The queen, [Mary Stuart's] mother-in-law, and Madame, the king's sister, also liked poetry, theatre, and music.

> La reine, sa belle-mère, et Madame, soeur du roi, aimaient aussi les vers, la comédie et la musique. (36)

□ □ □

> No woman at court would not have been flattered to have [Nemours] drawn to her.

> Il n'y avait aucune dame dans la cour dont la gloire n'eût été flattée de le voir attaché à elle. (37)

□ □ □

> The prince de Condé, in a small body that nature had not favored, had a great and noble soul, and a personality that made him attractive even to the most beautiful women.

> Le prince de Condé, dans un petit corps peu favorisé de la nature, avait une âme grande et hautaine, et un esprit qui le rendait aimable aux yeux même des plus belles femmes. (37)

In addition, each portrait underscores the fusion of politics and sentiment by illustrating the underlying principle that the real political realm is located on the interpersonal level and that political acts consist of confrontations between individual personalities. In describing Catherine de Médicis's political position, for example, Lafayette emphasizes her "ambitious temperament" ("humeur ambitieuse") as well as her personal relationship to Diane de Poitiers:

> Because of her ambitious temperament, the queen found much satisfaction in reigning; she seemed to bear without pain the king's affection for the duchesse de Valentinois, and she revealed no jealousy, but she concealed everything so well that it was difficult to judge her feelings, and politics obliged her to have contact with the duchess in order also to have contact with the king.

> L'humeur ambitieuse de la reine lui faisait trouver une grande douceur à régner; il semblait qu'elle souffrit sans peine l'attachement du roi pour la duchesse de Valentinois, et elle n'en témoignait aucune jalousie, mais elle avait une si profonde dissimulation qu'il était difficile de juger de ses sentiments, et la politique l'obligeait d'approcher cette duchesse de sa personne, afin d'en approcher aussi le roi. (35)

Although the queen's public role is not entirely effaced—Lafayette connects the verb "to reign" with Catherine rather than with her husband—the queen's politics are grounded in her relationship to Diane de Poitiers rather than in any public action. To politicize the interpersonal level, here and elsewhere, Lafayette alters her sources. Mézeray concentrates on the queen's personality:

> She saw his affections shared with her rivals, especially with the Valentinois woman: with whom she was so prudently able to adapt that she never gave her husband a reason to completely alienate himself from her. . . . As for her mind, it was extremely subtle, hidden, full of ambition and artifice. She knew how to adapt to all kinds of people, remain secretive in meetings, and carry out her designs with incredible patience.

> Elle vit partager ses affections avec ses rivales, spécialement avec la Valentinois: avec laquelle sa prudence sut si bien s'accommoder qu'elle ne donna jamais sujet à son mari de s'aliéner entièrement d'elle. . . . Pour son esprit, il était extrèmement subtil, caché, plein d'ambition, et d'artifices, qui savait s'accommoder avec toutes sortes de personnes, dissimuler dans les rencontres, et conduire ses desseins avec une incroyable patience.[28]

Lafayette retains the principal characteristics of her source but places them in a politicized framework. She channels Catherine's "ambition" into politics: because of this ambition, Catherine finds "much satisfaction in reigning." In addition, Lafayette shifts the focus away from Catherine's efforts to keep her husband and onto the political rivalry between women. Lafayette invests their relationship with political overtones: "Politics obliged her to approach this duchess." She also describes Diane de Poitiers in terms of political influence founded upon gallantry: Diane's power results from her amorous relationship to Henri II. Lafayette thus focuses attention on what are conventionally considered aspects of "la petite histoire"—amorous liaisons, family rivalries, personal disputes—and presents these court characteristics, the "particularities" of the court of Henri II, as the sole components of her historical vision. Moreover, by subsuming the official, well-known events of the past into the inner life of the court and positing affairs of the heart and mind as affairs of state, she transforms particular history into universal history.

　　With this particular orientation, Lafayette places the emphasis on marriage. Because marriages were an important political tool, allying families and realms, such unions obviously figure in Lafayette's sources. But in *La Princesse de Clèves*, this aspect of politics is placed in the forefront and has a personal as well as a political character. In addition, marriages are the structuring and unifying principle of the entire narrative. As Pierre Malandain notes, there is an extraordinary total of 106 allusions to marriage in the novel, referring to 41 different alliances. Many characters, such as Mlle de la Marck, who is "to be married" ("à marier" [35]), are identified in terms of their marital status and their relative importance in this area of the political arena. All the major historical events that Lafayette places at the foundation of her narrative are related to marriage. References to the marriage of Elisabeth de France, Henri II's daughter, to the king of Spain and to the marriage of Madame, the king's sister, to the duc de Savoie recur throughout and provide Lafayette with the occasion to describe court pageantry at length. The fatal tournament that marks a turning point in the composition of the court is held to celebrate Madame's marriage. And the possible marriage between the duc de Nemours and Queen Elizabeth of England gives rise to a long and complex explanation of the state of the British political realm (81).

Lafayette's emphasis on marriage leads Chamard and Rudler to conclude that one of the main characteristics of history in *La Princesse de Clèves*, in sharp contrast to the history in Lafayette's sources, is that "it doesn't seem very nationalist or political; the misfortunes and the glorious actions of France don't appear at all. . . . She gave history a dynastic quality."[29] To strengthen their argument, Chamard and Rudler point to Lafayette's long description of the marriages of Elisabeth de France and of Madame Marguerite and complain that the author inappropriately cites these unions as the principal articles of the Cateau-Cambrésis peace treaty.[30] Chamard and Rudler are in fact identifying Lafayette's variation on the historical narration in her sources and her specific historical perspective. Although their assessment is correct, Chamard and Rudler do not understand why the novelist changes the focus of her sources to exclude what they seem to consider the more important "misfortunes and . . . glorious actions of France."

Lafayette in fact transforms the conventional portrayal of what at this period was a political instrument of negotiation between nations by focusing on the conflict of personalities. For example, she uses Mézeray's description of Diane de Poitiers's marital manipulations because it is suitable for her construction of history. In describing Diane de Poitiers's influence, Mézeray states that

> The duchesse de Valentinois was on the lookout to prevent him [the duc de Guise] from gaining more favor. For, taking everything into account, she preferred the more moderate connétable, who had always gotten along well with her; she also feared the Lorraine princes' ambition. Feeling that way, she had done her best to delay the marriage between the dauphin and the princes' niece Mary Stuart, because she feared the mind of that young princess. . . . This is why, to strengthen her bond with the

Montmorencys, she secretly negotiated to give Henri, the connétable's second son, one of her granddaughters.

La Duchesse de Valentinois était désormais au guet pour l'empêcher d'empiéter davantage dans la faveur. Car tout considéré, elle aimait mieux le connétable plus modéré, lequel s'était toujours assez bien accommodé avec elle; et d'ailleurs redoutait l'ambition des Princes Lorrains. Avec cela, elle s'était efforcée de retarder le mariage du Dauphin avec Marie Stuart leur nièce, pour ce qu'elle redoutait l'esprit de cette jeune Princesse. . . . C'est pourquoi, afin de s'unir d'un lien plus étroit avec les Montmorencys, elle traita dès lors secrètement de donner à Henri second fils du Connétable, une sienne petite fille. (3:699)

Lafayette incorporates this entire passage into her text but with subtle transformations:

She had delayed, as much as she could, the marriage between the dauphin and the queen of Scotland: the beauty and the capable and progressive mind of this young queen, and the increased importance that this marriage gave to MM. de Guise [the princes] were unbearable to her. She especially hated the cardinal de Lorraine. . . . She saw that he was in collaboration with the queen; thus the connétable found her well disposed to unite with him and to create their alliance through the marriage of Mlle de la Marck, her granddaughter, with M. d'Anville, his second son.

Elle avait retardé, autant qu'elle avait pu, le mariage du dauphin avec la reine d'Ecosse: la beauté et l'esprit capable et avancé de cette jeune reine, et l'élévation que ce mariage donnait à MM. de Guise, lui étaient insupportables. Elle haïssait particulièrement le cardinal de Lorraine. . . . Elle voyait qu'il prenait des liaisons avec la reine; de sorte que le connétable la trouva disposée à s'unir avec lui, et à entrer dans son alliance par le mariage de Mlle de la Marck, sa petite-fille, avec M. d'Anville, son second fils. (38–39)

Lafayette was drawn to Mézeray's depiction because his treatment of the political marriage between the dauphin and Mary Stuart includes the conflict of personalities. Lafayette highlights this characteristic by reorganizing Mézeray's text to place Diane de Poitiers's personal reaction to Mary first. Mézeray attributes Diane's opposition first to her dislike of the Guise faction and only second to her fear of Mary's "mind." Lafayette strengthens her focus on female rivalry by adding "capable" and "beauty." At the end of the passage, Lafayette implicitly continues to emphasize women by mentioning the duchess's granddaughter before the connétable's son and by naming the granddaughter.

Mézeray continues his account by dismissing the preceding description as an aside of minor importance: "The court intrigues struggled along in this way. But the king continued the war, mounting great sieges; especially in Germany. . . . At that time there was the siege of Thionville; the conquest of Luxembourg depended on its capture" ("Les intrigues de la Cour se démenaient de la sorte. Mais le Roi continuant la guerre, faisait de grandes levées; spécialement en Allemagne. . . . C'était le siège de Thionville, de la prise de laquelle dépendait la conquête du Luxembourg" [3:699]). But in Lafayette's narrative, "the court intrigues" remain at the center of the stage, and the king's military maneuvers are excluded.

In dealing with the history of Marguerite's marriage to the duc de Savoie, Lafayette also amends her source to personalize state affairs, privilege the female component of the court, and depict women as active political agents. The source of her portrait of the king's sister is Brantôme's *Les Vies des dames illustres*. Brantôme accentuates Marguerite's love of learning and analyzes the negotiations for her marriage to the duc de Savoie. His portrait begins with a description of her as the quintessential learned women: "She had much wisdom and knowledge, which she always fostered by her constant studies, after-dinner discussions, and lessons with learned scholars whom she liked above all other people; thus they esteemed her as their goddess and patron" ("Elle avait beaucoup [de sapience] et de science aussi, qu'elle entretenait toujours par ses continuelles études, les après dînées, et les leçons qu'elle apprenait des gens savants qu'elle aimait par-dessus toute sorte de gens, aussi l'honoraient-ils comme leur Déesse et Patronne").[31]

His portrayal of her as a "goddess" among "learned scholars" perhaps drew Lafayette to this personage and inspired her to make Marguerite's marriage a primary event in *La Princesse de Clèves*. (Mézeray only mentions the alliance and does not provide a portrait of Marguerite.) But after elevating the princess to the level of "patron" within the court, Brantôme switches strategies and depicts her as a marital pawn in the political arena:

> She had a noble and lofty heart; King Henri once wanted to marry her to M. de Vendôme, first prince of the blood, but she answered that she would never marry the subject of the king, her brother. This is why she remained single for so long, until through the peace treaty between the two Christian and Catholic kings she was married to M. de Savoie, to whom she had aspired for a long time.

> Elle eut le coeur grand et haut, le Roi Henri la voulut une fois marier à Monsieur de Vendôme premier Prince du sang, mais elle fit réponse qu'elle n'épouserait jamais le sujet du Roi son Frère,

voilà pourquoi elle demeura si longtemps à prendre parti, jusqu'à
ce que par la paix faite entre les deux Roi Chrétiens et Catho-
liques, elle fut mariée avec Monsieur de Savoie, auquel elle aspi-
rait il y avait longtemps. (1:324)

Brantôme's description is ambiguous. On the one hand, he allows
Marguerite to object openly to one marriage and thus help shape her
own destiny. But on the other hand, he positions the princess as an
object for marital and political consumption, and he compounds the
objectification by reiterating the passive voice: "Marguerite was found
by M. de Savoie to be very pleasant, and very suitable for his son"
("Elle fut trouvée fort agréable à Monsieur de Savoie et fort propre
pour son fils" [1:325]). Marguerite passes from one patriarchal realm
to another, as the first male agent, Henri, is replaced by another,
M. de Savoie. Her own volition, although mentioned—"to whom she
had aspired for a long time"—is not the principal reason for her marriage. Brantôme concludes his portrait on a note of political commentary by lamenting Henri's decision to surrender Piedmont in return
for the marriage. He attributes this mistake to the fact that "King
Henri wanted peace and loved his sister so much that he did not want
to spare anything to establish her appropriately" ("le Roi Henri désir-
ait la paix et aimait sa soeur, qu'il ne voulut rien épargner pour la bien
colloquer" [1:325]). The alliance is placed in a negative light. According to Brantôme, the loss of Piedmont can be attributed to the irra-
tional whims of a king who "loved his sister."

Lafayette's rendering of Marguerite presents some fascinating
contrasts with her source in terms of historical perspective. First, instead of beginning with Marguerite's learnedness, she begins with
Marguerite's relationship to her brother: "This princess was very respected because of her influence over the king her brother; and this
influence was so great that, in negotiating the peace treaty, the king
agreed to give up Piedmont in order to have her marry the duc de
Savoie" ("Cette princesse était dans une grande considération par le
crédit qu'elle avait sur le roi son frère; et ce crédit était si grand, que le
roi en faisant la paix consentait à rendre le Piémont, pour lui faire épouser le Duc de Savoie" [42]). Lafayette chooses to focus first on the
princess's power and respected position within the court at large—
power and respect that derive from the "influence she had over the
king," which the novelist is careful to leave ambiguously vague. She
does not specify the king's feeling as love, as did Brantôme, and the
open nature of "influence" ("crédit") allows that term to be interpreted as having a meaning broader than the merely personal: Lafayette's ellipsis permits the reader to view Marguerite's "crédit" as
more political, in the conventional sense of the term, and as perhaps
deriving from her abilities as a political leader. This interpretation is
strengthened by the grammatical constructions used in the discus-

sion of Marguerite's marriage alliance. Only once is Marguerite the object—"to have her marry." In the rest of the passage, Marguerite is the agent, capable of making her own decisions and exerting "her influence over the king": "Even though she had always wanted to marry, she had wanted to marry only a sovereign, and she had therefore refused the roi de Navarre when he was the duc de Vendôme; [she] had always hoped for M. de Savoie. She had maintained a liking for him" ("Quoi qu'elle eût désiré toute sa vie de se marier, elle n'avait jamais voulu épouser qu'un souverain, et elle avait refusé pour cette raison le roi de Navarre lors qu'il était duc de Vendôme; et avait toujours souhaité Monsieur de Savoie. Elle avait conservé de l'inclination pour lui" [42]). Lafayette deletes the political implications of the marriage alliance to stress Madame's active role in the decision-making process.

Only at the end of Marguerite's portrait does the novelist evoke what in Brantôme's opening were the princess's personal qualities. Again Lafayette abridges her source: "As she had a lot of personality and great judgment concerning beautiful things, she attracted all the well-bred people, and there were certain hours when the whole court was at her residence" ("Comme elle avait beaucoup d'esprit et un grand discernement pour les belles choses, elle attirait tous les honnêtes gens, et il y avait certaines heures où toute la cour était chez elle" [42]). In condensing, Lafayette replaces Brantôme's precise references to Madame's intellectual qualities ("wisdom and knowledge") with valuable courtly attributes ("personality and . . . judgment concerning beautiful things"). In addition, Marguerite's personal influence is extended beyond Brantôme's "learned scholars" to "all the well-bred people." Thus, Marguerite is more fully integrated into the court and political arena and is transformed from the "goddess and patron" of an elite group of intellectuals to a presiding figure during "certain hours when the whole court was at her residence."

As is evident in Lafayette's revisionist depiction of marriage in *La Princesse de Clèves*, events of the court arena determine general history. In fact, occurrences situated outside of this realm, such as the wars of religion, are excluded from the novel unless they can be placed within the court and its personal politics. When well-known political events are alluded to in the novel, they are most often portrayed as resulting from personal relationships. For example, Lafayette attributes Henri II's fatal desire to joust against the comte de Montgomery to the king's love for Catherine: "[Henri II] answered that it was out of love for her [Catherine] that he was going to joust again, and he entered the arena" ("Il répondit que c'était pour l'amour d'elle qu'il allait courir encore et entra dans la barrière" [142]).[32] Lafayette's elevation of marriage and her concomitant personalization of this affair of state reflect the governing principle of her history, which privileges the court.

If this conception of history does not appear "very nationalistic or political," as Chamard and Rudler remark, that is not because of omission or negligence on Lafayette's part but, rather, because she refocuses events to revise the very notion of "politics" ("politique"). In *La Princesse de Clèves*, the particular intrigues of the court become the privileged realm of political activity. This reformulation of history creates a sphere of power not normally seen in official sixteenth- and seventeenth-century historical narrative—a sphere that, more importantly, is dominated by women. In a world where "every day there was hunting and tennis, ballets, races, or similar entertainment" ("c'étaient tous les jours des parties de chasse et de paume, des ballets, des courses de bagues, ou de semblables divertissements" [35]), where marriage is the predominant political tool, it is not surprising to find women maintaining a position equal to, and frequently stronger than, that of men in the balance of power. Lafayette includes only events, such as marriage, where women play an instrumental role, as opposed to battles, from which they are absent. In addition, she carefully filters official history to choose mainly marriages arranged by political matriarchs, avoiding marriages that depict women as political pawns of male heads of state. Only one marriage, that of Elisabeth to Philippe II of Spain, is clearly brought about by royal authority, with female desire subjugated. Even in this instance, a woman, Mary Stuart, eventually persuades Elisabeth to agree (83). The other marriages either reflect women's wishes or are actually arranged by women. References to the alliances arranged by women are frequent. As we have seen, Diane de Poitiers negotiates the marriage of her granddaughter to M. d'Anville (38). Also highlighted is the negotiating power of the duchesse de Lorraine, who, "while working toward the peace treaty, had also worked for the marriage of the duc de Lorraine, her son. It was concluded with Mme Claude de France, the king's second daughter" ("en travaillant à la paix, avait aussi travaillé pour le mariage du duc de Lorraine, son fils. Il avait été conclu avec Mme Claude de France, second fille du roi" [52]). Even the aborted marriage alliance between Elizabeth of England and Nemours has its origins in female desire and prerogative, as Elizabeth is "so filled with the duc de Nemours's reputation" ("si remplie de la réputation du duc de Nemours" [40]) that she initiates the negotiations. The "dynastic quality" that distinguishes Lafayette's history from her sources is accompanied by a predominantly female presence. Marriage ultimately controls dynasties and, in Lafayette's historical vision, marriage is frequently governed by women.

In *La Princesse de Clèves*, history is composed to feminize the conception of dynasty and, indeed, the conception of history itself. Furetière defines *dynastie* as "a historian's term that is used for a line or series of kings who have reigned one after another in a realm" ("terme d'Historiens, qui se dit d'une lignée ou suite de Rois qui ont régné l'un après l'autre dans un Royaume"). This conventional and patriarchal notion of dynasty is overturned in *La Princesse de Clèves* in favor of a history where women are the sovereigns of the royal court family. Lafayette chooses to situate her fiction in a period of transition to female rule, which the opening words of the novel underscore, specifying the time as "the last years of the reign of Henri II" ("les dernières années du règne de Henri second" [35]). To reinforce this ominous allusion to the king's death, the novelist weaves the prediction of Henri's demise into the historical fabric of her novel. By the end of the third part of *La Princesse de Clèves*, the patriarchal presence is effectively erased as the fatal blow is dealt by the duc de Montgomery. Catherine de Médicis assumes power as regent, accompanied by her daughter-in-law, Queen Mary Stuart. In fact, upon the death of Henri II a series of female reigns began—the regencies of Catherine de Médicis and Marie de Médicis, followed in the seventeenth century by that of Anne d'Autriche. To accentuate this passage to female political dominance, Lafayette concentrates on female rivalry at the moment of the king's death: "M. de Nemours led the queen mother. As they began to walk, she stepped back a few steps and said to the queen, her daughter-in-law, that she should go first, but it was easy to see that there was more bitterness than a sense of propriety in this compliment" ("M. de Nemours menait la reine mère. Comme ils commençaient à marcher, elle se recula de quelques pas et dit à la reine, sa belle-fille, que c'était à elle à passer la première; mais il fut aisé de voir qu'il y avait plus d'aigreur que de bienséance dans ce compliment" [144]). Lafayette lends her own interpretation to this scene, for the remark that Catherine de Médicis speaks with bitterness is not in any of her sources.

But Lafayette does not wait until the end of her history to undermine patriarchal power. When Catherine de Médicis becomes regent, she simply replaces the woman whose "colors and initials . . . appeared everywhere" ("couleurs et chiffres . . . paraissaient partout" [35]) from the opening pages of the novel—Diane de Poitiers. I will return later to the capital importance of this historical figure. For now, it is important to note that from the initial portrait, this history is dominated by Diane de Poitiers, in particular, and by the female members of the court, in general. Although the king is the first historical character mentioned, in the opening paragraph he is described uniquely with respect to Diane de Poitiers. Next, he is linked with the queen, whom he "had married while he was still the duc d'Orléans, while his older brother was the dauphin, who then died at Tournon, a prince whose birth and whose great qualities destined him to fill with dignity the place of François I, his father" ("avait épousée lorsqu'il était encore duc d'Orléans, et qu'il avait pour aîné le dauphin, qui mourut à Tournon, prince que sa naissance et ses grandes qualités destinaient à remplir dignement la place du roi François premier, son père" [35]). Lafayette thus includes Henri's genealogy, as Mézeray does, but whereas Mézeray begins with this lineage, she inserts it almost as an aside in her description of Catherine. She further diminishes Henri's importance by implicitly contrasting him with his brother, who would have been a worthy replacement for their father. Henri II's own qualities are not mentioned, and this ellipsis leads the reader to view him as a less-worthy second choice. Henri remains subservient to Catherine, who radiates the power usually associated with a king. Henri II "stayed at the queen's every day during the salon" ("demeurait tous les jours chez la reine à l'heure du cercle" [36]). For the next four paragraphs, Henri II continues to be the only male figure, while Mlle de la Marck, Catherine de Médicis, Elisabeth de France, Mary Stuart, and Madame, the king's sister, all make their entrance. This historical opening is decidedly feminocentric and corresponds to Montpensier's displacement of the king in her *Divers Portraits*. Only after depicting the people who are presented as the central figures on the historical stage does Lafayette turn to the general configuration of the court—the "princes and . . . great noblemen" ("princes et . . . grands seigneurs"). By separating the key female figures from the mass of portraits of those who constitute "the adornment and the admiration . . . of their century" ("l'ornement et l'admiration . . . de leur siècle"), Lafayette privileges the female component at court. She also limits the male courtiers' importance with the temporally precise "their century," whereas the preceding paragraph dedicated to the female figures begins, "Never has a court had so many beautiful people" ("Jamais cour n'a eu tant de belles personnes" [36]). Furthermore, like the king, the majority of men presented are described according to their relationship to the gallant, courtly world, with little attention accorded to their military prowess and feats.

Lafayette devotes much of her historical portrayal to describing the relationships among these *femmes fortes*. More important, she accentuates the political nature of these relationships and their effect on the court as a whole. By putting these affairs forward as the sole interest of the court as a whole, Lafayette further politicizes gallantry. The political realm of general history is evoked here exclusively in terms of the court and women's relationships:

> Ambition and gallantry were the soul of this court and occupied men and women equally. There were so many special interests and so many different plots, and women had so much a part in it that love was always mixed with business and business with love. No one was at peace or indifferent. One tried to get ahead, to please, to serve, or to injure. One did not know boredom or idleness and one was always occupied by pleasure or intrigue. The

women had their own attachments to the queen, to the queen dauphine, to the reine de Navarre, to Madame, the king's sister, or to the duchesse de Valentinois. Inclinations, reasons of propriety, or temperament created these different attachments.

L'ambition et la galanterie étaient l'âme de cette cour, et occupaient également les hommes et les femmes. Il y avait tant d'intérêts et tant de cabales différentes, et les dames y avaient tant de part que l'amour était toujours mêlé aux affaires et les affaires à l'amour. Personne n'était tranquille, ni indifférent; on songeait à s'élever, à plaire, à servir ou à nuire; on ne connaissait ni l'ennui, ni l'oisiveté, et on était toujours occupé des plaisirs ou des intrigues. Les dames avaient des attachements particuliers pour la reine, pour la reine dauphine, pour la reine de Navarre, pour Madame, soeur du roi, ou pour la duchesse de Valentinois. Les inclinations, les raisons de bienséance ou le rapport d'humeur faisaient ces différents attachements. (44–45)

Especially striking in this description is the universality bestowed on events that are normally relegated to the margins of the historical record. "The soul of this court"—the only historical locale represented, to the exclusion of the battlefield—is composed uniquely of "ambition" and "gallantry." Moreover, in this principally female realm, ambition and gallantry "occupied men and women equally," reinforcing the remark that Henri was "at the queen's every day during the salon." "Men and women" become further generalized as the subjects become "no one" and "one," and the universality is reinforced by repetition: "One tried . . . one did not know . . . one was always occupied by pleasure or intrigue." Seemingly no other occupations exist for these historical figures. The interests of the court are those in which women play the central role, a fact Lafayette further reinforces by enumerating the women's "own attachments." Such "attachments," and not attachments among men or even fidelity to the king, are the "soul of this court."

The historical "background" Lafayette constructs contrasts sharply with that found in any of her sources, primarily in its vision of politics dominated by women. Although Lafayette's sources supplied her with the basic facts about these female attachments, Lafayette herself made the decision to exclude all other information to highlight women's influence in the political realm. Throughout the history in her novel, Lafayette frequently alludes to women's power, and she chooses, amends, and even transforms her sources to create this specific ambience. Even the English court mirrors this political outlook, as Elizabeth accedes to the throne (40). The adjective "political" ("politique") to describe these women's actions recurs more frequently in *La Princesse de Clèves* than in Lafayette's many sources. She extends female influence at court to include the entire realm of politics.

Lafayette's revisions of her sources work to replace a patriarchal realm with an alternative, female-dominated one. To supplement her perspective and further develop it for her fiction, she inserts what critics normally view as historically grounded "digressions." The three principal figures of these internal narratives—Diane de Poitiers, Mary Stuart, and the vidame—are important forces behind the novel and their stories reflect the same principles as those underlying the overall historical climate. The three *H/histoires* are the models from which Lafayette's exceptional princess constructs her implausible world.

Historical "Digressions": A Feminist Pedagogy

In the history of the critical reception of *La Princesse de Clèves*, the internal narratives, like the historical introduction, have consistently met resistance and been viewed as unnecessary additions reminiscent of the outmoded heroic novel. It is especially interesting to note that, during the seventeenth-century quarrel, certain historical episodes draw the most critical fire within the general condemnation of the inclusion of history. Valincour asks his addressee,

> Don't you think . . . that Mme la Dauphine talks too much? Isn't she just wasting her time by recounting the history of the king of Scotland and Henry VIII to that young girl?

> Ne trouvez-vous pas . . . que Madame la Dauphine parle trop? N'est-ce bien perdre son temps, que d'aller conter à cette jeune fille l'histoire du Roi d'Ecosse, et de Henri VIII? (130)

□   □   □

> I hope you don't mind if I skip over the conversation that Mme de Chartres has with her daughter or, more precisely, her long introduction about the life of Mme de Valentinois: it is 32 or 33 pages long, during which there is not one word that is useful for Mme de Clèves's story.

> Vous voulez bien, Madame, que je passe la conversation de Madame de Chartres avec sa fille, ou plutôt la longue introduction qu'elle lui donne sur la vie de Madame de Valentinois: elle est de 32 ou 33 pages, dans lesquelles il n'y a pas un mot qui soit utile à l'histoire de Madame de Clèves. (138–139)[33]

Fontenelle pinpoints the same two episodes. He sees them, and the historical content in general, as detracting from what critics want to interpret as the "real" story. Fontenelle even speaks of intentional maliciousness on the part of the author, suggesting that she cruelly and unjustly forces the reader to divert her/his attention from M. de Nemours and Mme de Clèves for no apparent reason.[34] Only M. de Clèves's story of Mme de Tournon is accepted as a necessary addition to the fiction because it prefigures the princess's declaration scene. Yet, curiously, this is the one internal narrative that is not founded upon history. The narratives devoted to Diane de Poitiers, to Mary Stuart, and to the vidame—rejected as superfluous—are verifiable history. Lafayette includes these episodes and rewrites her authoritative sources to enhance subtly and subversively the story of her princess. By denying a purpose to these histories, critics separate the fiction from the history that this author uses to create her fiction's full significance and implications.[35]

Diane de Poitiers

From the beginning of the novel, Lafayette empowers one woman especially with ultimate political authority: Diane de Poitiers. The court superficially bears her imprint: "The colors and initials of Mme de Valentinois appeared everywhere" ("Les couleurs et les chiffres de Mme de Valentinois paraissaient partout" [35]). But these "colors and initials" do more than mark the court superficially. Throughout the novel, they tint and regulate all the court's functions and relationships. Diane de Poitiers is the political matriarch in this court arena, where one cannot define "political" without taking women into account. The duchess in fact usurps the monarch's absolute power, as she governs not only the various court factions but also Henri II himself: "Those whom favor or business brought close to [Henri] could not maintain [their position] unless they submitted themselves to the duchesse de Valentinois, and even though she no longer had youth or beauty, she governed him with such absolute authority that one can say she was mistress of his person and of the state" ("Ceux que la faveur ou les affaires approchaient de sa personne ne s'y pouvaient maintenir qu'en se soumettant à la duchesse de Valentinois, et, quoiqu'elle n'eût plus de jeunesse ni de beauté, elle le gouvernait avec un empire si absolu que l'on peut dire qu'elle était maîtresse de sa personne et de l'Etat" [38]). This description of Diane's political hold comes after a lengthy enumeration of the principal male court figures (36–38). In culminating the list with the duchess, Lafayette structurally subsumes them under the absolute empire of the king's mistress, just as she verbally renders Henri a mere object of matriarchal authority: "She governed him."[36] The entire court assiduously seeks the duchess's favor: "The court was divided between MM. de Guise and the connétable, who was supported by the princes of the blood. Both parties had always hoped to win the duchesse de Valentinois" ("La cour était partagée entre MM. de Guise et le connétable, qui était soutenu des princes du sang. L'un et l'autre parti[s]

avai[en]t toujours songé à gagner la duchesse de Valentinois" [38]).
Lafayette's characterization of the duchess's power goes beyond that
found in her sources. Mézeray, for example, says, "That shameless
Diane . . . was involved in everything, she could do anything" ("Cette
impudique Diane . . . se mêlait de tout, elle pouvait tout").[37] The
novelist enhances this general description by specifying that Diane is
"mistress of his person and of the state," thus rendering her omnipotent in both court and state, the particular and the public realms.

The political connotations of the dominance that Lafayette confers on the king's mistress within the context of this passage are reinforced later, at the time of Henri's death. In Lafayette's account of
the scene, Diane is again at the apex of the court hierarchy, and "mistress"/"maîtresse" and "master"/"maître" are actually conflated:

> The queen did not permit Diane to see the king, and sent some-
> one to her to demand the seals of this prince and the crown jew-
> els that she had. This duchess asked if the king were dead; and as
> she was told no: "I do not yet have a master," she responded,
> "and no one can force me to return what his trust has placed in
> my hands."

> La reine ne permit point qu'elle vît le roi et lui envoya demander
> les cachets de ce prince et les pierreries de la couronne qu'elle
> avait en garde. Cette duchesse s'enquit si le roi était mort; et
> comme on lui eut répondu que non:—Je n'ai donc point encore
> de maître, répondit-elle, et personne ne peut m'obliger à rendre
> ce que sa confiance m'a mis entre les mains. (143–144)

Diane's proud response reinforces the political structure present
throughout the novel. She does "not yet have a master." The temporal precision of the phrase underscores the fact that she herself has
been the "maître," and she will be the "maître" as long as Henri II
breathes. Diane is mistress and master of the patriarch.

The intentionality behind this elevation of Diane de Poitiers is
evident if one compares the preceding passage with its source, Brantôme's *Les Vies des dames galantes*. In Brantôme, Diane is the faithful
mistress instead of the political master:

> Someone was sent to ask her to return some rings and jewels
> that belonged to the crown. She suddenly asked the messenger,
> "What, is the king dead?" "No, Madame," the other responded,
> "but he will be soon." "As long as he has the least bit of life," said
> she, "I want my enemies to know that I do not fear them in the
> least; and that I will not obey them as long as he is alive. I am still
> unconquerable; but when he dies, I do not want to live after him;
> and all the bitterness that can be given to me will be sweetness
> compared to my loss."

On lui envoya demander quelques bagues et joyaux qui appartenaient à la Couronne, et eut à les rendre. Elle demanda soudain à Monsieur l'harangueur, comment, le Roi est-il mort? Non, Madame, répondit l'autre, mais il ne peut guère tarder. Tant qu'il lui restera un doigt de vie donc, dit-elle, je veux que mes ennemis sachent, que je ne les crains point; et que je ne leur obéirai tant qu'il sera vivant. Je suis encore invincible de courage; mais lors qu'il sera mort, je ne veux plus vivre après lui; et toutes les amertumes qu'on me saurait donner ne me seront que douceurs au prix de ma perte.[38]

Brantôme makes Diane's power entirely contingent upon the king. Moreover, he concentrates on the emotional bond between Diane and her lover and excludes any reference to her political influence.

Throughout the novel, Lafayette adopts the opposite stance. In *La Princesse de Clèves*, Diane's political maneuvers and strategies are privileged over her amorous relationship to the king. Lafayette chooses to concentrate on Diane's own exceptional qualities, negating the conventional association of female influence with ephemeral beauty to emphasize female political power. Diane's influence remains supremely unaffected by time: "The duchesse de Valentinois was part of all pleasures, and the king had the same attraction and the same attentions for her as in the beginning of his passion" ("La duchesse de Valentinois était de toutes les parties de plaisir, et le roi avait pour elle la même vivacité et les mêmes soins que dans le commencement de sa passion" [55]). Even though "she no longer had youth or beauty," traditional sources of female power, she continues to dominate the king absolutely. Diane does not fear being replaced by younger, more beautiful women such as Mary Stuart, for, according to Lafayette, "a too-long experience had taught her that she had nothing to fear concerning the king" ("une trop longue expérience lui avait appris qu'elle n'avait rien à craindre auprès du roi" [44]). By dissociating Diane from the traditional personal sources of female power, Lafayette can extend the duchess's influence further into the political realm. She uses the duchess to feminize her general portrayal of political power.

The figure of Diane de Poitiers thus presides over Lafayette's depiction of this sixteenth-century court and indirectly provides the fictional princess with an example of a woman's self-determination. Lafayette strengthens the duchess's influence within the novel by devoting the first internal narrative to her rise to power. The author's choice of Mme de Chartres to be the narrator of this history is curious, given the fact that Diane de Poitiers incarnates the antithesis of the model of female behavior that Mme de Chartres urges on her daughter.[39] For Mme de Chartres has taught the princess to value virtue and marital fidelity over all other qualities:

[Mme de Chartres] told [the princesse de Clèves] about men's in-sincerity, their deceptions, and their infidelity . . . and she made her see, on the other hand, the tranquility that accompanied the life of a virtuous woman, and to what degree virtue gave bril-liance and nobility . . . but she also made her see how difficult it was to maintain this virtue, [that it was possible only] by ex-tremely mistrusting oneself and by taking great care to attach oneself to the one thing that can make a woman happy, which is to love her husband and to be loved by him.

Elle lui contait le peu de sincérité des hommes, leurs tromperies et leur infidélité . . . et elle lui faisait voir, d'un autre côté, quelle tranquillité suivait la vie d'une honnête femme, et combien la vertu donnait d'éclat et d'élévation . . . mais elle lui faisait voir aussi combien il était difficile de conserver cette vertu, que par une extrême défiance de soi-même et par un grand soin de s'at-tacher à ce qui seul peut faire le bonheur d'une femme, qui est d'aimer son mari et d'en être aimée. (41)

Diane de Poitiers's story, as told by Mme de Chartres, provides a rival pedagogy that Lafayette endows with the same maternal authority as Mme de Chartres's lessons on virtue. This mother does not condone or understand the protagonist of her historical exemplum, but her lengthy discourse implicitly offers the princess an attractive alterna-tive model upon which to base her own comportment.

The unconventional nature of Diane's *puissant* relationship to Henri is what provokes this maternal pedagogy. Diane is a woman who transcends the boundaries of society and nature. The princess inquires of her mother, "Is it possible, madame, . . . that the king has been in love with her for such a long time? How could he be attracted to someone who was so much older than himself?" ("Est-il possible, madame, . . . qu'il y ait si longtemps que le roi en soit amoureux? Comment s'est-il pu attacher à une personne qui était beaucoup plus âgée que lui?" [55]). Mme de Chartres, in an explanation that displays one of the few moments of temporal precision in the novel, elevates the duchess over temporal constraints:

This passion has lasted over twenty years without being altered by either time or obstacles.

Il y a plus de vingt ans que cette passion dure sans qu'elle ait été altérée ni par le temps, ni par les obstacles. (57)

□　□　□

For the past twelve years . . . she has been the absolute mistress of everything.

Depuis douze ans . . . elle est maîtresse absolue de toutes choses. (59)

Diane defies time by perpetuating a seemingly eternal passion. In her description, Mme de Chartres's language echoes the narrator's: Diane is "absolute mistress" ("maîtresse absolue"), mistress and master in politics as well as in love.

Mme de Chartres's history of Diane de Poitiers provides an additional portrait of the court as a whole, a portrayal that confirms and enhances the perspective of Lafayette's history. She includes Diane's political negotiations, concentrating on the rivalry between Diane de Poitiers and the duchesse d'Estampes: "There had never been such hatred as between these two women" ("Jamais il n'y a eu une si grande haine que l'a été celle de ces deux femmes" [58]). Mme de Chartres specifies that "these intrigues were not limited to women's quarrels" ("ces intrigues ne se bornèrent pas seulement à des démêlés de femmes" [58]). This hatred is the cause of divisions at court that involve even the future king: "The division of the two brothers [the dauphin and the duc d'Orléans] gave the duchesse d'Estampes the idea of siding with the duc d'Orléans so that he would support her before the king, against the duchesse de Valentinois. . . . This created two plots in the court" ("La division des deux frères donna la pensée à la duchesse d'Estampes de s'appuyer de M. le duc d'Orléans pour la soutenir auprès du roi contre Mme de Valentinois. . . . Cela fit deux cabales dans la cour" [58]). As in the opening portrayal of the court, women are placed at the center of the political arena. Their influence extends even beyond the court and into the battlefield. For example, Mme de Chartres depicts the duchesse d'Estampes's effect on one particular battle:

The dauphin led the king's army in Champagne and reduced the emperor's army to such an extreme state that [the emperor's soldiers] would have all perished if the duchesse d'Estampes, fearing that such great gains would make us refuse a peace treaty and an alliance with the emperor favoring the duc d'Orleans, had not secretly warned the enemy to attack Epernay and Château-Thierry, which were full of supplies. They did so and thus saved their entire army.

M. le Dauphin commandait alors l'armée du roi en Champagne et avait réduit celle de l'Empereur en une telle extrémité qu'elle eût péri entièrement si la duchesse d'Estampes, craignant que de trop grands avantages ne nous fissent refuser la paix et l'alliance de l'Empereur pour M. le duc d'Orléans, n'eût fait secrètement avertir les ennemis de surprendre Epernay et Château-Thierry qui étaient pleins de vivres. Ils le firent et sauvèrent par ce moyen toute leur armée. (58–59).

Women affect the battles of public history as well as cause the battles of the particular, courtly realm. Mme de Chartres, like the narrator of the historical introduction, focuses on female intrigue and rivalry for the power and dominance that ultimately determine political alliances and affairs. In this *Histoire*, Mme de Chartres's intent is to instruct her daughter about the decisive victory of Diane de Poitiers over the duchesse d'Estampes. When François I died, "the duchesse de Valentinois took complete vengeance on that duchess, and on all those who had displeased her" ("la duchesse de Valentinois se vengea alors pleinement, et de cette duchesse, et de tous ceux qui lui avaient déplu" [59]). Having disposed of her rival, Diane is then free to exercise her authority over all, including the king. "Her power over the king's mind appeared more than when he was the dauphin. . . . She has control of positions and affairs" ("Son pouvoir parut plus absolu sur l'esprit du roi qu'il ne paraissait encore pendant qu'il était dauphin. . . . Elle dispose des charges et des affaires" [59]). Diane's biography is designed to illustrate the principle that love and personal alliances change the course of history.

Mme de Chartres ends her pedagogical history with a description of the king's attachment to this domineering mistress, putting her emphasis on Henri's fidelity: "Jealousy, which is bitter and violent in everyone else, is sweet and restrained in him because of the extreme respect he has for his mistress" ("La jalousie, qui est aigre et violente en tous les autres, est douce et modérée en lui par l'extrême respect qu'il a pour sa maîtresse" [59–60]). Although Mme de Chartres finds Henri's fidelity incomprehensible, she nonetheless values it. This fidelity, founded upon his "extreme respect . . . for his mistress," is the main reason Diane de Poitiers reigns supreme.[40] This eternal love, although inexplicable, is important for the freedom it affords Diane to exercise her power. As long as she retains Henri's respect, she remains at the top of the court hierarchy. Although women are thus occasionally dependent upon male authority in Lafayette's history, they nonetheless dominate men. The position at the top is passed on from one woman to another—from the duchesse d'Estampes to Diane de Poitiers to Catherine de Médicis. If a woman is mistress or, occasionally, queen, she pulls the strings guiding history within this female political genealogy.

The lesson Mme de Chartres passes on to the princess with this historical exemplum is thus threefold. Enduring passion such as that between Diane de Poitiers and Henri II is attainable, albeit exceptional. Fidelity founded upon passion is to be valued for providing women with the freedom to determine their own actions. Finally, a

woman can rise above court opinion and control her own destiny—
and, in the case of Diane de Poitiers, the destiny of a nation. As shall
become apparent, the princess internalizes her mother's historical
discourse and takes Diane de Poitiers as a model for her own heroic
actions.

Mary Stuart: Lafayette's Historienne

A second female historical figure shares the spotlight with Diane
de Poitiers in *La Princesse de Clèves*. Mary Stuart's role differs from that
of Diane de Poitiers in that she is privileged more for her qualities as a
female historian than for her role in the political arena. Yet Mary
Stuart's pedagogy is as essential to the princess's development as
Mme de Chartres's history.

Mary Stuart is responsible for integrating the princess into the
court. Mme de Clèves frequents the dauphine's salon, where she
learns of the various court intrigues and alliances. Mary Stuart proves
to be a willing and forthcoming teacher, as she apprises the princess
of present court politics as well as of past events. The princess learns
of Nemours's rejection of a possible marriage with Elizabeth of England from Mary Stuart's account of this historically accurate event
(81–82). In addition, Lafayette grants the dauphine the narrative authority to recount two internal narratives: the story behind her own
position at court, and the story of Anne Boleyn.

Mary Stuart's first historical intercession is provoked by her lack
of influence over the princess's own marriage. The dauphine's wishes
are thwarted by Catherine de Médicis and Diane de Poitiers. Mary
Stuart laments, "I am so hated by the queen and by the duchesse de
Valentinois that it is rare when either they or those under their rule do
not block all the things I desire" ("Je suis si haïe de la reine et de la
duchesse de Valentinois qu'il est difficile que, par elles ou par ceux
qui sont dans leur dépendance, elles ne traversent toujours toutes les
choses que je désire" [48]). Mary Stuart explains this "women's quarrel" ("démêlé de femmes") with the story of yet another quarrel, as
she describes her mother's disruption of three European courts. In
her feminocentric account, Mary ascribes the rivalry among the kings
of France, England, and Scotland to their desire for her mother, who
was very beautiful and seduced all of them: "This overturning [of the
promise that her mother would marry Henry VIII of England] almost
severed relations between the two kings [of England and of Scotland].
Henry VIII could not get over not having married the queen my
mother" ("Il s'en fallait peu même que ce manquement ne fît une rupture entre les deux rois. Henri VIII ne pouvait se consoler de n'avoir
pas épousé la reine ma mère" [48]). Mary's intricate and complex
description of the political maneuvers to secure her mother's hand
underscores the general revisionist tenet of Lafayette's historical foun-

dation, according to which women are the motivating forces behind the events of general history.

Mary Stuart continues her role of particular historian to the princess by recounting Anne Boleyn's misfortunes. This history complements the implicit pedagogy of Mme de Chartres, for Anne Boleyn's story is one of passion and jealousy which ultimately ends in the protagonist's death. The dauphine emphasizes Anne's initial power in attaining the position of queen, forming a marriage alliance that had grave political consequences: "Anne Boleyn, who was ambitious, viewed the divorce as a way by which she might reach the throne. . . . Finally, after nine years of passion, Henry married her without waiting for the dissolution of his first marriage . . . and dragged all England into the unfortunate turmoil in which you see it" ("Anne de Boulen, qui avait de l'ambition, regarda le divorce comme un chemin qui la pouvait conduire au trône. . . . Enfin, après une passion de neuf années, Henri l'épousa sans attendre la dissolution de son premier mariage . . . et entraina toute l'Angleterre dans le malheureux changement où vous la voyez" [90–91]). But just as Diane de Poitiers's power results partly from Henri II's fidelity, so Anne Boleyn's downfall results from her husband's inability to remain faithful to his passion. Convinced that his wife was having an affair with her own brother, and already in love with Jane Seymour, Henry VIII "tried this queen and her brother, had them beheaded, and married Jane Seymour. He than had many wives, whom he rejected or had killed" ("fit faire le procès à cette reine et à son frère, leur fit couper la tête et épousa Jeanne Seymour. Il eut ensuite plusieurs femmes, qu'il répudia ou qu'il fit mourir" [91]). Mary Stuart's "digression" thus provides a corollary to that of Mme de Chartres, as both *Historiennes* pinpoint the need for fidelity if a woman is to maintain her position, and the danger of founding one's power on passion. Mary Stuart also implicitly warns against marriage, for Henry VIII's nine-year passion vanished almost as soon as he married his mistress.

Mary Stuart's function in the novel is thus to complement the maternal discourse and to recount history from the same particular perspective that the narrator does. In addition, with this principal figure, Lafayette highlights female literary initiatives. In telling of Anne Boleyn, Mary Stuart identifies Marguerite de Navarre as a literary figure—"whose stories you have seen" ("dont vous avez vu les contes")—a characterization not found in any of Lafayette's sources.[41] This addition can be interpreted as the author's homage to a female literary precursor. Mary Stuart embodies the woman writer who follows in Marguerite's footsteps. In spirit and tone, the end of Mary's account of Anne Boleyn's history even resembles the conclusion of many of Marguerite's stories: "Henry VIII died, having become tremendously fat" ("Henri VIII mourut, étant devenu d'une grosseur prodigieuse" [91]). In choosing Diane de Poitiers and Mary Stuart as her principal female personages, Lafayette foregrounds woman as political matriarch and as literary creator. The princess will follow Mary Stuart's lead as she writes her own story and joins the tradition of women H/*historiennes*.

The Vidame and Nemours: Historical Warnings

A third historical figure hovers over *La Princesse de Clèves* and is granted a historically verifiable internal narrative. From the beginning of the novel, the vidame de Chartres is present as a strong, primarily negative influence on the princess.[42] Like Diane de Poitiers and Mary Stuart, the vidame fulfills a pedagogical function for his fictional niece. The lesson to be inferred is one of male deception in the volatile world of passion.

From the beginning of the novel, the vidame's position in the princess's life is ambiguous. As an uncle with numerous court connections, he would seem to be the perfect person to help Mlle de Chartres with her plans for marriage. However, he proves to be an obstacle to the most desirable alliances. The cardinal de Lorraine opposes the union of his son, the chevalier de Guise, with Mlle de Chartres because "this cardinal had such hate for the vidame, which was secret but which afterward exploded" ("ce cardinal avait une haine pour le vidame, qui était secrète alors, et qui éclata depuis" [46]). It is also because of the vidame that the protagonist loses Diane de Poitiers's favor: "[Diane de Poitiers] had such hatred for the vidame de Chartres . . . that she could not favorably consider someone who bore his name" ("Elle avait tant de haine pour le vidame de Chartres . . . qu'elle ne pouvait regarder favorablement une personne qui portait son nom" [44]). Even the princess's marriage to M. de Clèves is endangered by the vidame: M. de Clèves's father, the duc de Nevers, opposes the marriage because he does not want to anger Diane de Poitiers (44). M. de Clèves eventually succeeds in marrying the princess, but only because his father conveniently dies.

The negative nature of the vidame is clarified in the internal narrative of his amorous intrigues. He incarnates infidelity, as he passes from one mistress to the next and deceitfully covers his tracks by playing with appearances. His relationship with the queen is founded on appearances (*paraître*) as, contrary to his promises, he hides a relationship with another woman from the possessive and critical eyes of the queen (104). Lafayette embellishes the facts of general history, which records that the vidame was the confidant of Catherine de Médicis but does not develop the relationship. She constructs her account to stress the fusion of politics and love. The vidame loses his position at court when the queen discovers his true character. Lafayette portrays the queen as the one who, although deceived by the duplicitous vidame, ultimately defeats him. Catherine sets the conditions for their relationship—conditions that the vidame is incapable of meeting. She explains,

> I want you to be one of my friends . . . but in giving you this position, I do not want to be ignorant about your affections. See if you want to buy [my friendship] for the price of telling me about them: I will give you two days to think about it.

> Je veux que vous soyez de mes amis . . . mais je ne veux pas, en vous donnant cette place, ignorer quels sont vos attachements. Voyez si vous la voulez acheter au prix de me les apprendre: je vous donne deux jours pour y penser. (104)

□ □ □

> Remember that I want your complete fidelity; and I do not want you to have any friends except those that are agreeable to me, and I want you to abandon every other care except that of pleasing me.

> Souvenez-vous que je veux la vôtre [confidence] toute entière; que je veux que vous n'ayez ni ami, ni amie, que ceux qui me sont agréables, et que vous abandonniez toute autre soin que celui de me plaire. (106)

In the figure of Catherine de Médicis, the princess receives another role model, a *femme forte* who is capable of determining her surroundings and those of the people around her. Lafayette altered the accounts of her sources to emphasize Catherine's power over the vidame's fate. Le Laboureur suggests that the vidame's disgrace is due to the Cardinal de Lorraine as well as to the queen: "I don't know if the cardinal dismissed him, or if he left to satisfy his weakness which made him love all the women at court. In any case, [the vidame's disgrace] contributed to his ruin, either because the queen loathed his behavior or because the cardinal suspected a recurrence" ("Je ne sais pas si ce Cardinal l'en éloigna, ou si lui-même il lui quitta la place pour satisfaire à son inconstance, qui le rendit amoureux de toutes les Dames de la Cour. Quoi qu'il en soit, cela aida beaucoup à sa ruine, soit que la Reine eût conçu quelque aversion de sa conduite, ou que le Cardinal se défiat de quelque retour").[43] Lafayette unequivocally places the power in Catherine's hands.

> As for the vidame de Chartres, his relationship with the queen was ruined and, either because the cardinal de Lorraine had already become master of her mind or because the affair of this letter, which showed her that she had been deceived, helped her discover the other tricks the vidame had already played on her, it

is certain that he was never able to be reconciled with her. Their relationship was broken, and she then caused his ruin during the Amboise conspiracy, in which he was entangled.

> Pour le vidame de Chartres, il fut ruiné auprès d'elle, et, soit que le cardinal de Lorraine se fût déjà rendu maître de son esprit, ou que l'aventure de cette lettre qui lui fit voir qu'elle était trompée, lui aidât à démêler les autres tromperies que le vidame lui avait déjà faites, il est certain qu'il ne put jamais se raccommoder sincèrement avec elle. Leur liaison se rompit, et elle le perdit ensuite à la conjuration d'Amboise, où il se trouva embarrassé. (118)

As with the other "digressions," a lesson for the princess is embedded in the vidame's story. Appearances are deceiving, especially when they involve men's fidelity. A woman must follow the lead of Catherine de Médicis and determine her own relationships to men.

Lafayette draws the example of the vidame closer to the princess's own story by linking this shady character with Nemours, thus casting a shadow on "nature's masterpiece" ("un chef-d'oeuvre de la nature" [37]). From the beginning of the novel, the vidame is described in relation to the duke: "The vidame was the only one worthy of comparison with M. de Nemours" ("Il était seul digne d'être comparé à M. de Nemours" [37]). Lafayette refers to him as Nemours's "intimate friend" ("ami intime" [61, 66]). The vidame chooses Nemours to be the recipient of his pitiful tale and his accomplice in the effort to trick the queen. Upon hearing the story of the vidame's amorous exploits, Nemours himself draws a parallel between their two characters: "I am accused of not being a faithful lover and of having many affairs at the same time; but you go so far beyond me that I would not have dared even to imagine the things you have undertaken" ("On m'a accusé de n'être pas un amant fidèle et d'avoir plusieurs galanteries à la fois; mais vous me passez de si loin que je n'aurais seulement osé imaginer les choses que vous avez entreprises" [111]).

Nemours perhaps has not gone as far as his friend in the game of love, but Lafayette suggests that the possibility of such behavior is in Nemours's character. In her introduction, Nemours is described as having "such a tendency toward gallantry" ("tant de disposition à la galanterie") and consequently "many mistresses" ("plusieurs maîtresses" [37]).[44] The vidame's story and its connection to Nemours emphasize the possibility that the duke could be as despicable as his friend. This possibility partially materializes a few pages later, when Nemours reciprocates the vidame's confidence and indiscreetly repeats to "the man at court whom he loved the most" ("l'homme à la cour qu'il aimait le mieux" [126]) the princess's declaration to her husband, which he had secretly overheard: "Unable to keep to himself the amazement he had felt over Mme de Clèves's action, he told the vidame about it" ("Enfin ne pouvant renfermer en lui-même l'étonnement que lui donnait l'action de Mme de Clèves, il la conta au vidame" [126]).

Like the letter written by the vidame's mistress, the princess's story becomes an object for public consumption, thanks to male indiscretion.[45] She hears her own supposedly intimate discussion with her husband retold at court—made public by the vidame, who is incapable of keeping it to himself. In this way, Lafayette implicitly denounces both Nemours and the vidame and calls into question the characters of the two primary male personages. Valincour perhaps recognized this diminution of the male characters when he criticized this scene and Lafayette's depiction of Nemours. To Valincour, the retelling of the princess's story is done "at the expense of plausibility" ("aux dépens du vraisemblable" [50]) because a plausible Nemours would choose his confidant more carefully or would not reveal what he knows. Valincour queries, "But doesn't an adventure cost too much when it costs the hero of the book mistakes in judgment and behavior?" ("Mais une aventure ne coûte-t-elle point trop cher, quand elle coûte des fautes de sens et de conduite au Héros du livre?" [52]). Lafayette subverts the conventional mold of the hero.[46]

Through the internal narrative devoted to the vidame, Lafayette thus diminishes male power by simultaneously placing him and Nemours in a negative light and promoting a positive image of Catherine de Médicis. Like Diane de Poitiers, Catherine de Médicis controls her own plot. Lafayette highlights these two women to show that political power is generated from an interior, feminized space.

Feminized Historical Space

Lafayette reveals herself to be as gender-conscious in creating the theatres for her fictional princess's actions as in constructing the particular historical milieu of the introduction and internal narratives. She chooses specific historical places for the principal fictional events in order to develop her emphasis on female power. The locales of the determining fictional events are as gender-specific as the court.[47]

This historical fiction is oriented more toward description than toward action. Chamard and Rudler's research reveals Lafayette's extreme precision in describing historical details, as she remains as close as possible to her sources' descriptions of costumes and pageantry. For example, she scrupulously evokes the costumes and customs behind the two major historical events, the marriage of Madame to the king of Spain and the tournament that accompanies the festivities. She also evokes in detail the various locations, such as Coulommiers, where the fiction takes place. This attention to detail, specifically of physical locations, is a stylistic tendency of many seventeenth-century women writers, both memorialists and novelists. Like Montpensier and Villedieu, Lafayette constructs her history in such a way as to place depictions of history's actors and actresses and their various theatres in the forefront. She accentuates châteaux and salons—thus, interiors. In a fascinating article, Cuénin and Morlet-Chantalat remark that such descriptions of châteaux seem to be almost gender-specific.[48] They note that Saint-Réal, often cited as a proponent of particular history, does not include such descriptions in his novels but that the works of Scudéry, Villedieu, and Lafayette abound with them—a fact that is surely more than mere coincidence.

The choice of certain settings is far from gratuitous. *La Princesse de Clèves* presents a striking example of the importance that can be attached to descriptions of geographic locations. Cuénin reveals intriguing characteristics of one of the central stages in the novel, the princess's country estate at Coulommiers. This château is the setting for two of the most important scenes: the princess's declaration to her husband and her reverie in front of Nemours's portrait. Cuénin's research uncovers a conscientious effort on Lafayette's part to set these two key acts within a decor that would create another level of signification, besides linking the author herself with female memorialists and novelists.

The first reference to Coulommiers identifies it as "a beautiful house a day's journey from Paris that [M. and Mme de Clèves] were having *carefully* built" ("une belle maison à une journée de Paris, qu'ils faisaient bâtir avec *soin*" [120, my emphasis]). Two paragraphs later, the notion of "care" is reiterated with respect to this residence. Without care, M. de Nemours "got lost in the forest" ("s'égara dans la forêt" [120]), only to find himself conveniently near Coulommiers: "He reached the forest and wandered by chance along *carefully* constructed paths that he correctly judged led to the château" ("Il arriva dans la forêt et se laissa conduire au hasard par des routes faites avec *soin*, qu'il jugea bien qui conduisaient vers le château" [120, my emphasis]). The notion of careful construction appears yet again just before the princess's reverie scene: "[Mme de Clèves] went to Coulommiers; and as she left, she took *care* to have some large paintings brought there" ("Elle s'en alla à Coulommiers; et en y allant, elle eut *soin* d'y faire porter de grands tableaux" [152, my emphasis]). By repeating "care" and associating it with the château, Lafayette calls attention to her own work; her choice and use of this setting for the crucial events of her fiction are equally "careful" and deliberate.

Curiously, in situating these important scenes at Coulommiers, Lafayette abandoned the sixteenth-century milieu she had so meticulously researched and chose a residence that was not even in existence in 1558–1559, the year the action takes place.[49] Coulommiers, however, was very well known in the seventeenth century, so Lafayette expected its name to resonate in certain ways for her contemporaries.[50] According to Cuénin, Coulommiers "symbolizes, in the middle of the corruption of the court and of the century, a strength of spirit, a disdain for society, [and] piety" because of the activities of two of Coulommiers's illustrious occupants.[51] The first, Catherine de Gonzague, founded at least two convents, and the second, Marie d'Orléans-Longueville, sought the solitude of Coulommiers after the Fronde. Cuénin's interpretation of the significance of Coulommiers appears logical, especially because Lafayette portrays the château as a haven for the princess.

But piety and solitude are not the only connotations Lafayette hoped to evoke and exploit. Coulommiers has additional characteristics that take on special importance when seen in the overall context of women's history. First, Coulommiers was built by a woman, Catherine de Gonzague, the daughter of Henriette de Clèves, who transformed the château into a veritable monument to the glory of women, filling it with busts and statues of illustrious women from history and mythology.[52] The château continued its association with female historical figures with the next occupant, Marie d'Orléans-Longueville, the duchesse de Nemours, who played a very active role in the Fronde.[53] Lafayette is evoking not only a place of solitude but also, and more importantly, a milieu with specific affinities to female historical initiative. The "coincidence" (Cuénin's term) of the names Clèves and Nemours attests to Lafayette's meticulous attention to historical detail, and to her intentionality. The princess is onomastically identified with these illustrious women. In choosing such a historically charged setting, Lafayette indicates how the princess's actions should be interpreted. She makes it possible for the princess to be viewed as one of the heroic women who actually inhabited Coulommiers.

The crucial fictional events that take place at Coulommiers bear the imprint of the historical associations of the château and should be read with them in mind. Like the real historical figures who inhabited or ornamented Coulommiers, the princess is a heroic *femme forte* and acts in ways that Lafayette's contemporaries judged exceptional. She makes "a declaration that no one has ever made to her husband" ("un aveu que l'on n'a jamais fait à son mari" [122]), and she creates an ideal reverie of passion in front of Nemours's portrait. I will return to these central actions later.

Coulommiers is not the only domain associated with strong women that Lafayette chooses to foreground. The salons of Mary Stuart, Diane de Poitiers, Elisabeth de France, and Catherine de Médicis serve as the focal point for much of the action of *La Princesse de Clèves*. As we have seen, Lafayette characterizes the salons as rival centers of power focused on the principal court matriarchs. Politics are played out within circles that are centered on women but are far from female-exclusive.[54] Throughout *La Princesse de Clèves*, Lafayette privileges the salon milieu by situating a majority of the principal events within its confines. For instance, the princess is introduced to the court through these circles and meets the prince de Clèves at Madame Elisabeth's salon (43). The king's horoscope predicting his death is recounted at one of the queen's gatherings (87). The salons serve as places of communication for the advancement and regression of the love affair between the princess and Nemours. It is in the salon of Mary Stuart that Nemours receives his first encouragement and that the princess consciously acts upon her attraction to him by refusing to go to the maréchal de Saint-André's ball when she learns that Nemours believes a mistress should not attend (61–63). The dauphine's salon later provides the stage for the crucial retelling of the princess's confession to her husband, a scene at which the princess herself is present as addressee and critic (132). Finally, the prince de Clèves's suspicions about his wife and Nemours are confirmed in the same salon (149).

The salons, especially that of Mary Stuart, thus constitute an important influence within the fictional drama. At the same time, they are the place where history/*Histoire* is linked to story/*histoire* as the princess receives historical information about the court. This pedagogical function is performed through the recounting of stories, so that the oral transmission of historical knowledge is emphasized through the art of conversation. In composing her historical text, Lafayette thus shifts the focus of her history in order to become a woman's historian, echoing the efforts of Montpensier, among others. Although historical, the "context" of the fiction in Lafayette's novel has many strong ties with the seventeenth century. The novel's time period in fact resembles her own.

Historical Time: Formation and Negation

Literary critics past and present frequently attribute Lafayette's use of history to a desire to provide a rigid time frame for the novel's fictional events. But the use of history to establish time is not so easily explained. Like the historical context, the past's temporality undergoes reformulation. Critics inadvertently recognize this when they cite Lafayette's chronological inaccuracy and express contempt for her apparent inability to present history as a past world rather than as a reflection of her present one.[55] Such assessments point to the ambiguous nature of historical time in *La Princesse de Clèves*. When closely examined, the novel's conception of historical time appears simultaneously constructed and deconstructed in order to affect and reflect the fictional component of her novel.

Lafayette designs a precise temporal structure, choosing to situate her fictional drama within the span of one year. The year 1558–1559 is evoked in a variety of ways that illustrate the care she took to construct the temporal framework from her sources. Specific events, such as Queen Elizabeth's accession to the throne and the death of Henri II, identify the year and ground the fictional story in it. Lafayette develops certain events, such as the marriage between Elisabeth de France and the king of Spain and the tournament, to establish further the fictional story in a precisely defined sixteenth century.

Critics such as Ann Moore and Chamard and Rudler, who have examined the time frame, attest to the novelist's conscientiousness with respect to time.[56] Her sources provide an exact chronological framework for the construction of the novel. Mézeray's *Abrégé*, for example, precisely delineates chronology and even goes so far as to insert the exact months of events in the table of contents and present a continuous column of dates in the margins of the work.[57] Lafayette uses the temporality of her sources to make her fiction accord with the historical referent. Numerous critics have remarked on the exceptional relationship between the two. Malandain even goes so far as to say that "never has the relationship between history and fiction been so close and so musical."[58] Moore carefully plots the historical chronology against the fictional one and concludes that "the chronological structure is symmetrical, with the fictional and the historical crises occurring together near the year's mid-point."[59]

But the harmonious relationship delineated by Malandain and Moore is in fact deceptive. For although the time frame does orient the fiction chronologically, the general conception of time is problematic. Lafayette's historical chronology is carefully researched but does not simply correspond to the author's desire to create a historical time frame for her fiction. Lafayette makes her work difficult to verify because, as with Montpensier's *Mémoires*, there are few references to precise dates. The lack of a specified chronology can also be attributed, perhaps, to Lafayette's desire to keep open the option of changing dates when it would serve her fiction. The prince de Clèves, for example, conveniently dies four years earlier in the novel than he did in history, and Elizabeth falls in love with Nemours a few months earlier.[60] These deviations indicate Lafayette's desire to fuse her historical narrative and her fictional story to force the reader to interpret the two together.

From the beginning of the novel, Lafayette deconstructs the precise historical time frame of her sources by portraying a sixteenth-century court with the values and terms of the seventeenth century. As we have seen, she posits gallantry—associated more with Louis XIV's court than with a Renaissance atmosphere—as the guiding

force behind Henri II's court, and even Nemours becomes the quintessential seventeenth-century hero. Throughout the novel, the novelist strengthens the initial transposition of the sixteenth to the seventeenth century, for example, introducing Coulommiers anach-
ronistically to evoke certain connotations for her seventeenth-century
readers. In addition, the novel is intentionally situated at a time when
the names of the principal historical characters could still be recognized and have impact because of their continuation into the seventeenth century. Names such as Mlle de Montpensier and Mme de
Longueville, especially, evoke the well-known seventeenth-century
frondeuses perhaps more than their sixteenth-century ancestors. Such
references stimulate the reader to draw parallels between the historical events and similar occurrences in the seventeenth century. The
names of Montpensier and Longueville mentioned in the context of
Elisabeth's marriage to the king of Spain could call to mind Louis
XIV's marriage to a Spanish princess, given the fact that the seventeenth-century princesses of those two names had been present at
Louis's marriage.[61]

The seventeenth century is also present in Lafayette's focusing
of power on women. As we have seen, she glorifies a female intelli-
gentsia through the figure of Mary Stuart, known as "the educated
queen," who herself names Marguerite de Navarre, her predecessor
in that role.[62] The relationship between the two periods is strengthened by the fact that *H/histoires* are frequently recounted in Mary
Stuart's salon in the novel, just as Lafayette's *H/histoire* and those of
other novelists were told or discussed in seventeenth-century salons.

Lafayette presents a nonlinear vision of history in which human
nature and personalities, the foundation of her historical perspective,
are seen as continuous, determining factors of history. History is not
measured in years but, rather, in changes to court personages, positions, and intrigues.[63] This conception of time contrasts with the
accepted notions of historical time in the seventeenth century. Historical narrative under the Sun King depicts the past as a linear progression of events that lead to the apogee of Louis XIV's reign. The
narratives of royal historiographers function as affirmations of a historical progression towards perfection.[64]

Perrault's *Parallèle des Anciens et des Modernes* (1687) is an extreme
although not atypical example of this tradition. Perrault clearly states
that his purpose for writing his manifesto of modernism is to delineate precisely the nation's rise to a political and cultural superiority unparalleled in the past: "The objective is to examine in detail all arts
and sciences to see the degree of perfection they attained during the
apogee of antiquity, and at the same time to observe what reasoning
and experience have since added, and especially during our century"

("Car il s'agit d'examiner en détail tous les beaux Arts et toutes les Sciences, de voir à quel degré de perfection ils sont parvenus dans les plus beaux jours de l'antiquité, et de remarquer en même temps ce que le raisonnement et l'expérience y ont depuis ajouté, et particulièrement dans le Siècle où nous sommes").[65] Perrault aims to prove that "today we have a more perfect knowledge of all arts and all sciences than ever before" ("nous avons aujourd'hui une plus parfaite connaissance de tous les Arts et de toutes les Sciences, qu'on ne l'a jamais eue" [preface]). In this context, Lafayette's conception of time is politically subversive, as she places Henri II's court on a par with that of Louis. Valincour recognizes this deviance and criticizes Lafayette for not following the rules:

> The first four lines were extremely surprising to me. Can someone who knows today's court as well as the author seems to know it say that *magnificence and gallantry have never appeared in France with such brilliance as during the last years of Henri II's reign?* Without a doubt, he [the author] forgot that he was living during the reign of Louis XIV. He believed he was still in the time during which the story took place. Otherwise it would not have been difficult for him to say, *gallantry and magnificence had not yet appeared in France with such brilliance,* etc. In this way he would have given all the justice he felt necessary to Henri II's reign, and would not have insulted the reign during which we live.

> Les quatre premières lignes m'ont extrêmement surpris. Un homme qui connaît aussi bien la Cour d'aujourd'hui, que l'Auteur paraît la connaître, peut-il dire que *la magnificence et la galanterie n'ont jamais paru en France avec tant d'éclat que dans les dernières années du règne de Henri II?* Sans doute il ne s'est pas souvenu, qu'il vivait sous le règne de Louis XIV. Il a cru être encore au temps du Prince, sous lequel s'est passée l'histoire qu'il a écrite. Sans cela il ne lui eut pas été difficile de dire, *la galanterie et la magnificence n'avaient encore jamais paru en France avec tant d'éclat, etc.* Par ce moyen il eut rendu au règne de Henri II toute la justice qu'il s'est cru obligé de lui rendre, et n'aurait point fait d'injure au règne sous lequel nous vivons. (5–6)

Lafayette's rejection of a precisely delineated, linear time frame is perhaps due to the overall vision of history she seeks to present. In fact, the court of Henri II is portrayed as transcending time. The characteristics of this court resemble those of Louis XIV's as well as those of another, temporally undefined world. In the opening portrayal of the court, the novelist avoids mentioning specific dates and substitutes the temporal expression *jamais,* or "ever/never," to qualify this courtly world and those who people it:

Magnificence and gallantry have *never* appeared in France with
such brilliance. . . . *Never* has a court had so many beautiful
people. . . . A charm . . . that has *never* been seen except in
him. . . . The greatest magnificence that one has *ever* seen. . . .
Never has a woman been so charming and attractive.

La magnificence et la galanterie n'ont *jamais* paru en France avec
tant d'éclat. . . . *Jamais* cour n'a eu tant de belles personnes. . . .
Un agrément . . . que l'on n'a *jamais* vu qu'à lui seul. . . . La plus
grande magnificence qu'on eût *jamais* vue en un particulier. . . .
Jamais femme n'a eu tant de charmes et tant d'agrément dans sa
personne. (35, 36, 37, 39, 89; my emphasis)

Whereas Lafayette announces her intention of describing those who
were "the ornament and admiration of *their century*" ("l'ornement et
l'admiration de *leur siècle*" [36, my emphasis]) and consequently of a
past removed from her own society, in reality she portrays a series of
timeless paragons. In fact, *jamais* becomes the distinguishing characteristic of Henri II's court. In positing this time as the pinnacle of history, Lafayette in effect removes her history from its chronological
context and places it in the vague territory of *jamais*, of no time and
all time.

This temporality corresponds to the conception of time in the
fictional drama of the princess. *Histoire* and *histoire* are thus parallel
constructions. For, like the women established as historical exempla,
the princess transgresses time's boundaries and is presented as existing outside of time. The princess's fictional *histoire* is marked with the
same temporal adjective as the court she enters.[66] She possesses "a
brilliance that has *never* been seen except in her" ("un éclat que l'on
n'a *jamais* vu qu'à elle" [41, my emphasis]). "Mme de Chartres admired her daughter's sincerity . . . for *never* had someone had such
noble and natural sincerity" ("Mme de Chartres admirait la sincérité
de sa fille . . . car *jamais* personne n'en a eu une si grande et si naturelle" [51, my emphasis]). And like the sixteenth-century court personages, the princess transcends conventions of time regarding age:
"Even though she was extremely young, she had already had many
marriage proposals" ("quoiqu'elle fût dans une extrême jeunesse,
l'on avait déjà proposé plusieurs mariages" [41]).

As the novel progresses, the fictional story of the princess is
more and more located in this exceptional space. There are fewer references to history and more of an effort to portray the princess and
her story as exceptional. The term *jamais* frequently reappears to
qualify the various aspects of the fictional story, echoing this distinguishing quality of the historical court. Above all, the actions viewed
as *invraisemblable* by seventeenth-century readers—the princess's

declaration to her husband and her final rejection of Nemours—are marked with "jamais":

> I [the princess] am going to make a declaration to you that no one has *ever* made to her husband. . . . I have *never* shown any sign of weakness. . . . Consider [the fact] that to do what I am doing, one must have more friendship and more respect for a husband than one has *ever* had.

> Je vais vous faire un aveu que l'on n'a *jamais* fait à son mari. . . . Je n'ai *jamais* donné nulle marque de faiblesse. . . . Songez que pour faire ce que je fais, il faut avoir plus d'amitié et plus d'estime pour un mari que l'on en a *jamais* eu. (122, my emphasis)

□   □   □

> You seem to me [the prince] to be more worthy of respect and admiration than any woman who has *ever* been in the world; but I also consider myself to be the most unhappy man that has *ever* existed. . . . You make me unhappy by the greatest sign of fidelity that a woman has *ever* given to her husband.

> Vous me paraissez plus digne d'estime et d'admiration que tout ce qu'il y a *jamais* eu de femmes au monde; mais aussi je me trouve le plus malheureux homme qui ait *jamais* été. . . . Vous me rendez malheureux par la plus grande marque de fidélité que *jamais* une femme ait donnée à son mari. (123, my emphasis)

The extraordinary qualities of this action are reinforced in the parallel declaration scene between Nemours and the princess. When the princess admits her love to Nemours, Lafayette again depicts her as an exceptional woman:

> As you want me to speak, I will do so with a sincerity that you will not easily find among persons of my gender. . . . I admit that you have awakened feelings in me that I did not know before seeing you. . . . I make this declaration to you with less shame because I am making it at a time when I can do so without sin.

> Puisque vous voulez que je vous parle . . . je le ferai avec une sincérité que vous trouverez malaisément dans les personnes de mon sexe. . . . Je vous avoue que vous m'avez inspiré des sentiments qui m'étaient inconnus devant que de vous avoir vu. . . . Je vous fais cet aveu avec moins de honte, parce que je le fais dans un temps ou je le puis faire sans crime. (170–171)[67]

This "time when I can do so without sin" is the princess's personally constructed temporal space. At this point in the novel, she has made her decision to reject Nemours and to write the end of her own story. She recognizes her refusal to be part of a world that differs from the one she constructs. "It is true . . . that I am sacrificing a lot for a duty that exists only in my imagination" ("Il est vrai . . . que je sacrifie beaucoup à un devoir qui ne subsiste que dans mon imagination" [175]). Within this personal world, time ceases to exist. The duality of historical time in the novel—its existence and its subversion—mirrors the princess's personal dilemma: should she give in to the expectations of her society or remain outside the boundaries of the court? In the end, the princess enters her own world, which is a product of the historical world present in the text. Her fictional story overwhelms the historical referent while continuing its principal themes. The turning away from verifiable history is emphasized by the fact that all references to history disappear by the fourth part of the novel, when the princess retreats to Coulommiers with her historical portraits.

The final paragraph posits the princess as a paragon of virtue:

> Mme de Clèves lived in a manner that made it seem she could never return [to the court]. She spent part of the year in this convent and the other at her home; but in a retirement and occupied with activities more pious than those of the strictest convents; and her life, which was relatively short, left inimitable examples of virtue.

> Mme de Clèves vécut d'une sorte qui ne laissa d'apparence qu'elle pût jamais revenir. Elle passait une partie de l'année dans cette maison religieuse et l'autre chez elle; mais dans une retraite et dans des occupations plus saintes que celles des couvents les plus austères; et sa vie, qui fut assez courte, laissa des exemples de vertu inimitables. (180)

Although this ending underscores the exceptional qualities of the princess, it is not implausible, given the historical context Lafayette composes for her. Because of Lafayette's choice and rewriting of history, the princess's unparalleled qualities do not alienate her from all historical referents. *Histoire* and *histoire* are both out of the ordinary, *invraisemblable*, but *vraisemblable* within the economy of the novel.

The historical world that Lafayette develops from her many sources and the personal world the princess creates are complementary. Both offer an alternative order in which the patriarchal presence is displaced—and even eliminated—to establish a female-dominated world. Lafayette offers the princess as exemplum possessing the same authority as history because her actions are generated from official history. The ideal world, elevated to the degree of perfection inherent in *jamais*, expresses Lafayette's feminist pedagogy founded upon a revised notion of *vraisemblance*.

AGAINST CRITICAL NORMS: LAFAYETTE'S RESCRIPTED NOTION OF PLAUSIBILITY

When history and story in La Princesse de Clèves are interpreted together, the debate that followed the novel's publication can be viewed as an attack on a female notion of vraisemblance and on the maxims Lafayette advances. Valincour's judgment that the princess and her fiction are invraisemblable is a clear illustration of the use of the concept of vraisemblance for literary and societal censorship. In his Lettres, Valincour appropriates the concept of vraisemblance to prescribe the acceptable boundaries of female comportment in an effort to counter the example this novelist offers of a woman who intentionally steps outside those boundaries.

The prescriptive aspect of vraisemblance is not immediately apparent in definitions of the term. Furetière designates vraisemblance as the "quality or appearance of truth" ("caractère ou apparence de vérité"); thus, a vraisemblable action is one "that has the appearance of truth, that is in the realm of possibilities of events that have occurred or will occur" ("qui a apparence de vérité, qui est dans la possibilité des choses arrivées ou à arriver"). But as this definition illustrates, the concept does not correspond entirely to truth. Furetière's emphasis on "appearance" reflects the distance between vraisemblance and vérité. In fact, the example he offers to illustrate vraisemblance clearly distinguishes between the two: "The adventures in novels and in plays must be vraisemblable rather than true" ("Les aventures des Romans et des pièces dramatiques doivent être plutôt vraisemblables que vraies").

Furetière's example points to the prevalent use of vraisemblance to evaluate literary works in the seventeenth century. As we have seen, novelists have recourse to history to instill this essential quality. But historical truth alone does not ensure plausibility. As Huet remarks in his Traité sur l'origine des romans, "Plausibility, which is not always found in history, is essential for the novel" ("La vraisemblance qui ne se trouve pas toujours dans l'Histoire est essentielle au roman").[68] Huet's formulation alludes to the complex relationship between vraisemblance and vérité in the developing critical canon for the novel. In their analyses of the genre, critics attempt to elucidate what Furetière refers to as "the appearance of truth." Their commentaries reveal that, when employed for judging the novel, this appearance consists of a coupling of plausibility with the elusive notion of bienséance, or propriety. This combination of plausibility and propriety is clear in Du Plaisir's definition of vraisemblance: "Vraisemblance consists of saying only that which is morally believable. . . . Truth is not always vraisemblable" ("La vraisemblance consiste à ne dire que ce qui est moralement croyable. . . . La vérité n'est pas toujours vraisemblable").[69] Du Plaisir's contemporary, Rapin, further distinguishes *vraisemblance* from *vérité* and underscores the prescriptive nature of the former: "Truth presents things as they are, and *vraisemblance* presents them as they should be" ("La vérité ne fait les choses que comme elles sont, et la vraisemblance les fait comme elles doivent être").[70]

Thus, inherent in the concept of *vraisemblance* is a notion of *bienséance* that can be seen as an essential factor in the condemnation of Lafayette's masterpiece as *invraisemblable*. As Genette defines *vraisemblance*, it is "an ideology, that is, a body of maxims and prejudices that constitute concomitantly a vision of the world and a system of values."[71] Likewise, Miller argues that the concept of *vraisemblance* corresponds to a set of maxims both societal and literary, and thus that an action that is *invraisemblable* is one that does not correspond to a maxim.[72] The critical standard of *vraisemblance* is in reality a means of governing literary production and of making it conform to a system of values existing outside of the works themselves. A work is plausible insofar as it reflects the maxims of seventeenth-century society. And a text must be *vraisemblable* because it must not only conform to these values but also transmit them, given its dual purpose of pleasing and instructing.[73]

When Valincour exclaims at one point that "there is no truth in the entire work, except for a few passages from French history which, in my opinion, should not be there at all" (88), he is implicitly censoring Lafayette's mixture of fact and fiction. But given the rules governing novels, Valincour's admonition is incomprehensible. In fact, the story of the princess provokes Valincour to reject the critical constraints of *vraisemblance* and to wish that this particular fiction did not have any connection with reality. For, in his words, "Nothing shocks a reader more than to see presented as true something that is not true at all and that is even completely false" ("Il n'y a rien qui choque davantage un lecteur que de voir qu'on lui propose comme véritable, une chose qui ne l'est point, et qui est même entièrement fausse" [96]). Valincour does not wish to see *La Princesse de Clèves* as true history or even as plausible fiction. He rejects Lafayette's use of history because the resulting composition is not "morally believable," to borrow Du Plaisir's phrase.

Valincour's reaction attests to the fact that Lafayette constructs a text that transgresses seventeenth-century ideology. Presenting himself as society's spokesman, Valincour isolates many extraordinary and "unnatural" events in Lafayette's narrative, all of which can be seen as offering alternative modes of female behavior. Valincour finds the princess's trip to the jeweler shocking because she is unaccompanied and is given a task unsuitable for a woman her age: "Competent women maintain that a sixteen-year-old girl is never allowed to match gems; that the only thing a girl can do at that age is choose ribbons

and trimmings. . . . . In short, this is not plausible" ("Les femmes ha-
biles soutiennent qu'on n'a jamais laissé à une fille de seize ans, le
soin d'assortir des pierreries; que tout ce que l'on peut faire à cet âge-
là, c'est de choisir des rubens et des garnitures. . . . Enfin cela n'est
pas vraisemblable" [9–10]). The princess is thus given too much inde-
pendence and responsibility. Valincour also feels that Lafayette's heroine is too forward in her relationship with Nemours: "I am only
annoyed that the author has her make all the advances" ("Je suis
fâché seulement que l'Auteur lui fasse faire toutes les avances" [143]).
Nemours, in contrast, is not strong enough. According to Valincour,
his passion for the princess develops too slowly: "If only for the sake
of propriety, I would have preferred M. de Nemours's passion to have
begun at least a few days before that of Mme de Clèves. That would
have been more legitimate" ("Quand ce n'eut été que pour la bienséance, j'eusse voulu que la passion de M. de Nemours eût commencé au moins quelques jours avant celle de Mme de Clèves. Cela
eut été plus régulier" [13]). Valincour is thus primarily drawn to those
scenes in which characters do not conform to the behavior expected
of someone of their gender. Above all, the critic finds "extraordinary," "unnatural," and "implausible" those narrative moments designed to illustrate female expression and self-determination. This
logic leads him to condemn three scenes specifically: the princess's
declaration to her husband, her reverie of passion in front of
Nemours's portrait, and her final rejection of the duke. He calls the
declaration scene "one of the most extraordinary events one has ever
heard of" ("un des plus extraordinaires événements dont on ait jamais ouï parler" [39]) and asks, "Does one often find women who con-
fide in their husbands in this manner?" ("Se trouve-t-il souvent des
femmes qui fassent à leurs maris des confidences de cette sorte?"
[215]). Fontenelle echoes his contemporary's reaction, calling the declaration "the aspect that is so new and so remarkable" ("le trait si
nouveau et si singulier") and speaking of the princess's battle against
"an inclination she constantly tries to combat and overcome by making the strangest resolutions that the most austere virtue can inspire"
("un penchant qu'elle s'attache sans cesse à combattre et à surmonter
en prenant les plus étranges résolutions que la plus austère vertu
puisse inspirer").[74]

For his condemnation of the reverie scene, Valincour bestows
authority on a fictional woman of society. In the conversation he invents, he asks, "But, Madame, what do you think of Mme de Clèves,
who when she goes to Coulommiers has some large paintings brought
there. . . . I am sure you will answer first that this is inexcusable"
("Mais Madame, que vous semble de Mme de Clèves, qui en s'en allant à Coulommiers, y fait porter de grands tableaux. . . . Je suis sûr
que vous me répondrez d'abord que cela n'est pas excusable" [245–

246]). In her reply, the worldly woman does not entirely denounce the existence of the princess's passion but, rather, condemns the public expression of it: "To tell you the truth, the act appears to be a bit rash. . . . She would have done better to give her passion greater satisfaction, as long as it was more secret" ("A vous parler franchement, l'action me paraît un peu inconsidérée. . . . Elle eut mieux fait de donner à sa passion quelque satisfaction plus sensible, pourvu qu'elle eût été plus secrète" [247]). The reverie scene is "inexcusable" because the princess expresses her passion: "This is inexcusable; . . . it was already too much for a woman who prided herself on being virtuous to have such feelings in her heart, . . . she shouldn't have looked for ways to maintain and even strengthen them" ("Cela n'est pas excusable; . . . s'en était déjà trop pour une femme qui se piquait de vertu, que d'avoir dans son coeur les sentiments qu'elle avait, . . . il ne fallait pas chercher encore les moyens de les entretenir, et même de les fortifier" [246]). Female expression of passion is also at the heart of Valincour's criticism of the final scene between the princess and Nemours:

> Mme de Clèves says here everything that the duc de Nemours should say. She's the one who speaks to him about her passion . . . and who does it with a discipline and tranquility that do not reveal the uneasiness such a declaration always gives women who are somewhat reserved. One would think that she came only to speak and M. de Nemours to listen, whereas it should be just the opposite. . . . In truth, it would have been much more glorious for her to say nothing.

> Mme de Clèves dit ici tout ce que devrait dire M. de Nemours. C'est elle qui lui parle de sa passion . . . et qui le fait avec un ordre et une tranquillité qui ne ressent guère du trouble qu'un pareil aveu donne toujours aux femmes un peu retenues. L'on dirait qu'elle n'est venue là que pour parler, et M. de Nemours pour écouter au lieu que ce devrait être tout le contraire. . . . En vérité, il lui [Mme de Clèves] eut été bien plus glorieux de ne rien dire. (270–271)

The implicit maxims for female conduct become explicit. A woman should not usurp the male position of dominance. The preponderance of verbs related to expression (say, speak), which consistently have the princess as subject, points to her principal transgressive act: that of speaking. Nemours is relegated to the passive role of auditor, one that in fact parallels his earlier voyeuristic positions. He is present only "to listen" in this *monde à l'envers*.

In addition to speaking too openly, the princess transgresses Valincour's conception of acceptable female behavior by ultimately re-

rejecting a relationship that society would have condoned: "While her husband is alive she loves M. de Nemours. She does not find it a problem to have his portrait and to spend nights looking at it: and when her husband dies and she becomes her own mistress and can decide for herself what to do with her heart, she considers it a crime to give it to a man she passionately loves" ("Pendant la vie de son mari elle aime M. de Nemours; elle ne fait point de difficulté d'avoir son portrait, de passer les nuits à le regarder: et lors que par la mort de son mari elle devient maîtresse d'elle-même, et qu'elle peut disposer de son coeur, elle se fait un crime de le donner à un homme qu'elle aime passionnément" [273]). Valincour can envisage only two possibilities for a woman in the princess's position who becomes "her own mistress": she can either "follow these feelings to the end, . . . or stifle them and not reveal them at all" ("suivre ces sentiments jusqu'à au bout, . . . ou les étouffer et ne les point faire paraître" [272]). The princess remains an implausible mystery to him because she expresses a passion upon which she refuses to act according to expectations. "If she had enough strength to overcome her inclination, why didn't she have enough to hide it?" ("Si elle avait assez de force pour surmonter son inclination, pourquoi n'en avait-elle pas assez pour la cacher?" [271]) he wonders.

If Valincour finds the princess unacceptable, it is because he refuses another reading of the reverie scene and the final declaration, a reading in which the princess does not "overcome her inclination" but, rather, creates an ideal passion according to her own expectations and seeks to preserve it from destruction by an unworthy Nemours. Valincour negates the possibility that a woman who is "her own mistress" could write her own story outside of society's norms. Yet this is precisely what the three scenes that draw the most criticism suggest when they are interpreted in light of Lafayette's history. By composing the historical foundation of the novel to complement the fiction, Lafayette reinforces alternative maxims according to which a woman can construct and enunciate her own world. The historical text is written according to the same maxims. Lafayette highlights women as political leaders, creating their social world, and as storytellers in the salons, enunciating their vision of society.

Throughout *La Princesse de Clèves*, Lafayette anticipates and even provokes the accusation of *invraisemblable*. By subtly commenting on her H/*histoire*, she reveals that she is aware of the singularity of both her fiction and the history she constructs to make the fiction plausible. In each of the three principal scenes, she underscores her princess's exceptionality, which is generated by the historical subtext. Mme de Clèves's declaration to her husband at Coulommiers is the first step in her effort to write her own story following the example of her female models, especially Diane de Poitiers.[75] As we have seen,

Lafayette underscores the exceptional nature of the act by using the adverb *jamais* nine times in two pages, elevating the princess to the level of the inimitable. The prince's remark, "You make me unhappy by the greatest sign of fidelity that a woman has ever given to her husband," reveals that Lafayette intends the princess's action to be viewed as a positive act of strength, thus reflecting the heroic actions of Coulommiers's inhabitants. In fact, as DeJean has found, Lafayette uses the term *aveu*—avowal—in its legal sense of a loyalty oath.[76] Most translators and critics mistakenly translate it as "confession." But the princess's avowal is not due to weakness, nor is she in the guilty position of admitting fault, as "confession" connotes. In fact, she never admits any transgression and affirms only, "I will never displease you by my actions" ("Je ne vous déplairai jamais par mes actions" [122]). The princess's own rhetoric focuses on the strength of her act. She refers to herself as the "mistress of [my] behavior" ("maîtresse de [ma] conduite" [122]) and states: "The innocence of my behavior . . . gives me the strength" ("L'innocence de ma conduite . . . m'en donne la force" [122]) to make her declaration. She specifies that the declaration "has not been [made] out of weakness" ("n'a pas été [fait] par faiblesse" [123]).

Through this choice of vocabulary, Lafayette accentuates the exceptional, transgressive nature of the princess's act. The narrator remarks that "the singularity of such a declaration, for which she did not find a single example, made her see all the peril of it" ("la singularité d'un pareil aveu, dont elle ne trouvait point d'exemple, lui en faisait voir tout le peril" [126]). In addition, within the novel, Lafayette overtly denounces her fiction's *vraisemblance* by having the princess label her own declaration *invraisemblable*. Upon hearing her story, the princess says, "This story does not seem at all plausible to me, madame. . . . In fact I don't think it could be . . . and even if it were, where could it have been heard? One would not think that a woman who is capable of such an extraordinary thing would be so weak as to retell it" ("Cette histoire ne me paraît guère vraisemblable, madame. . . . Je ne crois pas en effet qu'elle le puisse être . . . et quand il serait possible qu'elle le fût, par où l'aurait-on pu savoir? Il n'y a pas d'apparence qu'une femme, capable d'une chose si extraordinaire, eût la faiblesse de la raconter" [132, 134]). The princess herself accentuates transmission of the story as the main criterion for the charge of *invraisemblable*. For, "even if it were" true, no plausible woman would "retell it." When she characterizes the declaration itself as "extraordinary," Mme de Clèves points to the inability of a self-determined woman to stay within the limits of plausibility and propriety. A woman who hopes to abide by the constraints of socially defined *vraisemblance* must not devise her own story.

Lafayette's history also reflects this preoccupation with women's creativity. As we have seen, Lafayette lends her authority as narrator to two other *Historiennes,* Mme de Chartres and Mary Stuart, so they can recount two histories. Lafayette can be seen as valorizing women as historians and storytellers. At one point especially, she overtly points to the tradition of women recounting history through conversation. Mme de Chartres says that she would have informed her daughter about the court earlier "if I did not fear . . . that you would say about me what is said about all women my age, that they like to tell stories of their past" ("si je ne craignais . . . que vous dis[s]iez de moi ce que l'on dit de toutes les femmes de mon âge, qu'elles aiment à conter les histoires de leur temps" [56]).

The second controversial scene, the princess's reverie of passion in front of Nemours's portrait, is the next step in her construction of her own implausible story. Once again, Lafayette subtly indicates the desired interpretation of the scene, this time by focusing our attention on the historical paintings the princess uses as props:

> She went to Coulommiers; and in parting, she took care to have transported there the large paintings that she had had copied from the originals that Mme de Valentinois had had made for her beautiful house at Anet. All the remarkable actions of the king's reign were in these paintings. Among others there was the siege of Metz, and everyone who had been valiant there was depicted very true to life. M. de Nemours was among this group.

> Elle s'en alla à Coulommiers; et, en y allant, elle eut soin d'y faire porter de grands tableaux qu'elle avait fait copier sur des originaux qu'avait fait faire Mme de Valentinois pour sa belle maison d'Anet. Toutes les actions remarquables, qui s'étaient passées du règne du roi, étaient dans ces tableaux. Il y avait entre autres le siège de Metz, et tous ceux qui s'y étaient distingués étaient peints fort ressemblants. M. de Nemours était de ce nombre. (152)

These paintings depict official history in its purest form—the military accomplishments of the king. Yet, in the famous voyeur scene at Coulommiers, the official history of depicting Nemours's military exploits at Metz is appropriated for the princess's particular—in the sense of both private and personal—interpretive reading. She

> took a candlestick and approached a large table in front of the painting of the siege of Metz, where the portrait of M. de Nemours was. She sat down and began to look at this portrait with such attention and reverie as only passion can give.

> prit un flambeau et s'en alla, proche d'une grande table, vis-à-vis du tableau du siège de Metz, où était le portrait de M. de Nemours;

elle s'assit et se mit à regarder ce portrait avec une attention et
une rêverie que la passion seule peut donner. (155)

Within the idyllic confines of Coulommiers, the princess freely creates her own work, a reverie of perfect, eternal passion that cannot be
destroyed by the whims of an untrustworthy Nemours. Public history
serves to create particular history, as the princess transforms her historical props with a vision that comes from female models. The historically grounded female pedagogy that enables the princess to
compose this *H/histoire* is evoked through the reference to Diane de
Poitiers, whose affair with the king is the referent for the princess's
own desire for fidelity. Significantly, Lafayette intentionally deviates
from history here, for these paintings never decorated Diane de
Poitiers's château at Anet.[77] Lafayette grounds this important action in
history to make it appear more plausible. She directs the reader to interpret the scene through her historical "digression" dedicated to
Diane de Poitiers, the most powerful figure at court and the symbol in
the novel of a woman who has managed to write her own story. Lafayette thus endows the princess's reverie with female creativity.

   This crucial scene can be read as a *mise-en-abîme* of Lafayette's
own narrative strategy, for, like her heroine, Lafayette constructs her
fiction using a historically verifiable framework. Lafayette is thus authorizing women writers both to create their fictions using history
and to revise history. She advocates the historical novel for her female
contemporaries as a means of transcribing and prescribing the world
according to a different premise of *vraisemblable* behavior for women.

   The final scene in which the princess rejects Nemours is also designed to illustrate the creative powers of female self-expression and
the transformation of a woman into an active writing subject. In re-
nouncing Nemours, the princess is again motivated by a desire to retain control over her own plot. She refuses Nemours primarily because
she does not believe he can live up to the ideal passion she has created. She explicitly states her belief:

> The certainty that I will no longer be loved by you the way I am
> now seems to me to be such a horrible misfortune that, even if I
> did not have insurmountable reasons for my duty, I doubt I could
> resolve to expose myself to that unhappiness. I know that you are
> free, and that I am, and that the situation is such that the public
> perhaps would have no reason to blame you, or me either. . . .
> But do men retain passion in these eternal engagements [mar-
> riage]? Must I expect a miracle in my favor?

> La certitude de n'être plus aimée de vous, comme je le suis, me
> paraît un si horrible malheur que, quand je n'aurais point de
> raisons de devoir insurmontables, je doute si je pourrais me

résoudre à m'exposer à ce malheur. Je sais que vous êtes libre,
que je le suis, et que les choses sont d'une sorte que le public
n'aurait peut-être pas sujet de vous blamer, ni moi non plus. . . .
Mais les hommes conservent-ils de la passion dans ces engagements éternels? Dois-je espérer un miracle en ma faveur? (173)

The princess's realization that Nemours's fidelity would be a "miracle" reveals that she is a good interpreter of her historical exempla,
especially the vidame's story, all of which disclose Nemours's unfaithful nature.[78] Mary Stuart's explanation of the English court and
her numerous allusions to Nemours's many love affairs—referring to
a personality trait that is historically accurate—all point to his inability to remain faithful and thus to conform to the princess's expectations of love based on the model offered by Diane de Poitiers. The
princess says, "You have already had many passions, you would have
more; I would not constitute your happiness" ("Vous avez déjà eu
plusieurs passions, vous en auriez encore; je ne ferais plus votre
bonheur" [174]). In this passage, the princess acknowledges society's
expectations but refuses to conform to them, choosing instead to
meet what she calls "an obligation that exists only in my imagination"
("un devoir qui ne subsiste que dans mon imagination" [175]). Her
reference to "devoir" echoes her mother's deathbed wish: "Consider
what you owe yourself" ("Songez ce que vous vous devez à vous-
même" [68]). The princess comes to the conclusion that the majority
of men must be excluded from the life she writes because the historical exempla force her to answer "no" to her own question, "Do men
retain passion in these eternal engagements?" Anne Boleyn provides
dramatic proof that passion and marriage cannot coexist. Mme de
Clèves does not reject her passion, as Valincour and many modern
critics argue, but channels it into a mode of action where it can be
perpetuated instead of destroyed. She assures Nemours that her love
in its ideal form will continue: "Believe that the feelings I have for you
will be everlasting" ("Croyez que le sentiment que j'ai pour vous
seront éternels" [175]).

Lafayette uses a meticulously constructed historical foundation
to ensure the *vraisemblance* of the princess's actions, subverting the expected use of history to propose her own conception of *vraisemblance*,
in which a woman can write her own story outside of society's norms
and openly express it. In denying the relevance of the history, critics
dismiss this threatening possibility in favor of a reading like Valincour's, for whom the princess is "a woman who fights against a passion that is stronger than she is, and that she is unable to conquer"
("une femme qui combat contre une passion qui est la plus forte, et
qu'elle ne saurait surmonter" [170]), an interpretation that places the
princess's actions into the desired category of plausible and accept-

able female behavior. In the eyes of a seventeenth-century public, an overly virtuous princess can more plausibly refuse her lover to keep the memory of her husband alive then from fear of rejection. Significantly, the only model Valincour can find for such an implausible character is that of another woman writer. He ridicules the princess's fear of Nemours's infidelity, saying, "Isn't that a great reason for not marrying a man? And since Sapho in *Le Grand Cyrus* has there ever been a woman with such a vision in her mind?" ("Voilà-t-il pas une belle raison pour ne pas épouser un homme? Et depuis la Sapho du *Grand Cyrus*, s'est-il rencontré une femme à qui cette vision soit tombée dans l'esprit?" [275]). Lafayette reaffirms the trajectory of a woman who is "her own mistress," as Scudéry had depicted in *Le Grand Cyrus*. Both Sapho and the princess live according to their own rules, passions, and desires.[79]

Given the implications of Lafayette's *vraisemblance* for women novelists as well as for her female contemporaries in general, it is not surprising that critics found it advisable to dismiss such actions as pure fiction and Lafayette's literary effort as a breach of critical norms. To Valincour, "Novelists are not permitted to abuse [poetic license] to the point of creating monsters and utopian dreams, nor to invent things that shock the mind of everyone who reads them" ("Il ne leur est pas permis d'en abuser, jusques à faire des monstres et des chimères, ni jusques à inventer des choses qui choquent l'esprit de tous ceux qui les lisent" [90]). Lafayette's fiction is not a "monstre" or a "chimère" if it is read in relation to the historical text she carefully constructs for it. But it is provocative, which is why there is still no "moyen de n'en pas parler."

Afterword

In 1667, Margaret Cavendish, duchess of Newcastle, an English contemporary of Montpensier, Lafayette, and Villedieu, prefaced her biography of her husband with a brief description of the state of historiography during the period. Within the genre as a whole, Cavendish isolates three types of narratives as "the chiefest. (1) general history. (2) national history. (3) particular history." She places her biography in the third category, which she characterizes as "the most secure because it goes not out of its own circle, but turns on its own axis, and for the most part, keeps within the circumference of truth."[1] According to Cavendish's distinctions, particular history is a separate version of historical events, a version she terms "heroical" as opposed to "political." In her view, particular history adds to the knowledge of the past but does not call into question "general" and "national" histories.

The works of Cavendish's French counterparts present a striking contrast to "particular" history as she defines it. Montpensier, Lafayette, and Villedieu all conceive of particular history as a political act. It is precisely while Louis XIV was consolidating his power that this group of women challenged his dominion and, especially, its representation in history. Their works are not just "a supplement to history," to return to Woolf's suggestion, but a conscious effort to confront the genre as a whole, especially its formulation in mid–seventeenth-century France, and to offer a revised version of it. These women appropriate the domain of particular history and use it for their own purpose: to oppose both a patriarchal system epitomized by Louis XIV and its written expression, history. These particular memoirs and novels are destined to go beyond their "own circle" to affect the very conception of history itself.

This collective effort among women writers to rewrite history is specifically a French seventeenth-century phenomenon that does not have a corollary in another country or another period. Kelly's recent reflections illuminate the underlying causes of this literary reaction. For Kelly, "an oppositional consciousness arises out of its antithesis, out of the discrepancy between the real and the ideal experienced by those who stand on the boundary of the dominant culture."[2] By the mid-seventeenth century, the "discrepancy between the real and the ideal" was especially apparent for French women within the political realm of the court. Women such as Montpensier, Lafayette, and Villedieu found themselves in a "real" milieu whose primary goal was to glorify a man who chose Apollo as his model. The "ideal" that contrasts with the "real" of Kelly's paradigm can be viewed as the preceding periods, when women like Diane de Poitiers, Catherine de Médicis, and the rebellious Montpensier asserted threatening matriarchal power. Having "as a weapon only the word," to use Montpensier's phrase, these women writers attempted to resurrect and glorify, on a literary level, the political struggles of the past.

In describing women's autobiographies, Stanton identifies their difference from men's as the very act of writing, a deviant and devious act when women hold the pens. In Stanton's words, "a symbolic order that equates the idea of the author with a phallic pen transmitted from father to son places the female writer in contradiction to the dominant definition of woman and casts her as the usurper of male prerogatives."[3] The female memorialists and novelists we have seen are double usurpers, for they not only seize the pen, but they also appropriate the ultimate expression of the universal symbolic order, history. By offering a revised vision of history, these women denounce the truth value of the official narrative and its superficial portrayal of power by disrupting the seemingly impenetrable relationship between monarch and history. They replace the traditionally male realm of political power, specifically war, with the court domain and reveal that this particular sphere is not a separate world but, rather, provides the key to a more complete vision of history and a better understanding of the course of human events. These writers challenge history as a reflection of a human universal and force us to take gender into account in interpreting their texts and forming our overall conception of history.

The rescripted history that emerges when memoirs and historical novels are read together addresses issues that transcend the elite group represented by Montpensier, Lafayette, and Villedieu and transcend, as well, their seventeenth-century context. Particular history as expressed in these texts is a feminized addition to the "so-called mainstream of historical writing" that concurrently calls into question the existence of this "mainstream," just as Davis does implicitly with "so-called."[4] These women force us to review our own literary, historical, and social categories—our conceptions of historical narrative and of what it should be, of male and female spheres of influence in the past and in the present, of literary genre distinctions, and of the purposes that inspired women to write.

These texts make clear the need to interpret women's works within their own cultural contexts. These memoirs and novels must be read in dialogue with the historical texts and contexts they were designed to oppose. They are part of a general phenomenon in seventeenth-century France that influenced men and women, writers of both sexes, and literary history as a whole. An explanation of this phenomenon is not complete unless women's participation is taken into account. Likewise, unless these works are read within their specific seventeenth-century context, the brand of feminism they project could appear naive, and these women's development of particular history could be mistakenly interpreted as a simplistic reaffirmation of the traditional gender dichotomy between public and private. To propose women and the court milieu as the motivating force of history may not appear revolutionary to a twentieth-century public accustomed to social history, but it certainly was in a world where social history did not yet exist and where history really was his-story. These women's memoirs and novels present a feminocentric history in the sense that women and the milieu they dominate, the court, replace the center of traditional history, the king and the military field. These literary endeavors are a herstory designed to illuminate not only women's past (satisfying Woolf's curiosity) but the past as a whole.[5]

In many respects, these seventeenth-century women writers create a feminist utopian dream, a *chimère*, as Valincour called *La Princesse de Clèves*. They write to oppose a system that relegates women to a sphere of silence, and they use a creative space, the novel and memoirs, to foster female expression. Even today, women writers continue to advocate literature as the space for feminist revisionary strategies. In *La Jeune Née*, Hélène Cixous, for example, seems to echo this vision:

> But somewhere else? There will be some elsewhere where the other will no longer be condemned to death. But has there ever been any elsewhere, is there any? While it is not yet "here," it is there by now—in this other place that disrupts social order, where desire makes fiction exist. . . . A place exists . . . that is not obliged to reproduce the system. That is writing. If there is a somewhere else that can escape the infernal repetition, it lies in that direction, where *it* writes itself, where *it* dreams, where *it* invents new worlds. (97, 72)

> Mais ailleurs?—Il y aura de l'ailleurs où l'autre n'y sera plus condamné à mort. Mais de l'ailleurs, est-ce qu'il y en a eu, est-qu'il y en a? S'il n'est pas encore "ici" il est déjà là,—en cet autre lieu qui dérange l'ordre social, où le désir fait exister la fiction. . . . Il existe un lieu qui . . . n'est pas obligé de reproduire le système et c'est l'écriture. S'il y a un ailleurs qui peut échapper à la répétition infernale, c'est par là, où ça s'écrit, où ça rêve, où ça invente les nouveaux mondes. (180, 131–132)[6]

The seventeenth-century women writers I have discussed use this "place" to revise history, to offer another vision of reality, and to comment on the polemical status of a woman within the "system" who seeks to express herself and to shape her own destiny. Their literary efforts bring history into conformity with women's vision of the past and hope for the future, as these women not only present "things as they are" but also prescribe "things as they should be."

N O T E S

INTRODUCTION

1. Virginia Woolf, *A Room of One's Own*, 47.

2. Ibid.

3. Saint-Réal's novel *Don Carlos* figures in the collected works of Marie-Catherine-Hortense Desjardins, Mme de Villedieu, into the eighteenth century.

4. For the development of the novel during this period, see, among others, Henri Coulet, *Le Roman jusqu'à la Révolution;* René Godenne, *Histoire de la nouvelle française au XVIIe et XVIIIe siècles;* Marie-Thérèse Hipp, *Mythes et réalités: Enquête sur le roman et les mémoires 1660–1700;* Maurice Lever, *Le Roman français au XVIIe siècle;* English Showalter, *The Evolution of the French Novel 1641–1782;* and Ian Watt, *The Rise of the Novel*.

5. In 1983, Joan DeJean edited a ground-breaking issue of *Esprit Créateur* devoted to the female literary tradition in seventeenth-century France. As she notes in her introduction, contrary to their fate in the twentieth century, "the female novelists of seventeenth-century France were widely revered as the undisputed 'masters' of their craft" (*Women's Writing in Seventeenth-Century France*, 3). Other works that elucidate this female tradition are DeJean, "Lafayette's Ellipses: The Privileges of Anonymity," and Nancy K. Miller, "Emphasis Added: Plots and Plausibilities in Women's Fictions." DeJean and Miller have recently collaborated on a special issue of *Yale French Studies* entitled *The Politics of Tradition: Placing Women in French Literature*. Throughout the present study, I attribute the development of the novel in France to women, a view not always held by specialists of early prose fiction. I base many of my claims on DeJean's unpublished research on the origin of the novel and on her forthcoming book, *Tender Geographies* (to be published by Columbia University Press, 1991). Many of the texts cited in the following pages lend support to such a view.

6. Micheline Cuénin, *Roman et société sous Louis XIV; Mme de Villedieu*.

7. DeJean has recently analyzed the fate of these women writers in the eighteenth and nineteenth centuries ("Classical Reeducation: Decanonizing the Feminine").

8. When she extols women's development of narrative genres, Genlis refers to these writers. She remarks that if women have not surpassed men in the genres of tragedy and epic, "They have often surpassed them in many works of another genre. No man has left a volume of personal letters that can be compared to Mme de Sévigné's or Mme de Maintenon's. *La Princesse de Clèves* . . . [and] the last two novels of Mme Cotin are infinitely superior to all those of the male French novelists" ("Elles les ont souvent surpassés dans plusieurs ouvrages d'un autre genre. Aucun homme n'a laissé un recueil de lettres familières que l'on puisse comparer aux lettres de Mme de Sévigné et à celles de Mme de Maintenon. *La Princesse de Clèves,* . . . les deux derniers romans de Mme Cotin sont infiniment supérieurs à tous ceux des romanciers français" [Stéphanie-Félicité de Genlis, *De l'influence des femmes sur la littérature comme protectrices et comme auteurs,* vii]).

9. Ibid., xxxiv.

10. This is not to say that no women wrote poetry or drama. Villedieu, for example, was a successful playwright.

11. Hipp, for example, does not interpret Motteville's and Montpensier's declarations of purpose as efforts to join their works with history (*Mythes et réalités*, 133). She classifies Montpensier and Henriette d'Angleterre among memorialists who "take refuge in remembrances" (14).

12. Villedieu devotes pages to listing the sources for her *Annales galantes*, for example. In "Les Sources historiques de *La Princesse de Clèves*," H. Chamard and G. Rudler point out the erudition behind *La Princesse de Clèves*.

13. Gustave Dulong, *L'Abbé de Saint-Réal: Etude sur les rapports de l'histoire et du roman au XVIIe siècle*, 349.

14. In now-classic studies, Georges May and English Showalter, for example, have thoroughly examined the advent of the novel and its relationship to succeeding manifestations of the genre. Both of them account for the novel's reliance on history by considering the reliance to be one stage in the novel's evolution toward realism (May, "L'Histoire a-t-elle engendré le roman?" Showalter, *The Evolution of the French Novel*). The term *vraisemblance* is difficult to translate precisely. It connotes both plausibility and propriety. As the English "verisimilitude" does not embrace both these connotations, I will continue to use the French.

15. Foremost among such efforts is Hipp's *Mythes et réalité*. In this comprehensive study, Hipp reviews all of the primary representatives of both genres, memoirs and fiction, and juxtaposes their style and content in an effort to unearth the various affinities between the two genres. In a similar vein, Marc Fumaroli has explored the question of memoirs during the classical period and their influence on the general development of French prose. In his opinion, the hybrid nature of memoirs, belonging to the domain of history yet frequently slipping into more fictional modes as they incorporate more personal experiences, exercised a strong influence on the development of seventeenth-century French prose ("Les Mémoires du XVIIe siècle au carrefour des genres en prose").

16. In "Gender and Genre: Women as Historical Writers 1400-1820," Natalie Zemon Davis was the first scholar to suggest that women's historical works may have gender-specific characteristics. Joan Kelly continues this line of investigation in "Early Feminist Theory and the Querelle des femmes, 1400-1789" (a chapter in her book, *Women, History and Theory*). See also Joan Wallach Scott, *Gender and the Politics of History*.

17. *The Female Autograph*, ed. Domna C. Stanton; *Interpreting Women's Lives: Feminist Theory and Personal Narratives*, ed. The Personal Narratives Group; *Life/lines: Theorizing Women's Autobiography*, ed. Bella Brodski and Celeste Schenck.

18. In *Le Pacte autobiographique*, Philippe Lejeune, for example, excludes almost all women's works from the genre of autobiography because they do not reflect his definition of the genre.

19. "Even where a verbal creation negates or surpasses all expectations, it still presupposes preliminary information and a trajectory of expectations [*Erwartungsrichtung*] against which to register the originality and novelty. This horizon of expectations is constituted for the reader from out of a tradition or series of previously known works, and from a specific attitude, mediated by one (or more) genre and dissolved through new works" (Hans Robert Jauss, "Theory of Genres and Medieval Literature," *Towards an Aesthetic of Reception*, 79).

20. May remarks, "This curious grafting of the novel onto history seems to have been above all a French phenomenon" ("L'Histoire a-t-elle engendré le roman?" 164). Fumaroli describes memoirs as they developed in mid–seventeenth-century France as "a specifically French genre" ("Les Mémoires au carrefour des genres en prose," 36).

21. For example, Arthur Flannigan relegates his discussion of history in Villedieu's *Les Désordres de l'amour* to a footnote (*Madame de Villedieu's "Les Désordres de l'amour": History, Literature and the Nouvelle Historique,* 42).

22. Paul Hazard, *La Crise de la conscience européenne,* 50; Orest Ranum, *Artisans of Glory: Writers and Historical Thought in Seventeenth-Century France.*

23. Carolyn C. Lougee, *Le Paradis des femmes: Women, Salons, and Social Stratification in Seventeenth-Century France;* Dorothy Backer, *Precious Women;* Ian Maclean, *Woman Triumphant (1610–1652).* The women's history that I view as an important context is very difficult to research. In fact, a women's history of the Fronde, for example, would be another book in itself. Many of the sources for such a history are the very texts I am studying here, especially women's memoirs.

24. May, "L'Histoire a-t-elle engendré le roman?" 157.

25. René Godenne isolates 1670–1680 as the crowning moment of the historical novel (*Histoire de la nouvelle française au dix-septième et dix-huitième siècles,* 84).

26. Godenne notes that after 1681, works of fiction had fewer historical pretensions (*Histoire de la nouvelle française,* 87).

27. I have selected *La Princesse de Clèves* from among Lafayette's literary works because in her other fictions—*La Princesse de Montpensier, Zaïde,* and *La Comtesse de Tende*—she makes much less use of history. The extensive use of history in *La Princesse de Clèves* is thus all the more clearly purposeful and not simply a generic convention. *La Princesse de Clèves* is also especially important because of the controversy its history incited.

CHAPTER ONE: PERSPECTIVES ON HISTORY

1. "It is strange that one takes such pleasure in putting oneself in danger, and that peril is as pleasant for literary people as for soldiers" (Buffet, "Au lecteur," *Les Illustres Savantes*).

2. *L'Histoire du roy,* ed. Daniel Meyer.

3. The fourteen tapestries are entitled the Coronation (1654), the Interview of the Two Kings (1660), the Marriage (1660), the Audience with the Comte de Fuentès (1662), the Entry into Dunkerque (1662), the Renewal of the Swiss Alliance (1663), the Capture of Marsal (1663), the Audience with the Nuncio Chigi (1664), the Siege of Tournay (1667), the Siege of Douai (1667), the Capture of Lille (1667), the Bruges Canal (1667), the Visit to the Gobelins (1667), and the Capture of Dole (1668).

4. The tapestries were produced for the last time in 1736.

5. It is interesting to note that Louis XIV appears much older in the civil scenes than in the military scenes. The tapestries are not direct representations of reality but, rather, creations designed to convey specific interpretations of reality.

6. Marie-Madeleine Pioche de la Vergne, comtesse de Lafayette, *La Princesse de Clèves,* 56.

7. Philippe Ariès, *Le Temps de l'histoire*, 135. See especially the chapter entitled "L'Attitude devant l'histoire: Le XVIIe siècle."

8. Ariès states that "history is thus written by continuators" (*Le Temps de l'histoire*, 135–136).

9. For an in-depth study of Mézeray's work, see Wilfred Hugo Evans, *L'Historien Mézeray et la conception de l'histoire en France au XVIIe siècle*.

10. For my description of Mézeray's position at court and his historical undertaking, I have relied on Ranum's chapter on the Mézeray phenomenon in *Artisans of Glory* and on Evans's biography.

11. Ranum, *Artisans of Glory*, 204.

12. François Eudes de Mézeray, Preface, *L'Histoire de France depuis Pharamond jusqu'à maintenant*, n.p.

13. Erica Harth, *Ideology and Culture in Seventeenth-Century France*, 153. See the chapter entitled "History and Fable," especially the section devoted to "The disappearance of history" (153–162). Harth states that "after the mid-century flourishing of François Eudes de Mézeray, there was not a single important historian of France" (129).

14. Ranum remarks that "the Fronde turned the man of letters increasingly toward the crown as the sole source of patronage and toward the French Academy as the principal center of literary and historical culture" (*Artisans of Glory*, 159).

15. Ranum, *Artisans of Glory*, 246.

16. Ranum (*Artisans of Glory*) describes the activities of this group in his chapter on Pellisson, especially 260 ff.

17. Paul Pellisson-Fontanier, *Histoire de Louis XIV*, 1:1–2. All further references to this work appear in the text.

18. Jean Racine, *Le Précis historique des campagnes de Louis XIV*, in *Oeuvres complètes*, 387. Very little of Racine's history is extant.

19. Louis XIV, *Mémoires*, 31. All further references to this work appear in the text.

20. As Ranum has remarked, in the *Mémoires* one clearly sees that Louis's "purpose [was] to raise the narrative of his actions and events during his reign to the level of a *politique*" (*Artisans of Glory*, 266).

21. In *Le Roi-machine*, Jean-Marie Apostolidès analyzes these spectacular events and their relationship to Louis's *politique*.

22. For an explanation of Versailles and its images, see Apostolidès, *Le Roi-machine*, 86–92, 135–137.

23. Apostolidès, *Le Roi-machine*, 145.

24. Louis Marin, *Le Récit est un piège*, 9.

25. Maurice Lever, *La Fiction narrative en prose au XVIIe siècle*.

26. *Histoire* is often capitalized when it refers to "history," whereas a lower-case *h* is used when the word should be translated as "story." In the seventeenth century, writers of fiction often used a capital *H* to pass their works off as true history.

27. Abbé Nicolas Lenglet Dufresnoy, *Méthode pour etudier l'histoire*, 1:5.

28. François Menestrier, *Les Divers Caractères des ouvrages historiques*. All further references to this work appear in the text.

29. In her discussion of Menestrier's text, Phyllis Leffler sees *l'histoire raisonnée* as one type of *histoire figurée* ("*L'Histoire raisonnée*: A Study of French

Historiography, 1660–1720," 6). I understand Menestrier's text to be more ambiguous and to conflate the two terms.

30. Harth remarks that "Louis's appointment in 1677 of Racine and Boileau as court historiographers was consistent with the devaluation of history" (*Ideology and Culture*, 153).

31. Hipp makes a similar distinction when discussing memoirs: "In general two ways of recounting historical events can be distinguished: one places the accent on the political and heroic history of great events. . . . In opposition to this documentary history is a humanized history which contains important and secret things" (*Mythes et réalités*, 140–141). I shall return to these distinctions in my analysis of Montpensier's *Mémoires*.

32. Throughout, I use "interior"/"exterior" to distinguish between the perspectives of the "particular" historian and the general historian. I wish to imply a difference both in location and in the type of event that is developed. For the most part, in an interior perspective the court is privileged and the historian uncovers motivations, whereas an exterior perspective locates most of the principal actions outside the court milieu, especially on the battlefield, and emphasizes events without delving below the surface.

33. César Vichard, Abbé de Saint-Réal, *De l'usage de l'histoire*, 1:326. All further references to this work appear in the text.

34. Charles de Marguetel de Saint-Denis, seigneur de Saint-Evremond, *Discours sur les historiens français*, in *Oeuvres meslées*, 7:56.

35. It is important to remember that Saint-Evremond wrote his commentary twenty years after the publication of *La Princesse de Montpensier* and six years after the publication of *La Princesse de Clèves*, two books that are based on this particular brand of history and may have influenced his conception of historical narrative.

36. Throughout this study I will translate "particulier" literally, as "particular." As shall become evident, I believe that what is referred to as "particular history" differs considerably from what twentieth-century historians refer to as "private history."

37. Antoine Varillas, Preface, *Anecdotes de Florence*.

38. Charles Sorel, *De la connaissance des bons livres*, 69–70.

39. Ibid., 83.

40. Adrien Baillet, *Jugement des sçavans sur les principaux ouvrages des auteurs*, 1:27.

41. Abbé Charles Batteux, *Principes de littérature*, 4:316.

42. Louis de Rouvroy, duc de Saint-Simon, *Mémoires*, 4.

43. Abbé Jean-Antoine de Charnes, *Conversations sur la critique de la Princesse de Clèves*, 135. All further references to this work appear in the text.

44. Saint-Evremond, *Discours sur les historiens français*, 7:67.

45. Lenglet Dufresnoy, *De l'usage des romans*, 108–109.

46. Ibid., 84.

47. Lenglet Dufresnoy, *De l'usage des romans*, the heading of chapter 2; and pp. 82 and 214. Lenglet Dufresnoy specifically mentions Lafayette, Scudéry, and d'Aulnoy, along with Villedieu.

48. Hazard, *La Crise de la conscience européenne*, 50.

49. For the sake of convenience, I will continue to translate *nouvelle historique* as "novel" or "historical novel."

50. For a history of the *nouvelle*, see especially Godenne, *Histoire de la nouvelle française*. Although Godenne limits his analysis to works that are actually entitled *nouvelle*, his study is a good bibliographical source and is useful for its distinctions among the various forms of the genre. See also Coulet, *Le Roman jusqu'à la Révolution*; Lever, *Le Roman français au XVIIe siècle*; and especially Showalter, *The Evolution of the French Novel*. I use the term "heroic novel" to refer to the *roman héroïque* as written by Scudéry. Showalter terms this form the heroic novel or romance.

51. Du Plaisir, *Sentiments sur les lettres et sur l'histoire avec des scrupules sur le style*, 87.

52. Jean-Regnault de Segrais, *Les Nouvelles françaises*, 240–241.

53. As Segrais was a close friend of Lafayette's, it is not surprising that his concept of the genre corresponds to the notion implicit in her works.

54. "Gallant (hi)stories" refers to the historical novel. "Gallant" is used here in the sense of "courtly."

55. Du Plaisir refers to Lafayette as a "historien" when he discusses *La Princesse de Clèves* in *Sentiments*. For the sake of convenience I will use the term "novelist" to refer to Lafayette and authors like her.

56. Modern studies of the development of the French novel refer to this fusion of history and fiction to remain within the critical constraints of *vraisemblance*. See in particular May, "L'Histoire a-t-elle engendré le roman?" especially 157–159 and 171; Hipp, *Mythes et réalities*; Adam, *Histoire de la littérature française au XVIIe siècle*.

57. Sorel, *La Bibliothèque française*, 157, 160.

58. Georges de Scudéry, Preface, *Ibrahim*, n.p. Showalter examines *vraisemblance* and the *roman héroïque* in *The Evolution of the French Novel*, 26–32.

59. Although heroic novels like Madeleine de Scudéry's are not revisions of the past, they can be interpreted as a form of contemporary history. It has often been remarked that *Le Grand Cyrus*, for example, is an à clé portrayal of the Fronde years.

60. For a discussion of the relationship between memoirs and the historical novel, see May, "L'Histoire a-t-elle engendré le roman?" and Hipp's in-depth study.

61. May, "L'Histoire a-t-elle engendré le roman?" 162.

62. In his study of Retz, J. T. Letts stresses the strong ties between memoirs and history in the seventeenth century: "The function of the memorialist in the seventeenth century was to furnish material to the historian" (*Le Cardinal de Retz: Historien et memorialiste du possible*, 19). Fumaroli gives the example of Louis XIV's own *Mémoires* as possibly composed for this same purpose ("Les Mémoires du XVIIe siècle au carrefour des genres en prose," 26–27).

63. Lenglet Dufresnoy, *De l'usage des romans*, 109–110.

64. Significantly, Montpensier finds the inspiration for her *Mémoires* in this same "Reine Marguerite."

65. Abbé Joseph de La Porte, *L'Histoire littéraire des femmes françaises*, 1:105. All further references to this work appear in the text.

66. Abbé Claude-François Lambert, *Histoire littéraire du règne de Louis XIV*, 2:25.

67. See, among others, May, *L'Autobiographie*; Derek Watts, "Self-

Portrayal in Seventeenth-Century French Memoirs"; and Hipp, *Mythes et réalités.*

68. For a discussion of the notion of biography in France, see Roland Desné's preface to René Vaillot's *Qui étaient Mme de Tencin . . . et le Cardinal?* It is interesting to note that in all the definitions Desné cites, biography is always associated with the adjective *particulier. Biographie* is a *vie particulière* and is therefore related to *histoire particulière.* For the development of autobiography in France, see May, *L'Autobiographie,* and Lejeune, *L'Autobiographie en France* and *Le Pacte autobiographique.*

69. See May's discussion of the distinction between memoirs and autobiography, which he posits as a common one, in *L'Autobiographie* (122). He traces these differences to the 1866 Larousse dictionary, which he quotes: "'For a long time, in England as in France, narratives left by important men in politics, literature, or the arts about their lives were called memoirs. But then on the other side of the Channel common usage gave the name autobiography to those memoirs that were concerned more with the men themselves than with the events in which the men were involved. Autobiography can be part of the composition of memoirs; but often, in these kinds of works, the place given to contemporary events, to history, is greater than that accorded to the personality of the author, in which case the term memoirs is better suited than autobiography'" (119). May's evaluation when he states, "This distinction, which is useful and largely accepted today, is not without inconveniences: it is often insufficient and misleading" (122). I do not, however, find his alternatives convincing or satisfactory, as shall become apparent in what follows.

70. May, *L'Autobiographie,* 123.

71. Hipp, *Mythes et réalités,* 28.

72. Marc Fumaroli, "Les Mémoires du XVIIe siècle au carrefour des genres en prose," 32. This article is the most thorough and comprehensive treatment of the genre to date. See also Watts, "Self-Portrayal in Seventeenth-Century French Memoirs."

73. When Fumaroli comments that, in this form, the genre is "not very compromising" ("peu compromettant"), he is explaining in part that aristocrats could take up the pen as memorialists because memorialists were not considered authors, a vocation viewed as unworthy of the nobility. But his characterization of the genre is debatable, especially in view of the fact that these texts were not published until the eighteenth century, often precisely because of their "compromising" material on the Fronde. Even when the texts did finally appear, as we shall see with Montpensier's, some of the material was censored. I also question the suggestion that these memorialists—in Fumaroli's example, all women—were eluding acknowledgment of authorship. Many of them, as we have seen, were already well known for their contributions to other literary genres.

74. In *The Revolt of the Judges,* A. Lloyd Moote recounts the Fronde from the parliamentary point of view.

75. Although the parliamentary Fronde and the princely Fronde can be distinguished for the sake of clarity, such a distinction is actually an oversimplification. The two waves were closely related. As Hubert Méthivier has justly remarked in *La Fronde,* "It is wrong to oppose the parliamentary and

the princely Frondes, for the first was supported by the majority of the princes, and it is better to call the latter the Condéen Fronde (1651–1652) because the parliament, which was against Mazarin, participated in both Frondes. One can say that in 1649 Condé's attitude was first determined by his hateful contempt of the parliament, which then turned to a haughty contempt for Mazarin, which created a group around him in which there were more swords than robes [of parliament] . . . except the robes of the women" (124).

76. The following genealogy situates the major participants:

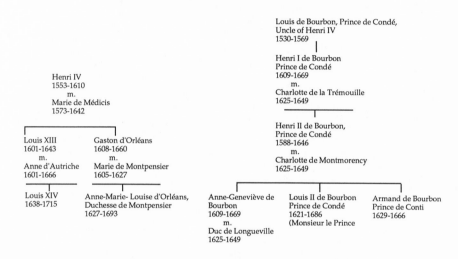

77. Moote, *The Revolt of the Judges*, 224.

78. Ibid., 225.

79. This alliance was so unstable that, in 1649, Retz was involved in a plot to kill Condé—an assassination attempt supported by Mazarin (Moote, 249).

80. Jeanine Delpech, *L'Ame de la Fronde*, 139.

81. Moote, *The Revolt of the Judges*, 310.

82. Méthivier and Pierre-Georges Lorris recognize the women's power and take it into account in their recent treatments of the Fronde. Maclean focuses entirely on women's roles.

83. See Delpech's biography for Longueville's complex role.

84. Kossmann, *La Fronde*, 240.

85. Backer's study is enlightening, but its findings are undercut by a mocking tone, as is evident here (*Precious Women*, 141).

86. In Albistur and Armogathe's opinion, for example, these women "only act for the love of intrigue. . . . The Grande Mademoiselle, the duchesse de Chevreuse, or Madame de Longueville associate themselves with political action only 'for the love of a love,' or for the hatred of another" (*Histoire du féminisme français du moyen âge à nos jours*, 136).

87. For a discussion of women's roles during the Fronde, see especially

Lorris, *La Fronde;* Ch.-L. Livet, "Les Femmes de la Fronde"; and Maclean, *Woman Triumphant.*

88. Backer discusses Rambouillet's *chambre bleue,* especially 58–130.

89. Marguerite Marie Thiollier, *Ces Dames du Marais.* Thiollier includes everyone and establishes the relationship between them.

90. Abbé Michel de Pure, *La Prétieuse ou le mystère des ruelles,* 1:49. For a discussion of the role of salons, see also Maurice Magendie, *La Politesse mondaine et les gens d'honnêteté.*

91. Maclean, *Woman Triumphant,* 149. He discusses the relationship between literature and the salons on pp. 140–154. Recent critics explain Molière's attack on the *précieuses* as directed not at the true *précieuses* such as Scudéry but at provincial pretenders. But it is possible to see Molière's attack in *Les Précieuses ridicules* and *Les Femmes savantes* as a frustrated response to a powerful and influential female public.

92. Elizabeth Goldsmith traces the influence of the art of conversation in *Exclusive Conversations: The Art of Interaction in Seventeenth-Century France.*

93. Portraits, for example, are frequently mentioned as characteristic of this different kind of history. In *Discours sur les historiens français,* Saint-Evremond stresses the need to portray individuals in history, to characterize each person. As we have seen, Mézeray calls attention to his inclusion of portraits. In *Sentiments sur les lettres,* Du Plaisir advocates the use of detailed portraits in fiction—thus pointing to the similarity of techniques in historical and fictional narratives.

94. Anne-Marie-Louise-Henriette d'Orléans, duchesse de Montpensier, *Le Recueil des portraits,* n.p. The preface is of uncertain authorship.

95. See Ariès, *Le Temps de l'histoire,* 166–169, for a summary of this fashion.

96. Albistur and Armogathe include a good discussion of the *précieuses'* views on marriage (*Histoire du féminism,* 140–144). They note that a father had the legal right to choose a husband for his daughter (138). See also Maclean, *Woman Triumphant,* 88–118.

97. Somaize, *Le Grand Dictionnaire historique des Précieuses,* 2:43–46.

98. Montpensier may have secretly married the comte de Lauzun, but if the union did take place, it was very short-lived.

99. Unfortunately, most of this correspondence has been lost. What remains is reprinted following Motteville's *Mémoires* in the Petitot edition.

100. Albistur and Armogathe, *Histoire du féminisme,* 141–142.

101. See the internal narrative devoted to Sapho in Scudéry's *Artamène ou le Grand Cyrus* 10:328–531. In *Fictions of Sappho, 1546–1937,* DeJean notes that in the seventeenth century the spelling "Sappho" was gallicized to "Sapho." I will use "Sapho" to refer to Scudéry's character. For an analysis of Scudéry's use of Sappho, see DeJean, *Fictions of Sappho,* 96–115.

102. Maclean, *Woman Triumphant,* 152.

103. Lafayette's correspondence with Segrais and Huet reveals her interest in Latin.

104. Jacquette Guillaume, *Les Dames illustres.* Her rhetoric is devoted to showing how women surpass men, and thus reflects the rhetoric of the sixteenth-century *querelle des femmes.*

105. Although one canonical woman novelist of the time, Lafayette, did not sign her works, this was not necessarily out of shame or modesty. In

"Lafayette's Ellipses: The Privileges of Anonymity," DeJean has convincingly demonstrated the power that could be derived from anonymity.

106. Albistur and Armogathe include a good bibliography of the anti-feminist works that continued to be produced (*Histoire du féminisme*, 122–123 and 134–135).

107. Albistur and Armogathe, *Histoire du féminisme*, 136.

108. In particular, Christine de Pizan expressed many of the same concerns in the fifteenth century. However, because she is never specifically cited by her seventeenth-century successors and her works were not easily available, an analysis of her examination of history would be superfluous here. I have analyzed Pizan's revisionist notion of history in an article entitled "Female Signatures: A Challenge to History" (forthcoming).

109. Madeleine de Scudéry, *Les Femmes illustres*, 1:46. All further references to this work appear in the text.

110. Scudéry was known to her contemporaries as Sapho. Davis uses the term "women worthies" to refer to women in the "collective memorials" that came into existence in the fifteenth century ("Women's History in Transition: The European Case").

111. Marguerite Buffet, *Nouvelles Observations sur la langue française*, n.p. All further references to this work appear in the text.

112. Montpensier, *Mémoires*, 41:8. All further references to this work appear in the text.

113. I am grateful to English Showalter for pointing out that Montpensier's use of the term *détail* is not synonymous with the English "detail" and thus does not mean a trivial element but, rather, a specific one.

114. Marie d'Orléans-Longuevillle, duchesse de Nemours, *Mémoires*. (All further references to this work appear in the text.) This edition was edited by Mlle de l'Héritier, herself a recognized author. L'Héritier's introduction is especially interesting. It refers to Nemours's *Mémoires* as a series of portraits: "She thought only of painting the truth, without anything relating to her interests or to her glory appearing in her portraits" ("Elle n'a uniquement pensé qu'à peindre la vérité, sans qu'aucun rapport ni à ses intérêts ni à sa gloire ait eu la moindre part dans ses Portraits" [*Avertissement*, n.p.]). L'Héritier uses her introduction to excuse Nemours for writing honest but frank portraits in the name of historical accuracy: "One should not be surprised to find paintings showing some weaknesses in the greatest men. . . . The illustrious person who wrote these memoirs believed she should not omit anything demanded by historical accuracy" ("Au reste qu'on ne soit pas surpris, si l'on trouve dans ces Mémoires la peinture de quelques faiblesses dans de fort grands Hommes. . . . L'illustre personne qui a écrit ces mémoires a crû ne devoir rien omettre de ce que demandait l'exactitude de l'Histoire"). This seems to be an excuse, almost as though l'Héritier were anticipating criticism of this different history founded upon portraits and personalities.

115. Marguerite de Valois, *Mémoires*, 36.

116. Lafayette, *Histoire de Madame Henriette d'Angleterre*.

117. Françoise Bertault, dame Langlois de Motteville, *Mémoires*, 1:305. All further references to this work appear in the text.

118. Although these women's texts were not published until the beginning of the eighteenth century, they were all composed approximately between 1655 and 1680.

119. Hortense Mancini, *Mémoires*, and Marie Mancini, *Mémoires*. Hortense's *Mémoires*, often attributed to Saint-Réal, was first published in 1676, and Marie's appeared in 1678.

120. Madame de Caylus, *Souvenirs*, 23. It is not known when Caylus wrote her *Souvenirs*. She died in 1729, so she most likely wrote it at the beginning of the eighteenth century. Her *Souvenirs* treats the 1680s especially and places the accent on Mme de Maintenon, her aunt. The *Souvenirs* was not published until 1770.

121. Nemours, *Les Mémoires de M.L.D.D.N.*, ed. Mlle l'Héritier.

122. Saint-Simon, *Mémoires*, 4.

123. Lafayette, *Correspondance*, 2:62–63. The authenticity of this letter has been contested but is generally still accepted. Lafayette did not acknowledge her authorship in this letter.

124. It is interesting to note that editors tried to erase novels' affiliations with history. The manuscript versions of Lafayette's first historical novel played on the ambiguity of the word *"histoire"* and bear the title *Histoire de la Princesse de Montpensier sous le règne de Charles IX roi de France*, a title that clearly stresses the novel's historical pretensions. In the first printed edition, however, the title was changed to *La Princesse de Montpensier*. If one believes Lafayette's letter to Lescheraine, a similar process occurred with *La Princesse de Clèves* vis-à-vis the term "memoirs" (André Beaunier, ed., *Histoire de la Princesse de Montpensier*, by Lafayette, 20.

125. Marie-Catherine-Hortense Desjardins, Mme Antoine Boesset de Villedieu, *Portrait des faiblesses humaines*, 1:215.

126. Villedieu, *Les Annales galantes*, in *Oeuvres* 1:iv.

127. Table of contents, *Les Annales galantes*.

128. Villedieu, *Les Amours des grands hommes*, in *Oeuvres* vol. 4, n.p. Villedieu is stressing her desire to humanize history, to put it at the level of everyday life. This is what Saint-Réal called for, as we have seen.

129. As May remarks, the vogue of deceptive prefaces (designed to fool the reader) did not really begin until the last years of the century, especially the period after 1685. ("L'Histoire a-t-elle engendré le roman?" 160). These prefaces often accompanied what were openly identified as "secret histories." The appellation "secret history" did not appear until the last quarter of the century (May, 172). As already stated, by 1681 novelists were moving away from deliberately conflating their work with history and were instead assigning it to the separate domain of secret history.

130. Caumont de la Force, Preface, *Histoire secrète de Catherine de Bourbon*.

131. Marie de Viche-Chamrond, Mme Du Deffand, letter to Walpole, 5 October 1770 (*Correspondance*, 2:100). I would like to thank Elizabeth Mac-Arthur for bringing this letter to my attention.

132. Germaine de Staël, *Essai sur les fictions*, 203.

133. Staël, *Delphine*. All further references to this work appear in the text.

134. Staël, *Essai sur les fictions*, 203.

135. Ibid., 205.

CHAPTER TWO: FROM MILITARY TO LITERARY *FRONDEUSE*

1. "I do not know what it means to be a heroine: I am of a lineage never to do anything except what is great and lofty. One can call this what one

wants; as for me, I call this following my own desires and going my own way; I was born to not go any other way" (Anne-Marie-Louise-Henriette d'Orléans, duchesse de Montpensier, *Mémoires*, 42:340). All further references to this work appear in the text.

2. Marguerite Duras, interview, *Elle* (October 1987).

3. Montpensier, *Le Manifeste de Mademoiselle*.

4. Domna Stanton identifies the notion of an intertext as an inherent aspect of the genre of autobiography: "The specific texture of an autobiography also represents the mediation of numerous contextual factors: a particular intertext, such as Rousseau's *Confessions* for George Sand and other nineteenth-century autobiographers; or a set of intertexts, such as hagiographies for Margery Kempe" ("Autogynography: Is the Subject Different?" 9).

5. Genlis, *De l'influence des femmes*, 78.

6. See, among many others, Vita Sackville-West, *Daughter of France;* Cécile Vincens, *Louis XIV and La Grande Mademoiselle;* Arvède Barine, *La Grande Mademoiselle;* Christian Bouyer, *La Grande Mademoiselle;* and Anne Andreu, *La Duchesse de Montpensier ou la grande Amazone*.

7. Montpensier's family tree illustrates her powerful lineage:

```
        Henri IV           m.          Marie de Médicis
        1553-1610                      1575-1642
  ┌───────────────────────────────────────────────────────┐
Louis XIII                Henriette de France        Gaston D'Orléans
1601-1643                 1609-1669                   1608-1660
m.                        m.                          m.
Anne d'Autriche           Charles I of England        Marie de Montpensier
1601-1666                 1625-1649                   1605-1627
  ┌──────────┐     ┌────────────┬───────────┬─────────┬────────────────────┐
Louis XIV  Philippe   Henriette    Charles II  James II   Anne-Marie-Louise d'Orléans,
1638-1715  d'Orléans  d'Angleterre of          of         Duchesse de Montpensier
           1640-1711  1644-1670    England     England    1627-1693
           m.         m.           1630-1685   1633-1701
           Henriette  Philippe
           d'Anglerre d'Orléans
           1644-1670  1640-1711
```

8. For an analysis of this phenomenon, see my "Rescripting Historical Discourse: Literary Portraits by Women."

9. For a description of this text, see Denise Godwin, *Les Nouvelles françaises ou les divertissements de la Princesse Aurélie de Segrais*.

10. Eglal Henein rightly underscores the historicity of Montpensier's various literary endeavors. In her opinion, for Montpensier all art is "a way of illustrating history" ("Mlle de Montpensier à la recherche du temps perdu," 47).

11. The dates of composition are identified in the *Mémoires*. Montpensier begins her work at St. Fargeau in 1653 (41:383). She stops in 1660 when she returns to the court, and picks up the narration again in 1677 (42:417).

12. Lejeune, *Le Pacte autobiographique*, 15.

13. The editor of the 1883 Garnier edition of La Rochefoucauld's *Mémoires*, for example, consistently refers to Montpensier's and Motteville's accounts to fill in the personal blanks of La Rochefoucauld's narrative.

14. François Marie Arouet de Voltaire, *Le Siècle de Louis XIV*, in *Oeuvres complètes*, 14–15: 108.

15. One hundred fifty years later, Sackville-West agrees with La Porte and Voltaire: "Nothing did escape her, except the important things" (*Daughter of France*, 172).

16. Jean Garapon, "Les Mémorialistes et le réel: L'exemple du Cardinal de Retz et de Mademoiselle de Montpensier," 187. All further references to this work appear in the text.

17. Garapon concludes his brief comparison between Retz and Montpensier by stating, "Certainly, when the memoirs of Retz and those of Montpensier are compared, clear differences in purpose become apparent, the former concentrating more on the reality of history and the latter on an intimate I" (188).

18. Saint-Simon, *Mémoires* (Pléiade), 1:123, n. 8.

19. Letts, *Le Cardinal de Retz: Historien et mémorialiste du possible*, 10.

20. Verdier states that editors revised the text of the *Mémoires*: "Words that were too concrete were replaced by more proper expressions; the ellipses were filled in and the conjunctions were varied to make the abrupt rhythm smoother and more polished. They went even further and suppressed the personal passages and added motivations in order to make Mlle's reactions and opinions appear less extravagant, less violent, more well thought out. They corrected one of the most striking aspects of her style, even more striking over the years, her use of direct discourse. The conversations are often transposed into indirect discourse, made more conforming to the rules of narrative, more distant, with the voices muffled" ("Mlle de Montpensier et le plaisir du texte," 19).

21. The *Mémoires* has recently been republished (Paris: La Fontaine, 1985).

22. Verdier speaks in terms of "the coexistence of contradictory codes" ("Mlle de Montpensier et le plaisir du texte," 27). It is precisely this "coexistence of contradictory codes" that I wish to elucidate here. Significantly, Henein remarks that Montpensier's other works are also judged "unclassifiable." She notes that Cioranescu groups all these works together "under the very ambiguous rubric of 'Editions'" ("Mlle de Montpensier à la recherche du temps perdu," 44).

23. White, "The Value of Narrativity in the Representation of Reality," 10.

24. I am using the term "discourse" as Genette delineates it in his discussion of the various functions of the narrator. The discourse corresponds to his fourth category of functions, that is, "the testimonial function, or function of attestation, . . . direct or indirect interventions about the story" ("Discours du récit," 262–263).

25. The early editors of Montpensier's *Mémoires* offer no justification for omitting these passages, which are first included in the 1735 edition—the fifth edition.

26. Lejeune, *L'Autobiographie en France*, 14.

27. Jean-François-Paul de Gondi, Cardinal de Retz, *Mémoires*, 127.

28. Patricia Cholakian, "A House of Her Own: Marginality and Dissidence in the *Mémoires* of La Grande Mademoiselle," 5.

29. Saint-Simon, *Mémoires*, 7:396.

30. Although the *Mémoires* was not published until the early eighteenth century, it may have been circulated before then. In any case, the pub-

lication history does not preclude Montpensier's inscribing a contemporary public in her work.

31. Lejeune identifies the "pacte" or contract as the agreement between the author and the reader that the latter is truly reading the former's life story and, indeed, that this story is addressed to her/him and was composed for the enjoyment and enlightenment of the public (*Le Pacte autobiographique*, 25–26).

32. Michel Beaujour, *Miroirs d'encre*.

33. In locating part of her narrative deviance in its chronological disorder, Montpensier anticipates her own critics, who often comment on this essential difference. La Porte, for example, states disdainfully, "[The *Mémoires*] is very muddled: all the facts are mixed up and confused to the point that it is almost impossible to follow them" ("[Les *Mémoires*] sont très embrouillés: tous les faits y sont mêlés et confondus à un point, qu'il est presque impossible de les suivre" [1:434]). White identifies order as an inherent aspect of historical narrative according to the conventional rules of narrativity ("The Value of Narrativity in the Representation of Reality," 23).

34. See also 40:407, where Montpensier describes her technique as writing "when something makes me remember" ("à mésure que quelque chose de particulier m'en fait souvenir"), and 43:486.

35. R. J. Knecht, *The Fronde*, 1.

36. Ranum, *Artisans of Glory*, 159, 168.

37. Ibid., 167.

38. Père M. A. Anselme, *Oraison funèbre de très-haute et très-puissante princesse Anne Marie Louise d'Orléans, duchesse de Montpensier, souveraine de Dombes*, 27–28.

39. Ibid., 28.

40. As cited by Kossmann, *La Fronde*, 197.

41. Ch.-G. Livet, "Les Femmes de la Fronde," 530.

42. Two examples of such biographies are Jeanine Delpech, *L'Ame de la Fronde: Mme de Longueville*, and Arvède Barine, *La Grande Mademoiselle*.

43. The term *mazarinades* refers to texts, about 5,000 in all, that were published during the Fronde and were directed against Mazarin.

44. Lorris, for example, warns against minimizing the importance of Montpensier's role and its political effect. "The Grande Mademoiselle's success, as novelistic as it seems, must not be underestimated: Orléans was an important place on the Loire, and its loss would have been very detrimental to the princely party, and even more so to Monsieur's prestige" (*La Fronde*, 306). Lorris also credits Montpensier with saving the princely party in Paris by firing upon her cousin, Louis XIV.

45. The following description of Bordeaux is typical of the *Mémoires*: "Bordeaux is in the most beautiful location in the world: nothing is more beautiful than the Garonne River and its port; the streets are beautiful, and the houses are well built; there are very decent people who are very witty. . . . They do things quickly, and lack good judgment" ("La ville de Bordeaux est dans la plus belle situation du monde: rien n'est plus beau que la rivière de la Garonne et son port; les rues sont belles, et les maisons bien bâties; il y a de fort honnêtes gens et fort spirituels. . . . Ils vont fort vite, et n'ont pas grand jugement" [41:109]).

46. Retz, *Mémoires*, 801. All further references to this work appear in the text.

47. La Rochefoucauld, *Mémoires*, 206.

48. Ibid.

49. Jouhaud analyzes the Fronde from the perspective of the "mazarinades" that proliferated throughout these years. In his opinion, "the written word became, in and of itself, an action, an absolute weapon at a moment when problems could not be resolved in any other way" (*La Fronde des mots*, 7).

50. Montpensier is very conscious of the general exclusion of women from history. Even in her *Histoire de la Princesse de Paphlagonie*, she recognizes this censoring and justifies her own feminocentric vision: "The History of Persia talks about his [Cirus's] conquest and the progress of his armies enough, without my having to speak about it: that is why I will remain with our women" ("L'Histoire de Perse fait assez de mention de ses [Cirus] Conquêtes, et du progrès de ses Armées, sans que j'en parle: C'est pourquoi je demeurerai toujours à nos Dames" [94]).

51. Hipp, *Mythes et réalités*, 27.

52. Mézeray is not the actual author of the account of Louis XIV's marriage. His narration stops with the year 1656 and is continued by Henri Philippe de Limiers. Limiers's addition, published separately in 1740, is entitled *Abrégé chronologique de l'histoire de France sous les règnes de Louis XIII et de Louis XIV pour servir de suite à* [to serve as a continuation of] *celui de François de Mézeray*. Editors tend to place the two together under Mézeray's name. In this chapter I am using an 1839 Paris edition entitled *Histoire de France par Mézeray: Edition populaire et permanente*. All further references to this work appear in the text.

53. Mazarin's niece Marie wrote her own detailed description of this aborted love affair (*Mémoires*).

54. Montpensier was incognito at the first marriage ceremony at Fontarabie because the king had first decided that the ceremony would be private, which infuriated her; but after what she describes as four hours of meetings she was finally allowed to go, alone and in disguise.

55. In fact, Montpensier declares herself against marriage for love: "I have always had a great aversion to love, even to legitimate love, because this passion appeared to me unworthy of a good, sound soul. . . . One is very lucky, when one wants to marry, if it is a marriage of reason, even if there is great dislike, I believe that people love each other more after [marriage]" ("J'avais toujours eu grande aversion pour l'amour, même pour celui qui allait au légitime, tant cette passion me paraissait indigne d'une âme bien faite. . . . L'on est bien heureux, quand on veut se marier, que ce soit par raison, même quand l'aversion y serait, je crois que l'on s'en aime davantage après" [41:399]).

56. The marriage with the king of Portugal never came about. Even if it had, Louis XIV's vision could hardly have materialized.

57. Marin, *Le Portrait du roi*. I am also using the English translation (*Portrait of the King*). Another fascinating study of the representation of Louis XIV is Apostolidès's *Le Roi-machine*. Apostolidès bases his analysis on the theory of the king's two bodies, according to which the king exists both as an individual and as the incarnation of the state, thus as *roi* and *Roi* (11). Apos-

tolidès analyzes the representation of these two bodies in the histories and ceremonies developed to celebrate Louis XIV.

58. Marin stresses the historical dimension of this representation: "But we must also notice that the king's portrait in its very dimension as sacramental, as presence of the king's body in painted, sculpted, or written currencies, is also and indissolubly a narrative and historical representation" (*Portrait of the King*, 12).

59. As Marin states, "Thanks to the confusion between the universal utterer who promulgates the rules of historical discourse and the single utterer who proposes to tell the historical narrative, the historical writing of Louis XIV—because it has precisely the king for object—will transform the paradigm "History" into a particular narrative and, inversely, make of this narrative a universal model. Louis XIV makes history, but it is history that is made in what he does, and at the same time his historian, by writing what he does, writes what must be written" (*Portrait of the King*, 41–42).

60. Louis XIV is not the first portrait in *Divers Portraits*, which Montpensier herself had printed in 1659. That position is taken by the princesse de Tarante. Louis's portrait appears near the end of the volume. Not surprisingly, his portrait regains its primary position in Barbin's 1659 edition of Montpensier's *Le Recueil des portraits*.

61. For St. Fargeau, see 41:413–414. For Choisy, see 43:412–414. For an interesting interpretation of Choisy, see Cholakian, "A House of Her Own," 14–15.

62. This utopia was short-lived, however. When Louis XV purchased Choisy in 1739, the name was again changed, this time to Choisy-le-Roi, the name it possesses today. For a history of Choisy, see La Croix, *Le Château de Choisy*.

63. Choisy in fact became a second Versailles after Louis XV acquired it. See *Le Château de Choisy*.

64. As the frontispiece to the first volume of her biography, Vincens reprints another portrait in which Montpensier is dressed as an Amazon. The helmet is the same as the one in the Bourguignon portrait.

CHAPTER THREE: *HISTOIRE DE MADAME HENRIETTE D'ANGLETERRE*

1. "If women had written books, I know for sure they would have been written differently" (Christine de Pizan, "Epistre au dieu d'amour," in *Oeuvres poétiques*, 2:1–27).

2. Hortense Mancini, *Mémoires*, 32. *Gloire* is difficult to translate precisely. Furetière defines it as "worldly honor, the praise given for men's merit, knowledge, and virtue" ("se dit . . . de l'honneur mondain, de la louange qu'on donne au mérite, au savoir et à la vertu des hommes").

3. DeJean has examined in depth the mystery of Lafayette's signature. Her study illuminates the conception of female authorship held in seventeenth-century France and calls into question the conventional ideas of women's literary anonymity ("Lafayette's Ellipses: The Privileges of Anonymity").

4. The title of this portrait and its signature are playful: "Portrait de

Madame la marquise de Sévigné par Madame la comtesse de La Fayette sous le nom d'un inconnu [under the name of an unknown person]."

5. In the introduction to her edition of the *Histoire*, Hipp explains the existence of so many extant manuscripts, although not the original, by hypothesizing that Lafayette's friends may have asked her to write about Madame's death because she was an eyewitness and a friend. Lafayette would then have attached the narrative she and Henriette had composed together to her account of Madame's death. Hipp suggests that one copy could have been intended for Mme de Sablé, who was Lafayette's and Henriette's close friend (introduction, *Vie de la princesse d'Angleterre*, iv).

6. As no autograph manuscript of the *Histoire* exists, one cannot attribute this term with absolute certainty to Lafayette herself. However, of the eight extant manuscripts, all but two are entitled *Histoire*. For her 1967 Droz edition, Hipp chose *Vie* because the only manuscript version she decided to follow is entitled "Fragmens de la vie. . . ." As Hipp offers no real proof that this version is any closer to the true original, I believe the correct title is indeed *Histoire*, for it is the one most editors, including the first, have used. According to Hipp, biographies were not common during this period. Aside from Motteville's, she cites DuFossé's biography of de Pontis and Courtilz de Sandras's work on Colbert. Hipp also attributes Marie Mancini's *Mémoires* to Saint-Réal, although his authorship of it has not been conclusively proven. In any case, both of the Mancini memoirs are written in the first person, so their form is not biographical.

7. Marie-Madeleine Pioche de la Vergne, comtesse de Lafayette, *Fatal Gallantry: Or, the Secret History of Henrietta Princess of England*, trans. Ann Floyd.

8. See Hipp's discussion in the introduction to her edition of the work, lx–lxi.

9. Lafayette, Letter no. 211, 30 June 1673 (*Correspondance*, 2:40).

10. In her introduction, Hipp notes the hybrid nature of the work: "[The Life] is situated halfway between memoirs, with which it shares historical interest and familiar names, and novels that resemble it by the analysis, the curiosity about people, [and] the experiences of life and love" (liii). Thus, "it is difficult to classify the *Life* under a traditional genre" (xvi).

11. I am using the Mercure de France edition of the *Histoire*, which is based on the first edition. All further references to this work appear in the text.

12. The term "lover" (*amant*) was not as strong in the seventeenth century as it is now and did not necessarily imply a sexual relationship.

13. Hipp remarks that Henriette "conceived of this project as a game" (Introduction, xxvi).

14. In this instance, I am using the double pronoun to refer to the narrator because I believe the narrator here is intentionally gender-neutral and unidentifiable. However, this is not always the case, as shall become apparent.

15. I have intentionally translated this passage literally to show how Lafayette frequently replaces all names with pronouns, often with confusing results. In this instance, the subjects are Lafayette and the predicates refer to Henriette.

16. In my analysis of the content of the *Histoire*, I will refer to Lafayette

as the author, even though Henriette had a part in the composition. I do so because I believe the content reveals that Lafayette's role in the actual construction of the text is dominant.

17. In this passage, "lui" can be interpreted as referring to either Mazarin or Marie.

18. P. 206, n. 2. The editor of the Mercure de France edition explains that Sévigné was accused of being Fouquet's mistress.

19. Lafayette's description of Henriette's political position just before her death is historically accurate. Henriette negotiated a secret armistice between France and England, and this was but the last in a series of important political actions. For example, in 1662 she helped the French buy Dunkerque back from the English. For more on Henriette's position at court, see Guy de la Batut, *Oraison funèbre d'Henriette d'Angleterre par Bossuet*.

20. In a similar reflection, the members of the Personal Narratives Group, the editors of *Interpreting Women's Lives*, remark, "Traditionally, knowledge, truth, and reality have been constructed as if men's experiences were normative, as if being human means being male" (3).

21. Lafayette, Letter no. 221, 13 April 1678 (*Correspondance*, 2:62–63).

22. Fumaroli speaks in similar terms about the relationship between memoirs and novels at this time: "Novelistic *vraisemblance* is defined in relation to the truth found in memoirs, which win a decisive victory over absent history, rather than in relation to the epic and its tie to history" ("Les Mémoires du XVIIe siècle au carrefour des genres en prose," 34).

CHAPTER FOUR: AN INJUDICIOUS HISTORIAN

1. "When one chooses a century that is not so distant that one can't know something particular about it, nor so close that one knows too well everything that happened; yet is distant enough so that one can include events a historian might plausibly not have known about, and even should not have said: there is the possibility of doing much better things" (Madeleine de Scudéry, "De la manière d'inventer une fable," in *Conversations sur divers sujets*, 2:43).

2. Pierre Bayle, *Dictionnaire historique et critique*, entry for Mlle Desjardins.

3. Of Saint-Réal's preface to *Don Carlos*, Dulong remarks: "Here one does not find the cheap, showy erudition that is ironic and goodnatured, that we would find in Mme de Villedieu. Evidently our author takes himself seriously. In writing a novel, he claims to be a historian" (*L'Abbé de Saint-Réal: Etudes sur les rapports de l'histoire et du roman au XVIIe siècle*, 118).

4. Ibid., 77.

5. Tallemant des Réaux, *Historiettes*, ed. Antoine Adam, 2:900. *Femelles* is pejorative and is used primarily to refer to animals. All further references to this work appear in the text.

6. Cuénin includes a detailed biography of Villedieu in her *Roman et société*. Her research shows that M. de Villedieu was already married, unbeknown to Desjardins.

7. Hipp frequently refers to Villedieu in her general study of seventeenth-century memoirs and novels. The first work devoted entirely to Vil-

ledieu is Bruce Morrissette's *The Life and Works of Marie-Catherine Desjardins (Mme de Villedieu) 1632–1683*. As previously mentioned, the most complete work on her is Cuénin's *Roman et société sous Louis XIV: Mme de Villedieu*.

8. In 1987, the North American Society for Seventeenth-Century French Literature devoted a session to Villedieu at its annual convention. The papers, including a summary of Villedieu scholarship, are published in the *Actes de Wakeforest*, ed. Milorad R. Margitic and Byron R. Wells. Flannigan's work, particularly his study *Mme de Villedieu's "Les Désordres de l'amour": History, Literature, and the Nouvelle Historique*, is very useful. Miller's article "Tender Economies: Mme de Villedieu and the Cost of Indifference" led the way for a feminist reassessment of Villedieu's work.

9. For a chronological survey of Villedieu's literary production, see Cuénin's second volume, which consists of useful summaries of all Villedieu's works.

10. The poem was considered scandalous. "Jouissance" connotes sexual pleasure. The Pléiade editor of Tallemant de Réaux's *Historiettes* even reprints the poem in his notes to support his author's condemnation of Villedieu.

11. Thiollier places Villedieu within the milieu of the Marais, where she lived all her adult life (*Ces Dames du Marais*, especially 178–191).

12. Villedieu, *Les Annales galantes* (1670). In an article much in line with my own work, Stanton has recently analyzed *Les Annales galantes* and its relationship both to official history and to the novel ("The Demystification of History and Fiction in *Les Annales galantes*").

13. The importance of this preface is evidenced by the fact that it is the only one Barbin included in his first (1702) edition of Villedieu's collective works (Cuénin, *Roman et société*, 1:280). Curiously, the *Annales* and the *Mémoires de la vie de Henriette-Sylvie de Molière* are the only works Villedieu did not sign (Cuénin, 1:282).

14. As Stanton remarks, Villedieu's accent on the details of history is provocative: "Because it exposes a lack, a defective incompleteness, the added detail is the excess that subverts the authority of History" ("The Demystification of History and Fiction," 343).

15. The first English translation contains only the last two parts of the novel. The editor remarks that the work met with success in Holland "and in other parts where it hath been several times printed" (MDVD, *The Disorders of Love Truly Expressed in the Unfortunate Amours of Givry and Mlle de Guise*). Cuénin notes that the *Désordres* continued to be read throughout the eighteenth century and, in 1762, even inspired a comedy, de Renout's *Le Caprice ou l'épreuve dangereuse* (*Roman et société*, 1:134).

16. Cuénin remarks that, "with the exception of *Don Carlos*, no other seventeenth-century historical novel is as close to history" (*Roman et société*, 1:305).

17. Flannigan usefully compares Villedieu's novel to Mézeray's work, but he ignores other possible influences, especially Marguerite de Valois's *Mémoires*. For the identification of Villedieu's sources, I am indebted to Flannigan's work and to Cuénin's introduction to her edition of the *Désordres*. Cuénin's edition also includes extensive footnotes, and she is especially attentive to Villedieu's use of Mézeray. I will refer to her work throughout this discussion.

18. As Flannigan notes, "*Les Désordres de l'amour* is predicated upon the assumption that the reader is already familiar with the basic facts of history" (*Mme de Villedieu's "Les Désordres*," 143). As a result, her novel is often elliptical and confusing to a modern reader.

19. Cuénin, Introduction, *Les Désordres de l'amour*, by Villedieu, xxx.

20. Cuénin, Introduction, *Les Désordres de l'amour*, by Villedieu, xxvii.

21. Villedieu, *Les Désordres de l'amour*, ed. Micheline Cuénin, 207. All further references to this work appear in the text.

22. In this instance it is noteworthy that Villedieu eliminated from her portrait of Henri III such characteristics as "a remarkable politeness, a pleasant gentleness in conversation, very eloquent and charming in his speech" ("une politesse singulière, une douceur agréable dans la conversation, beaucoup d'éloquence et de charme dans ses discours")—qualities that associate him with the realm of particular history.

23. Flannigan calls these "embedded maxims." He discusses maxims in depth in *Mme de Villedieu's "Les Désordres*," 53–75.

24. Flannigan remarks that, with the maxims, Villedieu "provides the plan, the 'roadmap' with which her text is to be read" (*Mme de Villedieu's "Les Désordres*," 57).

25. As Flannigan remarks, this narrative voice is not identified as female. He believes that "one is forced . . . to attribute a masculine 'posture' to its narrator" (*Mme de Villedieu's "Les Désordres*," 69). However, I do not believe the voice is gender-identified and will thus refer to the narrator as s/he.

26. Flannigan, *Mme de Villedieu's "Les Désordres*," 79.

27. Flannigan, "*Mme de Villedieu's Les Désordres de l'amour*: The Feminization of History," 100.

28. As Cuénin notes, the banishment of Marguerite de Valois's friend Torigini is historically accurate, although the event occurred later (Villedieu, *Les Désordres de l'amour*, 13, n. 31). Marguerite recounts the episode in her *Mémoires*.

29. The Apollo Fountain is situated between the main gardens and the Grand Canal and is therefore the focal point of the east-west axis of the park. Apollo and his chariot were constructed by Tubi in 1671 from a sketch by Le Brun.

30. Cuénin notes that the theme of Apollo and Daphne "is borrowed from the ballet of the birth of Venus danced at the Palais Royal by his majesty January 26, 1665. . . . Mme de Villedieu could have been invited by Saint-Aignan, since he had invited her to the 'Pleasure of the Enchanted Island'" (Villedieu, *Les Désordres de l'amour*, 22, n. 49).

31. In *Roman et société*, Cuénin reviews the discussion about the declarations in the two novels (1:303–305).

32. Cuénin, *Roman et société*, 1:83.

33. According to Furetière, *génie* means "natural talent." Villedieu is perhaps using the term in both that sense and the sense of "guardian angel."

34. Cuénin believes that the division into two parts is in fact artificial and corresponds to the publisher's desire for a collection with stories of uniform length (Introduction, *Les Désordres de l'amour*, by Villedieu, xxx).

35. Katharine Jensen examines the relationship among women, writ-

ing, power, and passion in this last story of *Les Désordres* and in Villedieu's epistolary work, *Les Billets galants* ("The Love Letter and the Female Writing Self: Masochism or Subversion? The Case of Madame de Villedieu"). Although she looks at the relationship in a different context from mine, my reading is indebted to her insights.

36. Miller sees this remark as underscoring Givry's inability to distinguish between the realms of love and state ("Tender Economies," 88).

37. As Jensen remarks, "As Freud had described them women's ambitions have traditionally been limited to the erotic. . . . In the *Désordres*, however, . . . the princess holds out the possibility for another expression of female ambition. . . . She as a writing subject is not recontained within erotic dependence" ("The Love Letter and the Female Writing Self," 465).

38. Miller, "Tender Economies," 91.

39. Showalter, *The Evolution of the French Novel*, 55. Although I would agree with Showalter that Bayle is criticizing Villedieu's type of history for undermining any attempt to build a scientific foundation for the genre, I would also maintain that, by specifically choosing Villedieu as his target, Bayle is reacting against her particular reconstruction of historical perspective.

CHAPTER FIVE: LAFAYETTE H/HISTORIENNE

1. "We talked about the *Princesse de Clèves*, for how can one not talk about it?" Jean-Baptiste Trousset de Valincour, *Lettres à Mme la Marquise de *** au sujet de la Princesse de Clèves*, 365–366. All further references to this work appear in the text.

2. The most comprehensive study of the critical reception of *La Princesse de Clèves* is Maurice Laugaa's *Lectures de Mme de Lafayette*. He discusses the seventeenth-century quarrel (20–111).

3. Introduction, *Lettres*, by Valincour, iii.

4. As I said previously, the many connotations of *vraisemblance* make the word impossible to translate precisely. I will therefore continue to use the French.

5. Charles Dédéyan claims that Lafayette dictated her defense to Charnes (*Madame de Lafayette*, 152). This, however, has not been conclusively proven.

6. Laugaa, *Lectures*, 25. He examines the role of the *Mercure Galant* (20–40).

7. Laugaa includes this letter in its entirety (*Lectures*, 20–25).

8. An explanatory note in the Tours edition explains that in the seventeenth century Amadis de Gaule was considered "the symbol of extravagant fiction."

9. Dédéyan, *Madame de Lafayette*, 124. Dédéyan's analysis of history in *La Princesse de Clèves* is primarily a resumé of the findings of Chamard and Rudler.

10. J. W. Scott, "The 'Digressions' of the *Princesse de Clèves*."

11. Bruce Morrissette, *The Life and Works of Marie-Catherine Desjardins*, 111.

12. Chamard and Rudler, "Les Sources historiques de *La Princesse de*

Clèves." Chamard and Rudler identify Lafayette's sources and juxtapose her text against these histories. Throughout this chapter, I have used their identifications of passages for my own comparisons.

13. Roger Francillon, *L'Oeuvre romanesque de Mme de Lafayette*, 119.

14. Claudette Sarlet, "Le Temps dans *La Princesse de Clèves*," 57.

15. Antoine Adam, Preface, *La Princesse de Clèves*, by Lafayette, 15, 17. Adam's remarks pertain to the introductory presentation of the court.

16. Letter (previously cited) from Lafayette to the chevalier de Lescheraine, 13 April 1678 (*Correspondance*, 2:63–64).

17. See the first article in the series, in which they identify Lafayette's sources (117).

18. Barbara Guetti refers to Lafayette's work as an effort "to produce a rival reality" ("'Travesty' and 'Usurpation' in Mme de Lafayette's Historical Fiction," 216).

19. Miller, *Subject to Change*, 57.

20. One of the few critics to examine history in *La Princesse de Clèves* along lines similar to my own is Pierre Malandain in "Ecriture de l'histoire dans *La Princesse de Clèves*," 19–36. Another article that has many points in common with my own work is Guetti's "'Travesty' and 'Usurpation,'" an analysis of history in the novel. I will have occasion to refer to Malandain's work during this chapter. Among other things, he analyzes the changes Lafayette makes in her sources. But although Malandain's approach is similar to mine, I do not believe that his final interpretation of history in *La Princesse de Clèves* goes far enough in explaining Lafayette's intentions with respect to her use of history. His reading falls short because he does not examine Lafayette's work within the context of the conventions of historical narrative and of women's historical writing—a context that I find essential for comprehending the historical aspect of *La Princesse de Clèves*.

21. "Au lecteur," *Mémoires*, by Pierre du Bourdeille, seigneur de Brantôme, 1:n.p.

22. As quoted in Laugaa, *Lectures*, 23.

23. Villedieu's and Saint-Réal's introductions, for example, consist of a few vague paragraphs designed merely to inform the reader of the choice of period and the principal characters.

24. Peter Brooks, *The Novel of Worldliness*. I argue, on the contrary, for the historical nature of the portrait in my "Rescripting Historical Discourse: Literary Portraits by Women."

25. In his definitions of *galant* and *galanterie*, Furetière associates the terms with the court and amorous intrigues: "*Galant:* a civil, decent man, who is knowledgeable concerning his profession. . . . Is also said of a man who has a courtly air, pleasant ways, who tries to please, especially with the fair sex. . . . In the feminine: . . . a gallant woman is one who knows how to live, who knows how to choose and receive her entourage" ("Homme honnête, civil, savant dans les choses de sa profession. . . . Se dit aussi d'un homme qui a l'air de la Cour, les manières agréables, qui tâche à plaire, et particulièrement au beau sexe. . . . Au féminin: . . . une femme galante, qui sait vivre, qui sait bien choisir et recevoir son monde"). "*Galanterie:* That which is gallant. . . . Is also said of the courtship of ladies. . . . It is also figuratively

and hyperbolically used as in 'That business is pure gallantry,' to mean it is not an important thing" ("Ce qui est galant. . . . Se dit aussi de l'attache qu'on a à courtiser les Dames. . . . On dit aussi figurément et avec hyperbole, 'Cette affaire-là n'est qu'une pure galanterie,' pour dire, ce n'est pas une chose de conséquence"). Lafayette extends the boundaries of *galanterie* to include political acts, and she endows these acts with great importance.

26. Lafayette, *La Princesse de Clèves*, 35. All further references to this work appear in the text.

27. Mézeray, *Histoire de France* (Paris: Guillemot, 1646–1651), 3:601. All further references to this work appear in the text.

28. It is interesting to note that this description of Catherine de Médicis appears as part of the portrait of Catherine that Mézeray adds in a separate section following his account of Henri II's reign (3:733–734). It is thus not integral to his portrayal of the period in general.

29. Chamard and Rudler, "Les Sources historiques," 7.

30. Ibid.

31. Brantôme, *Les Vies des dames illustres de France*, in *Mémoires*, (Leiden: Jean Sambix, 1665–1666), 1:324. All further references to this work appear in the text.

32. In contrast, Mézeray's account of Henri's death does not display Lafayette's interiorization: "When the tournament was almost finished, he informed the comte de Montgomery, . . . against whom he wanted to joust again. It then happened that Montgomery, having broken his lance on the breastplate, could not hold his arm back and thus hit him in the right eye with the piece" ("Or comme le Tournoi était presque fini . . . il avisa le comte de Montgomery . . . contre lequel il voulut encore faire une course. . . . Il arriva donc que Montgomery lui ayant brisé sa lance dans le plastron, ne pût retenir son bras: tellement qu'il l'atteignit dans l'oeil droit avec le tronçon" [3: 719–720]).

33. Valincour's critique of these episodes is almost a refrain in the *Lettres*. Earlier he speaks of "that long conversation in which [Mme de Chartres] tells [the princess] the entire history of the old court. I had trouble understanding what relationship there could be between what she tells her about Mme de Valentinois, Mme d'Estampes, [and] the death of the dauphin, and the story of the princesse de Clèves" ("cette grande conversation, dans laquelle elle lui fait toute l'histoire de la vieille cour. J'ai eu peine à comprendre le rapport qu'il peut y avoir entre ce qu'elle lui conte de Madame de Valentinois, de Madame d'Estampes, de la mort du Dauphin, et l'Histoire de la Princesse de Clèves" [18–19]).

34. He states, "The reader is so interested in M. de Nemours and Mme de Clèves that he always wants to see the two of them. It seems that a crime is committed by making him/her turn his/her regard elsewhere. . . . The episodes are not at all desirable" ("Le lecteur est si intéressé pour M. de Nemours et pour Mme de Clèves qu'il voudrait toujours les voir l'un et l'autre. Il semble qu'on lui fait violence pour lui faire tourner ses regards ailleurs. . . . On n'y voudrait point d'épisodes" [as quoted in Laugaa, *Lectures*, 23]).

35. Although many critics treat these historical episodes, few develop an interpretation that relates them convincingly to the fictional story of the

princess. One of the most successful studies to do so is John Lyons's "Narration, Interpretation and Paradox: *La Princesse de Clèves*," 383–400. He relates the princess's behavior to these essential intertexts.

36. Here I am opposed to those critics who place Henri II at the top of the court hierarchy. Byron Wells, for example, states that "the king, of course, remains at the apex of the pyramid, untouchable, omnipotent, the ultimate arbiter of human destinies: in short, the Father, the author of the law" ("The King, the Court, the Country," 567). Such an interpretation does not recognize Lafayette's essential revision of history.

37. Mézeray, *Abrégé* (Paris: Billaine, 1668), 2:935.

38. Brantôme, *Les Vies des dames galantes de son temps*, in *Mémoires* (Leiden: Jean Sambix, 1665–1666) 2:328.

39. Lyons discusses the contradictory nature of Mme de Chartres's discourse ("Narration, Interpretation and Paradox," 393). Much interesting work has been done on Mme de Chartres's role in the novel. See, in particular, Marianne Hirsch's "A Mother's Discourse: Incorporation and Repetition in *La Princesse de Clèves*."

40. According to Chamard and Rudler, the king's respect for Diane is not referred to in any of Lafayette's sources (*Les Sources historiques,* 305).

41. Chamard and Rudler, *Les Sources historiques,* 309. This reference also points to Lafayette's careful construction of her history. *L'Heptaméron* appeared in 1558–1559, exactly the time in which the novel is set.

42. A vidame was an officer who replaced ecclesiastics in military or judicial functions.

43. Jean LeLaboureur, ed., *Les Mémoires de Messieur Michel de Castelnau,* 466.

44. Mary Stuart reinforces this portrayal when speaking to the princess: "M. de Nemours was right . . . to approve of his mistress's going to the ball. So many women then held this position that, if they had not come, there would have been few people present" ("M. de Nemours avait raison . . . d'approuver que sa maîtresse allât au bal. Il y avait alors un si grand nombre de femmes à qui il donnait cette qualité que, si elles n'y fussent point venues, il y aurait eu peu de monde" [63]).

45. DeJean interprets this episode in the context of female authorship in seventeenth-century France ("Lafayette's Ellipses: The Privileges of Anonymity").

46. Pierre Bayle also criticizes Lafayette's handling of Nemours. He complains that the novelist has this historical character play a role unworthy of him. "If great minds thus ruin nature and truth, what will minor authors and poets do?" ("Si les grands esprits gâtent ainsi la Nature et la vérité, que fera ce des petits Auteurs et des Poëtes?" [*Nouvelles Lettres de l'auteur de la critique du Christianisme,* 658]).

47. Michael Danahy examines the spaces, political and otherwise, in *La Princesse de Clèves* and proposes an interpretation that is almost the direct opposite of mine ("Social, Sexual and Human Spaces in *La Princesse de Clèves*"). Although Danahy sees the court as gender-specific in terms of political power, the gender he sees in this space is male. According to him, the "virilocal society" (214) that Lafayette describes implicitly gives men complete power over women. The princess strives to create her own female space in the midst of

this male-dominated world. This vision of the princess's struggle is only partially correct. Danahy's assessment of the court as a male-dominated space ignores the textual effort Lafayette makes to revise such preconceived ideas about women's political position.

48. Micheline Cuénin and Chantal Morlet-Chantalat, "Châteaux et romans au XVIIe siècle," 101–123. Although this is one article, it is divided into two distinct parts, each identified with a single author. In future references, I will specify the name of the author of the part referred to.

49. Cuénin, "Châteaux et romans," 118.

50. As Cuénin notes, the château itself is never described. Lafayette is thus relying on the reader to complete the picture.

51. Cuénin, "Châteaux et romans," 119.

52. Ibid., 118.

53. One of Nemours's illustrious compatriots, Montpensier, also went into exile after the Fronde, retiring to her domain of St. Fargeau. This is not the only association one could make between La Grande Mademoiselle and the feminocentric milieu of Coulommiers. At the time *La Princesse de Clèves* was published, Montpensier was the owner of the Luxembourg Palace, a residence that bears a curious resemblance to Coulommiers. Like Coulommiers, the Luxembourg Palace was built for a woman, in this case Marie de Médicis. Under Marie's governance, the palace was also decorated to attest to women's glory and political power; Marie de Médicis commissioned Rubens to depict her reign as regent in a series of twelve enormous paintings, which she hung in her palace. (They are now in the Louvre.) Today the Luxembourg Gardens continue to glorify women's historical contributions: the walkways are lined with statues of famous women. Thus, like Coulommiers before it, the Luxembourg Palace is still associated with women's historical activities.

54. Danahy states that, "to a greater degree than men, females are kept outside the 'ordered agitation' of the military and political struggles that form a vital part of the courtly households" ("Social, Sexual and Human Spaces," 215). But Lafayette does not include these military and political struggles as recounted in her sources, except when they are generated by women from the interior milieu of the court. In fact, in the novel the "ordered agitation" to which Danahy refers is specifically associated with interior court politics. "All these different factions competed against and envied each other: the women who constituted them were also jealous. . . . Thus there was an agitation without disorder in this court" ("Toutes ces différentes cabales avaient de l'émulation et de l'envie les unes contre les autres: les dames qui les composaient avait aussi de la jalousie. . . . Ainsi il y avait une sorte d'agitation sans désordre dans cette cour" [*La Princesse de Clèves*, 45]).

55. Chamard and Rudler, for example, remark that Lafayette "did not make the slightest effort to go outside of her own time period" (*Les Sources historiques*, 20). They also contend that Lafayette "doesn't care about the chronology" (120). Similarly, Adam summarizes his discussion of the opening depiction of the court by saying, "It is clear that Mme de Lafayette [because of her accent on *galanterie*] cannot imagine the possibility of seeing and describing the life at court differently" (Introduction, *La Princesse de Clèves*, 16). Adam thus attributes Lafayette's anachronistic history to inability rather than to intentionality.

56. Ann Moore examines the relationship between the fictional and the historical chronologies to suggest the effect that time in the novel may have on the reader ("Temporal Structure and Reader Response in *La Princesse de Clèves*").

57. In his evaluation of various histories, Lenglet Dufresnoy cites Mézeray *Abrégé* for its chronological accuracy: "Mézeray's *Abrégé* is very highly regarded, and is very exact regarding the chronology; it is even the one that is most often cited" ("*L'Abrégé* de Mézeray est fort estimé, et plus exact pour la chronologie; c'est même celui qu'on cite le plus souvent" [*Méthode pour étudier l'histoire*, 2:95]).

58. Malandain, "Ecriture de l'histoire," 31.

59. Moore, "Temporal Structure," 564. See her chart for the precise correspondences.

60. Chamard and Rudler, *Les Sources historiques*, 101, 126. They cite other such "discrepancies" on 296 and 238–239.

61. Lafayette notes that at the wedding, Madame's dress was "carried by" ("portée par") Mlles de Montpensier and de Longueville (140).

62. Chamard and Rudler refer to Mary Stuart as "the educated queen" ("la reine lettrée" [*Les Sources historiques*, 2]).

63. Manfred Kusch speaks of the timeless quality of history in *La Princesse de Clèves* and the negation of a linear notion of time ("Narrative Technique and Cognitive Modes in *La Princesse de Clèves*"). His final evaluation, however, seems somewhat reductive. Kusch views history as "a settled affair" (314). Although Lafayette may view history as circular, I do not believe she implies that history is static—just repetitive. Malandain also points to time's synchronic nature in the novel ("Ecriture de l'histoire," 20).

64. For a detailed examination of the development of royal historiography under the Sun King, see Ranum's *Artisans of Glory*, especially chapters 4 and 5. In a similar vein, Marin's discussion of historiography under the Sun King accentuates the relationship between historical narrative and the development of a notion of political apotheosis, or at least an effort to portray Louis XIV's reign as the high point in history (*Le Portrait du roi*). See especially the chapter "The King's Narrative or How to Write History" ("Le Récit du roi ou comment écrire l'histoire").

65. Charles Perrault, Preface, *Parallèle des Anciens et des Modernes*.

66. Odette Virmaux examines the relationship between the princess and her historical milieu. In her view, "Mme de Clèves does not belong to the domain of history because she is a creature of eternity, an ideal figure compared so as to be highlighted by the disorder of real events. . . . She is detached from all historical context by her dignity" (*Les Héroïnes romanesques de Mme de Lafayette*, 51). Virmaux's interpretation, which is more categorical than mine, is justified if the princess is viewed with respect to history in general. I believe, however, that when the princess is interpreted through the history Lafayette creates for her—which itself, in many respects, is detached from the conventional historical narrative of Lafayette's sources—the princess's relationship to history is not so clear.

67. Nemours's response, like that of M. de Clèves, underscores the princess's exceptionality. "Finally, Madame, you are perhaps the only person in whom these two things [the qualities of both a mistress and a wife] have ever been found to the degree they are found in you" ("Car enfin, madame,

vous êtes peut-être la seule personne en qui ces deux choses se soient jamais trouvées au degré qu'elles sont en vous" [172]).

68. Pierre-Daniel Huet, *Traité sur l'origine des romans*, 49. Although in this context *roman* refers to earlier fictions such as the heroic novels by Scudéry, the same concept applies to the notion of *vraisemblance* in the *nouvelle historique*.

69. Du Plaisir, *Sentiments sur les lettres et sur l'histoire avec des scrupules sur le style*, 89.

70. Rapin, *Reflexions sur la poétique*, in *Oeuvres*, 2:115–116.

71. Genette, "Vraisemblance et motivation," *Figures II*, 73.

72. Miller, "Emphasis Added: Plots and Plausibilities in Women's Fictions," 36–37. Miller analyzes the relationship between *La Princesse de Clèves* and the conception of *vraisemblance* and identifies *vraisemblance* with the dominant, male culture. In her interpretation, to which I am indebted, women's works often consciously opposed these maxims. In her words, "To read women's literature is to see and hear repeatedly a chafing against the 'unsatisfactory reality' contained in the maxims" (46–47).

73. Selma A. Zebouni examines the notion of *vraisemblance* within the context of seventeenth-century classicism. She ascribes the need for *vraisemblance* to the emphasis placed on the pedagogical function attributed to literature during this period: "It is because it has something to say that classical art must be *vraisemblable*, because what it says must have truth value, given that it would be absurd to want to teach something that is false" ("Classicisme et vraisemblance," 68–69.) Zebouni stresses that the system of maxims controlling the notion of *vraisemblance* is limited to those standards that are most universal: "Classicism esteems truth to be only that which is common and universal, which is to say, that which is guaranteed by the experience of the greatest number. . . . The reality, truth, or essence of a thing is its resemblance with other things that exhibit the same characteristics. . . . Only that which is founded upon common experience, that is to say, the *vraisemblable*, can have truth value" (71–72).

74. As quoted in Laugaa, *Lectures*, 23.

75. Guetti comments on the link between Diane de Poitiers and the princess: "Mme de Clèves . . . inherits (or usurps) the status of her fictional predecessor, Diane de Poitiers. . . . Mme de Clèves becomes, like Diane de Poitiers, a woman with no peer, no rival" ("'Travesty' and 'Usurpation,'" 216).

76. For an interpretation of this scene, see DeJean, "Lafayette's Ellipses: The Privileges of Anonymity." DeJean explains: "In fact, *aveu* only came to be used in the sense of 'confession' in the mid-seventeenth century, when it was first used in the legal procedure by which criminals were forced to *avouer*, or admit their crimes. The princess, however, does not use the term in this sense. . . . Rather she is attempting to enact an *aveu* in the earlier legal sense of a loyalty oath. . . . The word originally meant 'a written declaration admitting the vassal's commitment to his lord, in exchange for the heritable estate (fief)' (Robert dictionary)" (896).

77. Cuénin, "Châteaux et romans," 121. DeJean convincingly proves "Lafayette's awareness of the potentially scandalous impropriety of the situation in which she staged female desire." See DeJean's interpretation of the reverie scene in "Female Voyeurism: Sappho and Lafayette," 212–215.

78. Lyons comes to a similar conclusion about the evolution of the prin-

cess throughout the novel. In his opinion, "she becomes a story for herself. She becomes able to compare what she finds in the stories of others with what she finds in herself" ("Narration, Interpretation and Paradox," 391).

79. As we have seen, in the internal narrative dedicated to Sapho in Scudéry's novel, Sapho retires to the country of the Sauromates. Her lover accompanies her and lives according to her rules.

Afterword

1. Margaret Cavendish, duchess of Newcastle, *The Life of the Thrice Noble, High and Puissant Prince William Cavendishe*, 10–11.

2. Kelly, *Women, History and Theory*, xxv.

3. Stanton, "Autogynography," 13.

4. Davis, "Gender and Genre," 157.

5. I am using "herstory" as it is defined in *A Feminist Dictionary:* "The human story as told by women about women (and, possibly, men); accounts of the human past and human activities that consider women as being at the center of society, and not at the margins; women's history."

6. Hélène Cixous, *La Jeune Née.* Tr. *The Newly Born Woman*, trans. Betsy Wing.

REFERENCES

Actes de Wakeforest. Edited by Milorad R. Margitic and Byron R. Wells. Paris: Biblio 17, 1987.

Adam, Antoine. *Histoire de la littérature française au XVIIe siècle.* 5 vols. Paris: Domat, 1948–1956.

Albistur, Maïté, and Daniel Armogathe, eds. *Histoire du féminisme française du moyen âge à nos jours.* Paris: Des Femmes, 1977.

Andreu, Anne. *La Duchesse de Montpensier ou la Grande Amazone.* Lausanne: Editions Rencontre, 1965.

Anselme, Père M. A. *Oraison funèbre de très-haute et très-puissante princesse Anne-Marie-Louise d'Orléans, duchesse de Montpensier, souveraine de Dombes.* Paris: Josse, 1693.

Apostolidès, Jean-Marie. *Le Roi-machine.* Paris: Minuit, 1981.

Ariès, Philippe. *Le Temps de l'histoire.* 1954. Paris: Seuil, 1986.

Backer, Dorothy. *Precious Women.* New York: Basic Books, 1974.

Baillet, Adrien. *Jugement des sçavans sur les principaux ouvrages des auteurs.* 9 vols. Paris: A. Dezallier, 1685–1686.

Barine, Arvède. *La Grande Mademoiselle.* 2 vols. New York: Knickerbocker Press, 1903.

Batteux, Abbé Charles. *Principes de littérature.* 5 vols. Paris: Saillant et Nyon, 1774.

Batut, Guy de la. *Oraison funèbre d'Henriette d'Angleterre par Bossuet.* Paris: Société française d'éditions littéraires et techniques, 1931.

Bayle, Pierre. *Dictionnaire historique et critique.* Rotterdam: R. Leers, 1697.

———. *Nouvelles Lettres de l'auteur de la critique du Christianisme.* Villefranche, 1685.

Beasley, Faith E. "Rescripting Historical Discourse: Literary Portraits by Women." *Papers on French Seventeenth-Century Literature* 14, no. 27 (1987): 517–535.

———. "Villedieu's Metamorphosis of Judicious History: *Les Désordres de l'amour.*" In *Actes de Wakeforest,* edited by Milorad R. Margitic and Byron R. Wells, 397–405. Paris: Biblio 17, 1987.

Beaujour, Michel. *Miroirs d'encre.* Paris: Seuil, 1980.

Bouyer, Christian. *La Grande Mademoiselle.* Paris: Albin Michel, 1986.

Brantôme, Pierre du Bourdeille, seigneur de. *Mémoires.* Leiden: Jean Sambix, 1665–1666.

Brooks, Peter. *The Novel of Worldliness.* Princeton: Princeton University Press, 1969.

Buffet, Marguerite. *Nouvelles Observations sur la langue française.* Paris: Cusson, 1668.

Caylus, Mme de. *Souvenirs.* 1770. Paris: Mercure de France, 1986.

Chamard, H., and G. Rudler. "Les Sources historiques de *La Princesse de Clèves.*" *Revue de seizième siècle* 2 (1914): 92–131, 289–321; 5 (1917–1918): 1–20, 231–243.

Charnes, Jean-Antoine, Abbé de. *Conversations sur la critique de la Princesse de Clèves.* 1679. Edited by François Weil et al. Tours: Université de Tours, 1973.

Cholakian, Patricia. "A House of Her Own: Marginality and Dissidence in the

Mémoires of La Grande Mademoiselle." *Prose Studies* 9, no. 3 (1986): 3–20.

Cixous, Hélène. *La Jeune Née*. Paris: 10/18, 1975 (Tr. *The Newly Born Woman*. Translated by Betsy Wing. Minneapolis: University of Minnesota Press, 1986.)

Coulet, Henri. *Le Roman jusqu'à la révolution*. 2 vols. Paris: A. Colin, 1967.

Cuénin, Micheline. *Roman et société sous Louis XIV: Mme de Villedieu*. 2 vols. Paris: Champion, 1979.

Cuénin, Micheline, and Chantal Morlet-Chantalat. "Châteaux et romans au XVIIe siècle." *XVIIe siècle* 118–119 (1978): 101–123.

Danahy, Michael. "Social, Sexual and Human Spaces in *La Princesse de Clèves*." *French Forum* 3 (1981): 212–224.

Davis, Natalie Zemon. "Gender and Genre: Women as Historical Writers 1400–1820." In *Beyond Their Sex: Learned Women of the European Past*, edited by Patricia H. Labalme, 153–182. New York: New York University Press, 1980.

———. "Women's History in Transition: The European Case." *Feminist Studies* 3, no. 3/4 (1976): 83–103.

Dédéyan, Charles. *Madame de Lafayette*. Paris: Société d'édition d'enseignement supérieur, 1965.

DeJean, Joan. "Classical Reeducation: Decanonizing the Feminine." *Yale French Studies* 75 (1988): 26–39.

———. "Female Voyeurism: Sapho and Lafayette." *Rivista di letterature moderne e comparate* 40, no. 3 (1987): 201–215.

———. *Fictions of Sapho, 1546–1937*. Chicago: University of Chicago Press, 1989.

———. "La Fronde romanesque: De l'exploit à la fiction." In *La Fronde en question*, edited by Roger Duchêne and Pierre Ronzeaud (181–192). Aix-en-Provence: Université de Provence, 1988.

———. "Lafayette's Ellipses: The Privileges of Anonymity." *PMLA* 99, no. 5 (1984): 884–900.

———, ed. *Women's Writing in Seventeenth-Century France*. Special issue, *Esprit Créateur* 23, no. 2 (1983).

DeJean, Joan, and Nancy K. Miller, eds. *The Politics of Tradition: Placing Women in French Literature*. Special issue, *Yale French Studies* 75 (1988).

Delpech, Jeanine. *L'Ame de la Fronde: Mme de Longueville*. Paris: Fayard, 1957.

Du Deffand, Marie de Viche-Chamrond, Mme. *Correspondance*. Geneva: Slatkine, 1971.

Dulong, Gustave. *L'Abbé de Saint-Réal: Etude sur les rapports de l'histoire et du roman au XVIIe siècle*. 1921. Geneva: Slatkine, 1980.

Du Plaisir. *Sentiments sur les lettres et sur l'histoire avec des scrupules sur le style*. 1683. Edited by Philippe Hourcarde. Geneva: Droz, 1975.

Duras, Marguerite. Interview. *Elle*. Paris, October 1987.

Evans, Wilfred Hugo. *Mézeray: l'histoire et la conception de l'histoire au XVIIe siècle*. Paris: Gamber, 1930.

The Female Autograph. Edited by Domna C. Stanton. 1984. Chicago: University of Chicago Press, 1987.

A Feminist Dictionary. Edited by Cheris Kramarae and Paula A. Treichler. New York: Pandora Press, 1985.

Ferguson, Moira. *First Feminists*. Bloomington: Indiana University Press, 1985.

Flannigan, Arthur. "Mme de Villedieu's *Les Désordres de l'amour:* The Feminization of History." *Esprit Créateur* 23, no. 2 (1983): 94–106.

———. *Madame de Villedieu's "Les Désordres de l'amour"*: History, Literature and the Nouvelle Historique. Washington, D.C.: University Press of America, 1982.

Force, Caumont de la. *Histoire secrète de Catherine de Bourbon*. 1703. Paris: Slatkine, 1979.

Francillon, Roger. *L'Oeuvre romanesque de Mme de Lafayette*. Paris: Corti, 1973.

Fumaroli, Marc. "Les Mémoires du XVIIe siècle au carrefour des genres en prose." *XVIIe siècle* 94–95 (1971): 7–37.

Furetière, Antoine. *Dictionnaire universel*. Paris, 1682.

Garapon, Jean. "Les Mémorialistes et le réel: L'exemple du cardinal de Retz et de Mademoiselle de Montpensier." *Littératures classiques* 2 (January 1989): 181–189.

Genette, Gérard. *Figures II*. Paris: Seuil, 1969.

———. "Discours du récit." In *Figures III*. Paris: Seuil, 1972.

Genlis, Stéphanie-Félicité de. *De l'influence des femmes sur la littérature comme protectrices et comme auteurs*. Paris: Maradon, 1811.

Gilbert, Sandra, and Susan Gubar. "Ceremonies of the Alphabet: Female Grandmatologies and the Female Autograph." In *The Female Autograph*, edited by Domna C. Stanton. 1984. Chicago: University of Chicago Press, 1987.

Glaserman, Rose Hughette. "Etude sur la Grande Mademoiselle et ses *Mémoires*." Ph.D. diss., City University of New York, 1981.

Godenne, René. *Histoire de la nouvelle française au dix-septième et dix-huitième siècles*. Geneva: Droz, 1970.

Godwin, Denise. *Les Nouvelles françaises ou les divertissements de la Princesse Aurélie de Segrais*. Paris: Nizet, 1983.

Goldsmith, Elizabeth. *Exclusive Conversations: The Art of Interaction in Seventeenth-Century France*. Philadelphia: University of Pennsylvania Press, 1988.

Gregorio, Laurence A. *Order in the Court: History and Society in "La Princesse de Clèves."* Stanford, Calif.: Stanford French and Italian Studies, 1986.

Guetti, Barbara Jones. "'Travesty' and 'Usurpation' in Mme de Lafayette's Historical Fiction." *Yale French Studies* 69 (1985): 211–221.

Guillaume, Jacquette. *Les Dames illustres*. Paris, 1665.

Harth, Erica. *Ideology and Culture in Seventeenth-Century France*. Ithaca: Cornell University Press, 1983.

Hazard, Paul. *La Crise de la conscience européenne*. Paris: Boivin, 1935.

Henein, Eglal. "Mademoiselle de Montpensier à la recherche du temps perdu." *Papers on French Seventeenth-Century Literature* 6 (1976–1977): 38–52.

Hepp, Noémi. "La Notion d'Héroïne." *Onze Etudes sur l'image de la femme dans la littérature française du XVIIe siècle*. Edited by Wolfgang Leiner. Tubingen: Gunter Narr Verlag, 1978.

Hipp, Marie-Thérèse. *Mythes et réalités: Enquête sur le roman et les mémoires 1660–1700*. Paris: Klincksieck, 1976.

Hirsch, Marianne. "A Mother's Discourse: Incorporation and Repetition in *La Princesse de Clèves*." *Yale French Studies* 62 (1981): 67–87.

L'Histoire du roy. Edited by Daniel Meyer. Paris: Editions de la Réunion des Musées Nationaux, 1980.

Huët, Daniel. *Traité sur l'origine des romans*. 1669. Paris: Charpentier, 1861.

Interpreting Women's Lives: Feminist Theory and Personal Narratives. Edited by the Personal Narratives Group. Bloomington: Indiana University Press, 1989.

Jauss, Hans Robert. *Towards an Aesthetic of Reception*. Minneapolis: University of Minnesota Press, 1982.

Jensen, Katharine A. "The Love Letter and the Female Writing Self: Masochism or Subversion? The Case of Madame de Villedieu." In *Actes de Wakeforest*, edited by Milorad R. Margitic and Byron R. Wells, 451–467. Paris: Biblio 17, 1987.

Jouhaud, Christian. *Mazarinades: La Fronde des mots*. Paris: Aubier Montaigne, 1985.

Kelly, Joan. *Women, History and Theory*. Chicago: University of Chicago Press, 1984.

Knecht, R. J. *The Fronde*. London: The Historical Association, 1975.

Kossmann, Ernst. *La Fronde*. Leiden: University of Leiden, 1954.

Kusch, Manfred. "Narrative Technique and Cognitive Modes in *La Princesse de Clèves*." *Symposium* 30 (1976): 308–324.

La Croix, Pierre de. *Le Château de Choisy*. Paris: Dumoulin, 1867.

Lafayette, Marie-Madeleine Pioche de la Vergne, comtesse de. *Correspondance*. Edited by André Beaunier. 2 vols. Paris: Gallimard, 1942.

———. *Fatal Gallantry: Or, the Secret History of Henrietta Princess of England*. Translated by Ann Floyd. London: Clay, 1722.

———. *Histoire de la Princesse de Montpensier sous le règne de Charles IX roi de France*. Edited by André Beaunier. 1661. Paris: La Connaissance, 1926.

———. *Histoire de Madame Henriette d'Angleterre*. 1720. Paris: Mercure de France, 1965.

———. *La Princesse de Clèves*. 1678. Edited by Antoine Adam. Paris: Garnier, 1966.

———. *Vie de la Princesse d'Angleterre*. 1720. Edited by Marie-Thérèse Hipp. Paris: Droz, 1967.

Lalanne, Ludovic. *Brantôme et "La Princesse de Clèves."* Paris, 1891.

Lambert, Abbé Claude-François. *Histoire littéraire du règne de Louis XIV*. Paris, 1751.

La Mothe le Vayer, François de. *De peu de certitude qu'il y a dans l'histoire*. In *Oeuvres*. Paris: Camusat, 1628.

La Porte, Abbé Joseph de. *Histoire littéraire des femmes françaises*. 5 vols. Paris: Lacombe, 1769.

La Rochefoucauld, François de. *Mémoires*. 1662. Paris: Garnier, 1883.

Laugaa, Maurice. *Lectures de Mme de Lafayette*. Paris: Armand Colin, 1971.

Le Laboureur, Jean, ed. *Mémoires de Michel de Castelnau*, by Michel de Castelnau. (Paris, 1660).

Leffler, Phyllis. "*L'Histoire Raisonnée*: A Study of French Historiography, 1660–1720." Ph.D. diss., Ohio State University, 1971.

Lejeune, Philippe. *L'Autobiographie en France*. Paris: Colin, 1971.

———. *Le Pacte autobiographique*. Paris: Seuil, 1975.

Lenglet Dufresnoy, Abbé Nicolas. *De l'usage des romans*. Amsterdam: De Poilras, 1734.

———. *Méthode pour étudier l'histoire*. Paris: Coustelier, 1713.

Letts, J. T. *Le Cardinal de Retz: Historien et memorialiste du possible*. Paris: Nizet, 1966.

Lever, Maurice. *La Fiction narrative en prose au XVIIe siècle*. 1976. Paris: Presses universitaires de France, 1981.

———. *Le Roman français au XVIIe siècle*. Paris: Presses universitaires de France, 1981.

Life/lines: Theorizing Women's Autobiography. Edited by Bella Brodski and Celeste Schenck. Ithaca: Cornell University Press, 1988.

Livet, Ch.-L. "Les Femmes de la Fronde." *Revue européenne* 3 (1859): 529–551, 726–758.

Lorris, Pierre-Georges. *La Fronde*. Paris: Albin Michel, 1961.

Lougee, Carolyn C. *Le Paradis des femmes: Women, Salons and Social Stratification in Seventeenth-Century France*. Princeton: Princeton University Press, 1976.

Louis XIV. *Mémoires*. 1806. Edited by Jean Longnon. Paris: Tallandier, 1978.

Lyons, John D. "Narration, Interpretation and Paradox: *La Princesse de Clèves*." *Romanic Review* 72 (1981): 383–400.

Maclean, Ian. *Woman Triumphant (1610–1652)*. Oxford: Oxford University Press, 1977.

MacRae, Margaret J. "Diane de Poitiers and Mme de Clèves: A Study of Women's Roles, the Victim and the Conqueror." *Papers on French Seventeenth-Century Literature* 12, no. 23 (1985): 559–573.

Magendie, Maurice. *La Politesse mondaine et les gens d'honnêteté*. 2 vols. Paris: Alcan, 1925.

Malandain, Pierre. "Ecriture de l'histoire dans *La Princesse de Clèves*." *Littérature* 36 (1979): 19–36.

Mancini, Hortense. *Mémoires*. 1676. Paris: Mercure de France, 1965.

Mancini, Marie. *Mémoires*. 1678. Paris: Mercure de France, 1965.

Marin, Louis. *Le Portrait du roi*. Paris: Minuit, 1981. (Tr. *Portrait of the King*. Translated by Martha M. Houle. Minneapolis: University of Minnesota Press, 1988).

———. *Le Récit est un piège*. Paris: Minuit, 1978.

May, Georges. *L'Autobiographie*. Paris: Presses universitaires de France, 1979.

———. *Le Dilemme du roman au XVIIIe siècle*. New Haven: Yale University Press, 1963.

———. "L'Histoire a-t-elle engendré le roman?" *Revue d'histoire littéraire de France* 55 (1955): 155–176.

Melchior-Bonnet, Bernardine. *La Grande Mademoiselle: Héroïne et amoureuse*. Paris: Librairie Académique Perrin, 1985.

Menestrier, François. *Les Divers Caractères des ouvrages historiques*. Paris: J. Collombat, 1694.

Méthivier, Hubert. *La Fronde*. Paris: Presses universitaires de France, 1984.

Mezeray, François Eudes de. *Abrégé chronologique ou extrait de l'histoire de France*. 3 vols. Paris, 1667–1668.

———. *Histoire de France depuis Pharamond jusqu'à maintenant*. 3 vols. Paris, 1643–1651.

————. *Histoire de France par Mézéray: Edition populaire et permanente.* Paris: Bureau Central, 1839.

Miller, Nancy K. "Emphasis Added: Plots and Plausibilities in Women's Fictions." *PMLA* 96, no. 1 (1981): 36–48.

————. *Subject to Change.* New York: Columbia University Press, 1988.

————. "Tender Economies: Mme de Villedieu and the Cost of Indifference." *Esprit créateur* 23, no. 2 (1983): 80–93.

Moers, Ellen. *Literary Women: The Great Writers.* 1963. New York: Oxford University Press, 1985.

Montpensier, Anne-Marie-Louise-Henriette d'Orléans, duchesse de. *Divers Portraits.* St. Fargeau, 1659.

————. *Histoire de la Princesse de Paphlagonie.* B.N. (Paris) Rés. 8° Lb³⁷.3299.

————. *Le Manifeste de Mademoiselle présenté à son Altesse Royale.* Paris: Jacques Beley, 1652.

————. *Mémoires.* 1718. Vols. 40–43, *Collection des mémoires relatifs à l'histoire de France.* Edited by M. Petitot. Paris: Foucault, 1825.

————. *Le Recueil des portraits.* Paris: Barbin, 1659.

Moore, Ann. "Temporal Structure and Reader Response in *La Princesse de Clèves.*" *French Review,* 56, no. 4 (1983): 563–571.

Moote, A. Lloyd. *The Revolt of the Judges.* Princeton: Princeton University Press, 1971.

Morrissette, Bruce A. *The Life and Works of Marie-Catherine Desjardins (Mme de Villedieu) 1632–1683.* St. Louis: Washington University Press, 1947.

Motteville, Françoise Bertault, dame Langlois de. *Mémoires pour servir à l'histoire d'Anne d'Autriche.* 1723. Edited by M. Petitot. Paris: Foucault, 1825.

————. *Mémoires pour servir à l'histoire d'Anne d'Autriche.* 1723. Paris: Charpentier, 1867.

Nemours, Marie d'Orléans-Longueville, duchesse de. *Les Mémoires de M.L.D.D.N.* Edited by Mlle L'Héritier. Cologne, 1709.

Nettement, Alfred. *Etudes critiques sur le feuilleton-roman.* Paris: Perrodil, 1864.

Newcastle, Margaret Cavendish, duchess of. *The Life of the Thrice Noble, High and Puissant Prince William Cavendische.* 1667. New York: Dutton and Co., 1915.

Pellisson-Fontanier, Paul. *Histoire de Louis XIV.* Paris: Rollin, 1749.

Pelous, Jean-Michel. *Amour précieux, amour galant (1654–1675).* Paris: Klincksieck, 1980.

Perrault, Charles. *Parallèle des Anciens et des Modernes.* 1687. Edited by Hans Robert Jauss. Munich: Eidos Verlag, 1964.

Pizan, Christine de. *Epistre au dieu d'amours.* 1399. Edited by Maurice Roy. In *Ouevres poétiques.* Paris: Furmin Didot, 1886–1896, 2:1–27.

Pollitzer, Marcel. *Les Amazones de la Fronde et le quadrille des Intrigants.* Paris: Aubanel, 1959.

Pure, Abbé Michel de. *La Prétieuse ou le mystère des ruelles.* Paris: Guillaume de Luyne, 1656.

Racine, Jean. *Le Précis historique des campagnes de Louis XIV.* 1730. In *Oeuvres complètes.* Paris: Seuil, 1962.

Ranum, Orest. *Artisans of Glory: Writers and Historical Thought in Seventeenth-Century France.* Chapel Hill: University of North Carolina Press, 1980.

Rapin, le Père René. *Reflexions sur la poétique.* In *Oeuvres.* Amsterdam, 1709.

Retz, Jean-François-Paul de Gondi, Cardinal de. *Mémoires.* 1717. Paris: Pléiade, 1984.

Rewriting the Renaissance. Edited by Margaret W. Ferguson, Maureen Quilligan, and Nancy J. Vickers. Chicago: University of Chicago Press, 1986.

Sackville-West, Vita. *Daughter of France.* London: M. Joseph, 1959.

Saint-Evremond, Charles de Marguetel de Saint-Denis, seigneur de. *Discours sur les historiens français.* In *Oeuvres meslées.* Paris: Barbin, 1684.

Saint-Réal, César Vichard de. *La Conjuration des Espagnols contre la République de Venise.* 1674. Geneva: Droz, 1977.

———. *De l'usage de l'histoire.* 1671. In *Oeuvres.* Paris: Huart, 1745.

———. *Don Carlos.* 1672. Geneva: Droz, 1977.

Saint-Simon, Louis de Rouvroy, duc de. *Mémoires.* 1743. Paris: Hachette, 1879.

———. *Mémoires.* 1743. Paris: Pléiade, 1949–1961.

Sarlet, Claudette. "Le Temps dans *La Princesse de Clèves.*" *Marche romane,* (April/June 1959): 51–58.

Scott, J. W. "The 'Digressions' of the *Princesse de Clèves.*" *French Studies* 11 (1957): 315–322.

Scott, Joan Wallach. *Gender and the Politics of History.* New York: Columbia University Press, 1988.

Scudéry, Georges. *Ibrahim.* Paris: Sercy, 1648.

Scudéry, Madeleine de. *Artamène ou le Grand Cyrus.* Paris: Barbin, 1653.

———. *Conversations sur divers sujets.* Amsterdam: Daniel du Fresne, 1682.

———. *Les Femmes illustres.* Paris: Antoine de Sommaville, 1642.

Segrais, Jean-Regnault de. *Les Nouvelles françaises.* Paris: Antoine de Sommaville, 1656.

Showalter, English, Jr. *The Evolution of the French Novel 1641–1782.* Princeton: Princeton University Press, 1972.

Somaize, Antoine Baudeau, sieur de. *Le Grand Dictionnaire historique des Précieuses.* 2 vols. Paris: Kibou, 1661.

Sorel, Charles. *La Bibliothèque française.* Paris, 1664.

———. *De la connaissance des bons livres.* 1671. Edited by Lucia Moretti Cererini. Rome: Bulzoni Editore, 1974.

Staël, Germaine de. *Delphine.* Paris: Furmin Didot, 1872.

———. *Essai sur les fictions.* In *Oeuvres complètes.* Paris: Treuttel et Wurtz, 1820–1821.

Stanton, Domna C. "Autogynography: Is the Subject Different?" In *The Female Autograph,* edited by Domna C. Stanton, 3–20. 1984. Chicago: University of Chicago Press, 1987.

———. "The Demystification of History and Fiction in *Les Annales galantes.*" In *Actes de Wakeforest,* edited by Milorad R. Margitic and Byron R. Wells, 339–360. Paris: Biblio 17, 1987.

Tallemant des Réaux. *Historiettes.* Edited by Antoine Adam. 2 vols. Paris: Pléiade, 1961.

Thiollier, Marguerite Marie. *Ces Dames du Marais.* Paris: Atelier Alpha Bleue, 1988.

Vaillot, René. *Qui étaient Mme de Tencin . . . et le cardinal?* Paris: Le Pavillon, 1974.

Valincour, Jean-Baptiste Trousset de. *Lettres à Mme la Marquise de* *** *au sujet de la Princesse de Clèves*. 1678. Edited by Jacques Chupeau et al. Tours: Université de Tours, 1972.

Valois, Marguerite de. *Mémoires*. 1628. Paris: Mercure de France, 1971.

Varillas, Antoine. *Anecdotes de Florence*. The Hague: A. Leers, 1685.

Verdier, Gabrielle. "Mlle de Montpensier et le plaisir du texte." *Papers on French Seventeenth-Century Literature* 10, no. 18 (1983): 11–33.

Vertron, Claude-Charles Guionet, seigneur de. *La Nouvelle Pandore ou les femmes illustres du siècle de Louis le Grand*. Paris: Mazuel, 1698.

Villedieu, Marie-Catherine-Hortense Desjardins, Mme Antoine Boesset de. *Les Amours des grands hommes*. 1671. In vol. 4, *Oeuvres*. Lyon: Baritel, 1694.

———. *Les Annales galantes*. 1670. In vol. 1, *Oeuvres*. Lyon: Baritel, 1697.

———. *Les Désordres de l'amour*. 1675. Edited by Micheline Cuénin. Geneva: Droz, 1970.

———. *Mémoires de la vie de Henriette-Sylvie de Molière*. 1674. Edited by Micheline Cuénin. Tours: Université de Tours, 1977.

———. *Portrait des faiblesses humaines*. 1685. In vol. 1, *Oeuvres*. Paris: Edition de la Compagnie des Libraires, 1720–1721.

Vincens, Cécile. *Louis XIV and La Grande Mademoiselle*. New York: Knickerbocker Press, 1905.

Virmaux, Odette. *Les Héroïnes romanesques de Mme de Lafayette*. Paris: Klincksieck, 1981.

Voltaire, François Marie Arouet de. *Le Siècle de Louis XIV*. In *Oeuvres complètes*. Paris: Garnier, 1878.

Watt, Ian. *The Rise of the Novel*. Berkeley: University of California Press, 1957.

Watts, Derek A. "Self-Portrayal in Seventeenth-Century French Memoirs." *Australian Journal of French Studies* 12 (1975): 263–285.

Weinburg, Kurt. "The Lady and the Unicorn, or Madame de Nemours à Coulommiers." *Euphorion* 71, no. 4 (1977): 306–335.

Wells, Byron. "The King, the Court, the Country: Theme and Structure in *La Princesse de Clèves*." *Papers on French Seventeenth-Century Literature* 12, no. 23 (1985): 543–558.

White, Hayden. *The Content of the Form: Narrative Discourse and Historical Representation*. Baltimore: Johns Hopkins University Press, 1987.

———. *Tropics of Discourse: Essays in Cultural Criticism*. Baltimore: Johns Hopkins University Press, 1978.

———. "The Value of Narrativity in the Representation of Reality." *Critical Inquiry* 7 (1980): 5–27.

Woolf, Virginia. *A Room of One's Own*. 1929. New York: Harcourt, Brace, Jovanovich, 1957.

Zebouni, Selma A. "Classicisme et vraisemblance." *Papers on French Seventeenth-Century Literature* 8 (1977–1978): 66–73.

Index